T0325187

Personalized Machine Learning

Every day we interact with machine learning systems offering individualized predictions for our entertainment, social connections, purchases, or health. These involve several modalities of data, from sequences of clicks to text, images, and social interactions. This book introduces common principles and methods that underpin the design of personalized predictive models for a variety of settings and modalities.

The book begins by revising 'traditional' machine learning models, focusing on how to adapt them to settings involving user data; then presents techniques based on advanced principles such as matrix factorization, deep learning, and generative modeling; and concludes with a detailed study of the consequences and risks of deploying personalized predictive systems.

A series of case studies in domains ranging from e-commerce to health plus hands-on projects and code examples will give readers understanding and experience with large-scale real-world datasets and the ability to design models and systems for a wide range of applications.

JULIAN MCAULEY has been a Professor at the University of California San Diego since 2014. Personalized Machine Learning is the main research area of his lab, with applications ranging from personalized recommendation to dialog, health care, and fashion design. He regularly collaborates with industry on these topics, including Amazon, Facebook, Microsoft, Salesforce, and Etsy. His work has been selected for several awards including an NSF CAREER award, and faculty awards from Amazon, Salesforce, Facebook, and Qualcomm, among others.

Personalized Machine Learning

JULIAN MCAULEY
University of California San Diego

CAMBRIDGE
UNIVERSITY PRESS

CAMBRIDGE
UNIVERSITY PRESS

University Printing House, Cambridge CB2 8BS, United Kingdom

One Liberty Plaza, 20th Floor, New York, NY 10006, USA

477 Williamstown Road, Port Melbourne, VIC 3207, Australia

314–321, 3rd Floor, Plot 3, Splendor Forum, Jasola District Centre, New Delhi – 110025, India

103 Penang Road, #05–06/07, Visioncrest Commercial, Singapore 23846

Cambridge University Press is part of the University of Cambridge.

It furthers the University's mission by disseminating knowledge in the pursuit of education, learning, and research at the highest international levels of excellence.

www.cambridge.org
Information on this title: www.cambridge.org/9781316518908
DOI: 10.1017/9781009003971

First published 2022

A catalogue record for this publication is available from the British Library.

ISBN 978-1-316-51890-8 Hardback

Contents

Notation

Common Mathematical Symbols

Machine Learning

y vector of labels

X matrix of features

x_i feature vector for the ith sample

$f(x_i)$ model prediction for the ith sample

r_i residual (error) associated with the ith prediction, $r_i = (y_i - f(x_i))$

θ vector of model parameters

σ sigmoid function $\sigma(x) = \frac{1}{1+e^{-x}}$

$\|x\|_p$ p-norm, $\|x\|_p = (\sum_i |x_i|^p)^{1/p}$

$\ell_1; \ell_2$ regularizers $\|\theta\|_1$ and $\|\theta\|_2$

λ regularization hyperparameter

$\mathcal{L}; \ell$ likelihood and log-likelihood

Users and Items

$u \in U$ user u in user set U

$i \in I$ item i in item set I

I_u set of items rated (or interacted with) by user u

U_i set of users who have rated (or interacted with) item i

$|U|; |I|$ number of users and number of items

$R_{u,i}$ measurement (e.g., a rating) associated with an interaction between user u and item i

$x_{u,i}$ model estimate of the compatibility between user u and item i

Recommender Systems

β_u bias term associated with user u

β_i bias term associated with item i

γ_u	vector of parameters describing a single user u
γ_i	vector of parameters describing a single item i
γ_U; γ_I	parameters for all users U or all items I
K	feature dimensionality (or number of latent factors)

Common Abbreviations

AUC	area under the ROC curve (eq. (5.26))
BER	balanced error rate (eq. (3.20))
BPR	Bayesian personalized ranking (sec. 5.2.2)
CNN	convolutional neural network (sec. 5.5.4)
FVU	fraction of variance unexplained (eq. (2.32))
FN/FNR	false negatives/false negative rate (sec. 3.3.1)
FP/FPR	false positives/false positive rate (sec. 3.3.1)
GAN	generative adversarial network (sec. 9.4)
LSTM	long short-term memory model (sec. 7.6)
MAE	mean absolute error (eq. (2.17))
MLE	maximum likelihood estimation (sec. 2.2.3)
MLP	multilayer perceptron (sec. 5.5.2)
MMR	maximal marginal relevance (sec. 10.3.1)
MRR	mean reciprocal rank (sec. 5.4.2)
MSE	mean squared error (sec. 2.2.1)
NDCG	normalized discounted cumulative gain (sec. 5.4.3)
RNN	recurrent neural network (sec. 7.6)
ROC	receiver-operating characteristic (sec. 3.3.3)
SVM	support vector machine (sec. 3.2)
TF-IDF	term frequency and inverse document frequency (eq. (8.8))
TN/TNR	true negatives/true negative rate (sec. 3.3.1)
TP/TPR	true positives/true positive rate (sec. 3.3.1)

1

Introduction

Machine learning encompasses a broad range of problems ranging from detecting objects in images, finding documents relevant to a given query, or predicting the next element in a sequence, among countless others. Traditional approaches to these problems operate by collecting large, labeled datasets for training, uncovering informative features, and mining complex patterns that explain the association between features and labels. Typically, labels are regarded as an underlying 'truth' that should be predicted as accurately as possible.

Increasingly, though, there is a need to apply machine learning in settings where the 'correct' outcome is subjective, or otherwise depends on the context and characteristics of individual users. As we browse online for movies to watch, products to buy, or romantic partners to connect with, we are likely engaging with these new forms of *personalized* machine learning: Results are tailored to us specifically, based on the types of movies, products, or partners that *we specifically* are likely to engage with.

Much like traditional machine learning algorithms, *personalized* machine learning algorithms are at their heart essentially forms of pattern discovery. That is, predictions are made *for you* by analyzing the behavior of people *similar to you*. A recommendation such as 'people who liked this also liked' is perhaps the most simple example of this type of personalized pattern discovery:[1] based on the contextual attribute of a user liking a particular item, recommendations are extracted based on users who share this common preference. At the other end of the spectrum are complex deep learning approaches that learn 'black box' representations of users in order to make predictions, though these too at their heart rely on the intuition that 'similar' users (in terms of some complex representation) will have similar interaction patterns.

---

[1] Though strictly speaking maybe not one that we would call 'machine learning.'

1.1 Purpose of This Book

We seek to introduce *Personalized Machine Learning* by exploring a family of approaches used to solve the aforementioned problems, and construct a narrative around the common methods and design principles involved. We show that even in applications as diverse as song recommendation, heart-rate profiling, or fashion design, there is a common set of techniques around which personalized machine learning systems are built.

By introducing this underlying set of principles, the book is intended to teach readers how modern machine learning techniques can be improved by incorporating ideas from personalization and user modeling, and to guide readers in building machine learning systems where accurately modeling the users involved is key to success.

There is currently an abundance of models, datasets, and applications that seek to capture human dynamics or interactions. Examples pervade in diverse areas including web mining, recommender systems, fashion, dialog, and personalized health, among others. As such, there is an emerging set of techniques that are used to capture the dynamics of 'users' in each of these settings. This book is designed to act as a reference point to explain these techniques, and explore their common elements. As a starting point, we will begin the book (chaps. 2 and 3) with a primer of machine learning (and especially supervised learning) that will bring readers up-to-speed on the basic techniques required later. Although this introductory material is likely familiar to many readers, we have a particular focus on user-oriented datasets, and show that even with 'standard' machine learning techniques, there is considerable scope for building personalized systems through careful feature engineering strategies that capture relevant user characteristics.

Following this, our main introduction to personalized machine learning will be to explore recommender systems (chaps. 4 and 5). Recommendation technology has traditionally relied on personalization and user modeling, whether through simple similarity functions among users ('people like you also bought', etc.) or through more modern approaches involving temporal pattern mining or neural networks.

More recently, the need to account for personalization and to model users has spread into a variety of new areas of machine learning. Following our study of recommender systems, exploring personalization and user modeling in these new areas—and giving readers the tools they need to design personalized approaches in new settings—is the main goal of this book.

1.2 For Learners: What Is Covered, and What Is Not

Although this book is primarily intended as a guide to the specific topics of personalization, recommendation, and user modeling (etc.), it should also serve as a relatively gentle introduction to the topic of machine learning in general. Topics such as web mining and recommender systems serve as an ideal starting point for learners seeking a more 'application oriented' view of machine learning compared to what is typically covered in introductory machine learning texts.

Throughout the book, we focus on building examples on top of large, real-world datasets, and exploring techniques that are practical to implement in projects and exercises. Our particular focus guides us toward (and away from) certain topics, as we describe below.

Regressors, Classifiers, and the Learning Pipeline: We give a detailed introduction of the end-to-end machine learning process in Chapters 2 and 3, which (while condensed) should be suitable for learners with no background in machine learning. When introducing basic machine learning concepts in Chapters 2 and 3, we limit ourselves to linear regression and linear classification (logistic regression), since these serve as building blocks for the methods we develop later. Consequently, we ignore dozens of alternative regression and classification methods that are often the core of standard machine learning texts (though we briefly discuss the merits of alternatives in sec. 3.2).

User Representations and Dimensionality Reduction: Many of the techniques we explore when learning user representations are essentially forms of manifold learning (or dimensionality reduction), and borrow ideas from related topics such as matrix factorization (sec. 5.1). While readers should have some basic familiarity with linear algebra, we carefully avoid a linear algebra-heavy presentation of 'traditional' dimensionality reduction techniques: in terms of actual implementation, these have little in common with the methods we develop (though we discuss the connection to, for example, the singular value decomposition in sec. 5.1).

Deep Learning: Any discussion of 'modern' machine learning approaches necessitates a fairly broad discussion of deep learning. For example, we discuss multilayer perceptron-based recommendation in Section 5.5.2, sequence models based on recurrent neural networks in Chapter 7, and models of visual preferences based on convolutional neural networks in Chapter 9. However in doing so we are merely scratching the surface of deep learning-based personalization, and will largely refer readers elsewhere for in-depth discussion of specific architectures, or for a first-principles presentation of deep learning methods.

Offline versus Online Learning: We largely limit ourselves to traditional offline, supervised learning problems, that is, uncovering patterns and making predictions from historical collections of training data. Generally, we prefer this setting since it allows us to focus on methods that we can develop on top of real-world, publicly available datasets. Of course, in practice, when deploying predictive models, data may be obtained in a streaming setting and updates must be made in real time. This type of training regime is known as *online learning*, which we briefly cover in Section 5.7; we also avoid discussion of (e.g.) reinforcement learning algorithms, though mention their use briefly in settings such as conversational recommendation (e.g., sec. 8.4.4).

Bias, Consequences, and User Considerations: By design, our study of personalization is largely confined to machine learning approaches. That is, we are generally concerned with building predictive systems that can estimate—as accurately as possible—how a particular user will respond to a given stimulus. By doing so, we can estimate preferences, predict future activities, retrieve relevant items, and so on.

Of course, we are mindful of the dangers associated with 'black-box' approaches to machine learning, and want to avoid the pitfalls of blindly optimizing model accuracy, such as filter bubbles, unwanted biases, or simply a degraded user experience. In Chapter 10 we discuss these issues, as well as potential approaches to address them.

Again our discussion is mostly limited to machine learning solutions, that is, we investigate *algorithmic* approaches to correct for biases, increase recommendation diversity, and so on. We note that algorithmic solutions are only part of the picture, and that while having better algorithms is critical, it is also critical that those algorithms are appropriately *used*. Our presentation is complementary to a large body of work that explores personalization from the perspective of human computer interaction, or user interface design, where the primary concern is maximizing the quality of the user experience (ease of finding information, satisfaction, long-term engagement, etc.).

Implementation and Libraries: All code examples are presented in *Python*. While we assume a working familiarity with data processing, matrix libraries (etc.), further links on our online resources page (sec. 1.4) will help users with less familiarity. When discussing deep learning approaches, and more generally when fitting complex models, we base our implementations on *Tensorflow*, though these examples can easily be interchanged with alternate libraries (PyTorch, Theano, etc.).

While we focus on implementation, we largely avoid 'systems building' aspects of personalized machine learning, such as concerns around deploying machine learning models on distributed servers (etc.), though we discuss high-level libraries and implementation of best practices throughout the book.

1.3 For Instructors: Course and Content Outline

This book is inspired by my own experience teaching classes on recommender systems and web mining at UC San Diego. Courses on these topics have proved extremely popular and are often chosen as learners' first exposure to machine learning.

One reason this topic acts as a good first contact with the machine learning curriculum is that it has a somewhat lower bar for entry than many machine learning courses, including (e.g.) courses on deep learning, or even many 'introductory' machine learning classes. Partly this is due to the material being less dependent on deep and complex theory, and partly it is due to the ability to quickly build working solutions that are fairly representative of the state-of-the-art, rather than mere proofs-of-concept. As such, a focus of this book is to quickly build working solutions, and covering a wide breadth of approaches, rather than diving too deep into the theory behind any one approach. This approach can be useful in helping learners to understand the practical considerations behind building predictive systems based on user data, and is complementary to the more theoretical treatment given in most introductory texts.

Another feature that has made this material popular among learners is the ability to work quickly with large, real-world datasets. The ability to work with collections of user data from *Amazon, Google, Steam* (etc.) on applications that are representative of real use cases, has proved immensely valuable for students building their project portfolios or preparing for interviews. As such, each chapter is paired with project suggestions, each of which would be suitable as a major class project. These projects aim to synthesize the material from each chapter, with more focus on system building considerations, design choices, and thorough model evaluation.

1.3.1 Course Plan and Overview

The content in this text is aimed at developing a quarter- or semester-long course, for students with some background in linear algebra, probability, and data processing. After revising basic material in Chapters 2 and 3, Chapters 4 and 5 cover the core material upon which the remainder of the book builds. Chapter 6–9 are somewhat more orthogonal, such that components can be selected and combined as time or student background allows. A final chapter on bias, fairness, and the consequences of personalization (chap. 10) provides an opportunity to revisit earlier material through a new lens.

Each chapter is paired with homework and a project. Again the focus on these components is mainly on developing practical implementations, working with real data, and understanding the design choices involved, rather than testing theoretical concepts. Below we briefly summarize the material from each chapter:

Machine Learning Primer (chaps. 2 and 3) 2–3 weeks. Introduces the foundational concepts of machine learning, feature design, and evaluation, via a selection of datasets that capture user interactions. Exercises range from simple data manipulation to building a working machine learning pipeline (training, validation, etc.). Exercises are mainly concerned with feature design, including projects (Projects 1 and 2) that involve experimenting with activity data involving temporal and geographical dynamics.

Recommender Systems (chaps. 4 and 5) 2–3 weeks. Introduces the core set of techniques used for recommendation. Traditional heuristics are presented in Chapter 4 followed by machine learning approaches in Chapter 5. Recommender systems are used to develop the concept of a *user manifold* which is used throughout the following chapters to capture variation among users in several settings (sec. 1.7). Exercises are mainly focused on the basics of building practical recommendation approaches, and projects (Projects 3 and 4) are concerned with building an end-to-end recommendation pipeline for a book recommendation scenario.

Content and Structure in Recommender Systems (chap. 6) 1 week. Explores how to incorporate features (i.e., side information) into personalization (mostly recommendation) approaches, and explores personalization in settings with additional structure, such as socially aware recommendation and settings involving price dynamics. A particular focus is given to leveraging side-information in *cold-start* scenarios, where interaction histories are not yet available (sec. 6.2). Some of these content-aware approaches (such as factorization machines) are revisited later in the book when developing more complex models based on (e.g.) temporal or sequential dynamics. A project

(Project 5) consists of developing recommender systems for use in cold-start settings.

Temporal and Sequential Models (chap. 7) 1–2 weeks. We revise some of the basic approaches to temporal and sequential modeling, such as autoregression and Markov chains, and later develop more complex personalized approaches based on recurrent neural networks. The *Netflix Prize* (sec. 7.2.2) is presented as a case study to explore the basic design principles of temporal modeling. A project (Project 6) compares various approaches to temporal recommendation.

Personalized Models of Text (chap. 8) 1 week. After revising some of the basic predictive models of text (such as bag-of-words representations), we explore how text can be used to understand the dimensions of preferences. We revisit sequential modeling by exploring techniques that borrow from natural language to model interaction sequences. We also visit methods for text *generation*, which can be personalized in settings ranging from conversation to justification of machine predictions. A project (Project 7) consists of building personalized systems for document retrieval.

Personalized Models of Visual Data (chap. 9) 1 week. Explores applications involving visual data, ranging from personalized image search, to applications in fashion and design. A project (Project 8) consists of building visually aware recommendation systems for applications in fashion.

The Consequences of Personalized Machine Learning (chap. 10) 1 week. The final chapter explores the consequences and pitfalls of developing personalized machine learning systems. Examples include filter bubbles, extremification, and issues of bias and fairness. The chapter has a significant focus on applied case studies, and allows us to revisit several of the topics from previous chapters through a new lens. A project (Project 9) consists of improving recommendation approaches in terms of gender parity and other fairness objectives.

1.4 Online Resources

To help readers with exercises, projects, and to collect resources including datasets and additional reading materials, an online supplement is available to augment the material covered here with working code and examples:

https://cseweb.ucsd.edu/~jmcauley/pml/

The online supplement includes:

- Code examples covering the material in each chapter. These cover complete worked examples from which the code samples presented in each chapter are drawn. Additional code samples are included that correspond to various figures and examples presented throughout the book.
- Solutions to all exercises from each chapter.
- Links to datasets used in the book (as well as various other personalization datasets), including small, processed datasets useful to complete the exercises.
- Links to additional reading, mostly focused on introductory material useful to learners less familiar with some of the background material described in Section 1.2.

1.5 About the Author

I have been a Professor at UC San Diego since 2014, following postgraduate training at Stanford University, and undergraduate and graduate training in Australia. *Personalized Machine Learning* is the main theme of my research lab at UCSD. Our lab's research has pioneered the use of images and text in recommendation settings (e.g., McAuley et al. (2015); McAuley and Leskovec (2013a)), with applications including fashion design, personalized question answering, and interactive dialog systems. Our lab has also studied personalization outside of typical recommendation settings, such as develop-

Figure 1.1 The author

ing personalized models of heart-rate profiles (Ni et al., 2019b), and systems for generating personalized recipes (Majumder et al., 2019).

Our lab regularly collaborates with industry to develop state-of-the-art systems for personalized machine learning. We have worked on problems including visually aware recommendation with *Adobe* and *Pinterest*, understanding user budgets and personalized price dynamics with *Etsy* and *Microsoft*, and question-answering and dialog systems with *Microsoft* and *Amazon*. We will explore several of these approaches through case studies throughout the book.

1.6 Personalization in Everyday Life

Other than introducing the techniques underlying personalized machine learning systems, one of our goals in this book is to explore the wide range of practical applications where personalization is applied, to explore the history of the topic, and eventually to explore the associated risks and consequences.

Personalized machine learning is increasingly becoming pervasive to the point that most of us are likely to interact with personalized machine learning systems every day. Systems that generate playlists based on our listening habits, mark e-mails as 'important,' suggest products or advertisements based on our recent activities, rank our newsfeeds, or suggest new connections on social media, all personalize their predictions or outputs in some way. Techniques range from simple heuristics (e.g., we're likely to become friends with somebody if we already share mutual friends), to complex algorithms that account for temporal patterns, or incorporate natural language and visual signals.

Below we will study a few common (and less common) scenarios in which personalization plays a key role, many of which will form the basis of case studies throughout this book.

1.6.1 Recommendation

Many of the examples we cover in this book will relate to *recommender systems*, and more broadly to modeling users' interactions with data collected from the web. Part of the reason for this focus is opportunistic: user interaction datasets are widely available, allowing us to build models on top of real data.

Pedagogically, recommender systems are also appealing as an introduction to personalized machine learning as they allow us to quickly implement working systems that are close to the state-of-the-art. As we will see, even widely deployed systems turn out to be surprisingly straightforward, relying on simple heuristics and standard data structures (sec. 4.5).

Ultimately though, our main reason for studying recommender systems is because they are a fundamental tool for modeling *interactions between users and items*. The basic techniques developed when building recommender systems can be applied in a variety of other situations where we want to predict how a user will respond to some stimulus. Many of the settings we describe later build on this general theme.

Recommender systems represent perhaps the purest settings where *variation among individuals* captures a large fraction of the variability in a dataset. To build recommender systems we must understand the underlying *preferences* of users and *properties* of items that explain why an item might be purchased by one user and not another. Users might vary due to subjective preferences, budgets, or demographic factors; both users and items might change over time due to social, temporal, or contextual factors (etc.).

Building on the techniques we develop for recommendation, we argue that there are countless settings where capturing variation among individuals is key to making meaningful predictions. In settings like personalized health, users may vary in terms of their physical characteristics, medical histories, or risk factors; or in settings involving natural language (or dialog), users may vary in terms of their writing styles, personalities, or their specific context.

Below we describe a few such examples, partly to highlight the wide range of settings where personalization is critical, but also to demonstrate the common set of ideas involved in modeling them.

1.6.2 Personalized Health

Beyond 'obvious' applications in electronic commerce or social media, personalization is increasingly playing a role in high-stakes and socially important problems. *Personalized health* is a key emerging domain for personalization: like recommendation, problems in health have the key characteristic that predictions are highly contextual and exhibit significant variation among individuals. Critically, when estimating symptoms, responses to medication, or heart-rate profiles, it would be impossible to make useful predictions *without* personalization.

Estimating what symptoms a patient will exhibit on their next hospital visit is a canonical task in personalized health, with applications in (e.g.) preventative treatment. This task closely resembles the settings we explore when developing recommender systems, given the goal to estimate patients' interactions with certain stimuli (symptoms) over time (Yang et al., 2014). As such, techniques for such tasks borrow ideas from recommender systems, especially temporal and sequential recommendation, as we develop in Chapter 7.

Beyond estimating patient symptoms, personalized machine learning techniques can be adapted to related tasks ranging from estimating the duration of surgical procedures (Ng et al., 2017), modeling the progression of heart-rate sequences in response to physical stimuli (Ni et al., 2019b), or estimating the distribution kinetics of drugs (such as anesthetics) (Ingrande et al., 2020). Modeling such problems requires understanding the characteristics of patients or physicians (and the interactions between them). Techniques range from simple regression (e.g., to predict surgery duration) to recurrent neural networks (e.g., to forecast heart-rate profiles).

Many problems in personalized health also depend upon natural language data, for example, modeling the characteristics of clinical notes or generating reports based on radiology images (Ni et al., 2020). Such applications build on techniques for personalized natural language processing and generation, as we develop in Chapter 8.

These techniques span the different 'types' of personalized learning systems (see sec. 1.7): some systems leverage traditional machine learning techniques, in which 'personalization' merely means extracting features that capture the relevant properties about users (or patients, physicians, etc.); others use complex deep-learning approaches, in which the underlying dimensions that capture patterns in behavior are harder to interpret.

1.6.3 Computational Social Science

Often the goal of modeling user data is not merely to *predict* future events or interactions, but to *understand* the underlying dynamics at play. Using machine learning and data-driven approaches to understand the underlying dynamics of human behavior from large datasets is one of the main goals of *computational social science*.

Likewise, for many of the models we develop, our goals are as much about building more accurate predictors as they are about understanding social or behavioral dynamics. When we develop regressors to predict content success on *reddit* (sec. 2.6.1), our main goal is to disentangle what factors lead to success, such as community dynamics, titles, submission times, and so on. Or, when building recommender systems our goals are to understand and interpret the underlying preference dimensions that guide users' decisions, and what causes those preferences to change over time, including how users acquire tastes, develop nostalgia for old items, or simply respond to changes in a user interface.

Finally, as we begin to explore the ethical consequences of personalization (which we introduce in sec. 1.8), we will underline the point that accurate prediction is rarely a desirable goal in and of itself. In Chapter 10, we will examine the long-term effects on users who interact with personalized systems: this includes studying what factors drive users to extreme content, and how to algorithmically mitigate such undesirable outcomes.

1.6.4 Language Generation, Personalized Dialog, and Interactive Agents

Finally, given the new modalities via which people interact with predictive systems, there are new demands for personalization.

For example, personalization is critical in a broad range of settings involving natural language. User-generated language data exhibit substantial variability due to differences in writing style, subjectivity, and so on. When dealing with such data, non-personalized models may struggle with this nuance. For example, automated systems for dialog, whether in task-oriented settings or for open-domain 'chit-chat,' can benefit from personalization, in order to generate responses that are more personalized or empathetic to the tone or context of individual users (Majumder et al., 2020).

We will see several instances of personalized language modeling throughout the book: language models are increasingly important to explain or interpret machine predictions (sec. 8.4.3), to facilitate new modalities of interaction with predictive systems (such as conversation, sec. 8.4.4), and to develop new kinds of assistive tools, for example, to help users respond to e-mail (sec. 8.5).

1.7 Techniques for Personalization

As mentioned in Section 1.1, one of the goals of this book is to establish a common narrative around the tools and techniques used to design personalized machine learning systems. Although we have shown that such systems are applied in domains as diverse as online commerce to personalized health, we find that the techniques used to implement these models follow a few common paradigms.

1.7.1 User Representations as Manifolds

One of the main ideas we will revisit throughout this book—and which allows us to adapt ideas from recommender systems to other types of machine learning—is that of a *user manifold*. That is, most of the personalized methods we will explore will involve *representations* of users that describe the common patterns of variation in their activities and interactions.

In the case of recommender systems, this 'user manifold' will be a vector that describes the principal dimensions that explain variance among user preferences (fig. 1.2). For example, we might discover that the principal dimensions that explain variance in preferences in a movie recommendation setting center around certain genres, actors, or special effects. Throughout the book, we will revisit the idea of user manifolds, as a general-purpose means of capturing common patterns of variation among users. Some examples include:

- In Chapter 5, we will use low-dimensional user representations to describe the dimensions of preferences and activities, which can be used to recommend items that users are likely to interact with.

Figure 1.2 The basic idea behind recommender systems, and various other types of personalized machine learning, is to represent users by *low-dimensional manifolds* that describe the patterns of variance among their interactions. In a recommendation setting, a low-dimensional user vector might describe my *preferences* while a low-dimensional item vector describes an item's *properties*; compatible users and items have vectors that point in the same direction (chap. 5).

- In Chapter 8, user representations can describe the topics users tend to discuss (e.g., when writing reviews), or individual characteristics of their writing styles.
- In Chapter 9, user representations will describe the visual dimensions that users are interested in, allowing us to rank, recommend, or generate images in a personalized way.
- Throughout various case studies, user representations will capture characteristics ranging from dietary preferences (sec. 8.4.2), fitness profiles (sec. 7.8), social trust (sec. 6.4.1), or fashion choices (sec. 9.3).

1.7.2 Contextual Personalization and Model-Based Personalization

Although this book will predominantly cover methods that explicitly model user terms (as earlier), we will also cover a variety of models that deliberately avoid doing so.

Starting with simple approaches such as 'people who bought X also bought Y,' many classical approaches for (e.g.) recommendation *leverage user data, but do not include explicit parameters* (i.e., a 'model') associated with a user. However, such models are still *personalized*, in the sense that different predictions will be made for each individual based on how they interact with the system. Simple machine learning techniques, such as those we develop in Chapters 2 and 3, where users are represented by a few carefully engineered features, also follow this paradigm.

We will distinguish between these two classes of approach using the terms *model-based* and *contextual* personalization. *Model-based* approaches learn an explicit set of parameters associated with each user, such as the 'user manifolds' described earlier (and in fig. 1.2); these models are typically intended to capture the predominant patterns of variation among users in a system, usually in terms of a low-dimensional vector. In contrast, *contextual* (also sometimes called 'memory-based,' as in chap. 5) approaches extract features from users' histories of recent interactions.

There are several settings in which contextual personalization may be preferable to explicitly modeling a user. When developing simple recommender systems in Chapter 4, and even more trivial personalized models in Chapters 2 and 3, we see that personalization can often be achieved with simple heuristics, or hand-crafted features or similarity measures. Such approaches may be desirable for a number of reasons: simple models may be more interpretable (and therefore preferable to expose to a user compared to 'black-box' predictions); or, we may lack adequate training data to learn complex representations from scratch.

1.8 The Ethics and Consequences of Personalization

Along with the increasing ubiquity of personalized machine learning systems, there is a growing awareness of the risks associated with personalization. Some of these issues have reached mainstream awareness, such as the idea that personalized recommendations can trap users in 'filter bubbles,' while other issues are considerably more subtle. For instance, considering the specific case of recommender systems, a naively implemented model can introduce issues including:

Filter Bubbles: Roughly speaking, recommendation algorithms rely on identifying specific item characteristics that are preferred by each user, and recommending items that most closely represent those characteristics. Without care, even a user with broad interests may be recommended only a narrow set of items that closely mimic their prior interactions.

Extremification: Likewise, a system that identifies features that a user is interested in may identify items that are most representative of those features, for example, a user who likes action movies may be recommended movies with *a lot* of action; in contexts such as social media and news recommendation this can lead to users being exposed to increasingly extreme content (the relationship between this and the previous issue is explained in chap. 10).

Concentration: Similar to the previous phenomenon, a user who has diverse interests may receive recommendations that only follow their most predominant interest (sec. 10.2). In aggregate, this may lead to to a small set of items being over-represented among all users' recommendations.

Bias: Given that recommenders (and many other personalized models) ultimately work by identifying common patterns of user behavior, users in the 'long-tail' whose preferences do not follow the predominant trends may receive sub-par recommendations.

Along with a rising awareness of these issues has come a set of techniques designed to mitigate them. These techniques borrow ideas from the broader field of fair and unbiased machine learning, whereby learning algorithms are adapted so as not to propagate (or not to exacerbate) biases in training data, though the fairness goals are often quite different. Diversification techniques can be used to ensure that predictions or recommendations balance relevance with novelty, diversity, or serendipity; related techniques seek to better 'calibrate' personalized machine learning systems by ensuring that predicted outputs are balanced in terms of categories, features, or the distribution over recommended items (sec. 10.3). Such techniques can mitigate filter bubbles by ensuring that model outputs are not highly concentrated around a few items, and more qualitatively can increase the overall novelty or 'interestingness' of model outputs. Other techniques follow more directly from fair and unbiased machine learning, ensuring that the performance of personalized models is not degraded for users belonging to underrepresented groups, or who have niche preferences (sec. 10.7).

PART ONE

MACHINE LEARNING PRIMER

2

Regression and Feature Engineering

In this chapter, we will cover the fundamental principles of machine learning (and in particular *supervised* learning), which will serve as a foundation for the remaining material in this book.

In the following text, we will cover essential building blocks including:

- Strategies for feature extraction and transformation, including real-valued and categorical data, and temporal signals (sec. 2.3).
- The general strategy of associating probabilities with model outcomes, and more broadly the relationship between fitting a model and likelihood maximization (sec. 2.2.3).
- Gradient-based approaches to model fitting (sec. 2.5), and (in chap. 3) their implementation via high-level languages such as *Tensorflow* (sec. 3.4.4).
- How to deal with outliers, imbalanced datasets, and general strategies for model evaluation (sec. 2.2).

Although we will only briefly touch upon *personalization* in this chapter, our examples will focus on the same types of user-oriented data that we will visit in later chapters. In particular, we will focus on datasets covering topics such as recommendation, sentiment, and predictive tasks involving, for example, demographic characteristics.

As such, the view we will take on 'personalization' in this chapter will consist of *extracting features from user data* in order to make predictions using traditional machine learning frameworks. Later, we will draw a distinction between this type of method—where we extract *features* about users—and methods where we explicitly *model* each user. This will drive our discussion of *contextual* versus *model-based* personalization (as we introduced in sec. 1.7), though we will discuss this distinction more precisely in Chapters 4 and 5. However, as we will see in this chapter (and in various examples throughout the book), even traditional machine learning techniques, paired

19

with appropriate feature extraction strategies, can lead to surprisingly effective models for personalized prediction.

Supervised Learning

All of the techniques presented in this chapter—and most of the personalization techniques we will explore throughout this book—are forms of *supervised learning*. Supervised learning techniques assume that our prediction tasks (or our datasets) can be separated into the following two components:

labels (denoted y) that we would like to predict, and

features (denoted X) that we believe will help us to predict those labels.[1]

For example, given a sentiment analysis task (chap. 8), our data might be (the text of) reviews from *Amazon* or *Yelp*, and our labels would be the ratings associated with those reviews.

Given this distinction between features and labels in a dataset, the goal of a *supervised learning* algorithm is to infer the underlying function

$$f(x) \to y \tag{2.1}$$

that explains the relationship between the features and the labels. Usually, this function will be *parameterized* by model parameters θ, that is,

$$f_\theta(x) \to y. \tag{2.2}$$

For example, in this chapter, θ might describe which features are positively or negatively correlated (or uncorrelated) with the labels; later, θ might capture the preferences of a particular user in a recommender system (chap. 5). Figure 2.1 explains how this type of supervised approach relates to other types of learning.

Throughout this chapter, we will assume that we are given *labels* in the form of a vector y and *features* in the form of a matrix X, so that each y_i is the label associated with the ith observation and x_i is a vector of features associated with that observation.

The two categories of supervised learning that we will cover in this and the next chapter include:

- *Regression*, in which our goal is to predict *real-valued* labels y as closely as possible (sec. 2.1). When building personalized models in later chapters,

---

[1] Generally, we will use X when referring to a feature matrix and x or x_i to refer to a vector of features associated with a single observation.

Supervised learning approaches are those that seek to directly learn the relationship between the observed data X and the labels y. Nearly all of the models in this book are forms of supervised learning, starting with regression and classification in this chapter, and continuing into later chapters as we build models to predict user activities.

In contrast, *unsupervised learning* approaches seek to find patterns in the data X, but are not specifically concerned with predicting any label; examples include techniques for clustering and dimensionality reduction.

Finally, *semi-supervised learning* approaches are somewhere in between, usually leveraging large datasets of *unlabeled* data to improve the performance of supervised models with a small number of labels.

Figure 2.1 Supervised, unsupervised, and semi-supervised learning

such targets may include ratings, sentiment, the number of votes a social media post receives, or a patient's heart rate.

- *Classification*, in which y is an element of a discrete set (chap. 3). In later chapters, these will correspond to outcomes such as whether a user clicks on or purchases an item. We will also see how such approaches can be adapted to learn rankings over items (sec. 3.3.3).

2.1 Linear Regression

Perhaps the simplest association we could assume between our features X and labels y would be a *linear* relationship, that is, the relationship between X and y is defined as

$$y = X\theta. \tag{2.3}$$

Using our notation from Equation (2.2):

$$f_\theta(X) = X\theta, \tag{2.4}$$

or equivalently for a single observation x_i (a row of X)

$$f_\theta(x) = x_i \cdot \theta = \sum_k x_{ik}\theta_i. \tag{2.5}$$

Here θ is our set of model *parameters*: a vector of unknowns that describes which features are *relevant* to predicting the labels.

Ignoring strict notation for now, a trivial example might consist of predicting a review's rating as a function of its length. To do so, let us consider a small dataset of 100 (length, rating) pairs from *Goodreads* fantasy novels (Wan and McAuley, 2018). Figure 2.2 plots the relationship between review length (in characters) and the rating.

Regression and Feature Engineering

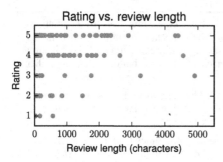

Figure 2.2 Ratings compared to review length (in characters), based on 100 reviews of fantasy novels from *Goodreads*

From Figure 2.2, there appears to be a (rough) association between ratings and review length, that is, more positive reviews tend to be longer. A very simple model might attempt to describe that relationship with a line, that is,

$$\text{rating} \simeq \theta_0 + \theta_1 \times (\text{review length}). \qquad (2.6)$$

Note that Equation (2.6) is just the standard equation for a line ($y = mx + b$), where θ_1 is a slope and θ_0 is an intercept.

If we can identify a line that approximately describes this relationship, we can use it to estimate a rating from a given review, even though we may never have seen a review of some specific length before. In this sense, the line is a simple *model* of the data, as it allows us to predict labels from previously unseen features. To do so, we formalize the problem of finding a *line of best fit*.

Specifically, we are interested in identifying the values of θ_0 and θ_1 that most closely match the trend in Figure 2.2. To solve for $\theta = [\theta_0, \theta_1]$, we can write out the problem as a system of equations in matrix form:

$$y \simeq X \cdot \theta, \qquad (2.7)$$

where y is our vector of observed ratings and X is our matrix of observed features (in this case the reviews' lengths).[2] For the first few samples of our *Goodreads* data, we have:

$$\underbrace{\begin{bmatrix} 5 \\ 5 \\ 5 \\ 4 \\ 3 \\ 5 \\ \vdots \end{bmatrix}}_{y} \simeq \underbrace{\begin{bmatrix} 1 & 2086 \\ 1 & 1521 \\ 1 & 1519 \\ 1 & 1791 \\ 1 & 1762 \\ 1 & 470 \\ \vdots & \vdots \end{bmatrix}}_{X} \cdot \underbrace{\begin{bmatrix} \theta_0 \\ \theta_1 \end{bmatrix}}_{\theta}. \qquad (2.8)$$

---

[2] We write $y \simeq X \cdot \theta$ in Equation (2.7) since the equation is an *approximation* (i.e., we cannot precisely solve for θ); however, we will typically write $y = X \cdot \theta$ when defining model equations.

The first column of the feature matrix X in Equation (2.8), and in most feature matrices throughout this chapter, is a column of 1s. To explain why we always have this feature, it is useful to expand the inner product $[1, \text{length}] \cdot [\theta_0, \theta_1]$ (e.g., as in eq. (2.8)) to confirm that it expands to the equation for a line $\theta_0 + \theta_1 \times \text{length}$. Without the constant term in our feature matrix, we would be implicitly assuming that the fitted line passes through $(0, 0)$.

Figure 2.3 Why is there a column of '1's in the feature matrix?

It is useful to compare Equations (2.6) and (2.8) to understand how the matrix expression above expands to include the slope ($\theta_1 \times$ (review length)) and intercept (θ_0) terms. We explain this construction more precisely in Figure 2.3.

We would like to solve Equation (2.8) for θ. Naively, we might attempt to multiply both sides of the equation $y = X \cdot \theta$ by X^{-1}; however, the inverse is not well defined since X is not a square matrix.

To obtain a square matrix, we (left) multiply both sides by X^T:

$$X^T y \simeq X^T X \theta, \tag{2.9}$$

resulting in a square (in this case 2×2) matrix $X^T X$. We can now multiply both sides by the inverse of this matrix:

$$(X^T X)^{-1} X^T y \simeq (X^T X)^{-1} (X^T X)\theta, \quad \text{or simply} \quad \theta = (X^T X)^{-1} X^T y. \tag{2.10}$$

The quantity $(X^T X)^{-1} X^T$ is known as the *pseudoinverse* of X.

Computing $\theta = (X^T X)^{-1} X^T y$ for our 100 ratings from *Goodreads* yields

$$\theta = \begin{bmatrix} 3.983 \\ 1.193 \times 10^{-4} \end{bmatrix}, \tag{2.11}$$

corresponding to the line

$$\text{rating} = 3.983 + 1.193 \times 10^{-4} \text{ (review length)}. \tag{2.12}$$

This line reflects a positive (albeit slight) trend between review length and ratings: For every additional character in a review, our estimate of the rating increases very slightly (by 1.193×10^{-4} points). This line of best fit is depicted in Figure 2.4.

More Complex Models: This reasoning generalizes to fitting more complex models than a simple line, for example, we could imagine that a rating could be related to both the length of the review and the number of comments the review received:

$$\text{rating} = \theta_0 + \theta_1 \times \text{(review length)} + \theta_2 \times \text{(n\_comments)}. \tag{2.13}$$

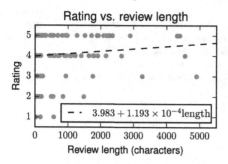

Figure 2.4 Line of best fit between ratings and review length (*Goodreads*)

This process—finding a line of best fit that best approximates the relationship between our observed features X and labels y—describes the basic concept of *linear regression*.

Adding More Dimensions: Just as Equation (2.6) corresponds to fitting a line in two dimensions, Equation (2.13) now corresponds to fitting a plane in three. But ultimately the procedure for fitting this model remains the same. We simply have an additional column in our feature matrix:

$$X = \begin{bmatrix} 1 & 2086 & 1 \\ 1 & 1521 & 1 \\ 1 & 1519 & 5 \\ 1 & 1791 & 1 \\ 1 & 1762 & 0 \\ & \vdots & \end{bmatrix}. \qquad (2.14)$$

Solving $\theta = (X^T X)^{-1} X^T y$ yields

$$\theta = \begin{bmatrix} 3.954 \\ 7.243 \times 10^{-5} \\ 0.108 \end{bmatrix} \begin{matrix} \text{intercept} \\ \text{slope for length} \\ \text{slope for number of comments} \end{matrix}. \qquad (2.15)$$

Interestingly, when we add this additional parameter θ_2, the values of θ_1 and θ_0 are different from those of the model we previously fit (compare eqs. (2.11) and (2.15)). Critically, the slope associated with the length term (θ_1) is reduced in our new model. We discuss how to interpret these parameters in Section 2.4.

2.1.1 Regression in *sklearn*

Various libraries support the basic machine learning techniques described in this chapter, and indeed they can be implemented relatively straightforwardly via standard linear algebra operations. Here we describe the implementation in *scikit-learn*, though other implementations follow similar interfaces. Once again note that detailed versions of all code examples are included in the online supplement (sec. 1.4).

First we load our dataset; here we read our sample (in this case a toy dataset of 100 reviews) in *json* format,[3] which results in a list of 100 dictionaries:

```
1  data = []
2  for l in open('fantasy_100.json'): # 100 reviews of fantasy
       novels from Goodreads
3      d = json.loads(l)
4      data.append(d)
```

Next, we extract labels and features from the dataset. In this case, we train a predictor to estimate ratings as a function of review length, as in Equation (2.6):

```
5  ratings = [d['rating'] for d in data] # The output we want
       to predict
6  lengths = [len(d['review_text']) for d in data] # The
       feature used for prediction
```

To regress on these data, we must first construct our matrix of features X and our vector of labels y; note the inclusion of a constant feature in our feature matrix:[4]

```
7  X = numpy.matrix([[1,l] for l in lengths])
8  y = numpy.matrix(ratings).T
```

From here, regressing is simply a matter of passing our features and labels to the appropriate model from *sklearn*. Having done so, we extract the coefficients θ:

```
9  model = sklearn.linear_model.LinearRegression(fit_intercept=
       False)
10 model.fit(X,y)
11 theta = model.coef_
```

Finally, we confirm manually that the pseudoinverse from Equation (2.10) yields the same result:

```
12 numpy.linalg.inv(X.T*X)*X.T*y
```

In both cases we find that $\theta = (3.983, 1.193 \times 10^{-4})$, as in Figure 2.4.

[3] *Json* is a structured data format, made up of key-value pairs (where values can in turn be lists or other *json* objects). See www.json.org/.
[4] Although in practice this can be excluded and θ_0 can be fit by the library by setting fit_intercept=True; here we include it manually.

2.2 Evaluating Regression Models

When developing the earlier linear models, we were somewhat imprecise about what is meant by a 'line of best fit' (or generally a model of best fit). Indeed, the pseudoinverse is not a 'solution' to the system of equations given in Equation (2.8), but is merely an approximation (naturally, the line of best fit does not pass through all points exactly).

Here, we would like to be more precise about what it means for a model to be 'good.' This is a key issue when fitting and evaluating any machine learning model: one needs a way of quantifying how closely a model fits the given data. Given a desired measure of success, we can compare alternative models against this measure and design optimization schemes that optimize the desired measure directly.

2.2.1 The Mean Squared Error

A commonly used evaluation criterion when evaluating regression algorithms is called the mean squared error, or MSE. The MSE between a model $f_\theta(X)$ and a set of labels y is defined as

$$\text{MSE}(y, f_\theta(X)) = \frac{1}{|y|} \sum_{i=1}^{|y|} (f_\theta(x_i) - y_i)^2, \qquad (2.16)$$

in other words, the average squared difference between the model's predictions and the labels. Often reported is also the root mean squared error (RMSE), that is, $\sqrt{\text{MSE}(y, f_\theta(X))}$; the RMSE is sometimes preferable as it is consistent in scale with the original labels.

With some effort, it can be shown that the linear model $f_\theta(X)$ that minimizes the MSE compared to the labels y is given by using the pseudoinverse as in Equation (2.10). We leave this as an exercise (Exercise 2.6).

2.2.2 Why the Mean Squared Error?

Although the MSE has a convenient relationship with the pseudoinverse, it may otherwise seem a somewhat arbitrary choice of error measure. For instance, it may seem more obvious at first to compute an error measure such as the mean absolute error (or MAE):

$$\text{MAE}(y, f_\theta(X)) = \frac{1}{|y|} \sum_{i=1}^{|y|} |f_\theta(x_i) - y_i|. \qquad (2.17)$$

Or, why not count the number of times the model is wrong by more than one star? For that matter, why not measure the mean *cubed* error?

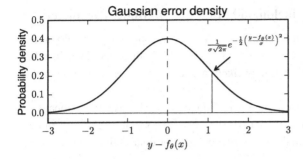

Figure 2.5 Gaussian error density

To defend the MSE as a reasonable choice, we need to characterize what types of errors are more 'likely' than others. Essentially, the MSE assigns very small penalties to small errors and *very* large penalties to large errors. This is in contrast to, say, the MAE, which assigns penalties precisely in proportion to how large the error is. What the MSE therefore seems to be assuming is that small errors are *common* and large errors are particularly uncommon.

What we are talking about informally here is a notion of how errors are *distributed* under some model. Formally, we say that the labels are equal to our model's predictions, plus some error:

$$y = \underbrace{f_\theta(X)}_{\text{prediction}} + \underbrace{\epsilon}_{\text{error}}, \tag{2.18}$$

and that our error follows some probability distribution. Our argument here said that small errors are common and large errors are very rare. This suggests that errors may be distributed following a *bell curve*, which we could capture with a Gaussian (or 'Normal') distribution:

$$\epsilon \sim \mathcal{N}(0, \sigma^2). \tag{2.19}$$

The density function for a (zero mean) Gaussian distribution is given by

$$f'(x') = \frac{1}{\sigma\sqrt{2\pi}} e^{-\frac{1}{2}\left(\frac{x'}{\sigma}\right)^2} \tag{2.20}$$

(we use the notation f' and x' to avoid confusion with f and x elsewhere). So, the probability density for an error of size $y_i - f_\theta(x)$ is given by

$$\frac{1}{\sigma\sqrt{2\pi}} e^{-\frac{1}{2}\left(\frac{y - f_\theta(x)}{\sigma}\right)^2}. \tag{2.21}$$

This density function is depicted in Figure 2.5.

2.2.3 Maximum Likelihood Estimation of Model Parameters

Having defined the density function, we can now reason more formally about what it means for a particular model to be a 'good' fit to the data. In other words, we would like to ask how *likely* a particular model is in terms of a given error distribution.

Specifically, the density function in Equation (2.21) gives us a means of assigning a probability (or likelihood) to a particular set of labels y, given features X, and a model θ, under some particular error distribution (in this case a Gaussian):

$$\mathcal{L}_\theta(y|X) = \prod_{i=1}^{|y|} \frac{1}{\sigma\sqrt{2\pi}} e^{-\frac{1}{2}\left(\frac{y_i - f_\theta(x_i)}{\sigma}\right)^2}. \tag{2.22}$$

Essentially, we want to choose θ so as to maximize this likelihood. Intuitively our goal is to choose a value of θ that is consistent with this error distribution, that is, a model that makes many small errors and few large ones.

Precisely, we would like to find $\arg\max_\theta \mathcal{L}_\theta(y|X)$. This procedure (finding a model θ that maximizes the likelihood under some error distribution) is known as maximum likelihood estimation (MLE). We solve this by taking logarithms and removing irrelevant terms (π, σ):

$$\arg\max_\theta \mathcal{L}_\theta(y|X) = \arg\max_\theta \ell_\theta(y|X) \tag{2.23}$$

$$= \arg\max_\theta \log \prod_{i=1}^{|y|} \frac{1}{\sigma\sqrt{2\pi}} e^{-\frac{1}{2}\left(\frac{y_i - f_\theta(x_i)}{\sigma}\right)^2} \tag{2.24}$$

$$= \arg\max_\theta \sum_i \log e^{-\frac{1}{2}\left(\frac{y_i - f_\theta(x_i)}{\sigma}\right)^2} \tag{2.25}$$

$$= \arg\max_\theta -\sum_i (y_i - f_\theta(x_i))^2 \tag{2.26}$$

$$= \arg\min_\theta \sum_i (y_i - f_\theta(x_i))^2 \tag{2.27}$$

$$= \arg\min_\theta \frac{1}{|y|} \sum_i (y_i - f_\theta(x_i))^2. \tag{2.28}$$

Note crucially in the above equation that *the maximum likelihood solution for θ under our Gaussian error model is precisely the MSE*. This demonstrates the relationship between the MSE and MLE (which we summarize in fig. 2.6).

These arguments may seem like just a mathematical curiosity, and indeed in practice we will often minimize the MSE without scrutinizing the decision to do so. But this relationship between error functions and probabilities will come up regularly when we develop models for classification (chap. 3),

The argument we made in sec. 2.2.2 explained our motivation behind the choice of the mean squared error (MSE): By choosing the MSE as our error metric, we are implicitly assuming that our model's errors follow a Gaussian distribution. This assumption is explained by the fact that minimizing the MSE maximizes the likelihood of the observed errors under a Gaussian error model.

Figure 2.6 The MSE and the MLE

recommender systems (chap. 5), and sequence mining (chap. 7). To summarize, a few key points are as follows:

(i) When we optimize a certain error criterion, we are often making implicit assumptions about how errors are distributed.
(ii) Sometimes a model will poorly fit a dataset because these assumptions are violated. Understanding the underlying assumptions gives us a chance to diagnose problems and attempt to correct them (sec. 2.2.5).
(iii) In many of the models we fit later (including when we develop classifiers in chap. 3), we will use this style of probabilistic language, that is, we will talk about some observed data having high *likelihood* under some model. Fitting such models will use this same strategy of selecting a model which maximizes the corresponding likelihood.

2.2.4 The R^2 Coefficient

Having motivated our choice of the MSE at some length, it is worth asking how low the MSE should be before we consider our model to be 'good enough'?

This quantity turns out not to be well defined: the MSE will depend on the scale and variability of our data, and the difficulty of our task. For example, predicted ratings on a 5-point scale would likely have lower MSEs than predicted ratings on a 100-point scale; on the other hand, this might not be the case if ratings on a 100-point scale were highly concentrated (e.g., nearly all ratings were in the 92–95 range). Finally, the MSE in either setting could be higher simply due to a lack of available features that allow us to predict ratings accurately.

As such, we would like a calibrated measurement of model error. As we just argued, the MSE is related to the *variance* of the data: this relationship is easy to see as follows:

$$\bar{y} = \frac{1}{|y|} \sum_i y_i, \tag{2.29}$$

$$\text{var}(y) = \frac{1}{|y|} \sum_i (y_i - \bar{y})^2, \tag{2.30}$$

$$\text{MSE}(y, f_\theta(X)) = \frac{1}{|y|} \sum_i (y_i - f(x_i))^2. \qquad (2.31)$$

In other words, the MSE would be equal to the variance if we had a trivial predictor that always estimated $f(x_i) = \bar{y}$.[5] Thus, the variance might be used as a way of normalizing the MSE:

$$\text{FVU}(y, f_\theta(X)) = \frac{\text{MSE}(f, f_\theta(X))}{\text{var}(y)}. \qquad (2.32)$$

This quantity, known as the *Fraction of Variance Unexplained (FVU)*, essentially measures the extent to which the model *explains variability* in the data, as compared to a predictor that always predicts the mean (i.e., one which explains no variability at all).

This quantity will now take a value between 0 and 1: 0 being a perfect classifier (MSE of zero) and 1 being a trivial classifier.[6]

Often, one reports the R^2 *coefficient*, which is simply 1 minus the FVU:

$$R^2 = 1 - \frac{\text{MSE}(y, f_\theta(X))}{\text{var}(y)}, \qquad (2.33)$$

which now takes a value of 1 for a perfect predictor and 0 for a trivial predictor. The name 'R^2' comes from a different way of deriving the same quantity, in terms of the correlation between the predictions and the labels.[7]

2.2.5 What to Do If Errors *Are Not* Normally Distributed?

Our abovementioned arguments characterized the relationship between the MSE and the normal (Gaussian) distribution. In summary, the MSE is a reasonable choice so long as our model errors are expected to be centered around zero, and not to have large outliers.

But what can we do if these assumptions do not hold? First, we consider how to validate the assumptions in the first place. Recall that our basic assumption asserts that the residuals

$$r_i = y_i - f_\theta(x_i) \qquad (2.34)$$

follow a normal distribution. To begin with, a simple plot may reveal whether the residuals follow the desired overall trend.

---

[5] Note that this is the best we could do if using a trivial predictor of the form $f(x_i) = \theta_0$ (Exercise 2.3).

[6] The FVU *could* be greater than 1, if our classifier were *worse* than a trivial one.

[7] We omit this alternate derivation for now, but revisit the idea of correlation briefly in Section 4.3.4.

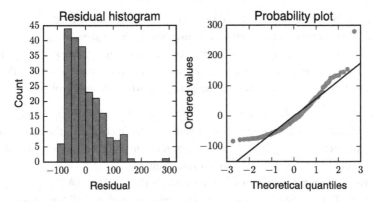

Figure 2.7 Histogram of observed residuals (left) and residuals compared to theoretical quantiles under a normal distribution

Figure 2.7 (left) shows a histogram of residuals r_i for a simple prediction task, in which we estimate review lengths as a function of user gender (covered later in sec. 2.3.2). Although the plot has a slight bell shape, it deviates from the normal distribution in several key ways, for instance:

- The residuals do not appear to be centered around zero. In fact, the *average* residual is zero,[8] though the largest bins in the histogram are somewhat below zero.
- The are some large outliers (i.e., extremely long reviews whose length was underpredicted).
- There are no small outliers, and there is almost no 'left tail,' that is, the model never significantly overpredicts.

Although the histogram in Figure 2.7 allows us to quickly assess whether the residuals follow a normal distribution, this can be visualized more precisely by comparing the theoretical quantiles of a normal distribution to the observed residuals, as in Figure 2.7 (right).[9] The plot essentially compares the (sorted) residuals to those we would expect if we were to sample the same number of values from a normal distribution: If our residuals followed a normal distribution, plotting these quantities against each other would result in a straight line. Again, the plot basically reveals that there is an unusual outlier, and that residuals are missing the left tail (i.e., overpredictions) that would be

---

[8] In fact, the average residual of this type of linear regression model is *always* zero (see Exercise 2.7).

[9] This type of diagnostic plot can be generated easily with a library function, for example, this one was generated with `scipy.stats.probplot`.

expected. Note that this same type of diagnostic tool can be used to compare our residuals against any hypothetical distribution in the same way.

While this is merely a diagnostic for determining *whether* the residuals followed a normal distribution, the more difficult question is how these discrepancies can be corrected. Some general guidelines are as follows:

Remove Outliers: The normal distribution (and thus the MSE) is especially sensitive to outliers due to how it penalizes large errors. To the extent that extremely long reviews do not conform to the usual behavior of the data, we could simply discard them before training.

Choose an Error Model Less Sensitive to Outliers: The MAE (e.g.) assigns a smaller penalty to large mispredictions, so outliers will have a smaller effect on the model.

Choose a Skewed Distribution: In this example we are predicting a length, which by definition is bounded below (at length zero) but not above. Thus, there will be a long tail of underpredictions but not large overpredictions. We might account for this by modeling the data using a skewed probability distribution (such as a Gamma distribution).

Fit a Better Model: Note that the diagnostic in Figure 2.7 is a function of the *errors* rather than the original data. Thus, for example, if we had a feature that allowed us to correctly predict the length of the unusually long review, the errors may become more consistent with a normal distribution.

Again, the MSE is generally a safe and reasonable choice, and can be used without too much scrutiny. Nevertheless, it is useful to have a sense of its underlying assumptions so that one can detect when they have been violated.

2.3 Feature Engineering

Along with the simple linear function relating features to labels as in Equation (2.3) come significant limitations in terms of what kinds of relationships can be modeled with linear regression techniques. When modeling asymptotic, periodic, or other nonlinear relationships between features and labels, it is not yet clear how this can be accomplished given the limitations of this type of model.

As we shall see, complex relationships can be handled within the framework of linear models, so long as we exercise care by appropriately transforming our features (and labels). In practice, the success or failure of our models will often depend on carefully processing our data to help the model uncover the most salient relationships. This process of *feature engineering* proves critical even when developing deep learning models based on images or text: in

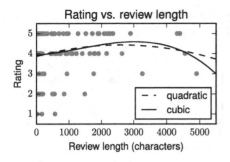

Figure 2.8 Quadratic and cubic polynomials of best fit

spite of the vague promise of learning complex nonlinear relationships automatically, extracting meaningful signals from data is often a matter of careful engineering, rather than selecting a more complex model.

2.3.1 Simple Feature Transformations

The first model we fit in Equation (2.6) revealed a positive association between review length and ratings. However, fitting the data with a line (fig. 2.4) does not seem to fit the data very accurately. Fitting the data with a line seems limiting, given that the trend may be better captured by a polynomial or asymptotic function (since the rating cannot grow above five stars).

Naively, we might think that this is a fundamental limitation of linear models. Note however that the assumption of linearity in θ (eq. (2.3)) does not prevent us from fitting (e.g.) a polynomial function. The polynomial equation

$$\text{rating} = \theta_0 + \theta_1 \times (\text{review length}) + \theta_2 \times (\text{review length})^2 \qquad (2.35)$$

is linear in θ, even though we have transformed the input features in X.

This idea can be applied straightforwardly to fit polynomial functions, as shown in Figure 2.8.[10]

2.3.2 Binary and Categorical Features: One-Hot Encodings

So far we have dealt with regression problems where we have both real-valued inputs (features X) and real-valued outputs (labels y). What can we do in cases where features are binary or categorical?

As an example, let us consider whether the length of a user's review can be predicted by (or more simply, is related to) their gender. To do so, we will

---

[10] Actually, these curves were generated using the feature $\frac{\text{length}}{1000}$, as the matrix inverse $(X^T X)^{-1}$ becomes numerically unstable given large values of $(\text{length})^3$.

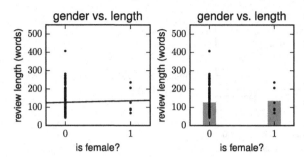

Figure 2.9 Gender versus review length (beer data). Visualized via a line of best fit (left) and a bar plot (right).

look at a different dataset (of a few hundred beer reviews from McAuley et al. (2012)) that includes the gender of its users.

That is, we would like a model of the form:

$$\text{length} = \theta_0 + \theta_1 \times \text{gender}. \qquad (2.36)$$

Obviously, gender (represented in this dataset as a string) is not a numerical quantity, so we need some appropriate *encoding* of the gender variable.

For the moment, let us treat gender as a binary variable. We will relax this assumption in a moment to allow for a non-binary gender variable (and allow for the possibility that the gender is missing, as it can be in this dataset), but for the moment let us encode the gender variable as:

$$\text{Male} = 0; \quad \text{Female} = 1. \qquad (2.37)$$

Alternately, this is just a binary indicator specifying whether this user is female. This encoding, although only one of a few we might have used, allows us to fit a linear model and estimate the values of θ_0 and θ_1. The model we fit (after removing users who did not specify a gender) is

$$\text{length (in words)} = 127.07 + 8.76 \times (\text{user is female}). \qquad (2.38)$$

With a little thought, we can interpret the model parameters as indicating that, on average, females write slightly longer reviews (by 8.76 words) compared to males. Note that 127.07 is not the population average, but rather the average for males (whose gender feature is zero).

A scatter plot of the data (i.e., the encoded gender attribute and the review lengths), as well as the line of best fit above is depicted in Figure 2.9. Note that although we have fit the data with a line (Fig. 2.9, left), the actual feature values only occupy two points (0 and 1); thus the fit is perhaps better represented with a bar plot (Fig. 2.9, right).

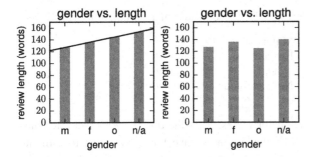

Figure 2.10 Categorical features with a naive sequential encoding (left), and a one-hot encoding (right)

Categorical Features

In practice, the gender attribute may assume more than binary labels in some datasets. To accommodate this, we might naively imagine extending our encoding from Equation (2.37) to include additional values:

$$
\begin{aligned}
\text{Male} &= & 0 \\
\text{Female} &= & 1 \\
\text{Other} &= & 2 \\
\text{Not specified} &= & 3 \\
\text{etc.}
\end{aligned}
\tag{2.39}
$$

Again we fit the same model as in Equation (2.36). Doing so we might obtain a fitted model like the one in Figure 2.10 (left).

Note that the model fit in Figure 2.10 (left) implicitly makes some dubious assumptions. For example, because the model is linear, it assumes that the difference between 'male' and 'female' lengths is *the same as* the difference between 'female' and 'other' lengths.[11]

This assumption is not supported by the data, and in fact would be different if we simply reordered our indices in Equation (2.39). Rather, we would like to associate different predictions to members of each group, as in Figure 2.10 (right). This can be achieved via a different encoding:

$$
\begin{aligned}
\text{Male} &= & [0,0,0] \\
\text{Female} &= & [0,0,1] \\
\text{Other} &= & [0,1,0] \\
\text{Not specified} &= & [1,0,0] \\
\text{etc.}
\end{aligned}
\tag{2.40}
$$

---

[11] That is, males receive the prediction θ_0; females receive $\theta_0 + \theta_1$; other receives $\theta_0 + 2\theta_1$, and so on.

We can quickly confirm that the model would make predictions as follows:

$$
\begin{array}{ll}
\text{Male:} & y = \theta_0 \\
\text{Female:} & y = \theta_0 + \theta_1 \\
\text{Other} & y = \theta_0 + \theta_2 \\
\text{Not specified} & y = \theta_0 + \theta_3 \\
\text{etc.} &
\end{array}
\qquad (2.41)
$$

That is, θ_0 is the prediction for males, θ_1 is the *difference* between females and males, and so on. Note that we now have four parameters to estimate four values, as opposed to two parameters as in Equation (2.39). As such, the model has sufficient flexibility to make different estimates for each group, as in Figure 2.10 (right).

This type of encoding, in which we have a separate feature dimension for each category, is called a *one-hot* encoding.

Note that to represent four categories in Equation (2.40) we only used *three*-dimensional features (or in general, for N categories, we could use an $(N-1)$-dimensional encoding). Possibly this seems slightly confusing compared to using a four-dimensional feature vector (e.g., Male = $[0, 0, 0, 1]$, etc.). Two reasons for using an $(N-1)$-dimensional feature vector are as follows:

(i) Using a four-dimensional encoding is not necessary; together with θ_0, the representation in Equation (2.40) uses four parameters to predict four values, so adding an additional dimension would add no more expressive power to the model and would be redundant.

(ii) Doing so could possibly be harmful. While adding redundant features seems harmless, in practice doing so means the system in Equation (2.7) would no longer have a unique solution, as the matrix $X^T X$ would be uninvertable.

Similarly, a *multi-hot* encoding can be used in cases where an instance can belong to multiple categories simultaneously, for example, for an 'ethnicity' feature, a user may associate with multiple ethnic groups (note that this is equivalent to a concatenation of several binary features).

2.3.3 Missing Features

Often datasets will have features that are missing, for example, the underlying data used for the example in Section 2.3.2 consisted of a gender attribute that many users may leave unspecified.

When dealing with binary or categorical features we dealt with these missing values quite straightforwardly—we simply treated 'missing' as an additional category.

But if a continuous feature, such as a user's age or income, were missing, we must think harder about how to handle it. Trivially, we might simply discard instances with missing features, though this strategy will harm model performance if it means discarding a substantial fraction of our data.

Alternately we might replace the missing entries by the average (or mode) value for that feature; this strategy is known as *feature imputation*. This may be more effective than discarding the feature, but may also introduce some bias, as (e.g.) users who choose to leave a feature unspecified may be quite different from the average or mode.

To avoid these issues, we would like a strategy that uses features when they are available, but makes separate predictions for those users when they are not. This can be achieved via the following strategy: for any feature x which is sometimes missing, replace it by two features x' and x'' as follows:

$$x' = \begin{cases} 1 & \text{if feature is missing} \\ 0 & \text{otherwise} \end{cases} \quad , \quad x'' = \begin{cases} 0 & \text{if feature is missing} \\ x & \text{otherwise} \end{cases} .$$

$$(2.42)$$

Following this parameters can be fit within a model as usual:

$$y = \theta_0 + \theta_1 x' + \theta_2 x''. \tag{2.43}$$

This representation may seem somewhat arbitrary, but makes sense once we expand the expression for missing and non-missing features. For example, when a feature is available predictions are made according to

$$y = \theta_0 + \theta_2 x, \tag{2.44}$$

whereas when a feature is missing predictions are made according to

$$y = \theta_0 + \theta_1. \tag{2.45}$$

This achieves the desired effect: when the feature is available we predict as normal, and when the feature is unavailable we predict using a learned value (θ_1). Note that this strategy is very similar to feature imputation, but rather than using a heuristic imputation strategy, the model will directly learn what is the best prediction to impute.

2.3.4 Temporal Features

Temporal features may make excellent predictors in various settings. Outcomes such as ratings, clicks, purchases (etc.) are often influenced by factors such as the day of the week, the season, or long-term trends that span several years.

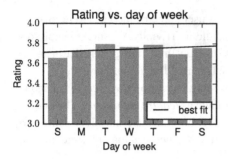

Figure 2.11 Ratings as a function of the weekday, and line of best fit

Let us explore an example in which we try to predict the rating of a book on *Goodreads* based on the day of the week that it was entered. Average ratings for each weekday[12] are shown in Figure 2.11.

As before, we might try to describe this relationship using a line, that is, to fit a model of the form

$$\text{rating} = \theta_0 + \theta_1 \times (\text{day of week}). \tag{2.46}$$

For this equation to make sense, we need to map the day of the week to a numeric quantity. A trivial encoding might assign numbers sequentially, for example,

$$\text{Sunday} = 1; \quad \text{Monday} = 2; \quad \text{Tuesday} = 3; \quad \text{etc.} \tag{2.47}$$

Fitting Equation (2.46) using this representation yields the line of best fit depicted in Figure 2.11, which reveals a slight upward trend as the days of the week progress.

The linear trend in Figure 2.11 seems a fairly poor fit to the data; we might think about fitting a more complex function (like a polynomial) to better capture the observed data. But consider that our model is essentially *periodic:* Sunday (represented by a 1) follows Saturday (represented by a 7), though we could just as easily have represented Wednesday as 1 and Tuesday as 7. These choices seem arbitrary, but impact our model in unexpected ways.

This point is perhaps clearer if we visualize our model's predictions over a period of two weeks, as in Figure 2.12: an encoding of the form in Equation (2.47) corresponds to an unrealistic 'sawtooth' pattern that repeats every week.

It might be tempting to model such data using a periodic function, for example,

$$\text{rating} = \theta_0 + \theta_1 \times \sin\left((\text{day} + \theta_2) \times \frac{2\pi}{7}\right). \tag{2.48}$$

---

[12] Again based on a small sample of reviews from the Fantasy genre.

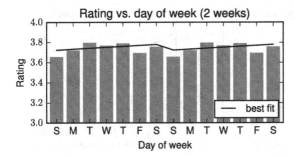

Figure 2.12 If we consider that our weekly measurements are periodic, we realize that fitting periodic data with a linear trend seems unrealistic.

Note however that this type of model is not linear (due to θ_2) and cannot be fit using the methods we have seen so far; furthermore, such a formulation is still quite restrictive and contains possibly unrealistic assumptions.

More straightforwardly, we can again use a one-hot encoding, as we did for gender in Equation (2.40) to encode the day of the week:

$$
\begin{aligned}
\text{Sunday} &= \quad [0,0,0,0,0,0] \\
\text{Monday} &= \quad [0,0,0,0,0,1] \\
\text{Tuesday} &= \quad [0,0,0,0,1,0] \\
\text{etc.}
\end{aligned}
\tag{2.49}
$$

Such a model can straightforwardly capture periodic trends (essentially corresponding to a 'step function,' much as we see in Figure 2.12). One could also combine several such encodings (e.g., for the hour of day, the month, etc.) to capture periodic patterns at different scales.

We will revisit the critical role of temporal dynamics (and explore more complex temporal representations) in Chapter 7.

2.3.5 Transformation of Output Variables

Finally, just as we saw how to transform features in Section 2.3.1, we can also transform our *output* variables.

For example, let us consider fitting a model to determine whether resubmitted posts on *reddit* (Lakkaraju et al., 2013) receive lower numbers of upvotes, that is,

$$
\text{upvotes} = \theta_0 + \theta_1 \times (\text{submission number})
\tag{2.50}
$$

(where the 'submission number' is '1' for an original submission, '2' for the first resubmission, etc.). This model, along with the observations on which it is based, are shown in Figure 2.13 (left).

Although the line of best fit indicates a slight downward trend, it does not appear to correspond closely to the overall shape of the data. Eye-balling the

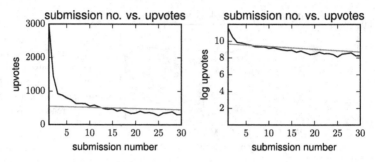

Figure 2.13 Number of upvotes versus submission number on *reddit*. The left plot shows the original data (with averaged upvote counts), the right plot shows the logarithm of the number of upvotes. Lines of best fit for both plots are included.

data in Figure 2.13, we might hypothesize that the data follows an exponentially decreasing trend, for example, every time you resubmit a post, you can expect to receive half as many upvotes.

Again, one might assume that this type of trend is something that cannot be captured by a linear model. But in fact we can possibly address this by transforming the *output* variable y. For example, consider fitting

$$\log_2(\text{upvotes}) = \theta'_0 + \theta'_1(\text{submission number}). \qquad (2.51)$$

Now, a unit change in the prediction corresponds to a post receiving *twice* as many upvotes. While this is still a linear model, the model corresponds to fitting

$$\text{upvotes} = 2^{\theta'_0 + \theta'_1(\text{submission number})}. \qquad (2.52)$$

The transformed data and line of best fit are shown in Figure 2.13 (right).

Arguably, this second line better captures the overall trend, and does not have the same issues with outliers. If we transform the fitted values from Equation (2.51) back to their original scale via Equation (2.52), the transformed values actually have a MSE about 10% lower than the model from Equation (2.50), indicating that the transformed data more closely follows a linear trend compared to the untransformed data.

2.4 Interpreting the Parameters of Linear Models

When analyzing the linear models developed so far, we have already talked about interpreting their parameters in terms of general trends, correlation, differences between groups, and so on.

Given a linear model $y = X\theta$ we should interpret a parameter θ_k as follows:

For every unit change in x_{ik}, our prediction of the output y_i would increase by θ_k, *if all other feature values remain fixed*.

It is important to note that we are talking about the model's *prediction* (rather than an actual change in the label), which could change if different features were included. And we must include the condition that other features remain constant, without which we would fail to account for the potential correlations among different features.

Figure 2.14 Interpreting the parameters of linear models

While is tempting to casually interpret the meaning of various features, we must be careful and precise when doing so.

First, we should be precise about the interpretation of our slope and intercept terms. For example, when we modeled ratings as a function of review length (eq. (2.12)), we stated that under our model, ratings increased fractionally (1.193×10^{-4}) for every character of a review.

This interpretation makes sense given a model containing only a single features, but as soon as we incorporate multiple features we must be more careful. Consider, for example, the model from Equation (2.15), in which we included both the length and number of comments as predictors. We could no longer state that under this model, the rating increases (by 7.243×10^{-5}) for every character in the review. Precisely, we must interpret the parameters as follows: *Our prediction of the rating increases by* 7.243×10^{-5} *for every character in the review, assuming the other features remain unchanged*. This definition is stated precisely in Figure 2.14.

Critically, features like review length and number of comments may be highly *correlated* (e.g., we may rarely see longer reviews without also seeing more comments). For example, when incorporating features based on polynomial functions (as in eq. (2.35)), or when dealing with one-hot encodings (as in eq. (2.39)), a feature *cannot* change without the other features changing.

Second, we should be clear when interpreting parameters that we are talking about *predictions* under a particular model rather than actual changes in the label y_i. These predictions can change as we include additional features; a feature that had previously been predictive may become less so in the presence of another (as we saw in Equation (2.15)). Likewise, we should be careful not to conclude that (e.g.) length is *not* related to the output variable, simply because another correlated feature has a stronger relationship.

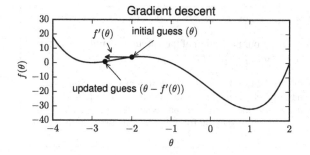

Figure 2.15 Gradient descent demonstration

Finally, we should be careful not to make statements about the *causal* effect of features on the output variable. Our line of best fit does not state that long reviews 'cause' positive opinions any more than it states that positive opinions cause long reviews.

2.5 Fitting Models with Gradient Descent

So far, when solving regression problems, we looked for *closed form* solutions. That is, we set up a system of equations (eq. (2.3)) in X, y, and θ, and attempted to solve them for θ (albeit approximately via the pseudoinverse).

As we begin to fit more complex models (including in Chapter 3), a closed-form solution may no longer be available.

Gradient descent is an approach to search for the minimum value of a function, by iteratively finding better solutions based on an initial starting point. The process (depicted in Figure 2.15) operates as follows:

(i) Start with an initial guess for θ.
(ii) Compute the derivative $\frac{\partial}{\partial \theta} f(\theta)$. Here $f(\theta)$ is the MSE (or whatever criterion we are optimizing) under our model θ.
(iii) Update our estimate of $\theta := \theta - \alpha \cdot f'(\theta)$.
(iv) Repeat Steps (ii) and (iii) until convergence.

During each iteration, the process now follows the path of steepest descent, and will gradually arrive at a minimum of the function f_θ.[13]

The above is a simple description of the procedure that omits many details. In practice, we will largely rely on high-level libraries to implement gradient-based methods (sec. 3.4.4). Briefly, to implement such techniques 'from scratch,' some of the main issues include:

---

[13] Assuming the function is 'well-behaved,' for example, the objective is bounded below, and the function is differentiable everywhere; though these are rarely issues when dealing with simple models and error functions like the MSE.

- Given the starting point in Figure 2.15, the algorithm would only achieve a *local* rather than a *global* optimum. To address this we could investigate ways to come up with a better initial 'guess' of θ, or investigate variants of gradient descent that are less susceptible to local minima.
- The step size α (step (iii)) must be chosen carefully. If α is too small, the procedure will converge very slowly; if α is too large, the procedure may 'overshoot' the minimum value and obtain a *worse* solution during the next iteration. Again, other than carefully tuning this parameter, we could investigate optimization methods not dependent on choosing this rate (see e.g., quasi-Newton methods such as L-BFGS (Liu and Nocedal, 1989)).
- 'Convergence' as defined in Step (iv) is not well-defined. We might define convergence in terms of the change in θ (or $f_\theta(X)$) during two successive iterations, or alternately we may terminate the algorithm once we stop making progress on held-out (validation) data (see sec. 3.4.2).

2.5.1 Linear Regression via Gradient Descent

To solidify the earlier ideas above, let us consider the specific example of minimizing the MSE of a linear model, that is,

$$\frac{1}{|y|} \sum_{i=1}^{|y|} (x_i \cdot \theta - y_i)^2. \tag{2.53}$$

The derivative $f'(\theta)$ can be computed as follows:

$$\frac{\partial f}{\partial \theta_k} = \frac{1}{|y|} \sum_{i=1}^{|y|} 2x_{ik}(x_i \cdot \theta - y_i). \tag{2.54}$$

Note that the above is a *partial* derivative in θ_k, which must be computed for each feature dimension $k = \{1 \ldots K\}$.[14]

2.6 Nonlinear Regression

So far, we have limited our discussion to models of the form $y = X\theta$, mostly because these offered us a convenient (closed form) solution to finding lines of best fit in terms of θ.

However, this type of model has several limitations that we might wish to overcome, such as:

---

[14] The derivative of Equation (2.54) is more obvious after expanding $x_i \cdot \theta = \sum_{k=1}^{K} x_{ik}\theta_k$.

- We cannot incorporate simple constraints on our parameters, such as that a certain parameter should be positive, or that one parameter is larger than another (which might be based on domain knowledge of a certain problem).
- Although we can manually engineer nonlinear transforms of our features (as we did in sec. 2.3.1), we cannot have the model learn these nonlinear relationships automatically.
- The model cannot learn complex *interactions* among features, for example, that length is correlated with ratings, but only if the user is female.[15]

These goals can potentially be realized if we are allowed to transform model *parameters*: for instance, we could ensure that a particular parameter was always positive by fitting

$$\theta_k = \log(1 + e^{\theta'_k}) \tag{2.55}$$

(this is known as a 'softplus' function; note that this function smoothly maps $\theta'_k \in \mathbb{R}$ to $\theta_k \in (0, \infty)$); or if we wanted one feature to be larger than another (e.g., $\theta_k > \theta_j$) we could simply add the positive quantity above to another feature:

$$\theta_k = \theta_j + \log(1 + e^{\theta'_k}). \tag{2.56}$$

Roughly speaking, fitting these types of nonlinear models (and especially models that deal with complex combinations of parameters) is the basic goal of *deep learning*. We will see various examples of nonlinear models in later chapters, including models based on deep learning (e.g., secs. 7.6 and 9.4). In Chapter 3 (sec. 3.4.4) we present the basic approach used to fit these types of models using high-level optimization libraries.

2.6.1 Case Study: Image Popularity on Reddit

Lakkaraju et al. (2013) used regression algorithms to estimate the success of content (e.g., number of upvotes) on *reddit*. Other than building an accurate predictor, their main goal is to understand and disentangle *which features are most influential in determining content popularity*.

Presumably, one of the biggest predictors of success is the quality of the content itself. Predicting whether a submission is of high quality (e.g., whether an

---

[15] To be precise, the linear model *does* consider relationships among features in the limited sense that parameters for one feature will change in the presence of other correlated features (sec. 2.4); and, the model *could* capture relationships between (e.g.) gender and length if we were to manually engineer a feature describing this relationship. Our point here is about whether the model can learn these relationships *automatically*.

image is funny or aesthetically attractive) is presumably incredibly challenging. To control for this high-variance factor of content quality, Lakkaraju et al. (2013) study *resubmissions*, that is, content (images) that has been submitted multiple times. This way, if one submission is more successful than another (of the same image), the difference in success cannot be attributed to the content itself, and must arise due to other factors such as the title of the submission or the community it was submitted to.

Having controlled for the effect of the content itself, the goal is then to distinguish between features that capture the specific dynamics of reddit itself, versus those that arise due to the choice of title (i.e., how the content is 'marketed'). Various features are extracted that model reddit's community dynamics, such as the following:

- One of the largest predictors of successful content is simply whether it has been submitted before (as we saw in Figure 2.13, which is based on the same dataset); this is captured via an exponentially decaying function.
- However, the above effect might be mitigated if enough time has passed between resubmissions (by when the original submission is forgotten, or the community has enough new users); this is captured using a feature based on the *inverse* of the time delta between submissions.
- Resubmissions might still be successful if they are resubmitted to largely non-overlapping communities (subreddits).
- Submission success may correlate with the time of day. For example, submissions may be most successful during the highest-traffic times of day, or alternately they may be more successful if submitted when there is less competition.

Whereas community effects are somewhat reddit-specific, measuring the effect of a particular choice of title can potentially be of broader interest. Understanding the characteristics of successful titles can have implications when marketing content (such as an advertising campaign) to a new market.

Several features can be extracted to capture the dynamics of a submission's title, including:

- Titles should differ from those previously used by submissions of the same content.
- Titles should align with the expectations of the community the content is submitted to. Interestingly, Lakkaraju et al. (2013) find that there is a 'sweet spot,' in the sense that titles should roughly follow the linguistic style of previous successful submissions in the same community, but

should not be *too* similar, to the point that they are not novel compared to previous submissions (we will discuss text similarity measures more in Chapter 8).

- Successful titles might have other features, in terms of length, sentiment, linguistic style, and so on.

Ultimately, all of these features are combined into a regression model that estimates the score (number of upvotes minus number of downvotes) that a particular submission will receive.

Due to the way that features are combined, the model is not linear in the parameters, so optimization proceeds by gradient descent (as in sec. 2.5). The method is evaluated in terms of the R^2 coefficient (sec. 2.2.4), with experiments revealing that community and textual features both play a key role in prediction. Finally, it is shown that the method can be used 'in the wild' to predict the success of actual reddit submissions.

Exercises

2.1   Using the *Goodreads* data (see, e.g., sec. 2.1), train a simple predictor that estimates ratings from review length, that is,

$$\text{star rating} = \theta_0 + \theta_1 \times (\text{review length in characters}).$$

Compute the values θ_0 and θ_1, and the MSE of your predictor.

2.2   Re-train your predictor so as to include a second feature based on the number of comments, that is,

$$\text{star rating} = \theta_0 + \theta_1 \times (\text{length}) + \theta_2 \times (\text{number of comments}).$$

Compute the coefficients and MSE of the new model. Briefly explain why the coefficient θ_1 in this model is different from the one from Exercise 2.1.

2.3   Show that $\theta_0 = \bar{y}$ is the best possible solution for a trivial predictor (i.e., $y = \theta_0$) in terms of the MSE (hint: write down the MSE of this trivial predictor and take its derivative).

2.4   Repeat Exercise 2.3, but this time show that the best trivial predictor in terms of the Mean *Absolute* Error (eq. (2.17)) is given by taking the *median* value of y.

2.5   In Equations (2.23) to (2.28) we motivated the choice of the MSE by explaining its relationship to a Gaussian error model. Likewise, show that minimizing the MAE is equivalent to maximizing the likelihood if errors follow a Laplace distribution (the Laplace distribution has probability density function $\frac{1}{2b} \exp\left(-\frac{|x-\mu|}{b}\right)$).

2.6 In Equation (2.10), we saw how to compute a line of best fit via the pseudoinverse, $\theta = (X^T X)^{-1} X^T y$; show that the parameters that minimize the MSE are found by taking the pseudoinverse, that is, $\arg\min_\theta \frac{1}{|y|} \sum_{i=1}^{|y|} (x_i \cdot \theta - y_i)^2 = (X^T X)^{-1} X^T y$ (i.e., find the stationary point where $\frac{\partial \text{MSE}}{\partial \theta} = 0$).

2.7 When minimizing the MSE with a linear model as in Exercise 2.6, show that the residuals $r_i = (y_i - x_i \cdot \theta)$ have average $\bar{r} = 0$.

Project 1: Taxicab Tip Prediction (Part 1)

Throughout the chapter, we have seen various strategies for dealing with features of different types. For our first project, we will look into building a prediction pipeline to estimate tip amounts from taxicab trips. For this project you might make use of publicly available data such as the *NYC Taxi and Limousine Commission Trip Record Data*.[16]

This project is mostly intended to introduce the end-to-end approach of exploring a new dataset, extracting meaningful information from it, and comparing alternative models. We break this down into the following parts:

(i) First, conduct *exploratory analysis* of the data. Just as we have done throughout the chapter, plot the relationship between the output (tip amount), and various features that you think might be related to this outcome.

(ii) Based on this analysis, consider what features might be useful for prediction. Consider, for example, features associated with the time of the trip, the start and end location, and the duration/distance of the trip.

(iii) How should these features be represented or transformed? For example, how can the timestamp be represented to capture variation at the level of time of day, day of week, or even the time of year (sec. 2.3.4); how might you represent the start and end locations? Are there any useful derived features that are useful for prediction, for example, speed = distance/duration?

[16] www1.nyc.gov/site/tlc/about/tlc-trip-record-data.page.

(iv) Is it useful to transform the *output* variable (sec. 2.3.5)? For example, rather than predicting the tip *amount*, it may make more sense to predict the tip *percentage*.

We will revisit and extend this project in Chapter 3 (Project 2) once we have further developed the learning pipeline, in order to more rigorously investigate and compare our modeling decisions.

3

Classification and the Learning Pipeline

So far, we have considered supervised learning tasks in which the output variable y is a real number, that is, $y \in \mathbb{R}$. Often, we will deal with problems with binary or categorical output variables, for example, we might be interested in problems such as:

- Will a user click on a product or advertisement? (binary outcome)
- What category of object does an image contain? (multiclass)
- What product is a user most likely to purchase next? (multiclass)
- Which of the two products would a user prefer? (binary)

In this chapter, we will explore how to design *classification* algorithms for tasks like those above, and in particular explore a classifier that extends the ideas behind regression from Chapter 2 to classification problems.

Logistic Regression sets up classification using a probabilistic framework, by transforming the predictions $X \cdot \theta$ that we used when building regressors into *probabilities* associated with observing a particular label y. By associating a probability with a particular label, and thereby to all of the labels in a dataset, we can again develop prediction frameworks that are differentiable and can be optimized using gradient-based approaches, much as we saw in Section 2.5.

Ultimately logistic regression is just one of dozens of classification schemes; we describe it here rather than alternatives (such as Support Vector Machines (Cortes and Vapnik, 1995), or Random Forest Classifiers (Ho, 1995)) mainly because logistic regression more closely matches the approaches we will develop in later chapters. This same type of modeling approach will be used throughout this book, when building Recommender Systems in Chapter 5, or generating fashionable outfits in Chapter 9, among others. We will briefly discuss the merits of alternative classification approaches in Section 3.2.

After exploring classification techniques in Section 3.1, we will explore evaluation strategies for classification models in Section 3.3, much as we did for regression models in Chapter 2.

Finally, we will explore the idea of the learning *pipeline*. Having developed techniques for regression (chap. 2), classification, and evaluation strategies for both, in Section 3.4 we will explore how to compare models, how to ensure that our results are significant, and how to ensure that our models generalize well to unseen data. This type of end-to-end strategy for model training will be used whenever we train supervised learning models throughout the remainder of the book.

3.1 Logistic Regression

When developing regular linear regressors in Chapter 2, we wanted a model f_θ whose estimates $f_\theta(x_i)$ were as close as possible to the (real-valued) labels y_i. When adapting a linear regression algorithm to classification, we might instead seek models that associate positive values of $x_i \cdot \theta$ with positive labels ($y_i = 1$), and negative values of $x_i \cdot \theta$ with negative labels ($y_i = 0$).

If we could do so, we could write down the *accuracy* associated with a particular model:

$$\frac{1}{|y|} \sum_{i=1}^{|y|} \underbrace{\delta(y_i = 0)\delta(x_i \cdot \theta \le 0)}_{\text{label is negative and prediction is negative}} + \overbrace{\delta(y_i = 1)\delta(x_i \cdot \theta > 0)}^{\text{label is positive and prediction is positive}} \qquad (3.1)$$

(here δ is an indicator function that returns 1 if the argument is true, 0 otherwise). The equation here, in spite of slightly confusing notation, is merely counting the number of times we correctly predict a positive score for a positively labeled instance, and a negative (or zero) score for a negatively labeled instance.

We now simply desire from our classifier θ that it maximizes the accuracy measured by Equation (3.1). Unfortunately, directly optimizing Equation (3.1) for θ is NP-hard (see, e.g., Nguyen and Sanner (2013)). To get a sense for why it is difficult, consider that the function in Equation (3.1) is essentially a *step* function (fig. 3.1, left), that is, it is flat (derivative zero) almost everywhere; it is therefore not amenable to techniques like gradient ascent as we saw in Section 2.5.

So, to optimize the accuracy approximately, we would like a function that is *similar to* Equation (3.1), but is more straightforward to optimize.

Logistic Regression achieves this goal by converting the outputs of a linear function $x_i \cdot \theta$ to *probabilities* via a smooth function. Our intuition is that large

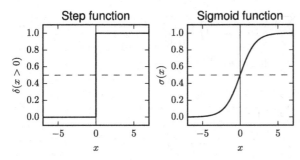

Figure 3.1 The sigmoid function (right), and the step function (left) that it approximates

values of $x_i \cdot \theta$ should correspond to high probabilities, and small (i.e., large negative) values of $x_i \cdot \theta$ should correspond to low probabilities.

This goal can be achieved via the *sigmoid function*:

$$\sigma(x) = \frac{1}{1 + e^{-x}}. \tag{3.2}$$

This function, depicted in Figure 3.1, maps a real value to the interval $(0, 1)$, and passes through 0.5 when $x = 0$. Thus it can be interpreted as a probability:

$$p_\theta(y_i = 1|x_i) = \sigma(x_i \cdot \theta) = \frac{1}{1 + e^{-x_i \cdot \theta}}. \tag{3.3}$$

Now, as a smooth surrogate for the expression in Equation (3.1), we can instead optimize

$$\mathcal{L}_\theta(y|X) = \prod_{y_i=1} p_\theta(y_i = 1|x_i) \times \prod_{y_i=0} (1 - p_\theta(y_i = 0|x_i)) \tag{3.4}$$

$$= \prod_{y_i=1} \frac{1}{1 + e^{-x_i \cdot \theta}} \times \prod_{y_i=0} \frac{e^{-x_i \cdot \theta}}{1 + e^{-x_i \cdot \theta}}. \tag{3.5}$$

This expression is a *likelihood function*, much like we saw in Equation (2.22). Intuitively, for this expression to be maximized we want positive instances ($y_i = 1$) to be associated with high probabilities, and negative instances ($y_i = 0$) to be associated with low probabilities.

3.1.1 Fitting the Logistic Regressor

Our goal is to maximize the abovementioned function, that is, to find $\arg\max_\theta \mathcal{L}_\theta(y|X)$. Short of a closed form solution, our approach is to take the logarithm $\ell_\theta(y|X)$ (since $\arg\max_\theta \mathcal{L}_\theta(y|X) = \arg\max_\theta \log(\mathcal{L}_\theta(y|X))$), to compute its gradient, and optimize via gradient ascent (as in sec. 2.5). We compute the gradient below as follows:

$$\ell_\theta(y|X) = \sum_{y_i=1} \log\left(\frac{1}{1 + e^{-x_i \cdot \theta}}\right) + \sum_{y_1=0} \log\left(\frac{e^{-x_i \cdot \theta}}{1 + e^{-x_1 \cdot \theta}}\right) \tag{3.6}$$

$$= \sum_i -\log(1 + e^{-x_i \cdot \theta}) + \sum_{y_i=0} -x_i \cdot \theta, \tag{3.7}$$

$$\frac{\partial \ell}{\partial \theta_k} = \sum_i x_{ik} \frac{e^{-x_i \cdot \theta}}{1 + e^{-x_i \cdot \theta}} - \sum_{y_i=0} x_{ik} \tag{3.8}$$

$$= \sum_i x_{ik}\,(1 - \sigma(x_i \cdot \theta)) - \sum_{y_i=0} x_{ik.} \tag{3.9}$$

Note carefully that the summation indices change between Equations (3.6) and (3.7), since both terms in Equation (3.6) have the same denominator.

3.1.2 Summary

Our development of logistic regression above is representative of the overall approach we will take later when developing models that estimate interactions, clicks, purchases, and so on:

- Rather than estimating an outcome directly, we associate a *probability* with each outcome. Associating a probability with the outcome allows us to replace discrete (e.g., $y_i \in \{0, 1\}$) outcomes with a continuous function ($f(x) \in (0, 1)$); this is accomplished via a transformation (such as the sigmoid function) which maps a real-valued output into the desired range.
- The model should associate positive (1) labels with high probabilities, and negative labels (0) with low probabilities. Likewise we can associate a probability to the entire dataset by taking a product of probabilities (or a sum of log-probabilities, as in eq. (3.6)).
- Ultimately these procedures allow us to associate the quality of a model (parameterized by θ) with a continuous function whose value we should try to maximize; we optimize the model via gradient ascent.

3.2 Other Classification Techniques

In our introduction to classification, we have only discussed a single classification technique: Logistic Regression. Our choice to explore this particular technique was largely a practical one: the idea of associating a probability with a particular outcome (as in eq. (3.5)) and estimating that probability via a differentiable function (to facilitate gradient ascent) will appear repeatedly as we develop more and more complex models.

However, the technique we have explored is only one class of approach to build classifiers. The specific choice to map binary labels to continuous probabilities via a smooth function has hidden assumptions and limitations, meaning that logistic regression is not the ideal classifier for every situation. Below we present a few alternatives, largely as further reading and to highlight specific situations where logistic regression may not be the preferable choice.

Support Vector Machines: While logistic regressors optimize a probability associated with a set of observed labels, they do not explicitly minimize the number of *mistakes* made by the classifier. Support Vector Machines (SVMs) (Cortes and Vapnik, 1995) replace the sigmoid function in Figure 3.1 with an expression that assigns zero cost to correctly classified examples,[1] and a positive cost[2] to incorrectly classified examples (in proportion to the confidence of the prediction $x \cdot \theta$). This distinction is fairly subtle: while *every* sample will influence the optimal value of θ for a logistic regressor, the solution found by an SVM is entirely determined by a few samples closest to the classification boundary, or those that are mislabeled. Conceptually it is appealing for a classifier to focus on the most 'difficult' samples in this way, though note that in many cases (and notably when building recommender systems) our goal is to optimize ranking performance rather than classification accuracy (as we will discuss in sec. 3.3.3), such that giving special attention to the most ambiguous examples is not necessarily desirable.

Decision Trees: Decision trees classify instances based on a sequence of binary decisions, each of which deals with a specific feature. Each node of the tree separates the data based on such a decision, with leaf nodes being responsible for determining an outcome. Decision trees straightforwardly facilitate learning nonlinear classifiers that capture complex interactions among features, for example, we can straightforwardly learn that a low price is associated with a positive review for young people, while a high price is associated with a positive review for older people: such an association is difficult for a linear classifier to learn if neither the 'age' nor 'price' feature is individually correlated with the outcome. Extensions such as *random forests* (Ho, 1995) (an ensemble of decision trees) remain popular forms of classification.

Multilayer Perceptrons: So far, we have focused on *linear* classifiers, which assume a simple relationship between features and predictions. Although we argued in Section 2.3 that such limitations could be overcome

---

[1] More precisely, correctly classified by some margin.
[2] Which is no longer interpretable as a probability.

by careful feature engineering, ideally we might like to learn such feature transformations automatically. Uncovering such complex relationships among features, and automatically learning nonlinear feature transformations is one of the main goals of *deep learning*. We will revisit such approaches as we develop more complex models throughout the book.

We exclude SVMs and decision trees from the remainder of this book mostly because they have little in common methodologically with the approaches we build in later chapters. We briefly introduce multilayer perceptrons in Section 5.5.2 when describing their use within deep learning-based recommendation techniques. As we try to reiterate throughout the book, multilayer perceptrons and various other state-of-the-art models are simply architectural choices that offer alternate ways to optimize the same objectives that we approach through simpler models. Having introduced the overall objectives, and the fundamentals of gradient-based optimization approaches, adapting them to alternate architectures is (relatively) straightforward.

3.3 Evaluating Classification Models

So far, when developing classifiers, we have focused on maximizing the alignment between the labels and the model's outputs. For example, in the case of logistic regression, we want the predicted probability $p_\theta(y_i = 1|x_i)$ to be as close as possible to the label y_i. Implicitly, when doing so, we are trying to maximize the model's *accuracy*:

$$\text{accuracy}(y, f_\theta(X)) = \frac{1}{|y|} \sum_{i=1}^{|y|} \delta(f_\theta(x_i) = y_i), \tag{3.10}$$

where δ is an indicator function, and $f_\theta(x_i)$ is the binarized output of the model (e.g., in the case of logistic regression, $f_\theta(x_i) = \delta(x_i \cdot \theta > 0)$).[3] Equivalently we are minimizing the *error*, that is,

$$\text{error}(y, f_\theta(X)) = 1 - \text{accuracy}(y, f_\theta(X)). \tag{3.11}$$

To motivate the difficulty of properly evaluating classifiers, consider the following classification task. We saw in Figure 2.9 that there was a slight relationship between gender and review length; now, let us see if we can develop a simple classifier that attempts to predict gender based on review length:

---

[3] Note that this is equivalent to the expression in Equation (3.1).

```
1  X = [[1, len(d['review/text'])] for d in data]
2  y = [d['user/gender'] == 'Female' for d in data]
3
4  mod = sklearn.linear_model.LogisticRegression()
5  mod.fit(X,y)
6  predictions = mod.predict(X) # Binary vector of predictions
7  correct = predictions == y # Binary vector indicating which
       predictions were correct
8  accuracy = sum(correct) / len(correct)
```

Surprisingly, the classifier produced by this code is 98.5% accurate. This result might seem implausible, but turns out to be a limitation of the error measure itself. Counting the number of negative labels in the dataset reveals that the data is 98.5% male (i.e., 98.5% negative labels). Not only does this reveal that the accuracy is unlikely to be an informative metric in this case, but it reveals that *our goal of optimizing the accuracy* caused us to learn a trivial classifier—the model simply predicts zero everywhere.

The aforementioned example demonstrates the problem with naively computing (or optimizing) model accuracy. Several situations where we might need more nuanced evaluation measures include:

- Datasets whose labels are highly imbalanced, such as the previous example.
- Situations where different types of errors have different associated costs. For example, failing to detect dangerous luggage in an airport is a more severe mistake than an erroneous positive identification.
- When we use classifiers for search or retrieval (as we will often do when developing recommender systems), we often care about the ability of the model to confidently identify a few positive instances (e.g., those surfaced on a results page), and are not interested in its overall accuracy.

Below we will develop error measures designed to handle each of these scenarios.

3.3.1 Balanced Metrics for Classification

The basic issue with the example presented here was that we allowed one of the two labels to dominate the classifier's objective. Although in some cases we may justifiably want a classifier that focuses more on the dominant label, in this example we would likely prefer a solution that had reasonable accuracy *per class*.

To achieve this we need evaluation metrics that consider the two classes (positive and negative, or female and male in our example) separately. To do so, we consider each of the four possible outcomes in terms of our prediction and label:

$$TP = \text{True Positives} \quad = |\{i \mid y_i \wedge f_\theta(x_i)\}| \qquad (3.12)$$

$$FP = \text{False Positives} \quad = |\{i \mid \neg y_i \wedge f_\theta(x_i)\}| \qquad (3.13)$$

$$TN = \text{True Negatives} \quad = |\{i \mid \neg y_i \wedge \neg f_\theta(x_i)\}| \qquad (3.14)$$

$$FN = \text{False Negatives} = |\{i \mid y_i \wedge \neg f_\theta(x_i)\}|. \qquad (3.15)$$

From these, we can define errors (or accuracies) that consider each of the two classes in isolation:[4]

$$TPR = \text{True Positive Rate} \quad = \frac{|\text{true positives}|}{|\text{labeled positive}|} = \frac{TP}{TP + FN} \qquad (3.16)$$

$$FPR = \text{False Positive Rate} \quad = \frac{|\text{false positives}|}{|\text{labeled negative}|} = \frac{FP}{FP + TN} \qquad (3.17)$$

$$TNR = \text{True Negative Rate} \quad = \frac{|\text{true negatives}|}{|\text{labeled negative}|} = \frac{TN}{TN + FP} \qquad (3.18)$$

$$FNR = \text{False Negative Rate} = \frac{|\text{false negatives}|}{|\text{labeled positive}|} = \frac{FN}{FN + TP}. \qquad (3.19)$$

Note that it is trivial to optimize any one of these criteria in isolation (e.g., we can achieve a True Positive Rate of 1.0 simply by always predicting positive). As such, we would normally optimize a criterion that considers both positive and negative labels together. One such measure is the balanced error rate (BER), which simply takes the average of the False Positive and False Negative rates:

$$\text{BER}(y, f_\theta(X)) = \frac{1}{2}(FPR + FNR) = 1 - \frac{1}{2}(TPR + TNR). \qquad (3.20)$$

In our motivating example, this now attributes half of the error to the 'Female' (positive) class and half of the error to the 'Male' (negative) class.

Note that an appealing quality of the BER is that (unlike the accuracy) it can no longer be minimized via trivial solutions: always predicting 'True,' or always predicting 'False,' or predicting at random, will all result in a BER of 0.5.

3.3.2 Optimizing the Balanced Error Rate

Having argued that the BER may be preferable to the accuracy if we wish to avoid trivial solutions, we next ask how to train a classifier to avoid producing trivial solutions in the first place.

Intuitively, the degenerate solutions we saw in Section 3.3 (i.e., a classifier which predicted zero everywhere) arose due to an imbalance in our training

---

[4] Various other terms exist for these expressions, for example, the terms *sensitivity*, *recall*, *hit rate*, and *true positive rate* are largely interchangeable.

data (that is, a high ratio of positive or negative labels). Trivially, we might correct this by *re-sampling* our training data: that is, sampling either a fraction of our negative instances, or sampling negative instances (with replacement) until we have an equal number of positive and negative instances.

While this is a common and reasonably effective strategy, the same goal can be achieved more directly simply by *weighting* the positive and negative instances. Note that in our objective for logistic regression:

$$\sum_{y_i=1} \log\left(\frac{1}{1+e^{-x_i \cdot \theta}}\right) + \sum_{y_1=0} \log\left(\frac{e^{-x_i \cdot \theta}}{1+e^{-X_I \cdot \theta}}\right), \qquad (3.21)$$

the two summations (over $y_i = 1$ and $y_i = 0$) essentially reward the model for correctly predicting positive instances and negative instances. The issue with this objective is that one of the two terms can dominate the expression in the event that positive or negative instances are over-represented in our dataset.

To address this, we can normalize the two expressions by the number of samples in the positive and negative classes:

$$\frac{|y|}{2|\{i \mid y_i = 1\}|} \sum_{y_i=1} \log\left(\frac{1}{1+e^{-x_i \cdot \theta}}\right) + \frac{|y|}{2|\{i \mid y_i = 0\}|} \sum_{y_1=0} \log\left(\frac{e^{-x_i \cdot \theta}}{1+e^{-X_I \cdot \theta}}\right). \quad (3.22)$$

By doing so, the left- and right-hand expressions have equal importance, such that *all* positively labeled instances have the same importance as *all* negative instances; in other words the two expressions (after normalization) roughly correspond to the True Positive *Rate* and True Negative *Rate*, as in Equation (3.20). Note that in addition to normalizing by the number of samples, both sides are multiplied by $\frac{|y|}{2}$; this is not strictly necessary but is done by convention such that the total 'weight' of all instances is still $|y|$.

This can be accomplished with the `class_weight='balanced'` option in sklearn as follows:

```
1  X = [[1, len(d['review/text'])] for d in data]
2  y = [d['user/gender'] == 'Female' for d in data]
3
4  mod = sklearn.linear_model.LogisticRegression(class_weight='
       balanced')
5  mod.fit(X,y)
```

Note that the same idea can be applied to problems including more than two categories, and that one can choose different weighting schemes, for example, to assign any desired relative importance to true positives versus true negatives (e.g., in the baggage-handling scenario we mentioned earlier).

3.3.3 Using and Evaluating Classifiers for Ranking

Often, the goal of training a classifier is not merely to generate exhaustive sets of 'true' and 'false' instances. For example, if we wanted to identify relevant webpages in response to a query, or to recommend items that a user is likely to purchase, in practice it may not matter whether we can identify *all* relevant webpages or products; rather, we might care more about whether we can surface *some* relevant items among the first page of results returned to a user.

Note that the type of classifiers we have developed so far can straightforwardly be used for *ranking*. That is, in addition to outputting a predicted label ($\delta(x_i \cdot \theta > 0)$ in the case of logistic regression), they can also output *confidence scores* (i.e., $x_i \cdot \theta$, or $p_\theta(y_i = 1|x_i)$). Thus, in the context of finding relevant webpages or products above, our goal might be to maximize the number of relevant items returned among the few most confident predictions. Furthermore, we might be interested in how the model's accuracy changes as a function of confidence; for example, even if the model's accuracy is low overall, is it accurate for the top 1%, 5%, or 10% of most confident predictions?

Precision and Recall

Precision and *Recall* assess the quality of a set of retrieved results in terms of two related objectives. Informally, *precision* measures the rate at which those items 'retrieved' by the model (i.e., those predicted to have a positive label by the classifier) are in fact labeled positively; *recall* measures what fraction of all positively labeled items our classifier predicted as having a positive label. For example, in a spam filtering setting (where positively labeled items are spam e-mails), *precision* would measure how often e-mails marked as spam are in fact spam, whereas *recall* would measure what fraction of all spam was filtered.

Formally precision and recall are defined as follows:

$$\text{Precision} = \frac{|\{\text{relevant items}\} \cap \{\text{retrieved items}\}|}{|\{\text{retrieved items}\}|} \tag{3.23}$$

$$\text{Recall} = \frac{|\{\text{relevant items}\} \cap \{\text{retrieved items}\}|}{|\{\text{relevant items}\}|}. \tag{3.24}$$

Alternately it is easy to verify that these expressions can be rewritten in terms of the number of true-positives, false positives, and false negatives, as in Equations (3.12) to (3.15):

$$\text{Precision} = \frac{TP}{TP + FP} \tag{3.25}$$

$$\text{Recall} = \frac{TP}{TP + FN}. \tag{3.26}$$

Finally we briefly show how these quantities can be computed for a given predictor (such as the one from the beginning of this section):

```
1  predictions = mod.predict(X) # binary vector of predictions
2
3  numerator = sum([(a and b) for (a,b) in zip(predictions,y)])
4  nRetrieved = sum(predictions)
5  nRelevant = sum(y)
6
7  precision = numerator / nRetrieved
8  recall = numerator / nRelevant
```

F_β **Score**

Note that neither precision nor recall are particularly meaningful if reported in isolation. For instance, it is trivial to achieve a recall of 1.0 simply by using a classifier that returns 'true' for every item (in which case, all relevant documents are returned); such a classifier would of course have low precision. Likewise, a precision close to 1.0 can often be achieved by returning 'true' only for a few items about which we are extremely confident; such a classifier would have low recall.

As such, to evaluate a classifier in terms of precision and recall, we likely want a metric that considers both, or otherwise to place additional constraints on our classifier (as we see below).

The F_β score achieves this by taking a weighted average of the two quantities:

$$F_\beta = (1 + \beta^2) \cdot \frac{\text{precision} \cdot \text{recall}}{\beta^2 \text{precision} + \text{recall}}. \tag{3.27}$$

In the case of $\beta = 1$ (which is normally called simply the 'F-score'), Equation (3.27) simply computes the harmonic mean of precision and recall, which is low if either precision or recall is low.

Otherwise, if $\beta \neq 1$, the F_β score reflects a situation where one cares about recall over precision by a factor of β.[5]

There are several situations where one might care about recall more than precision, or vice versa. For instance, considering the motivating examples from the start of this section, in a baggage-handling scenario we would likely care primarily about recall, and would be willing to sacrifice precision to achieve it; or, in a search or recommendation setting, we may be happy to retrieve only a few items, so long as some are relevant (i.e., high precision but low recall).

---

[5] Without going into detail, this motivation leads to the specific formulation in Equation (3.27) (Van Rijsbergen, 1979).

Precision and Recall @ K

One of our motivating examples when defining precision and recall considered cases where we may only have a fixed budget of results that can be returned to a user. In particular, we might be interested in evaluating the precision and recall when our classifier returns only its K most confident predictions. To do so, we begin by sorting the labels y_i according to their associated confidence scores (i.e., $x_i \cdot \theta$):

confidence $x_i \cdot \theta$: $\cdots$ 0.49 0.42 0.38 0.16 0.02 −0.02 −0.05 −0.05 −0.08 −0.10 $\cdots$
label y_i: $\cdots$ True True True True False True False False True True $\cdots$

$$(3.28)$$

Such tuples of confidence scores and labels can be generated as follows (in this case for a logistic regressor as in sec. 3.3):[6]

```
1  confidences = mod.decision_function(X) # real vector of
       confidences
2
3  sortedByConfidence = list(zip(confidences,y))
4  sortedByConfidence.sort(reverse=True) # sorted as in Equation
       3.28
```

Note that when evaluating our model's K most confident predictions, we are no longer interested in whether the actual scores are greater or less than zero (i.e., whether the classifier would output 'true' or 'false'): we are only interested in the *labels* among the top-K predictions.

The *Precision @ K* and *Recall @ K* now simply measure the precision and recall for a classifier that returns only the K most confident predictions. That is, precision@K measures what fraction of the top-K predictions are actually labeled 'true'; recall@K measures the fraction of all relevant documents that are returned among the top K. The main difference to note (compared to the definitions in eqs. (3.23) and (3.24)) is that the number of 'retrieved' documents is always K; that is, the 'retrieved' documents are always the K most confident, whether or not the classifier actually predicts a positive label (i.e., $x_i \cdot \theta > 0$).

Unlike precision and recall, precision@K and recall@K can be reported in isolation as they cannot be optimized by trivial solutions. Precision@10, for example, is an effective measure of a classifier's ability to return reasonable results among a page of ten retrieved items.

ROC and Precision/Recall Curves

Another holistic measure of a classifier's performance is to report the *relationship* between precision and recall, or between true and false positives.

---

[6] Strictly, we might adjust this sort to avoid sorting based on the labels if there are many ties in confidence scores.

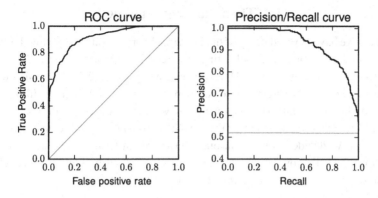

Figure 3.2 Examples of receiver-operating characteristic (left) and precision recall (right) curves

For example, the relationship between the number of true positives and false positives is known as the *receiver-operating characteristic* (ROC). It is so named because of its use in evaluating the performance of radar receiver operators: as an operator's threshold for detection decreases, both their true positive and false positive rates (TPR and FPR) will simultaneously increase; thus, we might evaluate a classifier by evaluating the TPR and FPR as we change the classifier's detection threshold.

The *precision recall curve* is developed following a similar line of reasoning: as we lower a classifier's detection threshold, the precision will decrease while the recall increases; thus we might evaluate a classifier by examining the relationship between precision and recall as the threshold changes.

To generate these curves, we sort the predictions of our classifier by confidence (much as we did in eq. (3.28)), which corresponds to gradually considering lower thresholds; at each step, we compute the precision and recall (i.e., we compute the precision and recall@K for each value of K). Together these values form the precision recall curve:

```
1  for k in range(1,len(sortedByConfidence)+1):
2      retrievedLabels = [x[1] for x in sortedByConfidence[:k]]
3      precisionK = sum(retrievedLabels) / len(retrievedLabels)
4      recallK = sum(retrievedLabels) / sum(y)
5      xPlot.append(recallK)
6      yPlot.append(precisionK)
```

Plotting these x and y coordinates results in the plot in Figure 3.2 (right); the ROC curve can be generated similarly.

We revisit evaluation techniques based on ranking in Section 5.4, when we explore evaluation strategies for recommender systems.

3.4 The Learning Pipeline

By now we have covered many of the individual components that go into build-ing a predictive model: model fitting (for regression models in sec. 2.1 and classification models in sec. 3.1), feature engineering (sec. 2.3), and evaluation (secs. 2.2 and 3.3). Bringing these components together still requires filling in some additional details. How can we know whether our model will work well when deployed (i.e., on *new* data), and what steps can be taken to ensure this? How can we decide between various alternatives in terms of feature design, and meaningfully compare those alternatives against each other? Collectively these steps are part of the *pipeline* of machine learning.

3.4.1 Generalization, Overfitting, and Underfitting

So far, when discussing model evaluation in Section 3.3 (and earlier in sec. 2.2), we have considered training a model to predict labels y from a dataset X; we have then evaluated the model by comparing the predictions $f(x_i)$ to the labels y_i. Critically, we're using the *same* data to train the model as we're using to evaluate it.

The risk in doing so is that our model may not *generalize* well to new data. For example, when fitting a model relating review length to ratings (as in figs. 2.4 and 2.8), we considered fitting the data with linear, quadratic, and cubic functions. Increasing the degree of the polynomial would continue to lower the errors of the predictor; alternately, we could have modeled review length using a one-hot encoding (so that there was a different predicted value for every length). Such models could fit the data very closely (in terms of their MSE), but it is unclear whether they would capture meaningful trends in the data or simply 'memorize' it.

To consider an extreme case, imagine fitting a vector y using only *random* features. The code below fits a vector of fifty observations using 1, 10, 25, and 50 random features, and then prints the R^2 coefficient of each model:

```
1   y = numpy.random.rand(50)
2   mod = linear_model.LinearRegression()
3   for n in [1,10,25,50]:
4       X = numpy.random.rand(50,n)
5       mod.fit(X,y)
6       print(mod.score(X,y))
```

Here, the R^2 coefficients take values of 0.07, 0.25, 0.35, and 1.0—once we include fifty random features, we can fit the data perfectly. Of course, given that our features were *random*, this 'fit' is not meaningful, and the model has merely discovered random correlations between the observed data and labels.

These arguments point to two issues that need to be addressed when training a model:

(i) We should not evaluate a model on the same data that was used to train it. Rather we should use a held-out dataset (i.e., a *test* set).

(ii) Features that improve performance on the training data will not necessarily improve performance on the held-out data.

Evaluating a model on held-out data gives us a sense of how well we can expect that model to work 'in the wild.' This held-out data, known as a *test set*, measures how well our model can be expected to *generalize* to new data.

Overfitting

Fundamentally, if our model works well on training data but not on held-out data, it must mean that certain characteristics of the training data are not representative of the held-out data. This could occur for various reasons. One possibility is that our held-out data is drawn from a different distribution than the training data. For instance, if we had withheld sales data from the most recent month, and trained on data from the previous eleven, the most recent month of observations may follow a different trend, or occur during a different season, and so on. In principle, one might address this simply by ensuring that the training and test sets are (non-overlapping) *random samples* of the data, such that both the training and test data will be drawn from the same distribution.[7]

Even if the training and held-out data are independently drawn samples from the same distribution, we may still observe significantly degraded performance on our held-out data. In such cases we are said to be *overfitting*.

A trivial demonstration of overfitting is shown in Figure 3.3. Here we show a dataset that follows a line, subject to some random perturbation. While a high-degree polynomial can fit the data very closely, we would not expect this complex function to generalize well to new data. We are said to have *overfit* when we fit a model that is highly accurate on the training data but that does not generalize well.

Note that we *expect* any model to perform somewhat worse when applied to new data compared to its training performance: in fact this is one of our 'theorems' about model performance that we present in Section 3.4.2. Rather our goal when tuning a model (or selecting among model alternatives) is to minimize this gap, typically by sacrificing training accuracy in order to improve generalization performance.

---

[7] Though if our goal is to *forecast* next month's sales, using the most recent data as our held-out sample may be the most appropriate decision.

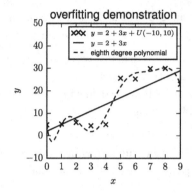

Figure 3.3 Overfitting demonstration. A high-degree polynomial fits the observed data accurately, but is unlikely to generalize well.

Underfitting

Just as we overfit by fitting a model whose good performance on a training set does not generalize to a held-out set, we *underfit* when our model is insufficiently complex to capture the underlying dynamics in a dataset. Again, this can occur for a variety of reasons. If we select too simple a model, for example, a linear function to capture the data in Figure 2.8 (which does not seem to follow a linear trend), no choice of parameters will lead to good training *or* held-out performance.

3.4.2 Model Complexity and Regularization

So far we have talked vaguely about what it means for a model to be 'too complex' (or too simple) and suggested that we should choose a model that is complex enough to fit the data but simple enough not to overfit. This idea is often referred to as *Occam's Razor*, a philosophical principle which states that among several alternate hypotheses that explain some phenomenon, one should favor the simplest.

However, for these notions to be useful, we must be precise about what it means for a model to be 'complex.' We would like to define complexity in terms of the parameters θ, such that given a fixed set of features and labels, we could select the 'simplest' θ that adequately explains (or models) the data.

We will discuss two candidate notions of 'simplicity' as follows:

(i) A simple model is one that includes only a few terms, that is, in which only a few values θ_k are nonzero.

(ii) A simple model is one in which all terms are about equally important, that is, one in which particularly large values of θ_k are rare.

These two potential notions of 'complexity' are captured by the following expressions:

$$\Omega_1(\theta) = \|\theta\|_1 = \sum_k |\theta_k|, \tag{3.29}$$

$$\Omega_2(\theta) = \|\theta\|_2^2 = \sum_k \theta_k^2, \tag{3.30}$$

that is, the sum of absolute values and the sum of squares, also called the ℓ_1 and (squared) ℓ_2 norms of θ. We state without proof that these expressions penalize models that have many nonzero parameters (eq. (3.29)) or large parameters (eq. (3.30)), though we further characterize their behavior later.

Regularization

In order to fit a model which simultaneously explains the data but is not overly complex (corresponding to our goal above), we write down a new objective that combines our original accuracy objective with one of the complexity expressions above (in this case the squared ℓ_2 norm). For a regression model we add the regularizer to the expression from Equation (2.16):

$$\underbrace{\frac{1}{|y|} \sum_{i=1}^{|y|} (x_i \cdot \theta - y_i)^2}_{\text{accuracy}} + \underbrace{\lambda \sum_k \theta_k^2}_{\text{model complexity } \|\theta\|_2^2}. \tag{3.31}$$

For a classification model, we *subtract* the regularizer, since we seek to maximize accuracy rather than minimizing error (so we maximize $-\lambda\|\theta\|_2^2$ rather than minimizing $\lambda\|\theta\|_2^2$):

$$\sum_i -\log(1 + e^{-x_i \cdot \theta}) + \sum_{y_i=0} -x_i \cdot \theta - \lambda\|\theta\|_2^2. \tag{3.32}$$

This procedure—where we add a penalty term to control model complexity—is known as *regularization*; the parameter λ, which controls the extent to which complexity is penalized, is termed a regularization parameter.

Note that we can straightforwardly adapt the derivatives (from eqs. (2.54) and (3.9)) to include the regularization term, $\lambda\|\theta\|_2^2$ by noting that $\frac{\partial}{\partial \theta_k}$ $\lambda\|\theta\|_2^2 = 2\lambda\theta_k$.

Hyperparameters

Our regularization parameter λ in Equation (3.31) is said to be a model *hyperparameter*. Hyperparameters are model parameters whose values control the model and influence other parameters (in this case λ controls the fitted values of θ). More complex models may have several tunable hyperparameters that control various model components. Note that generally we cannot fit hyperparameters in the same way that we fit model parameters (e.g., if we used our training set to choose λ in Equation (3.31), we would always choose a model that simply ignored model complexity in favor of accuracy). As such we need a separate strategy to tune model hyperparameters, which we explore when we introduce validation sets below.

Note that generally speaking the term θ_0, that is, the *offset* term, should not be included in the regularizer, that is, our regularizer should be $\sum_{k=1}^{K} \theta_k^2$ or $\sum_{k=1}^{K} |\theta_k|$. That is, our underlying assumption that few parameters are nonzero, or that parameters are small, should not apply to the offset term. If we were to include the offset term when regularizing, we would generally select a model which made systematically smaller (in magnitude) predictions.

Fitting the Regularized Model (Regression)

When introducing linear models in Section 2.1, we noted that the system in Equation (2.7) has a simple closed-form solution based on the pseudoinverse (eq. (2.10)). Briefly we note that this solution can be fairly straightforwardly modified to fit the *regularized* model as follows:

$$\theta = (X^T X + \lambda I)^{-1} X^T y \qquad (3.33)$$

(where I is the identity matrix). Generally, as we develop more complex models, we will move away from closed-form solutions, though this specific solution proves useful when fitting certain types of recommender systems in Chapter 5 (sec. 5.7).

Validation Sets

We now require a protocol for choosing the best value of the trade-off parameter λ in Equation (3.31). If we were to select λ based on the accuracy on the training set, we would always select $\lambda = 0$; ideally, we want to choose the value of λ that will result in the best performance on the held-out test set. However, we should be careful not to use the test set to compare alternative models: the test set is supposed to represent true held-out performance, and strictly speaking test performance should only be examined *after* we have selected our best model.

As such, we need a third data partition which can be used to select among alternative models. This *validation set* in some sense mimics the test set, in that it is not used to fit the model, but is used to give us an *estimate* of what we expect the test performance to be under a certain model.

A typical pipeline will consist of three partitions of our data, whose roles are summarized as follows:

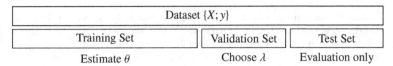

Figure 3.4 Basic roles of training, validation, and test sets

- The **training set** is used to optimize the parameters of a specific model. In the type of models we fit in this book, this usually refers to the parameters that can be fit via gradient ascent/descent (i.e., θ in this chapter).
- The **validation set** is used to select among model alternatives. 'Alternatives' may simply mean different values of λ in Equations (3.31) and (3.32), but could also mean different feature representation strategies, and so on. We discuss a few alternative uses below. Typically, we select the model with the highest accuracy/lowest error on the validation set.
- The **test set** is used to evaluate held-out model performance; ideally it should not be used to make any modeling decisions but should only be used to report performance.

The core use of our validation set is to estimate model hyperparameters such as λ above. Beyond regularization coefficients, 'hyperparameters' more broadly refer to any tunable model components that do not get optimized during the training phase. For example, when building models from text in Chapter 8, the number of words in our dictionary (from which we build features) would be an example of a hyperparameter, and could be chosen using our validation set to select the model that will generalize the best.

The relationship between training, validation, and test sets is shown in Figure 3.4, and some overall guidelines for building a validation set are shown in Figure 3.5.

Why Does the ℓ_1 Norm Induce Sparsity?

We stated briefly when introducing Equations (3.29) and (3.30) that an ℓ_1 regularizer will encourage a *sparse* parameter vector θ, while an ℓ_2 regularizer will result in a more balanced parameter distribution. Without formally proving this result, it is instructive to consider some simple geometric intuition as to why this should be the case. Figure 3.6 demonstrates (for a simple two-parameter model) why the ℓ_1 norm induces sparsity (i.e., few non-zero parameters) while the ℓ_2 norm results in a more uniform parameter distribution. Models with equivalent ℓ_1 norm lie along diamond-shaped contours (fig. 3.6, left) whereas models with equivalent ℓ_2 norm lie on a circle (fig. 3.6, right). Models with an

- Training, validation, and test sets should (generally speaking) be non-overlapping, random samples of a dataset. Some exceptions apply, for example when fitting temporal models in Chapter 7, we might build a test set out of the *most recent* observations in order to get a sense of how well a model would work *now* rather than how well it would work *on average*.
- The size of our training set may be driven by modeling as well as practical concerns. Our training set should be large enough that we can reasonably expect to fit our model on the data (as a guideline, we might hope to have an order of magnitude more training examples than model parameters); likewise, if we have a simple model with just a few parameters we need not train on millions of observations.
- Likewise the size of our validation and test sets should be large enough that we can be reasonably confident of our results. We briefly touch upon measuring significance in Section 3.5.1.

Figure 3.5 Guidelines for building training, validation, and tests sets

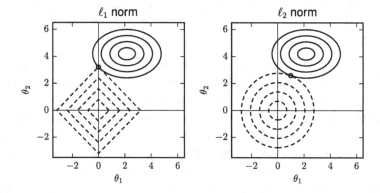

Figure 3.6 Demonstration of the regularization effect of the ℓ_1 (left) versus ℓ_2 norms. Dashed lines indicate models with equivalent norms (ℓ_1 or ℓ_2); solid lines indicate models with equivalent mean squared errors. The selected model in either condition is circled.

equivalent MSE lie along an ellipse. When balancing the error and the regularizer as in Equation (3.31), the best model will correspond to the point where the boundaries intersect. In the case of the ℓ_1 norm these curves intersect *on one of the vertices of the diamond*; for the ℓ_2 norm they do not; the former case corresponds to a model with only a few nonzero parameters. For a more rigorous explanation of this phenomenon, see, for example, Friedman et al. (2001).

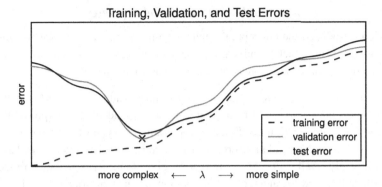

Figure 3.7 Example train, validation, and test curves, demonstrating the relationships between each type of error

'Theorems' Regarding Training, Testing, and Validation Sets

To solidify the roles of training, validation, and test sets, below we outline some theorems guiding the relationships among these sets, as the regularization hyperparameter λ changes.

Note that these are 'theorems' in the sense that they will be true in general, but only in the limit given large enough datasets, and assuming our training, validation, and test sets are drawn from the same distribution (etc.). As such, these theorems should mostly be regarded as guidelines to 'sanity check' the correctness of your model pipeline:

- The training error increases as λ increases; typically it will asymptote to some value, for example, a linear model might asymptote to the error of a trivial predictor (i.e., the variance of the label).
- The validation and test errors will be at least as high as the training error; intuitively, the algorithm will not work better on 'unseen' data than it did on training data.
- When λ is too small, a too-complex model achieves low training error, but high validation/test errors. In this case, the model is said to be *overfitting*.
- When λ is too large, a too-simple model has high training, validation, and test error. In this case, the model is said to be *underfitting*.
- Generally, there should be a 'sweet spot' between under- and over-fitting, which is determined using our validation set. This point (marked in fig. 3.7 with an 'x') corresponds to the model we expect to yield the best generalization performance on the test set.

3.4.3 Guidelines for Model Pipelines

Having introduced the conceptual details of a model pipeline, it is worth finishing with some practical advice on how to combine the various pieces and how to set the various tunable components of a model pipeline:

- If you do *not* see a 'sweet spot' between under- and over-fitting (as in the theorems above), it could mean that you have not adequately explored the range of regularization coefficients. For example, if you observe monotonically increasing validation errors, it may mean you have not considered sufficiently small values of λ. Alternately, given (e.g.) a simple linear model with only a few parameters, it may simply mean that your model is not capable of fitting (or overfitting to) a particular dataset.
- Regularization parameters such as λ do not have an absolute scale, and will vary depending on factors ranging from the model's tendency to overfit, to the specific scale of the features X and labels y. As a rough guideline, it is useful to consider setting λ by considering several different orders of magnitude (as we do in sec. 3.5), before honing in on a narrower range of values.
- When implementing iterative models (such as approaches based on gradient descent, as in sec. 2.5), the validation set can be used as a condition to cease further iteration. That is, we need not train models until convergence: if we are making no further improvements on the validation set (say, for a predetermined number of iterations), there is little reason to continue optimizing our model on the training set. Ideally, the model parameters θ might be chosen from whichever iteration yields the best *validation* performance.

3.4.4 Regression and Classification in *Tensorflow*

Below we describe an implementation of (regularized) linear regression in *Tensorflow*,[8] forming the basis of the overall pipeline we will use to develop more complex models in later chapters. Although widely associated with deep learning, *Tensorflow* can more simply be thought of as a general-purpose library for gradient-based optimization. *Tensorflow* computes derivatives *symbolically*, meaning that the programmer must only specify the *objective* to be optimized (e.g., eq. (3.31)), without having to compute gradients. This makes it easy to quickly experiment with model variants, even for models including complex transformations of model parameters.

---

[8] www.tensorflow.org/.

We first setup our observed variables (*X* and *y*) as *Tensorflow* data constants:

```
1  X = tf.constant(X, dtype=tf.float32)
2  y = tf.constant(y, dtype=tf.float32)
```

Next, we setup our model. Mostly this simply consists of defining the basic model components in terms of *Tensorflow* primitives:

```
3   class regressionModel(tf.keras.Model):
4       # Initialize with number of parameters and
            regularization strength
5       def __init__(self, M, lamb):
6           super(regressionModel, self).__init__()
7           self.theta = tf.Variable(tf.constant([0.0]*M, shape
                =[M,1], dtype=tf.float32))
8           self.lamb = lamb
9
10      # Prediction (for a matrix of instances) (eq. 2.7)
11      def predict(self, X):
12          return tf.matmul(X, self.theta)
13
14      # Mean Squared Error (eq. 2.16)
15      def MSE(self, X, y):
16          return tf.reduce_mean((tf.matmul(X, self.theta) - y)
                **2)
17
18      # Regularizer (eq. 3.30)
19      def reg(self):
20          return self.lamb * tf.reduce_sum(self.theta**2)
21
22      # Loss (eq. 3.31)
23      def call(self, X, y):
24          return self.MSE(X, y) + self.reg()
```

Next we define an *optimizer* to use (in this case the *Adam* optimizer from Kingma and Ba (2014)), and create an instance of our model. Here we create a model with regularization strength $\lambda = 1$:

```
25  optimizer = tf.keras.optimizers.Adam(0.01)
26  model = regressionModel(len(X[0]), 1)
```

Finally, we run 1,000 iterations of gradient descent. Gradients are computed automatically for the objective defined in call() with respect to the model's variables (θ):

```
27  for iteration in range(1000):
28      with tf.GradientTape() as tape:
29          loss = model(X,y)
30      gradients = tape.gradient(loss, model.
            trainable_variables)
31      optimizer.apply_gradients(zip(gradients, model.
            trainable_variables))
```

Again, although this code implements a simple model (which we could already compute in closed form), the value of *Tensorflow* is that we can easily adapt our model to handle different objectives, including complex, nonlinear transformations. For instance, we can easily replace our ℓ_2 regularizer above with an ℓ_1 regularizer:

```
32   def reg1(self):
33       return self.lamb * tf.reduce_sum(tf.abs(self.theta))
```

Finally, we note that *Tensorflow* is but one of many popular libraries (see, e.g., Theano, PyTorch, MXNet, etc.), though all implement the same basic functionality, in terms of performing gradient-based optimization on top of user-defined objectives.

Classification

Classification objectives can be built similarly. Given a vector of binary labels $y_i \in \{0, 1\}$, our prediction function is replaced by $\sigma(X \cdot \theta)$, and our objective is replaced by that of Equation (3.7) (along with a negative sign, so that we can still minimize the objective):

```
1    # Probability (for a matrix of instances)
2    def predict(self, X):
3        return tf.math.sigmoid(tf.matmul(X, self.theta))
4
5    # Objective as in Equation 3.6
6    def obj(self, X, y):
7        pred = self.predict(X)
8        pos = y*tf.math.log(pred)
9        neg = (1.0 - y)*tf.math.log(1.0 - pred)
10       return -tf.reduce_mean(pos + neg)
```

In practice, one rarely writes out such functions 'longhand,' as standard objectives are available as *Tensorflow* operations (e.g., the above is equivalent to a *binary cross-entropy* loss, `tf.keras.losses.BinaryCrossentropy()`).

3.5 Implementing the Learning Pipeline

Below, we briefly show how to practically apply the process from Section 3.4 to select a model based on training, validation, and test samples.

The actual features for this model are based on a sentiment analysis (regression) task from Chapter 8, in which we predict ratings based on words in a review; for the sake of demonstrating a model pipeline it is useful to consider a problem with high-dimensional features, such that the model is prone to overfitting if not carefully regularized (in this case, we consider 1,000-dimensional features on a dataset with only 5,000 samples).

First, we randomly shuffle the dataset and split it into non-overlapping training, validation, and test samples:

```
1   random.shuffle(data)
2   X = [feature(d) for d in data]
3   y = [d['review/overall'] for d in data]
4   Ntrain,Nvalid,Ntest = 4000,500,500
5   Xtrain,ytrain = X[:Ntrain],y[:Ntrain]
6   Xvalid,yvalid = X[Ntrain:Ntrain+Nvalid],y[Ntrain:Ntrain+
        Nvalid]
7   Xtest,ytest = X[Ntrain+Nvalid:],y[Ntrain+Nvalid:]
```

Next, we consider regularization coefficients λ ranging from $\lambda = 10^{-3}$ to $\lambda = 10^4$. For each value, we train a model on the training set and evaluate its accuracy on the validation set; during each step, we keep track of the best-performing model in terms of its validation accuracy. The Ridge model below implements regularized linear regression, as in Equation (3.31):

```
8   bestModel = None
9   bestVal = None
10  for l in [0.001, 0.01, 0.1, 1, 10, 100, 1000, 10000]:
11      model = sklearn.linear_model.Ridge(l)
12      model.fit(Xtrain, ytrain)
13      predictValid = model.predict(Xvalid)
14      MSEvalid = sum((yvalid - predictValid)**2)/len(yvalid)
15      print('l␣=␣' + str(l) + ',␣validation␣MSE␣=␣' + str(
            MSEvalid))
16      if bestVal == None or MSEvalid < bestVal:
17          bestVal = MSEvalid
18          bestModel = model
```

Finally, we evaluate the best-performing model (in terms of validation performance) on the test set. Note that this is the first and only time we use the test set:

```
19  predictTest = bestModel.predict(Xtest)
20  MSEtest = sum((ytest - predictTest)**2)/len(ytest)
```

Figure 3.8 shows the training, validation, and test performance found during the above steps; note the similarity to the hypothetical curves in Figure 3.7.

3.5.1 Significance Testing

Although not our focus in this chapter, it is worth briefly exploring how we can explicitly measure whether the performance of one model is 'better' than another, in terms of a formal statistical framework. So far, we have compared (regression) models in terms of their MSEs though as we explored in Section 2.2.2, the MSE was chosen based on an underlying assumption that model errors follow a Gaussian distribution.

Significance testing refers to the overall process of determining whether a statistical measurement would have been likely to have occurred due to chance alone (under the assumptions of some particular model). For example, if an

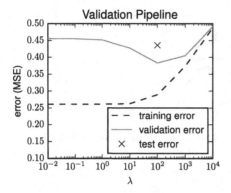

Figure 3.8 Training, validation, and test error on a real pipeline

established restaurant on *Yelp* has a rating of 4.3 stars based on fifty reviews, and a new restaurant has a rating of 4.5 stars based on four reviews, would you conclude that the new restaurant is better rated? Or would you conclude that the higher initial rating is likely to have occurred due to chance? Significance tests allow us to formalize these questions.

Formally, a *p*-value measures the probability that a result as (or more) extreme than the one we actually observed could have occurred due to chance (under some statistical model). For example, if we assume that users' ratings follow a Gaussian distribution, with what probability would the ratings of two restaurants deviate by (at least) 0.2 stars? In the case of this specific measurement, this probability would depend on (a) the *magnitude* of the difference between the two averages; (b) the *size* of the two samples (e.g., a difference of 0.2 stars might be significant of both restaurants had fifty ratings, but not if they had four); and (c) the *variance* of the two samples (e.g., if the two samples had highly concentrated ratings we might more quickly conclude that the difference was significant).[9]

When making comparisons between models, we will typically use a *p*-value to measure whether one model has residuals $(y - f_\theta(x))$ that are closer to zero than another (i.e., we are testing whether one model's predictions are closer to the labels than the other's). To do so we are measuring the difference in *variance* between two samples.

We will compute this quantity via an *F*-test. Other tests could also be used to compare the performance of two models, such as a likelihood ratio test, each of which has different underlying assumptions. Below we will compare the performance of two models for estimating a rating, using our beer review data as in Section 2.3.2:

---

[9] This specific probability would be measured via a *t*-test.

$$\text{model 1:} \quad \text{rating} = \theta_0 \tag{3.34}$$

$$\text{compared to model 2:} \quad \text{rating} = \theta_0 + \theta_1 \times (\text{ABV}). \tag{3.35}$$

One of the assumptions of this particular test is that one of the two models has a subset of the parameters of the other. As such we are really measuring whether the additional parameters significantly improve the model's performance (i.e., whether adding a term based on the ABV improves the performance of a model including only θ_0).

First, we generate features and labels for the two models (assuming the data has already been read, shuffled, etc.):

```
1  X1 = [[1] for d in data]
2  X2 = [[1, d['beer/ABV']] for d in data]
3  y = [d['review/overall'] for d in data]
```

Next, we fit the two models (on half of the data), and compute their residuals (on the other half):

```
4  model1 = sklearn.linear_model.LinearRegression(fit_intercept
       =False)
5  model1.fit(X0[:250], y[:250])
6  residuals1 = model1.predict(X1[250:]) - y[250:]
7  model2 = sklearn.linear_model.LinearRegression(fit_intercept
       =False)
8  model2.fit(X2[:250], y[:250])
9  residuals2 = model2.predict(X2[250:]) - y[250:]
```

The actual F statistic depends on the sum of squared residuals, the number of parameters in each model, and the size of the sample:

```
10  rss1 = sum([r**2 for r in residuals1]) # sum of squared
        residuals
11  rss2 = sum([r**2 for r in residuals2])
12  k1,k2 = 1,2 # Number of parameters of each model
13  n = len(residuals1) # Number of samples
```

Finally, we compute the F statistic and estimate the associated p-value using a method from *scipy*:

```
14  F = ((rss1 - rss2) / (k2 - k1)) / (rss2 / (n-k2))
15  scipy.stats.f.cdf(F,k2-k1,n-k2)
```

The obtained p-value is close to zero, indicating that the result (that ABV improves predictive performance) is statistically significant.[10]

---

[10] One can experiment with less-predictive features or a smaller test set to see how these influence the estimated p-value.

Note that this is just one example of a significance test, that works for a particular situation (albeit a fairly common one); in different situations alternative tests may be required, see, for example, Wasserman (2013) for a more comprehensive presentation.

In spite of the importance of rigorously demonstrating the significance of claimed model improvements, we will mostly avoid further discussing significance testing throughout the remainder of this book. Generally speaking, these types of tests are designed for small-sample contexts (e.g., surveys or clinical trials, etc.); on the types of large datasets we consider, even small differences between models will tend to yield extremely small (highly significant) *p*-values.

Exercises

3.1   In this exercise we will use the style of a beer (using the same data we have studied since, e.g., sec. 2.3.2) to predict its ABV (alcohol by volume). Construct a one-hot encoding of the beer style, for those categories that appear in more than 1,000 reviews. You can build a mapping of categories to feature indices as follows:

```
1  categoryCounts = defaultdict(int)
2  for d in data:
3      categoryCounts[d['beer/style']] += 1
4
5  categories = [c for c in categoryCounts if
       categoryCounts[c] > 1000]
6  catID = dict(zip(list(categories),range(len(categories)
       )))
```

Train a logistic regressor using this one-hot encoding to predict whether beers have an ABV greater than 5% (i.e., d['beer/ABV'] > 5). Report the True Positive, True Negative, and Balanced Error Rates of the classifier (see sec. 3.3).

3.2   The performance of the classifier above may be unsatisfactory due to the data being highly *imbalanced* (as in sec. 3.3.1). Implement a *balanced* version of the classifier using the class_weight='balanced' option in sklearn. Report the same metrics as above for the balanced classifier.

3.3   Generate precision and recall curves for the classifier you trained above.

3.4   Implement a complete learning and regularization pipeline with your balanced model. Split your data into 50%/25%/25% train/validation/test fractions. Consider values C in the range $\{10^{-6}, 10^{-5}, 10^{-4}, 10^{-3}\}$. Compute the train and validation BER for each value of C, and the BER for the classifier that performs best on the validation set.[11]

3.5 Naively, to build a classifier we might simply train a *regressor* by treating labels as real-valued quantities (e.g., predicting $-1/+1$). Perform a simple experiment to demonstrate that this naive model does not work as well as logistic regression. That is, select a dataset (such as the one you used in Exercise 3.1), a few features, a label to predict, and an appropriate classifier evaluation metric to show that the naive classifier is outperformed by logistic regression.

Project 2: Taxicab Tip Prediction (Part 2)

Below we will revisit Project 1 to (a) consider classification techniques and (b) more rigorously evaluate our models using a learning pipeline. Using the same data from Project 1, extend your project via the following steps:

(i) Carefully build a complete model pipeline. That is, split your data into train, validation, and test portions, and build a pipeline so that all models are trained on the training set and comparisons among models are performed on the validation set (similar to Exercise 3.4). Consider different ways to split the data, for example, is it better to split the data randomly, or is it better to withhold the most recent observations for testing for the sake of selecting the model most capable of *forecasting* future trends?

(ii) Rather than modeling the task as a regression problem, you could cast the problem as *classification* by estimating whether a tip will be above or below the median; this may be less sensitive to outliers. Consider the advantages and disadvantages of various formulations, as well as what evaluation metrics you might use.

(iii) Some of the features we used in Project 1 are potentially quite high dimensional, for example, if we encode timestamps using one-hot encodings for each possible day of the year, our model might be highly effective at capturing single-day trends (such as major holidays), but could also be prone to overfitting. Use your pipeline to select the best feature representation among alternatives (e.g., different levels of granularity for your temporal features, or otherwise), and to incorporate a regularizer into your model.

---

[11] C plays a similar role to λ in Equation (3.32), though it inverts the relationship between accuracy and complexity, that is, small λ is equivalent to large C. See documentation in `sklearn.linear_model.LogisticRegression`.

PART TWO

FUNDAMENTALS OF PERSONALIZED
MACHINE LEARNING

4

Introduction to Recommender Systems

In Chapters 2 and 3, when revising regression and classification, our only means of providing *personalized* predictions was to extract features associated with user characteristics (e.g., age, location, gender). The success of such models largely depends on our ability to extract features that adequately explain the variation in the labels we are trying to predict. While effective in a number of regression or classification scenarios, when modeling interactions in recommendation scenarios, it is less clear what features are predictive of users' actions, and less likely that those features could be collected in the first place. Consider, for example:

- What features would be useful to predict which movies a user would be likely to watch? 'Obvious' features such as user demographics may explain only a small fraction of the variation in interactions and preferences.
- How would you identify the types of features that would be useful for an obscure or unusual domain? For example, what features would you collect to recommend baby toys, toaster ovens, or temporary tattoos?
- Are such features likely to be available? In practice, we will often know little about a user, other than their interaction history.
- How can we make predictions in settings where *no* features are available?

Recommender systems are a fundamental tool to try and make predictions in such scenarios. At their core, recommender systems are concerned with understanding *interactions* between users and items. Roughly speaking, recommender systems operate by finding common patterns and relationships among users and items, so that recommendations for a user can be harvested from others who have similar interactions patterns.

In this chapter, we explore approaches based on simple similarity heuristics. Our basic goal is to identify *which items and which users are similar to each other*. Approaches range from simple heuristics like set overlap (sec. 4.3.2), to more complex approaches based on random walks (sec. 4.4). As we will discover, even simple heuristics can be surprisingly effective, and in practice drive high-profile industrial recommender systems, as we explore in our case study on *Amazon* recommendations (sec. 4.5).

Critically, the models we develop in this chapter are quite different from those we have seen so far, largely eschewing explicit features in favor of techniques more closely related to pattern mining. Note also that for the moment we will not use *machine learning* to build recommenders: we use this chapter to explore the overall problem setting and pipeline, before exploring machine learning (or so-called model-based) approaches in Chapter 5.

4.1 Basic Setup and Problem Definition

The typical modality of the data we are trying to model might consist of sequences of historical interactions between users and items, for example, we might have a collection of movie ratings such as:

$$
\begin{array}{llll}
(\text{Julian}, & \textit{The Godfather}, & 4, & \text{Jan 4 2019}) \\
(\text{Julian}, & \textit{Pulp Fiction}, & 3, & \text{Jan 6 2019}) \\
(\text{Laura}, & \textit{Seven Samurai}, & 5, & \text{Jan 8 2019}) \\
(\text{Laura}, & \textit{The Godfather}, & 4, & \text{Jan 11 2019}) \\
& \vdots &
\end{array}
\tag{4.1}
$$

which might further be anonymized in terms of user IDs, item IDs, and sequential timestamps:[1]

$$
\begin{array}{llll}
(264, & 547, & 4, & 1546588800) \\
(264, & 82, & 3, & 1546761600) \\
(3473, & 231, & 5, & 1546934400) \\
(3473, & 547, & 4, & 1547193600) \\
& \vdots &
\end{array}
\tag{4.2}
$$

Such a format is ubiquitous across many popular recommendation datasets and tasks, including (e.g.) the popular *Netflix Prize* dataset (sec. 7.2.2). Such data may include 'side information,' such as reviews, demographic information about the users, or metadata about the movies, but often it may not. In fact, in the simplest form it may not even include ratings or timestamps.

---

[1] The timestamp shown here is known as the *unix time*, representing the number of seconds since January 1970 (in UTC); such a representation is often useful as it allows straightforward comparison between timestamps.

Thus, in essence, the data we are trying to work with simply describe *interactions* among users and content. Such interactions could describe clicks, purchases, ratings, likes (etc.). In other settings the interactions could describe social connections among users, 'interactions' among compatible clothing items (sec. 9.3), among countless other possibilities.

Given interaction data such as that above, we would now like to ask questions such as:

- How will Laura rate *Pulp Fiction*?
- Given that Laura liked the *The Godfather,* which other movies will she like?
- Which movie is Laura likely to rate next?

Answering these questions seems difficult, as we seemingly know very little about the users and items involved. However, we do know, for instance, that both Laura and Julian (or users 3473 and 264) recently watched *The Godfather,* and gave it similar ratings; from this we could begin to reason that they may exhibit similar preferences with regard to other movies also.

Reasoning about these types of questions, and modeling these types of interactions, are the main goals of recommender systems.

How is Recommendation Different from Regression or Classification?

In Chapters 2 and 3, we saw several techniques that seem like they could already be used to predict outcomes like ratings and purchases. For example, predicting a rating (e.g., of a movie) seems like a traditional regression task, and we can imagine various user and movie features that might be associated with ratings. As such, naively we might try to extract user and movie features and fit a linear model of the form

$$\text{rating}(\text{user}, \text{movie}) = \langle \underbrace{\phi(\text{user}, \text{movie})}_{\text{user and movie features}}, \theta \rangle. \tag{4.3}$$

User features might include attributes like the user's age, gender, location, or other demographic features that might be associated with rating patterns; movie features could capture the length, MPAA rating, budget, or presence of certain actors (etc.). Assuming user and movie features can be collected independently, and since the model is linear, this could be rewritten as

$$\text{rating}(\text{user}, \text{movie}) = \langle \underbrace{\phi^{(u)}(\text{user})}_{\text{user features}}, \overbrace{\theta^{(u)}}^{\text{user parameters}} \rangle + \langle \underbrace{\phi^{(i)}(\text{movie})}_{\text{movie (item) features}}, \overbrace{\theta^{(i)}}^{\text{movie parameters}} \rangle. \tag{4.4}$$

When written this way, we can see that the prediction of the rating is the sum of two *independent* predictions: one for the user (say $f(u)$) and one for the item

> The main distinguishing feature of recommender systems compared to other types of machine learning is their goal of explicitly modeling *interactions* between users and consumed items based on historical patterns. This feature allows the models to understand which items are *compatible* with which users, and thus to make different recommendations to each user in a personalized way.

Figure 4.1 Recommender systems compared to other types of machine learning

(say $f(i)$). If we were to make recommendations based on these predictions, for example, by recommending whichever unseen movie a user would give the highest rating to, that is,

$$\arg\max_{i \in \text{unseen movies}} f(u) + f(i), \tag{4.5}$$

our recommendation *for every user* would simply be whichever movie had the highest predicted rating $f(i)$. In other words, every user would simply be recommended movies which had features associated with high ratings.

Critically, such a model could not *personalize* its recommendations to individual users. Even if the model achieved a reasonable MSE in terms of predicting ratings, it would not be an effective recommender system.

To overcome this limitation, a model must in some fashion capture *interactions* between users and items, for example, how compatible a user is with a particular movie. Explicitly modeling interactions between users and items is the main goal of recommender systems and is the main characteristic that differentiates them from other types of machine learning (fig. 4.1).

4.2 Representations for Interaction Data

There are several ways we could represent the interaction data described earlier. Formally, we might simply describe the dataset as a set of tuples (u, i, r, t), or $r_{u,i,t} \in \mathbb{R}$ indicating that a user u entered the rating r for item i at time t.

But conceptually it is easier to think about these data in terms of sets or matrices. Set representations will be useful when establishing similarity between users in terms of sets of items they have consumed (or likewise similarity between items in terms of sets of users who have consumed them); matrix representations will be useful when developing models based on the concept of matrix factorization (or dimensionality reduction).

Activities as Sets: For our simplest recommendation models, we can describe users in terms of the sets of items they have interacted with, for example, for a user u:

$$I_u = \text{set of items consumed by } u; \qquad (4.6)$$

likewise, we can describe items in terms of the sets of users who have interacted with them:

$$U_i = \text{set of users who consumed item } i. \qquad (4.7)$$

Activities as Matrices: Alternately, we can represent datasets of user/item interactions via matrices. Interaction matrices could describe which items a user has interacted with (C), or could augment our previous representations to capture real-valued interaction signals such as ratings (R):

$$R = \begin{bmatrix} 5 & \cdot & \cdot & 2 & 3 \\ \cdot & 4 & 1 & \cdot & \cdot \\ \cdot & 5 & 5 & 3 & \cdot \\ 5 & \cdot & 4 & \cdot & 4 \\ 1 & 1 & \cdot & 4 & 5 \end{bmatrix} \quad C = \begin{bmatrix} 1 & \cdot & \cdot & 1 & 1 \\ \cdot & 1 & 1 & \cdot & \cdot \\ \cdot & 1 & 1 & 1 & \cdot \\ 1 & \cdot & 1 & \cdot & 1 \\ 1 & 1 & \cdot & 1 & 1 \end{bmatrix} \Bigg\} \text{ users.} \qquad (4.8)$$
$$\underbrace{\qquad\qquad}_{\text{items}} \qquad \underbrace{\qquad\qquad}_{\text{items}}$$

Each row of R represents a single user, and each column represents a single item. A particular entry $R_{u,i}$ indicates the rating the user u gave to item i. Note that the vast majority of entries in such a matrix would typically be missing (most users do not rate most items); indeed, the missing entries are exactly the quantities that we would like to predict.[2]

Naturally, the set and matrix representations can be written in terms of each other, for example, our set representation is equivalent to:

$$I_u = \{i \mid R_{u,i} \neq 0\} \qquad (4.9)$$
$$U_i = \{u \mid R_{u,i} \neq 0\}. \qquad (4.10)$$

Both our set and matrix representations of interactions may seem limited— neither conveys the timestamps associated with the ratings (or any other side-information), and the set-based representation does not even encode users' ratings. Nevertheless, they are useful for reasoning about the basic principles behind recommender systems, which will become the building blocks behind more sophisticated approaches.

---

[2] It should be carefully noted that our matrix representation is largely conceptual: it is rarely feasible to enumerate a complete interaction matrix, which could have millions of rows (users) and columns (items). In practice we will represent interaction matrices using sparse data structures mapping user/item pairs to observed values.

The approaches we study in Section 4.3 make recommendations by writing down similarity functions that take as input user and item interaction histories. There is no *model* (i.e., no parameters) associated with each user or item; the original data are used as an input to the similarity functions. Such systems are referred to as *memory-based* (or neighborhood-based) recommenders. In contrast, the techniques we will develop in Chapter 5 learn *representations* of each user and item, such that the original data generally is not used directly when making predictions at test time. Such systems are referred to as *model-based* recommenders.

Figure 4.2 Memory-based and model-based recommender systems

4.3 Memory-Based Approaches to Recommendation

Perhaps the simplest (and most ubiquitous) approaches to recommendation are based on some notion of 'similarity' among items. That is, an item is recommended to a user because it is similar to one that they have recently clicked, liked, or consumed.

'People who viewed X also viewed Y' (or 'people who bought X also bought Y,' etc.) features are familiar examples of such similarity-based recommenders. Items are recommended to a user on the basis of how *similar* they are to an item the user is currently browsing.

For such a recommender to be effective depends on choosing an appropriate similarity function. The similarity function that guides such models might be based on click or purchase data (as we see in sec. 4.5); but even then, by what metric should we consider patterns of clicks to be 'similar'? Should we count the number of users who have clicked on both items? Or do we need some kind of normalization? Or should we consider temporal recency?

Appropriately designing such similarity functions, and recommending on the basis of such similarity, is the task of so-called memory-based recommender systems. Such systems are said to be 'memory'-based since they make predictions directly from data (rather than from the parameters of a model derived from data). Most of the approaches we will see below are alternatively titled *neighborhood-based* recommender systems, in which items are recommended due to being in the *neighborhood* of (i.e., similar to) other items.[3] We summarize this distinction in Figure 4.2, which we discuss further when presenting model-based approaches in Chapter 5.

---

[3] Alternately various types of recommender systems are also termed *collaborative filtering*, though we generally avoid the term. Such models are 'collaborative' in the sense that the predictions of one user or item are based on those of others.

4.3.1 Defining a Similarity Function

Defining a similarity-based item-to-item recommender essentially requires that we define a similarity function among items:

$$\text{Sim}(i, j), \tag{4.11}$$

and then given a query item i, recommend a set of items j that maximize the given similarity.

Let us consider a small toy example, with four items, and sets of users (or rather user IDs) who have consumed each:

$$
\begin{aligned}
U_1 &= \{1, 3, 4, 8, 12, 15, 17, 24, 35, 39, 41, 43\} \\
U_2 &= \{2, 3, 4, 5, 9, 12, 13, 16, 19, 24, 27, 31\} \\
U_3 &= \{4, 5, 9, 12\} \\
U_4 &= \{4, 9\}
\end{aligned}
\tag{4.12}
$$

(recall that in our notation U_1 represents the set of users who have bought item 1). Naively, we might assume that an item-to-item recommender (e.g., 'people who bought X also bought Y') is simply counting the number of users who purchased both items in common. In our set notation, this would be:

$$\text{Sim}(i, j) = |U_i \cap U_j|. \tag{4.13}$$

Computing some similarities under this model we would find:

$$\text{Sim}(1, 2) = 4; \quad \text{Sim}(2, 3) = 4; \quad \text{Sim}(3, 4) = 2; \quad \text{etc.,} \tag{4.14}$$

that is, we would rate items 1 and 2, or items 2 and 3, as being *more similar* than items 3 and 4.

We should examine whether these relative scores seem reasonable. Items 1 and 2 are *popular* items, which most users did *not* purchase in common; whereas items 3 has *half* of its users in common with item 4. If we were to build recommenders on this basis, we might recommend (e.g.) a popular album as being highly similar to a popular pair of jeans, simply on the basis that they have many users in common. In general, such a system would tend to identify popular items (such as items 1 and 2 in eq. (4.12)) as being similar. 'Niche' items with fewer associated purchases (such as items 3 and 4 in eq. (4.12)) would rarely be recommended.

In most cases, this is not the outcome we want; such a system would make generic recommendations of popular items, that likely would not seem specific to the context of a given query item.

This toy example is intended to demonstrate that 'similarity' is not something easy to define, and that different definitions have implicit assumptions

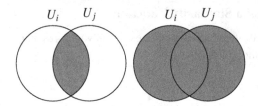

Figure 4.3 The similarity between two items i and j can be computed in terms of the intersection (left) and union (right) between the sets of users U_i and U_j who have consumed each

with nonobvious consequences. Presumably, we should improve our similarity function so that it has some appropriate normalization to account for item popularity, as we will see below.

4.3.2 Jaccard Similarity

Our first attempt at correcting these issues is to normalize similarity scores in a way that considers the popularity of each item. The *Jaccard Similarity*, or 'intersection over union,' does so by computing

$$\text{Jaccard}(i, j) = \frac{|U_i \cap U_j|}{|U_i \cup U_j|}. \tag{4.15}$$

This similarity function is perhaps best visualized by a Venn diagram such as that in Figure 4.3.[4] The Jaccard similarity takes a value between 0 (when U_i and U_j do not overlap at all, and thus have no intersection) and 1 (when the intersection is equal to the union, that is, the items were consumed by *exactly* the same set of users).

To demonstrate the Jaccard similarity in action, let us consider computing the similarity among items in terms of past purchases from *Amazon.com*. We will consider *Amazon*'s publicly available dataset of around 900,000 reviews from the *Musical Instrument* category.[5]

We first build some data structures to store the sets of items consumed by each user (or the sets of users who have consumed each item), that is, I_u and U_i:

```
1  usersPerItem = defaultdict(set)
2  itemsPerUser = defaultdict(set)
3
4  for d in dataset:
5      user, item = d['customer_id'], d['product_id']
6      usersPerItem[item].add(user)
7      itemsPerUser[user].add(item)
```

---

[4] Or more generally, for any two sets A and B, we have $\text{Jaccard}(A, B) = \frac{|A \cap B|}{|A \cup B|}$.

[5] Available from `https://s3.amazonaws.com/amazon-reviews-pds/tsv/index.txt`.

We can also implement the Jaccard similarity straightforwardly:

```
8    def Jaccard(s1, s2):
9        numerator = len(s1.intersection(s2))
10       denominator = len(s1.union(s2))
11       return numerator / denominator
```

Now, *recommendation* consists of finding the items with the highest Jaccard similarity compared to some given query (i.e., 'people who bought X also bought Y'):

```
12   def mostSimilar(i, K): # Query item i, and number of results
                            K to return
13       similarities = []
14       users = usersPerItem[i] # Users who have purchased i
15       for j in usersPerItem: # Compute similarity against each
                                 item
16           if j == i: continue
17           sim = Jaccard(users, usersPerItem[j])
18           similarities.append((sim,j))
19       similarities.sort(reverse=True) # Sort to find the most
                                          similar
20       return similarities[:K]
```

Finally, let us examine some recommendations, e.g. of the *'AudioQuest LP record clean brush'* (product ID *B0006VMBHI*). The five most similar items (i.e., mostSimilar('B0006VMBHI', 5)) are:

Shure SFG-2 Stylus Tracking Force Gauge
Shure M97xE High-Performance Magnetic Phono Cartridge
ART Pro Audio DJPRE II Phono Turntable Preamplifier
Signstek [...] Long-Playing LP Turntable Stylus Force Scale Gauge Tester
Audio Technica AT120E/T Standard Mount Phono Cartridge

All of the recommended items are also related to record players (which make up only a fraction of items in the category), which seem semantically reasonable given the query.

Using just a few lines of code, and using a (reasonably large) real-world dataset, we have implemented our first recommender system. Our solution is simple (and our implementation is fairly inefficient[6]), but nevertheless quickly produced reasonable recommendations. These simple types of similarity-based recommendations drive many of the most high-profile recommender systems on the web, as we study in Section 4.5.

---

[6] In particular, it is not necessary to iterate over *all* items; rather one can quickly compute a candidate set of only those items that could potentially have a non-zero Jaccard coefficient; see Exercise 4.1.

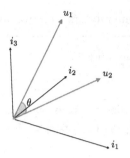

Figure 4.4 The cosine similarity is defined in terms of the angle between two vectors, here describing users u_1 and u_2

4.3.3 Cosine Similarity

The Jaccard similarity captures our intuition about what items ought to be similar to each other, but is only defined if interactions are represented as *sets*. We would like more nuanced similarity measures for data where feedback is associated with each interaction; for example, we might not regard two users as 'similar' if both had watched the *Harry Potter* movies, in the event that one of them liked the series and the other disliked it.

The *Cosine Similarity* achieves this by representing users' (or items') interaction histories in terms of *vectors* rather than *sets*. An example is shown in Figure 4.4, in which we have three items (i_1, i_2, and i_3) and two users (u_1 and u_2) who have each interacted with two of them.

In our previous (set) representation, we would write $I_{u_1} = \{i_2, i_3\}$ and $I_{u_2} = \{i_1, i_3\}$ to describe the sets of items that u_1 and u_2 have interacted with. In vector representation we could simply describe u_1 and u_2 in terms of *vectors* describing which items they interacted with. Such vectors are equivalent to rows of our interaction matrix R (eq. (4.8)), that is, $R_{u_1} = (0, 1, 1)$ and $R_{u_2} = (1, 0, 1)$.

The Cosine Similarity (in this case between two users u_1 and u_2) is now defined in terms of the *angle* between the vectors u_1 and u_2. Recall that the angle between two vectors a and b is defined as:

$$\theta = \mathrm{Cos}^{-1}\left(\frac{a \cdot b}{|a| \cdot |b|}\right); \quad \text{or} \quad \mathrm{Cos}(\theta) = \frac{a \cdot b}{|a| \cdot |b|}. \tag{4.16}$$

The angle θ measures the extent to which the two vectors point in the same direction; in the case of interaction data, the angle will range between $0°$ (if the two users have interacted with exactly the same items) and $90°$ (if the interaction vectors are orthogonal, that is, if the users have interacted with

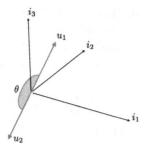

Figure 4.5 The cosine similarity for two users who rated the same items, but with opposite sentiment polarity

non-overlapping sets of items). The actual cosine similarity is the cosine of this angle, for example, between two users u and v:[7]

$$\text{Cosine Similarity}(u, v) = \frac{R_u \cdot R_v}{|R_u| \cdot |R_v|}. \tag{4.17}$$

For (binary) interaction data, the cosine of the angle is now between 1 (when the angle is zero, and the interactions are identical) and 0 (when the interactions are orthogonal).

It is instructive to compare Equations (4.15) and (4.17). In the case of binary interaction data, both expressions take values of 1 when the interactions are identical, and 0 when the interactions are non-overlapping. For binary interactions the numerator $R_u \cdot R_v$ in Equation (4.17) is equivalent to $|I_u \cap I_v|$, as in Equation (4.15). The two differ only in their denominators, both of which are essentially forms of normalization based on the size of the sets I_u and I_v (and both denominators will take the same value when I_u and I_v are equal).

Of course, the cosine similarity is more interesting once we consider numerical interactions, that is, interactions associated with *feedback*, rather than just binary (0/1) data. For example, consider data where each interaction is associated with a 'thumbs-up' or 'thumbs-down' rating. We might represent this via an interaction matrix R such that $R_{u,i} \in \{-1, 0, 1\}$ (where $-1/1$ indicates thumbs-down/thumbs-up, and 0 indicates an item the user has not interacted with).

In this case, the Jaccard similarity would not be well-defined. But the cosine similarity can still be computed on rows (or columns) of R. An example is shown in Figure 4.5. Here, user u_1 has interacted with two items (i_2 and i_3), and liked both; u_2 has interacted with the *same* items, but disliked both. The two user vectors now point in opposite directions, that is, they have an angle of 180° and a cosine similarity of -1.

---

[7] Or it can be straightforwardly defined for *item* similarity by interchanging users and items.

With some effort we can adapt our code above for the Jaccard similarity to implement the cosine similarity. Here we use an auxiliary data structure (ratingDict) that retrieves ratings for a given user/item pair:

```
1  def Cosine(i1, i2):
2      # Between two items
3      inter = usersPerItem[i1].intersection(usersPerItem[i2])
4      numer = sum([ratingDict[(u,i1)]*ratingDict[(u,i2)] for u
             in inter])
5      norm1 = sum([ratingDict[(u,i1)]**2 for u in usersPerItem
             [i1]])
6      norm2 = sum([ratingDict[(u,i2)]**2 for u in usersPerItem
             [i2]])
7      denom = math.sqrt(norm1) * math.sqrt(norm2)
8      if denom == 0: return 0 # If one of the two items has no
             ratings
9      return numer / denom
```

Doing so (for the same query item), the top recommendation remains the same (Shure SFG-2 Stylus Tracking Force Gauge). Among the next few recommendations, there are many ties (i.e., identical cosine similarities); upon inspection these turn out to be items with only a single (overlapping) interaction. In this case, such items are preferred by the cosine similarity (and not the Jaccard) since the denominator grows quickly for items with many associated interactions (whereas the union term in Equation (4.15) grows more slowly, assuming many of the interactions overlap).

Which Similarity Metric is 'Better'? In this example, the Jaccard similarity seemed to work 'better' than the cosine similarity, but our argument about the difference between the two is somewhat imprecise. Note that this argument largely applies to this specific dataset (or even the specific query item we chose). Ultimately, these similarity measures are essentially *heuristics*; whether one is 'better' than another depends on our own assumptions and intuition about what similarity ought to mean. This is in contrast to the machine learning approaches we saw in previous chapters in which we had a specific objective (i.e., a measure of success) that we were trying to optimize. We will revisit this question when we examine model-based recommender systems in Chapter 5.

4.3.4 Pearson Similarity

We motivated the Jaccard similarity by considering binary interaction data (i.e., sets), and the cosine similarity by considering polarized interactions like 'thumbs-up's and 'thumbs-down's.

Consider how these similarity measurements would operate on numerical feedback scores such as star ratings (as in eq. (4.8)). Take the users represented

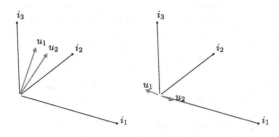

Figure 4.6 Pearson similarity. Two users have rating vectors that point roughly in the same direction (left); after subtracting the average from each, they point in opposite directions (right).

in Figure 4.6 (left) as an example. Here two users have rated the same items (i_2 and i_3); user u_1 rated them 3 and 5 stars (respectively); user u_2 rated them 5 and 3.

According to the Jaccard similarity (based only on interactions), we would consider the two users to be identical (Jaccard similarity of 1); according to the cosine similarity, we would regard them as being very similar, since the angle between the two vectors is small. However, one could argue that these users are polar opposites of each other: if we consider 5 stars to be a *positive* rating and 3 stars to be a *negative* rating, then these two users indeed have opposite opinion polarity.

Our definition of the cosine similarity does not account for this interpretation, essentially because it depends on the interactions already having explicitly positive or negative polarity. To correct this we might appropriately normalize our ratings: if we subtract the average for each user (4 stars for both u_1 and u_2), we find that their ratings are each 1 star above or below their personal average. After doing so, the example becomes very similar to the one from Section 4.3.3 (see fig. 4.6, right).

This is essentially the idea captured by the Pearson Similarity. The *Pearson Correlation Coefficient* is a classical measurement for assessing the relationship between two variables, that is, whether they trend in the same direction, regardless of scale and constant differences between them. The Pearson Correlation between two vectors x and y is defined as

$$\text{Pearson Correlation}(x, y) = \frac{\sum_{i=1}^{|x|} (x_i - \bar{x})(y_i - \bar{y})}{\sqrt{\sum_{i=1}^{|x|} (x_i - \bar{x})^2} \sqrt{\sum_{i=1}^{|y|} (y_i - \bar{y})^2}}. \tag{4.18}$$

Compare this definition to that of the cosine similarity in Equation (4.17): the only difference is that from each measurement we subtract the mean ($\bar{x}$ or $\bar{y}$) of the corresponding vector. We summarize the relationship between the Jaccard, Cosine, and Pearson similarities in Figure 4.7.

Our comparison of the Jaccard, Cosine, and Pearson similarities can be summarized as follows:

- The *Jaccard Similarity* computes the similarity between *sets*. The basic idea is to find items that have been purchased (or interacted with) in common by many users (or users who have purchased many items in common); the set union is used to normalize the quantity, so that the measure does not overly favor popular items (or highly active users).
- The *Cosine Similarity* instead represents interactions as vectors (basically, rows or columns of our interaction matrix R). Similarity is then computed in terms of the angle between vectors for two items (or users). This definition allows similarity to be computed for numerical interaction data, especially if a polarity (i.e., positive or negative) is associated with each interaction.
- Finally, the *Pearson Similarity* was motivated by the idea that numerical feedback may need to be properly calibrated in order to associate a polarity to each score. For instance, a rating of '3.5' might be positive for one user but negative for another. The Pearson similarity calibrates this polarity simply by subtracting the average for each user (or item); after this calibration the definition is similar to that of the cosine similarity.

Figure 4.7 Summary of similarity measures

When applying this concept to rating data, we should be careful not to regard unobserved ratings (i.e., missing values of $R_{u,i}$ in eq. (4.8)) as zeros—doing so would distort our estimate of the user mean. Thus we might define the similarity between two users u and v (or similarly, items) only in terms of items they have both interacted with:

$$\text{Pearson Similarity}(u, v) = \frac{\sum_{i \in I_u \cap I_v} (R_{u,i} - \bar{R}_u)(R_{v,i} - \bar{R}_v)}{\sqrt{\sum_{i \in I_u \cap I_v} (R_{u,i} - \bar{R}_u)^2} \sqrt{\sum_{i \in I_u \cap I_v} (R_{v,i} - \bar{R}_v)^2}}. \quad (4.19)$$

Our choice to define the Pearson similarity by considering only *shared* items is somewhat arbitrary; we could instead have considered *all* items rated by each user in the denominator. Using our definition (which appears in, e.g., Sarwar et al. (2001)), we regard users as maximally similar if they have rated shared items in the same way; if we considered all items rated by each user in the denominator, we would regard users as less similar if they had also rated some different items. Remember that these similarity functions are merely heuristics—neither option should be considered more 'correct,' but rather we should choose the definition that suits our intuition (or generates the most satisfactory results) in a particular situation.

Our code for the cosine similarity above can easily be adapted to implement the Pearson similarity (noting the details above). Here we have an additional data structure (`itemAverages`) recording the mean rating for each item:

```
1   def Pearson(i1, i2):
2       # Between two items
3       iBar1,iBar2 = itemAverages[i1], itemAverages[i2]
4       inter = usersPerItem[i1].intersection(usersPerItem[i2])
5       numer = 0
6       denom1 = 0
7       denom2 = 0
8       for u in inter:
9           numer += (ratingDict[(u,i1)] - iBar1)*(ratingDict[(u
                ,i2)] - iBar2)
10      for u in inter: # Alternately could sum over
            usersPerItem[i1]/[i2]
11          denom1 += (ratingDict[(u,i1)] - iBar1)**2
12          denom2 += (ratingDict[(u,i2)] - iBar2)**2
13      denom = math.sqrt(denom1) * math.sqrt(denom2)
14      if denom == 0: return 0
15      return numer / denom
```

Fitting the Pearson similarity given the query item from Section 4.3.2 does not produce particularly satisfactory results; using $U_i \cap U_j$ in the denominator of Equation (4.19) results in many items with a similarity of 1.0 (usually just due to a single overlapping interaction); using U_i and U_j separately in the denominator of Equation (4.19) generates more meaningful results, though they come from a broad category of items that do not seem closely related.

Possibly these results are unsatisfactory simply because ratings of (e.g.) a record cleaning brush are not due to factors that meaningfully transfer to other items. One likely purchases a record cleaning brush for its utility rather than because of their personal preference toward such items. If variability in ratings is primarily due to build quality, or effectiveness (e.g.), then the Pearson similarity might identify other items with 'similar' build quality or effectiveness, but those may not be semantically similar items. In this particular example, the Jaccard similarity—which defines similarity in terms of *what* was purchased— seems more appropriate than the Pearson similarity, which defines similarity in terms of preferences.

Again though, possibly this measure is simply not suitable for this dataset or this query item. Let us try again on another dataset, this time from the *Amazon Video Games* category. Given the query *One Piece: Pirate Warriors*, the five most similar items in terms of Pearson similarity[8] are:

> *Full Metal Alchemist: The Broken Angel*
> *Monster Rancher 4*
> *FINAL FANTASY X X-2 HD Remaster*
> *BlazBlue: Continuum Shift EXTEND Limited Edition*
> *Killzone 3* (etc.)

---

[8] Again using U_i and U_j separately in the denominator.

These recommendations look more reasonable. In addition to being for similar platforms (e.g., PlayStation) most are reasonably similar in terms of genre and style (e.g., Japanese, based on anime, etc.). Seemingly, in this setting features like style and genre better explain variation in ratings, making the Pearson similarity more effective.

Finally, these similarity measures need not be used directly for recommendations as we have done here (i.e., simply retrieving the most similar item given a query). In practice they might be subroutines that guide more complex algorithms. For example, to recommend items to a user we might first find similar users, and recommend items that many of those users liked, rather than simply relying on item-to-item similarity directly (see, e.g., sec. 4.5 and Exercise 4.3).

4.3.5 Using Similarity Measurements for Rating Prediction

In Chapter 5, we will contrast the similarity-based recommendation approaches above with machine learning (or 'model-based') approaches which directly seek to predict ratings (or interactions) as accurately as possible.

However, these two goals (measuring similarity versus predicting ratings) are not at odds with each other, and indeed one can use a measure of similarity as a means of predicting ratings.

The essence of such an approach is that the rating a user will give to an item can be estimated from ratings that user has given to *similar* items (again, for some appropriate definition of 'similarity'). One such definition (from Sarwar et al. (2001)) predicts the rating as a weighted sum of other items the user has rated:

$$r(u, i) = \frac{\sum_{j \in I_u \setminus \{i\}} R_{u,j} \cdot \mathrm{Sim}(i, j)}{\sum_{j \in I_u \setminus \{i\}} \mathrm{Sim}(i, j)}, \tag{4.20}$$

where $\mathrm{Sim}(i, j)$ could be any item-to-item similarity function such as those above. Note here that $r(u, i)$ is a prediction, whereas $R_{u,i}$ is a historical rating.

The intuition behind the above equation is simply that the most similar items should be the most relevant when predicting future ratings, so the user's past ratings of those items are given the highest weights. Again though this is just a heuristic for predicting ratings and could be defined differently. For example, we could write the same definition in terms of user similarity:

$$r(u, i) = \frac{\sum_{v \in U_i \setminus \{u\}} R_{v,i} \cdot \mathrm{Sim}(u, v)}{\sum_{v \in U_i \setminus \{u\}} \mathrm{Sim}(u, v)}, \tag{4.21}$$

or, we, could possibly improve performance by weighting deviations from the average rating, rather than ratings directly:

$$r(u, i) = \bar{R}_i + \frac{\sum_{j \in I_u \setminus \{i\}} (R_{u,j} - \bar{R}_j) \cdot \text{Sim}(i, j)}{\sum_{j \in I_u \setminus \{i\}} \text{Sim}(i, j)}, \qquad (4.22)$$

Using our video game data from Section 4.3.4 and following the prediction function from Equation (4.22) (with the Jaccard Similarity as our similarity function), the MSE of predicted ratings compared to the true labels is 1.786, compared to 1.838 when always predicting the mean.

Code to implement the rating prediction model of Equation (4.22) is included below. Here we use the Jaccard similarity, though any item-to-item similarity metric could be used in its place. Note that for the sake of evaluating such algorithms, we must be careful to exclude the query item (i) from all summations:[9]

```
1   def predictRating(user,item):
2       ratings = [] # Collect ratings over which to average
3       sims = [] # and similarity scores
4       for d in reviewsPerUser[user]:
5           j = d['product_id']
6           if j == item: continue # Skip the query item
7           ratings.append(d['star_rating'] - itemAverages[j])
8           sims.append(Jaccard(usersPerItem[item],usersPerItem[
                j]))
9       if (sum(sims) > 0):
10          weightedRatings = [(x*y) for x,y in zip(ratings,sims
                )]
11          return itemAverages[item] + sum(weightedRatings) /
                sum(sims)
12      else:
13          # User hasn't rated any similar items
14          return ratingMean
```

4.4 Random Walk Methods

So far we have developed recommender systems in which user interaction data were represented as sets or matrices. Based on these two types of representations methods, based on set (sec. 4.3.2) and vector (sec. 4.3.3), similarity arose naturally.

A third possible representation of user interaction data is to treat interactions as a *bipartite graph* (fig. 4.8). Here users and items are each a set of nodes, and edges between users and items represent user interactions (where edges may be weighted by a rating or interaction frequency).

---

[9] Strictly, our auxiliary data structures that store average ratings should also be adjusted to exclude the query interaction.

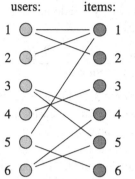

users: items:

Figure 4.8 User interactions can be represented as a *bipartite graph* connecting users and items. Recommendations can be made by simulating random walks on the graph, such that 'nearby' items are considered similar.

Based on this representation, *Random Walk*-based methods assess the relatedness or 'closeness' of nodes by simulating a walker that traverses the graph by randomly following its edges. Specifically, random walk-based methods attempt to assess the strength of a relationship between two nodes x and y by assessing *the probability that a random walk starting on node x will terminate on node y*.

Relation to *PageRank*: Note that this closely resembles algorithms like *PageRank* or *HITS* (Brin and Page, 1998; Kleinberg, 1999). These algorithms also model random walks on graph data; there the goal is to compute a stationary distribution π, where π_x represents the probability that a walker will visit node x at any given step. This is computed by defining the relation

$$\pi^{(t)} = \pi^{(t-1)}P \tag{4.23}$$

(where P is a matrix of transition probabilities) and computing $\pi = \lim_{t \to \infty} \pi^{(t)}$. This can be computed by power iteration (i.e., iteratively computing the relation from eq. (4.23)), which will converge to the principal eigenvector of P (Brin and Page, 1998). *PageRank* includes an additional detail, a *damping factor d*, which simulates the 'click-through probability' that a random walker will terminate (and randomly restart) their walk at any step. Without this term, the stationary probability π_i would become dominated by 'sink' pages (i.e., with no outgoing links). See Brin and Page (1998) for a full description.

When using the abovementioned approach in the context *PageRank* or *HITS*, we generally treat π_x as an overall measure of the 'quality' or 'authoritativeness' of a page. In a recommendation setting, we might instead be interested in transition probabilities, that is, the probability that a random walker will visit item j having started from item i.

To do so, we start with a *transition probability* $p(j|i)$ between nodes; this represents the probability that a walker currently at node i will visit node j during the next step (we give a few examples of such transition probabilities below). These probabilities can be aggregated into a transition matrix P (where $P_{i,j} = p(j|i)$). These *first-order* probabilities represent the probability that a random walker at node i would visit j in the next step; to compute the probability that the walker will eventually visit j on *some* step, we can take powers of the transition matrix P:

$$P^* = \sum_{n=1}^{\infty} \frac{(dP)^n}{|(dP)^n|}. \tag{4.24}$$

Here d is again a damping factor. The damping factor prevents the probability from becoming saturated by the walker eventually transitioning to popular items (Yildirim and Krishnamoorthy, 2008).

Representative papers include Li et al. (2009), which most closely follows the setting (and notation) above. They use this type of paradigm for the setting of grocery recommendations. They start by defining transition probabilities between users and items (on a bipartite graph similar to that in fig. 4.8):

$$p(i|u) = \frac{f(u,i)}{(\sum_j f(u,j))^{\alpha_1}}; \quad p(u|i) = \frac{f(u,i)}{(\sum_v f(v,i))^{\alpha_2}}. \tag{4.25}$$

Here $f(u,i)$ measures the historical purchase frequency between the user u and the item i; α_1 and α_2 penalize users or products associated with many transactions. The transition probability between items ($p(j|i)$) can then be found by summing over all users:

$$p(j|i) = \sum_{u=1}^{|U|} p(j|u)p(u|i). \tag{4.26}$$

Li et al. (2009) compare similarity functions like that of Equation (4.24) with traditional item-to-item similarity functions like those in Section 4.3.

Others adopt similar approaches, albeit with different ways of defining transition probabilities between items; Liu and Yang (2008) define transition probabilities between items in terms of the ratings those items have received.

Note that the idea behind random walk-based methods is quite general; above we describe only the simplest setting where (bipartite) graphs are defined in terms of user and item similarities. Other approaches based on this paradigm establish more complex graph structures to uncover different types of relationships among users, items, or other features. For example, *authors* from *organizations* may publish *papers* in *venues* (essentially a 'four-partite' graph) (Dong et al., 2017b); or richer item relationships could be defined in terms of which items were co-purchased in the same basket (in addition to user-to-item relationships) (Wan et al., 2018). Ultimately graph-based representations give us a straightforward means to incorporate several types of relationships via a common framework. We study a specific instance that models interactions within sessions in Section 7.3.2.

4.5 Case Study: Amazon.com Recommendations

In a 2003 paper (Linden et al., 2003), researchers described the techniques underlying *Amazon*'s recommendation technology. The paper described systems that recommend related items, for example, 'Customers who bought items in your shopping card also bought.'

The first recommendation method the paper describes is based on the Cosine Similarity (sec. 4.3.3). Interestingly, cosine similarity is defined between *users*, rather than between items as we did in Section 4.3.2; the goal is then to recommend items that have previously been purchased by similar customers. The paper discusses the issues of scaling this type of similarity computation to the large number of *Amazon* users, and discusses an alternative strategy to *cluster* users based on a user-to-user similarity metric; similar customers to a given user can then be found by determining the user's cluster membership (which is cast as a classification problem).

Although Linden et al. (2003) go into little detail about the specifics of what is implemented by *Amazon,* their work does stress the key point that real-world, large-scale recommenders need not be based on complex models. Rather, primary considerations include building models that are simple but scale well.

Following Linden et al. (2003), a follow-up paper was published describing more modern recommendation techniques on *Amazon* (Smith and Linden, 2017). The paper starts by describing minor modifications to the algorithms described earlier. For instance, they describe an item-to-item-based approach which is more reminiscent of that in Section 4.3.2 and describe how most of the computation for this type of problem can be done offline. Smith and Linden (2017) also stress the importance of choosing a good similarity heuristic and discuss some strategies for doing so. Finally, Smith and Linden (2017) discuss the importance of considering temporal factors when designing recommenders, which is our main focus in Chapter 7.

Exercises

4.1   *These exercises could be completed using any dataset with users, items, and ratings* (including the same dataset used in Project 3, below). The

Jaccard similarity-based recommender we implemented in Section 4.3.2 proved an effective recommender, though our implementation was inefficient. The main source of inefficiency was due to iteration over *all* items. A more efficient implementation might first build smaller a *candidate set* of items, by noting that only those items with at least one user in common with the query could potentially have non-zero Jaccard similarity. This candidate set can be built by taking all users who have purchased the query i, and taking the union over *other* items they have purchased (other than i), that is, $\bigcup_{u \in U_i} I_u \setminus \{i\}$. After modifying our implementation from Section 4.3.2 to use this candidate set, confirm that it produces identical recommendations, and compare its running time to the naive implementation.

4.2 Although we discuss evaluation in detail in Chapter 5, in this exercise we will build a simple quality measure for similarity-based recommenders. Specifically, an item-to-item recommender might be considered 'useful' if it tends to rate items i and j that are both purchased by u as being *more similar* than two items *not* purchased by the same user. For each user, randomly sample two of their interactions i and j, and a third interaction $k \in I \setminus I_u$ *not* purchased by u. Measure how often the system rates $\text{Sim}(i, j) \geq \text{Sim}(i, k)$. Compute this measure for the Jaccard, Cosine, and Pearson similarities (or other variants) to a measure which is best suited to a particular dataset.[10]

4.3 The code we developed in Section 4.3.2 (and in Exercise 4.1) is so far just an item-to-item recommender, and does not produce recommendations based on the user's *history*. However it could be adapted to do so in several ways, for example:

• Recommend an item i based on the *average* similarity compared to all items j from the user's history;
• rather than averaging over *all* items from the user's history, average over only the last K, or otherwise weight the average by recency;
• select an item consumed by a highly similar user;
• and so on.

Explore alternatives such as those above to determine which is best at recommending users' future interactions based on their history. For the sake of evaluation, it is useful if variants associate a *score $r(u, i)$* with each candidate recommendation; for example, the score could be the average cosine similarity between i and items j in u's history; or the score could be the Jaccard similarity between u and the most similar

---

[10] Also consider the most effective way to handle ties; ties could either be counted as a failure of the algorithm, or could be counted separately from successes or failures.

user v who has consumed i. Methods may then be compared using a similar approach to Exercise 4.2: that is, does the method tend to assign higher scores to (withheld) items the user interacted with compared to randomly chosen items.[11]

4.4 Implement rating prediction models following the formulas in Equations (4.20) to (4.22). Compare the three in terms of their MSE (using either the entire dataset or a random sample).

Project 3: A Recommender System for Books (Part 1)

In this project we will build recommender systems to make recommendations related to book reviews from *Goodreads* (which we studied a little in chap. 2). Here, we will build simple similarity-based recommenders before continuing this project with more complex recommendation approaches in Chapter 5 (Project 4). We will also use this project to set up an evaluation pipeline for this type of task (though we discuss evaluation strategies for recommender systems in more detail in chap. 5).

While this project could be completed using any dataset that includes users, items, and ratings, we suggest using a small subset of *Goodreads* data (e.g., reviews from the *Poetry* or *Comic Book* categories) for the sake of quickly benchmarking alternative methods.

(i) First, implement simple item-to-item recommendation strategies, as in Exercise 4.3 (you may follow a similar evaluation strategy as in that exercise).

(ii) Although the approaches explored in this chapter were largely *not* based on machine learning, there is no reason why we could not train a *classifier* to predict (or rank) books that a user is likely to read. We will explore more complex methods for this setting in Chapter 5, but for the moment let us see how far we can get by trying to extract some simple features to describe user/item interactions. Start by building a training set consisting of all pairs (u, i) of books i that user u has read; next build an (equally sized) set of *negative* pairs (u, j) of books the user *has not* read (e.g., by sampling randomly). Now, we want to build a feature vector $\phi(u, i)$ that can be used to predict whether a user u has read book i or not. To build a

---

[11] When withholding an interaction for evaluation, be careful to ensure the interaction is also withheld from any auxiliary data structures you've built. If using a sparse dataset, it is likely that many candidates will have scores of zero; you might consider using a denser dataset, or revisiting the exercise once we develop more sophisticated evaluation techniques in Section 5.4.

useful recommender system, we must include features that describe *inter-actions* between the user and the book. Examples of features you might use could include:

- The popularity of the book (e.g., the number of times item i appears in the training set, or its average rating);
- the Jaccard similarity (or any other similarity measure) between i and the *most similar* book the user u has read (i.e., $\max_{j \in I_u} \text{Sim}(i, j)$);
- likewise, the similarity between the *user* u and the most similar user who has read i;
- any other similarity measures, user, or item features.

Your classifier can be evaluated using standard accuracy or ranking metrics (though we further discuss evaluation in this setting in sec. 5.4). Compare this classification-based approach to methods like those from Exercise 4.3.[12]

(iii) Finally, consider using the data to predict ratings, as in Exercise 4.4. We will compare these predictions to model-based approaches in Project 4.

---

[12] If implemented properly, the classification approach should perform better since other similarity measures are used as *features* by the classifier; in essence, our classifier is implementing a simple form of *ensembling*.

5

Model-Based Approaches to Recommendation

So far when developing recommender systems in Chapter 4 we have avoided any discussion of *machine learning*. Although the types of 'memory-based' recommender systems (see fig. 4.2) we have developed so far can be used to make predictions (either by estimating the next item or predicting a rating as in sec. 4.3.5), they were in some sense not *optimized* to do so. That is, we used *heuristics* to rank items and predict ratings. This is in contrast to the approaches we developed in Chapters 2 and 3, where we were concerned with *objectives* to be optimized (involving an accuracy or error term), in terms of several model parameters.

In this chapter, we develop *model-based* approaches to recommendation, which adapt the regression and classification approaches from Chapters 2 and 3 to problems of estimating interactions between users and items. That is, we are concerned with fitting models that take a user u and item i as inputs in order to estimate an interaction label y (such as a purchase, click, or rating):

$$f(u, i) \rightarrow y. \tag{5.1}$$

Superficially, solving such a prediction task seems no different than the regression or classification scenarios we have already developed: naively, we might imagine collecting some appropriate user or item features and applying the techniques we have already developed. However, as we began to discuss in Chapter 4 (sec. 4.1), certain characteristics of this setting render traditional regression and classification approaches ineffective, and demand that we explore new approaches specifically designed to capture the dynamics of interaction data. Specifically:

- Most of the techniques we will develop in this chapter discard features altogether, and make predictions purely on the basis of historical interactions.

This owes partly to the difficulty of collecting useful features, and also to the complex semantics that underlie people's preferences and behavior.

- As such, rather than having parameters associated with features as we did in Chapters 2 and 3, the models we will develop here have parameters associated with individual *users* (or items). This shall be our introduction to the idea of *model-based* personalization, as we discussed in Section 1.7.2.
- To model users (and items) we will introduce the concept of *latent spaces* in Section 5.1, whereby we automatically discover hidden dimensions that explain the variation in people's opinions—without necessarily knowing exactly what the dimensions correspond to.

Our discussion of recommender systems will form the basis of many of the models we develop throughout the remainder of this book. Although in this chapter we will build predictive models based purely on interaction histories, later we will show how similar models can be extended by incorporating features (chap. 6) and temporal information (chap. 7). Later, as we further develop personalized models of text (chap. 8) and images (chap. 9) this same notion of modeling users via latent spaces will appear repeatedly.

In contrast to 'memory-based' recommendation approaches, *model-based* approaches seek to learn parameterized representations of users and items, so that recommendations can be made in terms of the learned parameters. Model-based approaches are typically cast in terms of supervised learning, so that the goal is to predict ratings, purchases, clicks (etc.) as accurately as possible. We summarize the differences between these two classes of approach in Figure 5.1.

The *Netflix Prize*

In 2006, *Netflix* released a dataset of 100,000,000 movie ratings (across 17,770 movies and around 480,000 users). Their dataset took exactly the form described in Section 4.1, that is, it consisted purely of (user, item, rating, timestamp) tuples. Associated with the dataset was a competition (Bennett et al., 2007) to reduce the RMSE (on a test set of withheld ratings) by 10% compared to *Netflix*'s existing solution. The first team to do so would win a $1,000,000 prize.

The competition's history is itself interesting. Early leaders joined forces to develop ensemble approaches, and the winning teams were nearly tied in a nail-biting finish. The competition also led to a broader discussion around the value of such high-profile competitions, as well as the question of whether narrowly reducing a MSE actually improves recommendations. It also led to a lawsuit against *Netflix* following de-anonymization of the competition data

There are a variety of reasons why one might choose a model-based or memory-based approach. We summarize a few of the advantages and disadvantages as follows:

Training and Inference Complexity Model-based approaches often require (expensive) offline training; on the other hand, once trained, recommendations can potentially be retrieved quickly, for example, by retrieving a nearest neighbor or a maximum inner product in parameter space (sec. 5.6). In contrast, memory-based approaches, while requiring no training, may depend on computationally intensive heuristics.

Interpretability Often, simple recommendations may be preferable simply because they are easy to explain to a user. In contrast, machine learning-based recommendations may make users uncomfortable due to their 'black box' nature (we explore notions of explainability and interpretability a little further in sec. 8.4.3).

Accuracy Model-based systems are appealing because they directly optimize a desired error measure. On the other hand, error measures that are tractable may not be those that relate meaningfully to user satisfaction, and may distract from qualitative improvements.

Figure 5.1 Memory-based versus model-based approaches

(Narayanan and Shmatikov, 2006).[1] Finally there is the question of whether the complex models that achieved the best competition performance—which have many complex, interacting, and carefully tuned components, and are expensive to train—can really be *deployed*.

Other than the specifics of the prize itself, the dataset and high-profile competition spawned a great deal of research on recommender systems in general, especially the specific setting of rating prediction. In particular, winning approaches were model-based solutions based on matrix factorization, as we begin to develop below.

5.1 Matrix Factorization

The basic assumption made by model-based recommenders is that there is some underlying low-dimensional *structure* among the interactions we are trying to predict. Put differently, model-based recommender systems are essentially a form of dimensionality reduction.

In simple terms, we assume that users' opinions, or the properties of the items they consume, can be efficiently summarized. Do you tend to like action movies (and is this an action movie)? Do you tend to enjoy movies with a

---

[1] This too is an interesting story, as the competition data, with anonymized user and item IDs, at first glance appears to be sufficiently anonymized.

high budget, certain actors, or a long runtime? To the extent that purchases, clicks, or ratings can be explained by such factors, the goal of model-based recommendation is to discover them.

Considering data of the form in Section 4.1, this seems a difficult process: we have no knowledge of the necessary *features* that would be needed to discover these important factors (i.e., we do not know which movies are action movies, which movies have a long runtime, etc.). But surprisingly one can still uncover these underlying dimensions without them. As a motivating example, consider the interaction (e.g., click) data depicted below:

$$R = \begin{bmatrix} 1 & \cdot & 1 & \cdot & \cdot \\ 1 & 1 & 1 & \cdot & \cdot \\ \cdot & 1 & 1 & \cdot & \cdot \\ \cdot & \cdot & \cdot & 1 & 1 \\ \cdot & \cdot & \cdot & 1 & \cdot \end{bmatrix} \begin{matrix} u_1 \\ u_2 \\ u_3 \\ u_4 \\ u_5 \end{matrix} \qquad (5.2)$$
$$\quad\ \ i_1\ \ i_2\ \ i_3\ \ i_4\ \ i_5$$

The matrix appears to decompose roughly into two 'blocks': if we wrote

$$\begin{aligned} \gamma_{u_1} &= [1,0] & \gamma_{i_1} &= [1,0] \\ \gamma_{u_2} &= [1,0] & \gamma_{i_2} &= [1,0] \\ \gamma_{u_3} &= [1,0]\ ; & \gamma_{i_3} &= [1,0]\ , \\ \gamma_{u_4} &= [0,1] & \gamma_{i_4} &= [0,1] \\ \gamma_{u_5} &= [0,1] & \gamma_{i_5} &= [0,1] \end{aligned} \qquad (5.3)$$

then we could (approximately) summarize the matrix R in Equation (5.2) by writing $R_{u,i} = \gamma_u \cdot \gamma_i$. The two blocks in R might conceivably correspond to some feature in the data, e.g., male and female users who buy men's and women's clothing. If so, the values in Equation (5.3) would correspond to genders for users and items. Note critically though that we discovered these factors simply because they *summarized the structure of the matrix*, rather than needing to rely on observed features.

Matrix Factorization follows this same idea, again by looking for underlying structure that explains observed interactions.

Essentially, our goal is to describe a (partially observed) matrix in terms of lower-dimensional factors, that is,

$$\underbrace{\begin{bmatrix} R \end{bmatrix}}_{|U| \times |I|} = \underbrace{\begin{bmatrix} \gamma_U \end{bmatrix}}_{|U| \times K} \times \underbrace{\begin{bmatrix} \gamma_I^T \end{bmatrix}}_{K \times |I|} . \qquad (5.4)$$

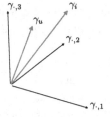

Figure 5.2 Represen-
tation of a user u and
item i in a latent factor
model

That is, we are assuming that the matrix R, of dimension $|U| \times |I|$ (the number of users times the number of items), can be approximated by a 'tall' matrix γ_U and a 'wide' matrix γ_I. Now, a single entry $R_{u,i}$ can be estimated by taking the corresponding row of γ_U and column of γ_I:

$$R_{u,i} = \gamma_u \cdot \gamma_i, \tag{5.5}$$

as in our motivating example here. $\gamma_u \in \mathbb{R}^K$ is now a latent vector that describes a user, and $\gamma_i \in \mathbb{R}^K$ describes an item.

Examples of such vectors are depicted in Figure 5.2. Intuitively, γ_u might be thought of as describing the 'preferences' of the user u, whereas γ_i describes the 'properties' of item i. Then, the user u will like (e.g., give a high rating to or interact with) the item i if their preferences are *compatible* with the item's properties (i.e., they have a high inner product). The latent dimensions, $\gamma_{\cdot,1}$, $\gamma_{\cdot,2}$ (etc.) now describe those latent factors that best explain variability in R. For example, if such a model were trained on the *Netflix* dataset they might measure the extent to which a movie is a comedy or a romance, or the quality of its special effects. Again though, these factors are *latent* and are discovered purely so as to maximally explain the observed interactions; models based on the principle of matrix factorization are commonly referred to as *latent factor models*.

Relationship to the Singular Value Decomposition

Briefly, we note that the factorization described in Equation (5.4) is closely related to the *Singular Value Decomposition* (SVD). Under the Singular Value Decomposition, a matrix M is decomposed as

$$M = U\Sigma V^T, \tag{5.6}$$

where U and V are left and right singular values of M (eigenvectors of MM^T and M^TM), and Σ is a diagonal matrix of eigenvectors of MM^T (or M^TM). Critically, *the best possible rank K approximation of M (in terms of the MSE) is found by taking the top K eigenvectors/eigenvalues in U, Σ and V* (Eckart-Young theorem). While this appears to give us a recipe for choosing the best possible γ_u and γ_i in Equation (5.5), the Singular Value Decomposition is defined only for *fully observed* matrices, rather than partially observed interactions as in R. Even if this could be addressed (e.g., via a data imputation strategy on the missing values), it would not be practical to compute the SVD on a matrix that could potentially have millions of rows and columns. As such, in practice we will not compute eigenvectors and eigenvalues, and will instead resort to gradient-based approaches, as described below. Nevertheless, the relationship to the SVD gives us a hint as to the type of factors to which γ_u and γ_i are likely to correspond.

5.1.1 Fitting the Latent Factor Model

So far we have described the intuition behind modeling interactions in terms of latent user and item factors, but have not yet described how to fit a model based on this principle. That is, we would like to choose γ_U and γ_I so as to fit the interaction data most closely, for example, by minimizing some loss such as the MSE, following the setting of the *Netflix Prize* above:

$$\underset{\gamma}{\arg\min} \frac{1}{|R|} \sum_{(u,i)\in R} (f(u,i) - R_{u,i})^2, \tag{5.7}$$

where $f(u,i)$ is our prediction function $f(u,i) = \gamma_u \cdot \gamma_i$.

As mentioned when discussing the SVD above, we seek a solution based on gradient descent. When minimizing the MSE, the solution is similar to the one we saw in Section 2.5. Note that as usual we should be careful to split interactions $(u,i) \in R$ into training, validation, and test sets, and to include a regularizer to avoid overfitting, as we describe below.

User and Item Biases

Before describing the gradient-descent-based solution to fitting models like those in Equation (5.7), we first suggest some steps to augment the model that will improve prediction accuracy.

Although a simple solution of the form $r(u,i) = \gamma_u \cdot \gamma_i$ seems to capture the types of interactions we want, it is difficult to regularize. Consider adding a simple ℓ_2 regularizer such as

$$\Omega(\gamma) = \sum_{u=1}^{|U|} \sum_{k=1}^{K} \gamma_{u,k}^2 + \sum_{i=1}^{|I|} \sum_{k=1}^{K} \gamma_{i,k}^2. \tag{5.8}$$

This regularizer (for large λ) will encourage the parameters to be close to zero; as such the predictions $\gamma_u \cdot \gamma_i$ will also be pushed toward zero, and the system will systematically underpredict ratings.

There are several ways this could be avoided. Trivially, we might simply subtract the mean ($\bar{R}$) from all ratings before training so that they are centered around zero. Alternately, recall as in Section 3.4.2 that we were careful to exclude the intercept term θ_0 from our regularizer. Although our current model lacks such an intercept term, we can straightforwardly add one:

$$r(u, i) = \alpha + \gamma_u \cdot \gamma_i. \tag{5.9}$$

Note that we would still regularize as in Equation (5.8).

Although the offset term α corrects the problem of systematically underpredicting ratings, it retains a similar issue at the level of individual users or items. Again, the regularizer pushes γ_u and γ_i toward zero, and therefore pushes predictions toward α. But individual users or items may tend to systematically give much higher (or lower) ratings than α, meaning that our regularizer again encourages us to systematically under (or over) predict.

Again we correct for this by adding additional bias terms, this time at the level of individual users or items:

$$r(u, i) = \alpha + \beta_u + \beta_i + \gamma_u \cdot \gamma_i. \tag{5.10}$$

β_u now encodes the extent to which user u's ratings trend higher or lower than α, and β_i encodes the extent to which item i tends to receive higher or lower ratings than α.[2]

Adding these bias terms introduces an additional $|U| + |I|$ parameters to the model. Whether these terms should be included in the regularizer Ω is arguable: on the one hand they are similar to offset terms, which we would normally not regularize (for the same reason we do not regularize α); on the other hand, failing to regularize them may lead to overfitting. In practice, the terms may simply be included in the regularizer:

$$\Omega(\beta, \gamma) = \sum_{u=1}^{|U|} \beta_u^2 + \sum_{k=1}^{K} \gamma_{u,k}^2 + \sum_{i=1}^{|I|} \beta_i^2 + \sum_{k=1}^{K} \gamma_{i,k}^2. \tag{5.11}$$

Alternately one could regularize β and γ with different strengths (since we generally expect β to have larger values):

$$\lambda_1 \Omega(\beta) + \lambda_2 \Omega(\gamma) = \lambda_1 \left(\sum_{u=1}^{|U|} \beta_u^2 + \sum_{i=1}^{|I|} \beta_i^2 \right) + \lambda_2 \left(\sum_{u=1}^{|U|} \sum_{k=1}^{K} \gamma_{u,k}^2 + \sum_{i=1}^{|I|} \sum_{k=1}^{K} \gamma_{i,k}^2 \right), \tag{5.12}$$

though doing so is difficult as it results in multiple regularization constants to tune.

---

[2] Note that we are careful not to refer to α as an 'average' rating, and indeed in general once we fit the model $\alpha \neq \bar{R}$, just as the offset θ_0 is not the average $\bar{y}$ in a linear regression model.

Gradient Update Equations

Under this new model of Equation (5.10), the objective we wish to minimize (on a training set of interactions $\mathcal{T}$) is

$$\text{obj}(\alpha; \beta; \gamma | \mathcal{T}) = \frac{1}{|\mathcal{T}|} \sum_{(u,i) \in \mathcal{T}} (r(u, i) - R_{u,i})^2 + \lambda \Omega(\beta, \gamma) \tag{5.13}$$

$$= \frac{1}{|\mathcal{T}|} \sum_{(u,i) \in \mathcal{T}} (\alpha + \beta_i + \beta_u + \gamma_i \cdot \gamma_u - R_{u,i})^2 + \lambda \Omega(\beta, \gamma). \tag{5.14}$$

Assuming the regularizer takes the form given in Equation (5.11), the partial derivatives (for α, β_u, and $\gamma_{u,k}$) are given by:

$$\frac{\partial \text{obj}}{\partial \alpha} = \frac{1}{|\mathcal{T}|} \sum_{(u,i) \in \mathcal{T}} 2(r(u, i) - R_{u,i}), \tag{5.15}$$

$$\frac{\partial \text{obj}}{\partial \beta_u} = \frac{1}{|\mathcal{T}|} \sum_{i \in I_u} 2(r(u, i) - R_{u,i}) + 2\beta_u, \tag{5.16}$$

$$\frac{\partial \text{obj}}{\partial \gamma_{u,k}} = \frac{1}{|\mathcal{T}|} \sum_{i \in I_u} 2\gamma_{i,k}(r(u, i) - R_{u,i}) + 2\gamma_{u,k}. \tag{5.17}$$

Note the change of summation in the last two terms: the derivative for user u is based only on items I_u that they consumed (in the training set). Derivatives for β_i and $\gamma_{u,k}$ can be computed similarly.

Other Considerations for Gradient Descent: When we first introduced gradient descent in Section 2.5, we noted some potential issues in terms of local minima, learning rates, and so on. It is worth revisiting some of those issues in light of the more complex model we are fitting here:

- The problem in Equation (5.14) is certainly non-convex and has many local minima.[3] Surprisingly though, this problem is not prone to 'spurious' local optima, and if carefully implemented, should converge to a global optimum (Ge et al., 2016).
- Nevertheless the problem is sensitive to initialization. For example, if multiple columns of γ_U and γ_I are initialized to the same value, they will have identical gradients and will remain in 'lock step' during successive iterations. This can normally be avoided simply by random initialization.
- Rather than computing the full gradient (as in eqs. (5.15) to (5.17)), alternate approaches such as stochastic gradient descent, or alternating least squares,

---

[3] The proof can roughly be sketched as follows. The objective is smooth, and given any global optimum γ_U, γ_I, any permutation applied to both (i.e., $\gamma_U \pi$ and $\gamma_I \pi$) will result in an *equivalent* local optimum.

may converge faster or require less memory.[4] See, for example, Bottou (2010); Yu et al. (2012).

5.1.2 What Happened to User or Item Features?

It is interesting to briefly consider that between our regression models in Chapter 2 and the model-based recommender systems we developed above, we have gone from models that *completely depend* on features to models that *completely avoid* them.

This can come as a surprise when first exploring recommender systems: obviously, features such a movie's budget or its genre ought to be predictive of users' preferences toward it. However, to the extent that a feature is predictive, it will already be captured by γ_u or γ_i. These parameters will capture whatever dimensions *maximally explain variance* in interactions, without any need to explicitly measure that feature.

As such, one might argue that if we observe enough interactions, γ_u and γ_i will capture whatever user and item characteristics are useful. We will revisit this argument in later chapters and explore various exceptions, for example, what can we do if we *do not* have sufficient interaction data (e.g., for new users or items, as in sec. 6.2), or what should we do if user preferences or item properties are not stationary over time (chap. 7).

5.2 Implicit Feedback and Ranking Models

So far, our discussion of (model-based) recommender systems has focused on predicting real-valued outcomes such as ratings, using objectives based on the MSE. That is, we have described model-based recommendation in terms of *regression* approaches.

Just as we developed separate approaches for neighborhood-based recommendation when considering click, purchase, or rating data (sec. 4.3), here we consider how our regression-based approaches should be adapted to handle binary outcomes (such as clicks and purchases).

Naively, we might imagine that we could adapt our regression-based approaches to handle binary outcomes in much the same way we that developed logistic regression in Chapter 3. That is, we could pass the model output (eq. (5.10)) through a sigmoid function, such that positive interactions are

---

[4] Alternating Least Squares notes that the optimization problem in Equation (5.14) has a closed form if either γ_U or γ_I is fixed; optimization proceeds by alternately fixing one term and optimizing the other.

associated with high probabilities, and negative interactions are associated with low probabilities.

However, when dealing with click or purchase data, we should consider that items which have not been clicked or purchased are not necessarily *negative* interactions—in fact, items that *have not* been clicked or purchased are exactly the ones we intend to recommend.

Several techniques have been proposed to handle recommendation in this context. Often this setting is referred to as *one-class* recommendation, as only the 'positive' class (clicks, purchases, listens, etc.) is observed. The setting is also referred to as *implicit feedback recommendation*, given that the signals (whether or not to buy something) only implicitly measure whether we like or dislike an item.

5.2.1 Instance Re-weighting Schemes

One category of methods for dealing with implicit feedback data attempts to reweight instances as having various 'confidences' of being positive or negative.

Hu et al. (2008) consider cases where positive instances are associated with 'confidence' measures $r_{u,i}$, which could measure, for example, the number of times a user listened to a song or watched a particular program. Negative instances still have $r_{u,i} = 0$, such that the model essentially assumes that negative instances are necessarily associated with low confidence, whereas confidence may vary substantially among positive instances.

Ultimately, the goal is still to predict a binary outcome $p_{u,i}$, and the model is trained to predict

$$p_{u,i} = \begin{cases} 1 & \text{if } r_{u,i} > 0 \\ 0 & \text{otherwise} \end{cases}. \tag{5.18}$$

The form of the predictor is similar to that of Equation (5.14), that is, latent user and item factors are used to predict $p_{u,i}$ using a (regularized) MSE. The main difference is that the MSE is weighted according to the confidence of each observation:[5]

$$\arg\min_{\gamma} \sum_{(u,i)\in\mathcal{T}} c_{u,i}(p_{u,i} - \gamma_u \cdot \gamma_i)^2 + \lambda\Omega(\gamma), \tag{5.19}$$

where $c_{u,i}$ is a weighting function associated with each observation, which ultimately is a monotone transform of $r_{u,i}$, for example

---

[5] For brevity we will sometimes omit the normalization $\frac{1}{|\mathcal{T}|}$ from our training objective. In practice this term is optional as it simply scales the objective by a constant.

$$c_{u,i} = 1 + \alpha r_{u,i}; \quad \text{or} \quad c_{u,i} = 1 + \alpha \log(1 + r_{u,i}/\epsilon), \tag{5.20}$$

where α and ϵ are tunable hyperparameters. Note that the transform $c_{u,i}$ ensures that negative instances have small but non-zero weight, whereas positive instances receive increasingly higher weight according to their associated confidence.

Pan et al. (2008) approach the problem in a similar way, also fitting a function of the form in Equation (5.19), though their weighting scheme is applied to *negative* instances. Several schemes are proposed, two of which are as follows:

$$c_{u,i} = \alpha \times |I_u|; \quad \text{or} \quad c_{u,i} = \alpha(m - |U_i|). \tag{5.21}$$

The first (which they call 'user oriented' weighting) suggests that a negative instance should be weighted higher if the corresponding *user* has interacted with many items; the second assumes that a negative instance should be weighted higher if the corresponding *item* has few associated interactions.

Although the schemes above are ultimately simple heuristics for reweighting the model we developed in Equation (5.14), experiments in Hu et al. (2008) and Pan et al. (2008) show that these schemes outperform models that try to predict $p_{u,i}$ (or $r_{u,i}$) directly.

5.2.2 Bayesian Personalized Ranking

While the above reweighting schemes demonstrate the importance of treating 'negative' and 'positive' feedback carefully in implicit-feedback settings, they ultimately optimize *regression* objectives, and therefore still seek to assign 'negative' scores to unseen instances.

A potential objection to such an approach is that the unseen instances are exactly the ones we *want* to recommend, and thus we should not encourage a model to assign them a negative score. A weaker assumption might state that while unseen instances should have *lower* scores than positive instances, they need not have negative scores. That is, items that we know a user likes are 'more positive' than unseen items, but unseen items could still have positive scores.

Rendle et al. (2012) built models based on the above principle by borrowing ideas from ranking. Recall from Section 3.3.3 that the above principle is similar to our goal when adapting classifiers for ranking: while positive (or relevant) items should appear near the top of a ranked list, we are not concerned with their actual (positive or negative) scores.

> The type of predictor we develop in Equation (5.25)—which compares two samples *i* and *j*, rather than assigning a score to a single sample—is known as a *pairwise* predictor.
>
> *Pointwise predictors* estimate a score or label associated with a particular sample *i*. All of the regression and classification models from Chapters 2 and 3 are examples of pointwise predictors, as are our latent factor models from Section 5.1.
>
> *Pairwise predictors* compare two samples *i* and *j*. Such predictors are often preferable when training ranking functions (since they act as proxies for objectives like the AUC, as in eq. (5.26)). They are often used in implicit feedback settings, where neither sample has a 'negative' label, but we can still assume that positive instances should rank higher. We will also use such predictors in cases where outcomes are associated with pairs of samples, such as when generating compatible outfits in Chapter 9.

Figure 5.3 Pointwise versus pairwise recommendation

Likewise, the principle behind their method, Bayesian Personalized Ranking (BPR), is that we should generate ranked lists of items such that positive items appear first. This is achieved by training a predictor $x_{u,i,j}$ that assigns a score based on which of the two items (*i* or *j*) is preferred (i.e., ranked higher) by *u*:

$$x_{u,i,j} > 0 \rightarrow u \text{ prefers } i \tag{5.22}$$

$$x_{u,i,j} \leq 0 \rightarrow u \text{ prefers } j. \tag{5.23}$$

Now, if we know that *i* is a positive and *j* is a negative (or unseen) item for user *u*, then a good model should tend to output positive values of $x_{u,i,j}$. This type of prediction strategy (which compares two samples, rather than assigning a score to a single sample) is known as a *pairwise* model (fig. 5.3).

$x_{u,i,j}$ could be any predictor, though the most straightforward option is to define it in terms of *difference* between predictions, for example:

$$x_{u,i,j} = \underbrace{x_{u,i}}_{u\text{'s preference toward } i} - \underbrace{x_{u,j}}_{u\text{'s preference toward } j}. \tag{5.24}$$

Compatibility $x_{u,i}$ could be defined via a latent factor model, similar to that of Equation (5.10):[6]

$$x_{u,i,j} = x_{u,i} - x_{u,j} = \gamma_u \cdot \gamma_i - \gamma_u \cdot \gamma_j. \tag{5.25}$$

Again, note that our goal is not that $\gamma_u \cdot \gamma_i$ should be positive for the positive item, nor that $\gamma_u \cdot \gamma_j$ should be negative for the unseen item, only that the *difference* is positive, that is, the positive item has a higher compatibility score.

---

[6] The implementation of BPR in Rendle et al. (2012) does not include bias terms β_i or β_j, though they can straightforwardly be included in Equation (5.25).

We can now define our objective in terms of whether the model correctly outputs positive values $x_{u,i,j}$ given a positive item i and an unseen item j. Ideally, we would like to count how often the model is able to correctly rank positive items higher than unseen items. For a specific user u, we have:

$$\text{AUC}(u) = \frac{1}{\underbrace{|I_u|}_{\text{positive items for user } u}\underbrace{|I \setminus I_u|}_{\text{unseen items for user } u}} \sum_{i \in I_u} \sum_{j \in I \setminus I_u} \delta(x_{u,i,j} > 0). \qquad (5.26)$$

The name 'AUC' stands for 'Area Under the ROC Curve' (as this measure is equivalent to computing the area under the ROC curve as we introduced in sec. 3.3.3). For an entire dataset, we average the above across all users:

$$\text{AUC} = \frac{1}{|U|}\text{AUC}(u). \qquad (5.27)$$

Note that this quantity takes a value between 0 and 1, where an AUC of 1 means that the model always ranks positive items higher than unseen items; an AUC of 0.5 means that the model is no better than random.

Optimizing the above presents two issues. First, it is not feasible to consider all (u, i, j) triples; to address this, one can randomly sample a fixed number of unseen items j per positive item i.[7]

Second, the objective in Equation (5.26) is a step function whose derivative is zero almost everywhere. This is much the same issue we encountered when developing logistic regression in Section 3.1; as such we can take the same approach by replacing the step function $\delta(x_{u,i,j})$ with a differentiable surrogate such as the sigmoid function (see fig. 3.1). Using the sigmoid function allows us to interpret $\sigma(x_{u,i,j})$ as a probability:

$$p(u \text{ prefers } i \text{ over } j) = \sigma(x_{u,i,j}). \qquad (5.28)$$

From this point, optimization proceeds in much the same way as we developed logistic regression: we use $\sigma(x_{u,i,j})$ to define a (log-)probability of a model given a training set, and subtract a regularizer:

$$\text{obj}^{(\text{BPR})} = \ell(\gamma; \mathcal{T}) - \lambda\Omega(\gamma) \qquad (5.29)$$

$$= \sum_{(u,i,j) \in \mathcal{T}} \log \sigma(\gamma_u \cdot \gamma_i - \gamma_u \cdot \gamma_j) - \lambda\Omega(\gamma). \qquad (5.30)$$

---

[7] Furthermore, the sampled items could change during each iteration of training.

Assuming an ℓ_2 regularizer $\Omega(\gamma) = \|\gamma\|_2^2$, we can compute the derivative, for example, with respect to $\gamma_{u,k}$:

$$\frac{\partial \text{obj}}{\partial \gamma_{u,k}} = \frac{\partial}{\partial \gamma_{u,k}} \sum_{(u,i,j)\in\mathcal{T}} \log \sigma(\gamma_u \cdot \gamma_i - \gamma_u \cdot \gamma_j) - \lambda\|\gamma\|_2^2 \tag{5.31}$$

$$= \frac{\partial}{\partial \gamma_{u,k}} \sum_{(u,i,j)\in\mathcal{T}} -\log(1 + e^{\gamma_u \cdot \gamma_j - \gamma_u \cdot \gamma_i}) - \lambda\|\gamma\|_2^2 \tag{5.32}$$

$$= \sum_{(i,j)\in I_u} (\gamma_{i,k} - \gamma_{j,k})(1 - \sigma(\gamma_u \cdot \gamma_i - \gamma_u \cdot \gamma_j)) - 2\lambda\gamma_{u,k} \tag{5.33}$$

(we abuse notation slightly so that $(i, j) \in I_u$ includes both positive and unseen items sampled from a user's history). Derivatives of other terms can be computed similarly. In practice, it is often preferable to use libraries that compute such derivatives automatically, as we explore in Section 5.8.3.

5.3 'User-free' Model-Based Approaches

At the beginning of this chapter, we drew a distinction between memory-based versus model-based recommenders. Roughly, *memory-based* approaches make recommendations using algorithms that operate on *histories* associated with users and items; *model-based* approaches generally distill these histories into low-dimensional user and item representations.

In practice, this distinction is not always so clear. Below we study two models that learn item representations but eschew user representations. At inference time, predictions are made in terms of parameters associated with items in a user's history, though users themselves are not associated with any parameters as such.

Such models may be preferable for a few reasons. First, avoiding user terms and directly making use of their interaction history can make models easier to deploy: the model does not have to be updated as new user interactions are observed. Second, this approach can be preferable when user interactions are *sparse*, meaning that we can fit complex item representations but cannot reliably fit parameters like γ_u. Third, when we explore sequential settings in Chapter 7, there may be important information in the user's history (such as the order in which items are consumed) which is not captured by user representations.

We briefly explore a few such methods below, which we summarize in Table 5.1.

Table 5.1 *Summary of user-free recommendation models. References: Kabbur et al. (2013); Ning and Karypis (2011).*

Ref.	Method	Description
NK11	Sparse Linear Methods (SLIM)	Each user is associated with a linear model weighting their interactions over past items; sparsity-inducing regularizers are used to deal with the large number of model parameters (sec. 5.3.1).
K13	Factored Item Similarity Models (FISM)	Replaces the user term in a latent factor model with a second term that represents the user by averaging over item representations from their history (sec. 5.3.2).

5.3.1 Sparse Linear Methods (SLIM)

A direct way to avoid including an explicit user term (i.e., γ_u) is to describe all of a user's interactions in terms of a binary feature vector enumerating which items they have interacted with (i.e., a vector of length $|I|$). To predict the score associated with an item i, we can then train a linear model (again with $|I|$ parameters), much as we did in Chapter 2:

$$f(u, i) = R_u \cdot W_i. \tag{5.34}$$

Here R_u is a (sparse) vector describing all of a user's interactions, that is, equivalent to a row of the interaction matrix R from Equation (4.8).

Fitting such a model naively is not straightforward, given the high-dimensional feature and parameter vectors involved. Ning and Karypis (2011) attempt to fit this type of model by exploiting the specific sparsity structure of the vector R_u, noting that Equation (5.34) can be rewritten in terms of just the items I_u that the user has interacted with:

$$f(u, i) = \sum_{j \in I_u} R_{u,j} W_{i,j}. \tag{5.35}$$

Here W is an $|I| \times |I|$ parameter matrix that essentially measures item-to-item compatibilities (or similarities).

Conceptually, Equation (5.35) is similar to the simple heuristic we developed in Section 4.3.5, in which we predicted a rating using a weighted average of previous ratings, where the weighting function was determined by an item-to-item similarity measure (such as the cosine similarity). Essentially, SLIM follows the same reasoning but replaces the heuristic item-to-item similarities from Section 4.3.5 with a learned matrix W.

The main challenge in fitting W is that it has dimension $|I| \times |I|$. Were W a dense matrix (i.e., every item interacts with every item) training and inference would be expensive; this is circumvented by using a regularization approach which ensures that W is sparse.[8] Sparsity is achieved via a regularization strategy which includes both an ℓ_2 and ℓ_1 regularizer:

$$\arg\min_{W} \|R - RW^T\|_2^2 + \lambda\Omega_2(W) + \lambda'\Omega_1(W)$$

$$\text{s.t.} \quad W_{i,j} \geq 0; \quad W_{i,i} = 0.$$

(5.36)

Note that $\|R - RW^T\|_2^2$ is merely a matrix shorthand for the predictions made for all interactions (u, i) following Equation (5.35). The first constraint in Equation (5.36) ensures that all terms in the weighting function are positive; the second constraint ($W_{i,i} = 0$) ensures that each item i's rating is predicted only based on interactions with *other* items j. Ω_1 is an ℓ_1 regularizer (i.e., $\Omega_1(W) = \sum_{i,j} |W_{i,j}|$); as we discussed in Section 3.4.2, ℓ_1 regularization leads to sparsity of the matrix W.

Ning and Karypis (2011) discuss various merits of this approach. Notably the rapid inference time (i.e., the rate at which recommendations can be made) compared to standard recommendation approaches, and also the *long-tail* performance of the approach. For the latter, compared to (e.g.) latent factor approaches—whose representations tend to favor whichever types of items predominate in the data, but fail to capture the dynamics of rarer items—SLIM maintains (relatively) good performance even for tail items.

5.3.2 Factored Item Similarity Models (FISM)

Factored Item Similarity Models (Kabbur et al., 2013) attempt to replace the user term γ_u in a latent factor model (eq. (5.10)) with a term that aggregates item representations from a user's history. Specifically, the user term in Equation (5.10) is replaced with an average over *item* terms for all items consumed by that user:

$$f(u, i) = \alpha + \beta_u + \beta_i + \frac{1}{|I_u \setminus \{i\}|} \sum_{j \in I_u \setminus \{i\}} \gamma'_j \cdot \gamma_i$$

(5.37)

(recall that I_u is the set of items consumed by user u, and we exclude the query item i during model training). Note that the item term γ_i is separate from the

---

[8] Though in practice experiments are conducted with moderate item vocabularies (e.g., $|I| \simeq 50000$), and various computational tricks are used to allow for parallelization and efficient inference.

term used to average user actions γ'_j, i.e., the model learns *two* sets of latent factors per item.[9]

Spiritually, the average $\frac{1}{|I_u|} \sum_j \gamma'_j$ fulfils the same role as γ_u, by summarizing the dimensions that are compatible with a particular user.

Kabbur et al. (2013) consider variants of Equation (5.37) for both rating prediction and ranking problems (i.e., to optimize the MSE as in sec. 5.1.1 or the AUC as in sec. 5.2.2).

Kabbur et al. (2013) argue that the above approach is particularly useful in *sparse* datasets (presumably, datasets where *users* have few associated interactions, while items have several). That is, a traditional latent factor model as in Equation (5.10) would struggle to meaningfully fit γ_u for a user who has only a few interactions; whereas if item histories are denser, a reasonable estimate of user preferences can be made by averaging over item terms. Indeed, experiments in Kabbur et al. (2013) show that the settings in which FISM are effective are closely related to dataset sparsity.

5.3.3 Other User-free Apporaches

Although we have only presented two examples of user-free models above, we will revisit user-free approaches throughout the book as we develop more complex models based on deep learning (sec. 5.5.3), sequences (sec. 7.7), and text (sec. 8.2.1). We briefly preview a few examples here just to give a sense of the overall approaches.

AutoRec: In Section 5.5.3 we discuss *AutoRec* (specifically *AutoRec-U*), an autoencoder-based recommendation model (Sedhain et al., 2015). Spiritually, this model is similar to FISM, in the sense that an explicit user term is replaced by a function that aggregates (representations of) all items from a user's history; the main difference being that the autoencoder framework allows for the inclusion of various nonlinear operations.

Item2vec (Barkan and Koenigstein, 2016) is an adaptation of *word2vec*, a natural language model that learns representations that describe semantic relations among words (sec. 8.2). Just as word2vec discovers which words appear in the same context in a sentence (essentially 'synonyms'), item2vec learns item representations γ_i that are capable of predicting which items occur in the same context in an interaction sequence.

---

[9] Strictly speaking, FISM is not 'user-free' in the sense that it includes a bias term β_u; however including this term requires only a single parameter per user, or could be excluded.

Sequential Models: Many of the neural network-based sequential models we discuss in Section 7.7 are also user-free. Like item2vec, such models also borrow ideas from natural language processing, generally treating items (or item representations) as a sequence of 'tokens' in order to predict which token comes next. As such there is no user representation, and the user is represented implicitly via some latent state of the model.

5.4 Evaluating Recommender Systems

So far, when developing models to predict ratings as in Section 5.1, we have done so by optimizing objectives based on a *sum of squared errors* (or equivalently, a MSE). Recall that in Section 2.2.2, we discussed the motivation behind the MSE, as well as some potential pitfalls when using it.

In the case of recommender systems, we must be aware of the same pitfalls, but also some different ones. Critically, since the system is likely used to provide ranked lists of items to the user, actual prediction of ratings may not be critical so long as desirable items appear near the top of the ranking. Consider, for example, some potential problems with the MSE in a recommendation context:

- Using the MSE, mispredicting a 5-star rating as 4-stars incurs a smaller penalty than mispredicting 3-stars as 1-star. Arguably, the latter should have a smaller penalty, as it concerns an item which should never have been recommended anyway.
- Similarly, mispredicting ratings of 3 and 3.5 as 4 and 4.5 (respectively) would incur a larger penalty than mispredicting them as 3.5 and 3. However the former preserves the *ordering* of the two items, whereas the latter does not.
- As we saw in Section 2.2.2, the MSE corresponds to an implicit assumption that errors are normally distributed; critically this assumes that outliers are extremely rare and should be penalized accordingly. In practice, outliers may be common, or alternately errors could be bimodal (or otherwise violate our model assumptions).
- Bellogin et al. (2011) noted the issue of 'popularity bias,' whereby strong performance on popular items can mask performance issues for less-popular ones.[10]

Ultimately, such problems raise the question of whether reductions in MSE actually correspond to increased utility of a recommender system.

---

[10] Though this is not an issue with the MSE specifically, but rather a general problem of evaluation in imbalanced datasets.

Interestingly, it is reported in Koren (2009) that a carefully implemented model with temporally evolving bias terms (which we discuss in sec. 7.2.2) out-performed *Netflix*'s previous solution (*Cinematch*) in terms of the RMSE. Critically, a system without any interaction terms (e.g., γ_u or γ_i) can do little more than recommend popular items over time; as such their experiment suggests that the system with a better MSE is not necessarily the better recommender.

Some of the above issues suggest the use of alternative regression metrics, such as the Mean Absolute Error, which (e.g.) is less sensitive to outliers, as we argued in Section 2.2.5. Others suggest that perhaps a recommender system should be evaluated less like a regression problem and more like a ranking problem. That is, so long as items matching a user's interests have the *highest* predicted scores, the precise accuracy of our predictions is unimportant.

Arguably, such problems with the MSE are driving research toward set-tings that rely on implicit feedback (clicks, purchases, etc.) rather than ratings; alternately, these settings may be preferable simply because such data is more available than explicit feedback (few users rate items, but *every* user clicks on them). More crudely, optimizing clicks or purchases may simply cor-respond more closely to business goals compared to identifying highly-rated items.

We already saw in Section 5.2.2 one technique to train recommender sys-tems to optimize a ranking loss based on implicit feedback, namely the AUC. Conceptually, the AUC reflects our ability to guess which of two items is 'rel-evant:' an AUC of 1 means that we always select the correct item, whereas an AUC of 0.5 means our guesses are no better than random.

However, the AUC is but one choice of ranking loss, and was primarily chosen for its convenience when formulating the optimization problem in Equation (5.30). As in Section 3.3.3, when considering cases where recom-mendations are surfaced to a user via an interface, we may be particularly interested in how the recommender system performs among the top K ranked items.

Below we present a few alternative evaluation functions to measure recom-mendation performance, most of which are focused on achieving high accuracy among the top-ranked items.

5.4.1 Precision and Recall @ K

When we evaluated classifiers in Section 3.3, we motivated the precision and recall@K as useful metrics in the context of evaluating user interfaces, where we have a fixed budget (K) of results that can be returned. Likewise, when recommending items, we might consider whether relevant items (e.g., those that a user eventually interacts with) are given a high ranking.

For convenience, when evaluating recommenders in this setting, it is useful to define a variable $\text{rank}_u(i)$ that specifies in what position an item i was ranked for a particular user u. That is, given a compatibility function $f(u, i)$, and a set of N items that can potentially be recommended (potentially excluding, for example, interactions that already appeared in the training set), then $\text{rank}_u(i) \in \{1 \ldots N\}$ is defined such that

$$\text{rank}_u(i) < \text{rank}_u(j) \Leftrightarrow f(u, i) > f(u, j) \tag{5.38}$$

$$\text{rank}_u(i) = \text{rank}_u(j) \Leftrightarrow i = j. \tag{5.39}$$

Now, given a test set of observed interactions I_u, we define the precision@K (for a particular user u) as

$$\text{precision@}K(u) = \frac{|\{i \in I_u \mid \text{rank}_u(i) \leq K\}|}{K}. \tag{5.40}$$

As in Equation (3.23), the numerator is the number of relevant items that were retrieved, while the denominator is the number of retrieved items. Now to compute the precision@K we simply average over all users:

$$\text{precision@}K = \frac{1}{|U|} \sum_{u \in U} \text{precision@}K(u). \tag{5.41}$$

Likewise the recall@K is defined similarly:

$$\text{recall@}K = \frac{1}{|U|} \sum_{u \in U} \frac{|\{i \in I_u \mid \text{rank}_u(i) \leq K\}|}{|I_u|}. \tag{5.42}$$

5.4.2 Mean Reciprocal Rank

The *Mean Reciprocal Rank* (MRR) is another metric to assess whether a recommender system (or any classifier) ranks positive items highly; unlike the precision and recall@K this expression does not depend on a particular size of the returned set of items, but rather rewards methods for ranking relevant items near the top of the list.

Traditionally, in search settings, the Mean Reciprocal Rank is defined in terms of the *first* relevant item among a ranked list of retrieved results, though in recommendation settings the metric is typically used by building a test set that consists of only a single relevant item per user, i_u. Then, the Mean Reciprocal Rank is defined in terms of the inverse (reciprocal) of the rank of the relevant item:

$$MRR = \frac{1}{|U|} \sum_{u \in U} \frac{1}{\text{rank}_u(i_u)}.$$ (5.43)

A score of 1 means the relevant item is always ranked in the first position; a value of $1/n$ would mean items are on average ranked in the nth position.

5.4.3 Cumulative Gain and NDCG

The *Cumulative Gain* (and its variants) aim to measure ranking performance in a setting that resembles a user browsing a page of search results: relevant results should be among the top K results, and ideally should be close to the top of the ranked list. The *Cumulative Gain* (here for a particular user u) simply counts the number of relevant items among the top K results:

$$\text{Cumulative Gain}@K = \sum_{i \in \{i | \text{rank}_u(i) \leq K\}} y_{u,i},$$ (5.44)

where $y_{u,i}$ is either a binary label (e.g., whether an item was purchased) or a relevance score (such as a rating). That is, the Cumulative Gain will be high if there are many relevant items (or highly rated items) among the top K results.

Ideally, relevant results should appear closer to the top of the list; the *Discounted* Cumulative Gain (DCG) accomplishes this by discounting the reward for items in lower ranks:

$$\text{DCG}@K = \sum_{i \in \{i | \text{rank}_u(i) \leq K\}} \frac{y_{u,i}}{\log_2(\text{rank}_u(i) + 1)}.$$ (5.45)

This expression is often normalized by comparison against an idealized ranking function to obtain the *Normalized* Discounted Cumulative Gain (NDCG):

$$\text{NDCG}@K = \frac{\text{DCG}@K}{\text{IDCG}@K}$$ (5.46)

where $\text{IDCG}@K$ is the 'ideal' discounted cumulative gain, that is, the discounted cumulative gain that would have been achieved via an optimal ranking function $\text{rank}_u^{\text{opt}}(i)$ (i.e., where labels $y_{u,i}$ are sorted in decreasing order of relevance). This normalization, and the specific choice of logarithmic scaling in Equation (5.45) are theoretically justified in Wang et al. (2013).

5.4.4 Evaluation Metrics Beyond Model Accuracy

Finally, it should be noted that there are several other qualities we might desire from a recommender system beyond its immediate utility to users (i.e., its ability to predict the next action). For example, we might be interested in exposing users to diverse viewpoints, ensuring that recommendations are not biased against certain groups, that users do not get pushed toward 'extreme' content, and so on. We will revisit these issues in Chapter 10, when we consider the broader consequences and ethics of personalized machine learning. Several are backed by user studies aimed at determining the qualitatively desirable features of recommender systems.

5.5 Deep Learning for Recommendation

Increasingly, state-of-the-art recommendation models are based on deep learning approaches. In principle, the appeal of deep learning-based recommenders is that they can capture complex, nonlinear relationships among users and items, beyond what is possible with the simple aggregation functions such as those in Equation (5.10). Later, deep learning-based approaches will allow us to uncover complex sequential patterns (chap. 7), or incorporate complex features from text (chap. 8) and images (chap. 9). For the moment, we explore a few of the main approaches to model interaction data in 'traditional' settings, though revisit deep learning-based models repeatedly in future chapters.

5.5.1 Why the Inner Product?

To motivate the potential of deep learning for recommendation, it is worth briefly revisiting our specific choice of the objective in Section 5.1, in which we computed compatibility between users and items via an inner product, that is,

$$\text{Compatibility}(u, i) = \gamma_u \cdot \gamma_i. \tag{5.47}$$

This seemed a reasonable enough choice and was motivated by a connection to matrix factorization and the Singular Value Decomposition. However, it should be carefully noted that this is only one choice of compatibility function and is by no means sacred. For instance, consider measuring compatibility between representations via a (squared) distance function:

$$\text{Compatibility}(u, i) = \|\gamma_u - \gamma_i\|_2^2. \tag{5.48}$$

Figure 5.4 shows recommendations that might be generated under these two compatibility conditions. Conceptually, these recommendations have quite different semantics: roughly, inner product-based compatibility (eq. (5.47)) implies that a user who likes action movies should be recommended movies with *a lot* of action, whereas a distance-based compatibility suggests that users who like action movies should be recommended other movies with a *similar amount* of action.

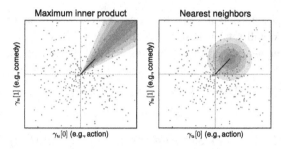

Figure 5.4 User vectors γ_u in latent space, and candidate items to be recommended. Highly compatible items appear in the highlighted region under inner product (left) and Euclidean (right) compatibility models.

Neither compatibility function is 'better,' and either could be preferable under certain conditions. Ideally, deep learning-based recommenders could give models the flexibility to determine the right compatibility functions for a particular scenario.

Zhang et al. (2019) discuss various potential benefits and limitations of deep learning-based recommender systems. Arguably, the main benefit of deep learning-based models is the ability to uncover complex, nonlinear relationships between user and item representations. For example, later we will study various settings (e.g., sec. 7.5.3) where the Euclidean distance may be preferable to the inner product when comparing representations. In principle, deep learning approaches could learn more flexible aggregation functions, reducing the need for manual engineering.

Zhang et al. (2019) suggest other appealing properties of deep learning-based recommenders, including the effectiveness of deep learning when dealing with structured data such as sequences, images, or text, and the ubiquity of high-level libraries that facilitate straightforward implementation. We revisit these topics throughout the book.

Conversely, there is some question as to whether deep learning-based recommender systems over-promise in terms of their perceived value, or whether 'traditional' recommender systems might still deliver better results if carefully tuned. We discuss these questions in Section 5.5.5.

5.5.2 Multilayer Perceptron-Based Recommendation

Multilayer perceptrons (MLPs) are a staple of artificial neural networks, offering a straightforward way to learn nonlinear transformations and interactions among features.

Roughly speaking, a 'layer' of a multilayer perceptron transforms a vector of input variables to a (possibly lower-dimensional) vector of output variables; typically the output variables are related to the input variables via a linear transformation followed by a nonlinear activation, for example:

$$f(x) = \sigma(Mx). \tag{5.49}$$

Here x is a vector of input variables, $f(x)$ is a vector of output variables, and M is a learned matrix, such that each term in Mx is a weighted combination of the original features in x. The sigmoid function (or some other nonlinear activation) is applied elementwise, in this case transforming the output variables to lie in the range $(0, 1)$.

While this is just one *layer* of a multilayer perceptron, several such layers can be 'stacked' in order for the network to learn complex nonlinear functions. Eventually, the final layer predicts some desired output, for example, a regression or classification objective. For example, the final layer might simply take a weighted combination of features from the previous layer:

$$f(x) = \sigma(\theta \cdot x), \tag{5.50}$$

that is, similar to the output of a logistic regressor (for a classification task).

We depict a multilayer perceptron in Figure 5.5. Note that a trivial linear model of the form $y = X\theta$ would be depicted by a similar figure in which the inputs were connected directly to the output.

Ultimately, multilayer perceptrons handle similar modalities of data and problems to those we saw in Chapters 2 and 3, that is, feature vectors as inputs and regression or classification targets as outputs; the main difference compared to our earlier models is simply their ability to learn complex nonlinear transformations and relations among features.

Neural Collaborative Filtering

He et al. (2017b) attempted to apply the benefits of multilayer perceptrons to latent factor recommender systems. The essential idea is fairly straightforward: rather than combining user and item latent factors via an inner product (as in eq. (5.10)), γ_u and γ_i are combined via a multilayer perceptron to predict the model output (note that both the latent factors and the MLP parameters are learned simultaneously). As we discussed in Section 5.5.1, the inner product function is only one possible choice when combining user and item preferences and other choices (such as a Euclidean distance) may be more appropriate in other settings; conceptually, the promise of a solution based on a multilayer perceptron is that one can be agnostic to these choices with the expectation that the model will learn the correct aggregation function automatically. While

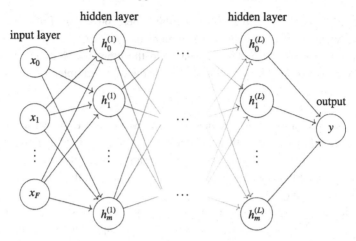

Figure 5.5 Representation of a multilayer perceptron with L layers. Here for simplicity each layer has the same number (m) of units, and we have only a single output y (so that the inputs and outputs are similar to the regression and classification problems we studied in chaps. 2 and 3).

He et al. (2017b) showed this method to be effective in some settings, there has recently been some question as to the value of this type of technique: while MLPs can in principle learn quite general functions, in practice specific functions (like the inner product) are not easily recoverable by such models, meaning that simpler models may still outperform these more complex approaches. We discuss this issue further in Section 5.5.5.

5.5.3 Autoencoder-Based Recommendation

Roughly speaking, the role of an *autoencoder* is to learn a low-dimensional representation of some input data that preserves the ability to reconstruct the original (high-dimensional) data from the low-dimensional representation. The basic principle of an autoencoder is depicted in Figure 5.6. Here an input vector x is projected into a lower-dimensional space via a function $g(x)$ (following an approach similar to that of a multilayer perceptron above), which may include several layers. The low-dimensional representation is then mapped back into the original space via $f(g(x))$; the goal is that $f(g(x))$ should match the original data x as closely as possible. In this way $g(x)$ acts as a 'bottleneck,' forcing the model to learn a compressed representation that succinctly captures the meaningful information in x. Several variants of autoencoders exist, for instance

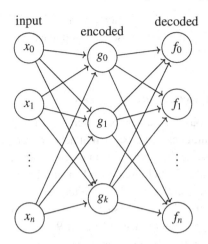

Figure 5.6 Autoencoder. g_i and f_i are shorthand for $g(x)_i$ and $f(g(x))_i$ respectively. Either of the encoding or decoding operations could include multiple layers.

denoising autoencoders partially corrupt the input in order to learn representations that are robust to noise; *sparse autoencoders* attempt to learn compressed representations that are sparse, and so on.

Zhang et al. (2019, 2020) survey various ways that autoencoders can be used in the specific context of recommendation, including methods that use autoencoders as a component in complex recommendation frameworks, autoencoders that model sequential dynamics (as in chap. 7, see, e.g., Sachdeva et al. (2019)), and so on. Below we explore a single approach that is representative of the general setup.

AutoRec

Sedhain et al. (2015) adapt the principle of autoencoders to recommendation problems. In their setting the data to be encoded is a vector of ratings for an item i, or equivalently a column of an interaction matrix $R_{.,i}$. Since $R_{.,i}$ is only partially observed (rather than a dense vector as in a traditional autoencoder), the compressed representation is only responsible for (and gradient updates are only applied to) the observed entries $R_{u,i}$. At inference time, the compressed representation can then be used to estimate the entries for unobserved pairs. Sedhain et al. (2015) term this version of the model *AutoRec-I*, since an autoencoder is used to learn compressed item representations; alternately, AutoRec-U consists of the same approach applied to user vectors $R_{u,.}$.

Note that AutoRec-U lacks any user parameters (and likewise AutoRec-I lacks item parameters). As such it is a form of *user-free* personalization (like those from sec. 5.3) that personalizes predictions using a model that aggregates data from the entire user history rather than 'memorizing' user preferences via an explicit parameter.[11] We further explore such notions of user-free personalization when exploring methods based on sequences in Section 7.7.

5.5.4 Convolutional and Recurrent Networks

Finally, Zhang et al. (2019) survey various recommender systems based on recurrent networks and convolutional neural networks. Recurrent networks are typically chosen as a way of exploring *sequential* dynamics in user activities; we explore this type of approach in Chapter 7, including deep learning-based approaches in Section 7.7. Convolutional neural networks are often used as a means of incorporating representations of rich content (such as images) into recommender systems; we explore this type of approach in Chapter 9.

Zhang et al. (2019) also discuss potential limitations of deep learning-based approaches, including the challenges involved in interpreting the predictions of deep learning systems, and the difficulty of tuning hyperparameters in systems with many complex, interacting parts. They also highlight the potential lack of interpretability of deep learning-based models (though this is to some extent a challenge with any model based on latent representations), as well as the 'data hungriness' of deep learning approaches. The latter issue arises whenever fitting models with a large number of parameters, and indeed is also a problem when fitting traditional latent factor models as in Section 5.1.1. On the one hand, this may narrow the conditions under which deep learning-based approaches are effective, for example, they may underperform in cold-start situations (sec. 6.2) where few interactions are available per user or per item. On the other hand, deep learning approaches may extend the modalities of data that can be incorporated into recommendation approaches (including in cold-start settings), for instance, by leveraging text or image data; we explore such approaches in Chapters 8 and 9.

We summarize the methods from this section in Chapter 6 (table 6.1), after presenting additional deep learning-based recommenders that make use of content and structure.

5.5.5 How Effective are Deep Learning-Based Recommenders?

In spite of the proliferation of deep learning-based approaches to recommendation, their benefit over simpler, more traditional forms of recommendation

---

[11] Note that AutoRec-U (and not AutoRec-I) is what we term the 'user-free' version: its input is a set of items a user has interacted with; as such a user is described in terms of an aggregation of item representations in a user's history, which is spiritually similar to FISM (sec. 5.3.2).

is perhaps questionable. Dacrema et al. (2019) conducted a thorough evaluation of several of the predominant deep learning-based recommender systems (including several of the approaches discussed earlier), and found that deep learning approaches were often outperformed by simpler methods, so long as those methods were carefully tuned. Most of the models for recommendation we have seen so far involve many tunable factors (e.g., number of factors, regularization schemes, and details of the specific training approaches), as well as choices in terms of dataset selection, pre-processing, and so on, that can favor certain models over others. Although the evaluation in Dacrema et al. (2019) was limited to a few specific (but popular) approaches, it raised broader issues of evaluation and benchmarking in recommender systems. Some general points raised include the difficulty in reproducing reported results (while releasing research code is common practice, releasing exact hyperparameter settings or tuning strategies is not), and the proliferation of datasets, metrics, and evaluation protocols that make fair comparison difficult.

Rendle et al. (2020) explored the same issue, focusing on the comparison of inner product-based recommendation versus solutions based on multilayer perceptrons. They reiterate the main point from Dacrema et al. (2019) that simpler methods remain competitive so long as they're carefully tuned. They also argue that in spite of the hope that multilayer perceptrons can learn complex, nonlinear relationships, that in practice even simple functions (like the inner product) are difficult for such models to reproduce.

Finally, both Dacrema et al. (2019) and Rendle et al. (2020) discuss issues of computational complexity, and whether the marginal benefits of deep learning-based approaches justify the substantial added complexity. Rendle et al. (2020) argue that simpler models may be preferable in production environments, especially when considering the efficiency of item retrieval (as we discuss below).

Note that these criticisms are not an indictment of deep learning-based approaches in general, but only with respect to their ability to model specific types of interaction data (essentially the same settings discussed in this chapter). In later chapters we will explore the use of deep learning-based approaches in a variety of other settings, in order to model sequence, text, and image data, with goals ranging from cold-start performance to interpretability.

5.6 Retrieval

Briefly, it is worth discussing one of the fundamental considerations when deploying a recommender system, namely, how to efficiently retrieve items.

Naively, having defined a compatibility function $f(u, i)$ between a user and an item (as in eq. (5.1)), our goal might be to rank (unseen) items according to their compatibility, that is,

$$rec(u) = \arg\max_{i \in I \setminus I_u} f(u, i). \tag{5.51}$$

Presumably, recommendations must be made rapidly, for use in interactive settings. Given a large vocabulary of items, this procedure is likely to be prohibitively expensive if we were to attempt to enumerate scores for all items $i \in I$; as such it is worth thinking about what types of relevance functions $f(u, i)$ admit efficient solutions to Equation (5.51).[12]

Euclidean Distance: Perhaps the most straightforward function for efficient retrieval is a Euclidean distance function, that is,

$$f(u, i) = \|\gamma_u - \gamma_i\|. \tag{5.52}$$

In this case, retrieval can be done efficiently (i.e., $O(\log(|I|))$ on average) using traditional data structures such as a KD-tree. A KD-tree (Bentley, 1975) is a data structure that represents K-dimensional points (in this case γ_i for each item) in such a way as to allow efficient retrieval given a query (γ_u); such data structures predate recommender systems and have classical applications (e.g.) in nearest-neighbor retrieval for classification.

Inner Product and Cosine Similarity: Bachrach et al. (2014) showed that the same types of data structure can be adapted for other types of relevance function. Fundamentally, they showed that both inner product and cosine similarity-based relevance functions can be related to nearest neighbor search (as above) via appropriate transformations:

$$\arg\max_i \|\gamma_u - \gamma_i\| \quad \text{nearest neighbor (NN)} \tag{5.53}$$

$$\arg\max_i \gamma_u \cdot \gamma_i \quad \text{maximum inner product (MIP)} \tag{5.54}$$

$$\arg\max_i \frac{\gamma_u \cdot \gamma_i}{\|\gamma_u\|\|\gamma_i\|} \quad \text{maximum cosine similarity (MCS).} \tag{5.55}$$

Doing so allows the same data structures that facilitate nearest-neighbor search to be used for recommenders based on inner products (as in sec. 5.1) or cosine similarity (as in sec. 4.3.3).

---

[12] The setting of Equation (5.51) is admittedly oversimplified; computing such a ranking is likely one piece in a more complex pipeline.

Approximate Search and Jaccard Similarity: In practice, efficient retrieval may be accomplished via approximation schemes, such as techniques based on locality-sensitive hashing (whereby 'similar' items are hashed to the same bucket). Versions of locality-sensitive hashing can be used to retrieve similar items based on similarity functions, including Euclidean distance (Indyk and Motwani, 1998), Jaccard (Broder, 1997), and Cosine similarity (Charikar, 2002). Bachrach et al. (2014) compare exact techniques for retrieval (as described earlier) to these types of hashing-based approximations, as well as other exact techniques for recommendation (Koenigstein et al., 2012). Search techniques like those here are implemented in libraries such as *FAISS*.[13]

5.7 Online Updates

Our presentation of recommender systems has so far assumed we have access to historical interaction data from which we can train a model to make predictions. That is, we have assumed we can train the model *offline*. In practice, when deploying such a system, we may continually collect new interactions (as well as new items and new users). Given the complexity of model training, it is naturally impractical to retrain the model 'from scratch' for every new interaction, item, or user. Although our focus in this book is not on model deployment, below we outline some of the general strategies for dealing with new interactions in an *online* setting.

Regressing on γ_u or γ_i: Most straightforwardly, we can update *some* parameters of a model without retraining the entire model. In particular, note that the model of Equation (5.5) (and its variants) is what is termed *bilinear* in γ_u and γ_i: if either of γ_u or γ_i is fixed (i.e., treated as a constant), fitting the remaining part of the model becomes equivalent to linear regression (and can be solved as in eq. (2.10) or eq. (3.33)). Doing so allows us to take a fitted model and include new user or item terms based on a few observations (or likewise, to update γ_u or γ_i for existing users and items without updating the entire model). This specific approach only applies to a limited class of models for which individual parameters can be updated in closed form, though alternately one can use gradient-based approaches to update only a selection of model parameters.

Cold-start and user-free Models: Other models are specifically designed to deal with new users and items. In Section 6.2 we explore models designed

---

[13] https://github.com/facebookresearch/faiss

for cold-start scenarios (i.e., users and items with few or no associated interactions). Such models generally make use of features or side-information to
compensate for a lack of historical observations. A second class of models
avoids modeling users altogether and directly makes use of an interaction history at inference time (meaning such models can naturally adapt to
user cold-start settings), including approaches like those we explored in
Section 5.3.

Strategies for Online Training: Finally, we mention schemes that are
designed specifically to handle model updates in online settings. Such
approaches generally follow the outline we described earlier, that is, efficiently updating a subset of model parameters in the presence of an otherwise
fully trained model. See, for example, Rendle and Schmidt-Thieme (2008),
which outlines efficient gradient descent-based update schemes under this
setting.

5.8 Recommender Systems in Python with *Surprise* and *Implicit*

Although the types of recommender systems we have seen so far can (with
some effort) be implemented 'from scratch' either by computing the gradient
expressions as in Equations (5.15) to (5.17) or by using high-level optimization
libraries like *Tensorflow* (we will explore a *Tensorflow* implementation in sec.
5.8.3), the recommendation techniques we have covered so far are reasonably
well-supported by popular Python libraries.

Here we examine two specific libraries, *Surprise* and *Implicit* for latent factor recommendation (as in sec. 5.1) and Bayesian Personalized Ranking (as
in sec. 5.2.2). However, these examples serve more to introduce the overall
recommendation pipeline, rather than to dive deeply into the specifics of these
libraries.

5.8.1 Latent Factor Models (*Surprise*)

Surprise (Hug, 2020) is a library that implements various recommendation
algorithms based on *explicit feedback* (e.g., ratings). Below we show how to
use *Surprise*'s implementation of a latent factor model as in Equation (5.10)
('SVD' as in Koren et al. (2009)).

First, we import the model ('SVD'), and utilities to read and split the dataset:

```
1  from surprise import SVD, Reader, Dataset
2  from surprise.model_selection import train_test_split
```

While the library has various routines to read data, the most straightforward is to read from a *csv/tsv* file. Here we have processed the *Goodreads* 'fantasy' data to extract just the 'user_id,' 'book_id,' and 'rating' fields, though this example could be applied to any similar dataset. After reading in the data, we split it into train and test fractions, with 25% of the data withheld for testing:

```
3   reader = Reader(line_format='user␣item␣rating', sep='\t')
4   data = Dataset.load_from_file('goodreads_fantasy.tsv',
        reader=reader)
5   dataTrain, dataTest = train_test_split(data, test_size=.25)
```

Next we fit the model, and collect its predictions on the test set:

```
6   model = SVD()
7   model.fit(dataTrain)
8   predictions = model.test(dataTest)
```

From 'predictions' we can then extract and compare the model's prediction (p.est) and the original value (p.r_ui), in this case to compute the MSE.

```
9    sse = 0
10   for p in predictions:
11       sse += (p.r_ui - p.est)**2
12
13   MSE = sse / len(predictions)
```

5.8.2 Bayesian Personalized Ranking (*Implicit*)

Implicit[14] is a library for recommender systems that operate on implicit feedback datasets. Here we show how to use the library for Bayesian Personalized Ranking, as in Section 5.2.2.

First, we read in the data. This time, the required data format is a *sparse* matrix describing all user/item interactions. Despite this matrix having hundreds of thousands of rows and columns, only observed interactions are stored:

```
1   from implicit import bpr
2
3   Xiu = scipy.sparse.lil_matrix((nItems, nUsers)) # Initialized
        after extracting the number of users and items
4   for d in data:
5       Xiu[itemIDs[d['book_id']],userIDs[d['user_id']]] = 1 #
            Only storing positive feedback instances
6
7   Xui = scipy.sparse.csr_matrix(Xiu.T)
```

---

[14] https://github.com/benfred/implicit.

Next, we initialize and fit the BPR model:

```
8   model = bpr.BayesianPersonalizedRanking(factors = 5)
9   model.fit(Xiu)
```

Having fit the model, we can retrieve the user and item factors γ_u and γ_i, as well as recommendations (high $\gamma_u \cdot \gamma_i$) and similar items (high similarity to γ_i):

```
10   itemFactors = model.item_factors
11   userFactors = model.user_factors
12
13   recommended = model.recommend(0, Xui) # Recommendations for
         the first user
14   related = model.similar_items(0) # Highly similar to the
         first item (cosine similarity)
```

5.8.3 Implementing a Latent Factor Model in *Tensorflow*

Following our introduction to *Tensorflow* in Section 3.4.4, it is now fairly straightforward to implement more complex models such as those developed in this chapter. Here we fit a latent factor model following Section 5.1.1.

We start by initializing our model, which takes as parameters the model dimensionality K and the regularization strength λ. Here we define our variables to be fit ($\alpha, \beta_u, \beta_i, \gamma_u, \gamma_i$). In practice, appropriate initialization of such variables is important; here alpha is initialized to the mean rating μ while all other parameters are initialized following a normal distribution:

```
1   class LatentFactorModel(tf.keras.Model):
2       def __init__(self, mu, K, lamb):
3           super(LatentFactorModel, self).__init__()
4           self.alpha = tf.Variable(mu)
5           self.betaU = tf.Variable(tf.random.normal([len(
                userIDs)],stddev=0.001))
6           self.betaI = tf.Variable(tf.random.normal([len(
                itemIDs)],stddev=0.001))
7           self.gammaU = tf.Variable(tf.random.normal([len(
                userIDs),K],stddev=0.001))
8           self.gammaI = tf.Variable(tf.random.normal([len(
                itemIDs),K],stddev=0.001))
9           self.lamb = lamb
```

Next we define our function (a method in the same class) that makes a prediction for a given user/item pair, that is, $f(u,i) = \alpha + \beta_u + \beta_i + \gamma_u \cdot \gamma_i$ as in Equation (5.10):

```
10      def predict(self, u, i):
11          p = self.alpha + self.betaU[u] + self.betaI[i] +\
12              tf.tensordot(self.gammaU[u], self.gammaI[i], 1)
13          return p
```

Similarly we define our regularizer as in Equation (5.8) (which could easily be adapted to include different coefficients for different terms, for example):

```
14    def reg(self):
15        return self.lamb * (tf.reduce_sum(self.betaU**2) +\
16                             tf.reduce_sum(self.betaI**2) +\
17                             tf.reduce_sum(self.gammaU**2) +\
18                             tf.reduce_sum(self.gammaI**2))
```

Finally we define the function to compute the squared error for a single sample, which will be called when computing gradients:

```
19    def call(self, u, i, r):
20        return (self.predict(u,i) - r)**2
```

5.8.4 Bayesian Personalized Ranking in *Tensorflow*

Bayesian Personalized Ranking (as in sec. 5.2.2) can be implemented similarly. Again we initialize our model variables (this time only β_i, γ_u, and γ_i) are included:

```
1  class BPR(tf.keras.Model):
2      def __init__(self, K, lamb):
3          super(BPR, self).__init__()
4          self.betaI = tf.Variable(tf.random.normal([len(
               itemIDs)],stddev=0.001))
5          self.gammaU = tf.Variable(tf.random.normal([len(
               userIDs),K],stddev=0.001))
6          self.gammaI = tf.Variable(tf.random.normal([len(
               itemIDs),K],stddev=0.001))
7          self.lamb = lamb
```

Our prediction function estimates the unnormalized score $x_{u,i} = \beta_i + \gamma_u \cdot \gamma_i$:

```
8     def predict(self, u, i):
9         p = self.betaI[i] + tf.tensordot(self.gammaU[u],
               self.gammaI[i], 1)
10        return p
```

Finally we define our loss for a single sample, this time including a user u, and items i and j that they did and did not interact with:

```
11    def call(self, u, i, j):
12        return -tf.math.log(tf.math.sigmoid(self.predict(u,i
               ) - self.predict(u,j)))
```

5.8.5 Efficient Batch-Based Optimization

Although the abovementioned implementations are straightforward, they are not particularly efficient if we attempt to compute the complete MSE (eq. (5.14)) or likelihood (eq. (5.30)) across the entire dataset. Instead, we compute gradients and update parameters in *batches* consisting of a random sample of our data.

First, we generate our sample; for a BPR-like model, this consists of three lists, corresponding to user, positive item, negative item triples (u, i, j):

```
1  sampleU, sampleI, sampleJ = [], [], []
2  for _ in range(Nsamples):
3      u,i,_ = random.choice(interactions) # positive sample
4      j = random.choice(items) # negative sample
5      while j in itemsPerUser[u]:
6          j = random.choice(items)
7      sampleU.append(userIDs[u])
8      sampleI.append(itemIDs[i])
9      sampleJ.append(itemIDs[j])
```

Next, we must redefine our score function to operate over a sample rather than a single data point. Note that rather than merely iterating over all points, estimates for all samples in our batch are computed using efficient vector operations:

```
10      def score(self, sampleU, sampleI):
11          u = tf.convert_to_tensor(sampleU, dtype=tf.int32)
12          i = tf.convert_to_tensor(sampleI, dtype=tf.int32)
13          beta_i = tf.nn.embedding_lookup(self.betaI, i)
14          gamma_u = tf.nn.embedding_lookup(self.gammaU, u)
15          gamma_i = tf.nn.embedding_lookup(self.gammaI, i)
16          x_ui = beta_i + tf.reduce_sum(tf.multiply(gamma_u,
                   gamma_i), 1)
17          return x_ui
```

The 'call' function is similarly modified:

```
18      def call(self, sampleU, sampleI, sampleJ):
19          x_ui = self.score(sampleU, sampleI)
20          x_uj = self.score(sampleU, sampleJ)
21          return -tf.reduce_mean(tf.math.log(tf.math.sigmoid(
                   x_ui - x_uj)))
```

For the complete implementation (including various 'boilerplate' components), see the online supplement (sec. 1.4).

5.9 Beyond a 'Black-Box' View of Recommendation

Finally, we should mention that our view of recommendation through the lens of machine learning represents only part of the study of recommender systems. For the most part, we have taken a 'black box' view in which we regard the 'recommender system' as merely a model that predicts user/item interactions (clicks, purchases, ratings, etc.) as accurately as possible.

Although high-fidelity prediction is clearly necessary to build a successful recommender, it is only part of the picture. For example, we have not considered broader questions of what makes a recommender system 'usable' or would ultimately drive user satisfaction or engagement. For example, if a user watches *Harry Potter* should they be recommended its sequel, or another movie from the same genre? The former might maximize some naive metric like click probability, whereas the latter is more likely to generate a suggestion that the user is not already aware of. But either could be a legitimate goal of building a recommender system: helping a user quickly navigate a user interface by predicting their next interaction is just as important as recommending for novelty or discovery.

Such questions go beyond the black-box supervised learning view of recommendation: they are less questions about how to accurately predict the next action, and more about what we should do with that prediction. At the very least such questions require more nuanced evaluation metrics, if not user studies. While this book largely avoids discussion of user interface design, in Chapter 10 we will revisit the consequences of how recommender systems are applied, and look at strategies to improve personalized recommendation beyond simply optimizing prediction accuracy.

5.10 History and Emerging Directions

So far we have attempted to construct something of a narrative behind the development of recommender systems: we started with simple 'memory-based' solutions (chap. 4), followed by 'model-based' approaches such as latent factor models (chap. 5); later, we argued about the benefits of leveraging implicit feedback (clicks, purchases, etc.) rather than relying on ratings (sec. 5.2.2); finally, we began to discuss emerging trends in neural network-based recommendation (sec. 5.5). While this narrative reflects current thinking on the topic, the actual history of recommender systems is substantially more complicated; for example, one survey paper (Burke, 2002) points out that even neural-network-based recommender systems have been proposed since the early nineties (Jennings and Higuchi, 1993).

To a large extent, research on recommender systems has been driven by the release and adoption of large-scale benchmark datasets. High-profile competitions such as the *Netflix Prize* (Bennett et al., 2007) have driven widespread interest in recommendation problems: the specific nature of the data (purely based on interactions with no side-information); the choice of metrics used (the MSE); and the specific dynamics of the data itself (e.g., the critical role of temporal dynamics), all show their influence in the models we have explored throughout this chapter. Likewise other datasets and competitions, including industrial datasets (e.g., *Yelp, Criteo*) and academic projects (e.g., *MovieLens* (Harper and Konstan, 2015)), have inspired models based on alternate settings and evaluation metrics.

A constant theme in such research is the extent to which new models must be designed to adapt to the specific dynamics of new datasets. As we will explore in upcoming chapters, research on recommender systems has sought to incorporate rich signals in the form of text, temporal and social signals, or images. Such factors serve not only to improve the predictive accuracy of recommendation models but can also help to make recommendation models more interpretable, and to deal with modalities of data not supported by traditional recommendation approaches. We revisit such *content aware* approaches throughout the remainder of this book as we begin to develop techniques that make use of social (chap. 6), temporal (chap. 7), textual (chap. 8), and visual (chap. 9) signals.

Methodologically, recent research on recommender systems has been dominated by deep learning-based approaches, as we discussed a little in Section 5.5. Besides models based on multilayer perceptrons, convolutional neural networks, or autoencoders, a major trend has been to incorporate ideas from natural language processing. Roughly speaking, models of natural language are concerned with modeling the semantics of sequences of discrete tokens (i.e., words or characters), and thus translate naturally to recommendation problems involving sequences of interactions over a discrete set of items. Recommender systems based on natural language models (e.g., *Self-Attention, Transformer, BERT*, etc.) arguably represent the current state-of-the-art (Kang and McAuley, 2018; Sun et al., 2019). We will explore this relationship in Chapters 7 and 8 when developing general-purpose models of sequences and text.

The study of complex recommender systems that make use of data from images, text, and other forms of structured side-information will dominate our discussion for the next several chapters. Partly these complex forms of side-information allow us to build increasingly more accurate recommender systems that leverage complex signals (chap. 6). They also facilitate novel types of recommendation, such as generating sets of compatible items (chap. 9) or recommender systems with natural-language interfaces (chap. 8). We will also argue that *personalization* in such domains goes well beyond recommendation, playing a role in several settings where differences among individuals explains significant variance in data.

Several survey papers present more detailed histories of recommender systems. Konstan et al. (1998) discuss early research from the *GroupLens* project, several of whose papers and datasets we discuss throughout this book. Their survey gives an interesting early perspective on recommender systems, with their focus mainly centering around memory-based methods (as in sec. 4.3), but also discussing broader topics such as user interfaces and benchmarking beyond accuracy. Burke (2002) discuss *hybrid* recommender systems—systems that combine multiple types of recommendation, feature representation, or knowledge extraction approaches. Their survey focuses on the setting of restaurant recommendation, though it broadly serves as an excellent introduction to a breadth of recommendation techniques, their trade-offs, and how they can be effectively combined. More recent surveys include Bobadilla et al. (2013), which provides a high-level survey of many of the same techniques we have presented so far, as well as those we will explore in later chapters such as socially aware and content-based approaches; other surveys focus on specific collections of techniques such as deep-learning-based recommendation (Zhang et al., 2019).

Exercises

5.1 *All of the exercises in this section can be completed on any dataset involving users, items, and ratings.* Before implementing the latent factor recommender system described in Equation (5.10), it is instructive to implement simpler variants in order to understand the model-fitting procedure. Implement a *bias-only* model, that is, one that makes predictions according to $r(u, i) = \alpha + \beta_u + \beta_i$. This can be achieved either by computing derivatives for this simplified model (as we did in sec. 5.1.1), or more simply by discarding the latent factor terms from the *Tensorflow* code from Section 5.8.3. Implement this model and compare its performance (in terms of the MSE) to one which always predicts the average rating. Find the items with the largest values of β_i, and compare them to the items with the highest average ratings.[15]

5.2 Implement a complete latent factor model, either by computing derivatives for all terms ($\frac{\partial \text{obj}}{\partial \gamma_{i,k}}$, $\frac{\partial \text{obj}}{\partial \gamma_{u,k}}$, etc.) in the objective from Equation (5.14), or by following the *Tensorflow* implementation. For your model to

---

[15] Consider why these two lists might not be the same: for example, a mediocre item which tends to be rated by 'generous' users (high β_u) could have a high average rating but a low value of β_i.

outperform the bias-only model from Exercise 5.1, you'll need to carefully experiment with the number of latent dimensions K, initialization strategies, and regularization.[16]

5.3 In Exercise 5.2 we predicted star ratings using a model that optimized the MSE. However the ratings we are predicting in many datasets are *integer* valued, for example, $r_{u,i} \in \{1, 2, 3, 4, 5\}$. In light of this, it might be tempting to round the predictions of our model to the nearest integer. Surprisingly, this type of rounding is generally not effective, and results in a *higher* MSE compared to non-rounded values. Explain why this might be the case (e.g., by constructing a simple counterexample), and consider whether other rounding strategies might be more effective (e.g., rounding ratings above 5 or below 1).

5.4 Implement Bayesian Personalized Ranking (starting from the code in sec. 5.8.4 or otherwise), and compare this method to simpler approaches based on item-to-item or user-to-user compatibility such as those we studied in Chapter 4 (e.g., recommend items with high Jaccard similarity compared to those the user has recently consumed). In doing so, consider several of the evaluation metrics from Section 5.4, such as the AUC, Mean Reciprocal Rank, and so on.

Project 4: A Recommender System for Books (Part 2)

Here we will extend our work from Project 3 to incorporate and compare model-based recommendation techniques.

(i) Start by comparing model-based approaches to the similarity-based recommenders you developed in Project 3. Start by comparing rating prediction approaches (e.g., models like those of eq. (4.20) to (4.22)) to latent-factor modeling approaches (as in sec. 5.1). It can be useful to develop your model in several stages: for example, starting with (a) a model including only an offset $f(u, i) = \alpha$; (b) using only an offset and biases $f(u, i) = \alpha + \beta_u + \beta_i$; (c) using latent factors $f(u, i) = \alpha + \beta_u + \beta_i + \gamma_u \cdot \gamma_i$.

(ii) Next, compare *implicit feedback* models, such as the Bayesian Personalized Ranking model from Section 5.2.2. Much as we measured the performance of BPR in terms of evaluation metrics like the AUC

---

[16] When debugging gradient-descent models, it can be instructive to isolate individual terms (i.e., updating only a single parameter or a subset of parameters at a time) to determine that each update results in an improvement of the objective; it can also be useful to start with only a *single* latent factor (i.e., $K = 1$) before experimenting with higher-dimensional models.

(eq. (5.26)), simple memory-based ranking schemes such as those we developed in Project 3 can also be evaluated based on how effectively they distinguish interactions (positive samples) from non-interactions.

(iii) Try to thoroughly tune and regularize the latent factor model you developed above. Some factors you might consider include (a) the number of latent factors K; (b) the regularization approach, for example, you might be able to improve performance by using separate regularizers for the bias terms and latent factors, that is, $\lambda_1 \Omega(\beta)$ and $\lambda_2 \Omega(\gamma)$; (c) other factors, such as learning rates, initialization schemes, and so on.

(iv) Experiment with fast retrieval techniques (or libraries) such as those we examined in Section 5.6.

6

Content and Structure in Recommender Systems

So far, the systems we have built for personalized recommendation have been based purely on interaction data. We argued in Chapters 4 and 5 as to why interactions are often sufficient to capture all of the critical signals that we need, simply by finding patterns among users and items that maximally explain variance. This argument holds in theory under certain conditions, though is quite limited. For one, collecting sufficient interaction data to fit parameter-hungry latent factor models is not feasible when we consider the long-tail of new users and rarely consumed items. Even when we can harvest sufficient interaction data, several recommendation settings simply do not conform to the canonical setting of predicting an interaction given a user-item pair.

In practice, several situations deviate from the classical setting we have described so far, and require more complex models that leverage side-information or problem structure to improve performance. Leveraging content and structure can be useful in a variety of situations, for example:

- Only a limited amount of interaction data may be available. Our argument that interaction data is sufficient to capture subtle preference signals applies only in the limit, that is, when a large number of interactions are available for each user (or item). When few interactions are available (or none, in *cold-start* settings), one must instead rely on user or item *features* to estimate initial preference models.
- Beyond improving performance, incorporating features into recommender systems may be desirable for the sake of model interpretability. For example, we may wish to understand how a user will react to a change in price; doing so effectively may require that price features are appropriately 'baked in' to the model (we study this specific case in sec. 6.5).
- User preferences or item properties may not be *stationary*. Even the simple fact that Christmas movies are unlikely to be watched in July cannot

be captured simply by adding more latent dimensions. Although not the topic of this chapter, we will revisit models of such temporal and sequential dynamics in Chapter 7.

- Many settings simply do not follow the setup we developed in Chapters 4 and 5. For example, many recommendation scenarios have a social component (dating, bartering, etc.), or other constraints that must be accounted for in addition to user-to-item compatibility.

In this chapter we will develop models that help us to adapt to these situations. First, we will explore general-purpose strategies to incorporate *content* (or simply *features*) into recommender systems, starting with factorization machines in Section 6.1. For the most part, our goal is to study strategies to incorporate simple numerical and categorical features; we develop strategies for the specific cases of temporal, textual, and visual features in Chapters 7 to 9. We are especially interested in how features can be incorporated for the sake of solving so-called *cold-start* problems (sec. 6.2), whereby we have little (or no) data associated with new users or items, as must infer an initial model of their preferences.

Beyond incorporating features into recommender systems, we will also explore various modalities of recommendation that deviate from the basic setup in Chapter 5. We will explore examples including online dating (sec. 6.3.1), bartering (sec. 6.3.2), social and group recommendation (sec. 6.4), among others. In exploring such settings, our goal is not only to explore a few specific applications of interest, but more importantly to understand the overall process of designing and adapting personalized machine learning techniques for situations that exhibit additional structure, or otherwise do not perfectly align with traditional settings.

6.1 The Factorization Machine

Factorization Machines (Rendle, 2010) are a general-purpose approach that seeks to incorporate features into models that capture pairwise interactions (such as interactions between users and items).

In essence, the factorization machine extends the approach behind the latent factor model (sec. 5.1). The latent factor model embeds users and items into low-dimensional space via γ_u and γ_i, and then models the interaction between them via an inner product; the factorization machine extends this approach to incorporate arbitrary pairwise interactions between users, items, and other features.

　The input to the model is a feature matrix X and a target y. In the simplest case, X might simply encode the identity of the user and item via a one-hot encoding, though can be extended to incorporate any additional properties associated with the interaction:

$$
\begin{bmatrix}
1000000 \ldots 000100000 \ldots 0001000 \ldots 15.95 \\
0001000 \ldots 000000010 \ldots 0001000 \ldots 12.25 \\
0100000 \ldots 000100000 \ldots 0000010 \ldots 15.00 \\
0000100 \ldots 010000000 \ldots 0010000 \ldots 17.50 \\
1000000 \ldots 000000010 \ldots 1000000 \ldots 19.95 \\
0000100 \ldots 000010000 \ldots 0000010 \ldots 10.15
\end{bmatrix} .
$$

(6.1)

$$
\underbrace{}_{\text{user}} \quad \underbrace{}_{\text{item}} \quad \underbrace{}_{\text{weekday}} \underbrace{}_{\text{price}}
$$

　The basic idea of the factorization machine is then to model *arbitrary* interactions between features. Each feature dimension is associated with a latent representation γ_i; the model equation is then defined in terms of all *pairs* of (non-zero) features (with feature dimensionality F):

$$
f(x) = \underbrace{w_0 + \sum_{i=1}^{F} w_i x_i}_{\text{offset and bias terms}} + \underbrace{\sum_{i=1}^{F} \sum_{j=i+1}^{F} \langle \gamma_i, \gamma_j \rangle x_i x_j}_{\text{feature interactions}}.
$$

(6.2)

　It is instructive to consider the case where the interaction matrix in Equation (6.1) includes *only* a user and item encoding. In such a case, Equation (6.2) expands to be equivalent to a latent factor model (as in eq. (5.10)), that is, the only interaction term is $\gamma_u \cdot \gamma_i$ for a user u and item i.

　As such, the factorization machine can be viewed as a generalization of a latent factor model, that allows for additional types of interactions to be considered. For example, if we include an additional one-hot feature in Equation (6.1) that encodes the *previous* item the user consumed, then the factorization machine will include an expression encoding the compatibility of the next item with the previous one, that is, the model can learn how *contextually relevant* the previous item is compared to the next one. It will be useful to compare this approach to the models we design specifically to handle sequential inputs in Chapter 7 (sec. 7.5). Rendle (2010) discuss such topics, describing the extent to which the general-purpose factorization machine formulation subsumes various approaches designed to handle specific types of features.

　Rendle (2010) describe how the model equation of Equation (6.2) can be computed efficiently (and how parameter learning can be done efficiently), by showing that the interaction term can be rewritten as

$$\sum_{i=1}^{F}\sum_{j=i+1}^{F}\langle\gamma_i,\gamma_j\rangle x_i x_j = \frac{1}{2}\sum_{f=1}^{K}\left(\left(\sum_{i=1}^{F}\gamma_{i,f}x_i\right)^2 - \sum_{i=1}^{F}\gamma_{i,f}^2 x_i^2\right), \qquad (6.3)$$

which allows for computation in $O(KF)$ (the dimension of the latent factors multiplied by the feature dimensionality).

6.1.1 Neural Factorization Machines

As we saw in Chapter 5 (sec. 5.5), deep learning-based models can potentially be used to improve the performance of traditional recommender systems, essentially by learning complex nonlinear relationships among latent features. Likewise, *Neural Factorization Machines* (He and Chua, 2017) generalize factorization machines by using a multilayer perceptron to learn complex non-linear feature interactions. The idea is similar to what we presented in Chapter 5 (sec. 5.5.2): just as user and item embeddings were combined by He et al. (2017b) to develop neural collaborative filtering, He and Chua (2017) combine the embeddings of several terms (users, items, previous items, etc.). The main additional component compared to neural collaborative filtering is a *pooling* operation, which aggregates the pairwise interactions among latent representations into a single feature vector so that they can be passed to a multilayer perceptron.

Wide and Deep Learning for Recommender Systems: The model architecture of the *Wide & Deep* model of Cheng et al. (2016), while not precisely a factorization machine, is inspired by the setting of factorization machines, as well as the neural collaborative filtering model from Chapter 5. Cheng et al. (2016) note that while neural networks can potentially learn complex interactions among latent features, they may nevertheless struggle to learn trivial but useful pairwise interactions among features. The wide and deep architecture essentially extends an architecture like the one above (the *deep* component) by adding a path that allows the model to 'circumvent' the multilayer part of the model using simple linear interactions (the *wide* component). The wide component is based on a simple linear model (i.e., $x \cdot \theta$), which includes (among other components) simple binary combinations of features. This allows the wide component to focus on important but simple feature interactions, while the deep component can focus on more complex interactions.

Finally we mention Guo et al. (2017a) (DeepFM), which adopts the same wide & deep architecture from Cheng et al. (2016). Their presentation is more

Table 6.1 *Deep learning-based recommendation techniques. References: Cheng et al. (2016); Guo et al. (2017a); He et al. (2017b); He and Chua (2017); Sedhain et al. (2015).*

Ref.	Technique	Description
H17	neural collaborative filtering	Uses multilayer perceptrons to learn complex interactions between user and item latent factors (chap. 5).
HC17	neural factorization machines	Similar to the above, but using multilayer perceptrons within a factorization machine framework.
C16	wide & deep learning for recommendation	Includes a 'wide' component to help the model capture pairwise feature interactions directly, allowing the deep component to focus on more complex hidden interactions.
G17	deep factorization machines	Similar to the above; incorporates the wide & deep architecture with the specific components of factorization machines.
S15	AutoRec	Learns compressed representations of item (or user) interaction vectors; the compressed representations can be used to estimate scores associated with unobserved interactions (chap. 5).

closely built around, and adopts the specific components of, the factorization machine architecture from Section 6.1.

Table 6.1 summarizes a few deep learning-based recommendation models (including some from Chapter 5); note that this is only a small sample intended to cover the variety of techniques and architectures involved (see, e.g., Zhang et al. (2019) for a more complete survey).

6.1.2 Factorization Machines in Python with *FastFM*

As we saw earlier, factorization machines are a highly flexible, general-purpose technique to incorporate numerical or categorical features into recommender systems. Later in this chapter, and in Chapter 7, we will explore specific types of dynamics that can be captured via factorization machines, but for the moment we will explore an implementation of a 'vanilla' factorization machine via the *FastFM* library (Bayer, 2016) (in this case using *Goodreads* data, as in Project 4).

First, we read our dataset and construct a mapping from each user to a specific index (from 0 to $|U| - 1$); this index will be used to associate each user and item with a feature dimension in our one-hot encoding (as in eq. (6.1)):

```
1  userIDs,itemIDs = {},{}
2  for d in data:
3      u, i = d['user_id'], d['book_id']
4      if not u in userIDs: userIDs[u] = len(userIDs)
5      if not i in itemIDs: itemIDs[i] = len(itemIDs)
6
7  nUsers, nItems = len(userIDs), len(itemIDs)
```

Next, we build our matrix of features associated with each interaction. Each feature is simply the concatenation of a (one-hot encoding of) a user ID and an item ID. Note that we use a sparse data structure (lil_matrix) to represent the feature matrix. Although we only use user and item IDs here, these feature vectors could straightforwardly be extended to include other features, such as those we explore later in the chapter:

```
8   X = scipy.sparse.lil_matrix((len(data), nUsers + nItems))
9   for i in range(len(data)):
10      user = userIDs[data[i]['user_id']]
11      item = itemIDs[data[i]['book_id']]
12      X[i,user] = 1 # Essentially a row from Equation 6.1
13      X[i,nUsers + item] = 1
14
15  y = numpy.array([d['rating'] for d in data])
```

Finally, we split the data into training and test fractions, fit the model, and compute its predictions on the test set:

```
16  X_train, y_train = X[:2000000], y[:2000000]
17  X_test, y_test = X[2000000:], y[2000000:]
18
19  fm = fastFM.als.FMRegression(n_iter=1000, init_stdev=0.1,
        rank=2, l2_reg_w=0.1, l2_reg_V=0.5)
20
21  fm.fit(X_train, y_train)
22  y_pred = fm.predict(X_test)
```

The model has several tunable parameters: n_iter controls the number of iterations; init_stdev controls the standard deviation of random parameter initialization; rank controls the number of latent factors (K); l2_reg_w and l2_reg_V control the regularization for the model's linear and pairwise terms (similar to λ_1 and λ_2 in eq. (5.12)).

6.2 Cold-Start Recommendation

So far, the recommendation approaches we have developed have depended on having detailed *interaction histories* associated with users and items. Naturally, we cannot find similar users (as in sec. 4.3) to a user who has no purchase history; likewise, we cannot estimate latent parameters γ_u (or even a bias β_u) for a user who has never rated or purchased any items (as in sec. 5.1).

As such, we need to develop recommendation approaches that can be useful in so-called *cold-start* scenarios. Depending on the setting, either users or items may be 'cold' (i.e., have zero associated interactions).

We will investigate two categories of approaches to deal with cold-start problems. First, one may attempt to deal with cold-start situations via the use of *side information* about users or items. Side information could range from product images to text or social interactions. In each case, side information gives clues as to the properties of an item, whether by learning user preferences toward observed item features (sec. 6.2.1), harvesting weaker signals such as the preferences of a user's friends (sec. 6.4.2), or by using item features to estimate item latent factors (sec. 9.2.1). We explore some of the simpler methods below but revisit the use of side information throughout the book. Second, we will explore methods that directly seek to elicit preferences from new users through surveys (sec. 6.2.2).

6.2.1 Addressing Cold-Start Problems with Side Information

In the absence of historical interaction data associated with users or items, one option is to resort to secondary signals. Park and Chu (2009) consider cold-start settings in the context of movie recommendation. For movies, associated features are available such as the release year, genre, (etc.), which can be encoded (e.g.) as a one-hot vector. For users, demographic features are used, such as a user's age, gender, occupation, or location. These features are captured via user and item feature vectors x_u and z_i for each user u and item i.

Recall that at the beginning of Section 4.1, we discussed the differences between recommendation and regression and argued that recommendation was fundamentally different from simple linear regression on user and item features. Critically, we argued that recommender systems must model the *interaction* between users and items, in order to be able to meaningfully personalize predictions for each user.

In order to capture interactions, Park and Chu (2009) use what is termed a *bilinear* model (we briefly mentioned bilinearity in sec. 5.7) to estimate the compatibility between user and item features. The model parameters can then be described via a matrix W, and user/item compatibility can be written as

$$s_{u,i} = x_u W z_i^T = \sum_{a=1}^{|x_u|} \sum_{b=1}^{|z_i|} x_{u,a} z_{i,b} W_{a,b}. \tag{6.4}$$

Here, unlike the linear regression model from (e.g.) Equation (4.4), W now encodes how user features should *interact* with item features. That is, a parameter $W_{a,b}$ encodes the extent to which the ath user feature is compatible with the bth item feature. So, the model can learn (e.g.) the extent to which users in the 35–50 age demographic will respond positively to the teen romance genre.

Both x_u and z_i include a constant feature. These features (or rather the corresponding entries in W) roughly fill the role of bias terms (i.e., α, β_u, and β_i in eq. 5.10)), that is, they allow the model to learn the extent to which users in a certain demographic, or movies of a certain genre, tend to yield higher or lower ratings than others.

The model is trained so that the compatibility $s_{u,i}$ should align with observed interactions (e.g., ratings). Park and Chu (2009) achieve this using a specific type of pairwise loss (i.e., a loss that considers two items at a time, similar to the BPR loss of eq. (5.30)), though this is an implementation detail that is not critical to the main idea of the method.

Ultimately, the method is evaluated on two movie datasets (*MovieLens* and *EachMovie*). Cold users and items in these datasets are simulated, simply by withholding interactions from a subset of users and items at training time, with interactions from those users being used to evaluate the system at test time. Experiments show that when considering cold users and/or items, the method outperforms alternatives that do not make use of features.

6.2.2 Addressing Cold-Start Problems with Surveys

An alternative to relying on side information in user cold-start settings is simply to directly solicit the preferences of new users once they first interact with the system.

Rashid et al. (2002) investigated strategies for generating initial user surveys. 'Surveys' in this setting simply consist of collecting ratings about an informative set of items in order to most quickly learn the preference dynamics of new users. Several strategies are investigated for selecting informative items. Surfacing *popular* items has the advantage that users will generally have interacted with them (and can thus provide an informed opinion), though opinions may not be informative if all users generally like the most popular items. In contrast, an *entropy*-based strategy selects items where opinions are highly varied: each rating provides more information, but users may be unable to rate a large number of unknown items. Beyond these, they explore hybrid strategies that balance popularity and entropy, as well as *personalized* strategies that (once a few known items are found) survey similar items that a user is likely to have interacted with.

Zhou et al. (2011) investigate more elaborate strategies based on the same principle, where a decision tree is constructed over items (where a user can provide positive, negative, or 'unknown' feedback at each step) to iteratively choose the most informative items to surface to the user.

Of course, this setting is only appropriate for settings where users can realistically be expected to already have experience with a reasonable fraction of the items (Rashid et al. (2002) and Zhou et al. (2011) consider movie recommendation scenarios). We will revisit the topic of cold-start recommendation regularly in later chapters, as well as 'cool-start' settings (where we have only a few interactions per user or item), as we develop systems that operate on features from sequences, text, and images. Whether explicitly designed for cold-start or not, such methods often seek to use side information to circumvent the paucity of available interaction data.

6.3 Multisided Recommendation

So far, our view of recommendation and personalization has consisted of maximizing some predicted utility for each user, for example, estimate their ratings or which items they'll interact with. Furthermore, every user has predictions made independently of each other.

Such a setting seems natural when considering contexts such as movie recommendation, but there are several cases where such models are inappropriate. For example, recommendation on an online dating platform would require quite different assumptions. For instance, the problem has symmetries in the sense that the users being recommended are also receiving recommendations— as such, users must be interested in their matches, but the matches must have a reasonable chance of reciprocating. Likewise, we must ensure not only that everyone receives recommendations but that everyone *is recommended to somebody*.

These types of problems are referred to as *multisided* or *multistakeholder* recommendations (Abdollahpouri et al., 2017). Such constraints appear in several settings, many of which we will visit throughout the book. In Section 6.4.3 we will look at *group* recommendations, where recommendations must simultaneously satisfy the interests of multiple users in a group. And in Section 6.7, we will consider advertising settings, where we must consider not only user preferences but also the budgets of individual advertisers (which prevent us from recommending the most compatible ads to everyone). Finally, we will revisit the topic in depth in Chapter 10, where we consider issues of fairness, calibration, balance, and so on. For example, when recommending movies we might want reasonable coverage of different genres (Steck, 2018), or when recommending authors, we might want our recommendations not to be too narrow in terms of gender or nationality (Ekstrand et al., 2018b).

For now, we will consider two specific examples of multistakeholder recommendation, namely online dating and bartering (i.e., recommending trading partners).

6.3.1 Online Dating

Pizzato et al. (2010) studied recommendations in the context of online dating. Online dating has several constraints not present in the types of recommendation problems we have seen so far, in particular, due to the fact that the users receiving recommendations are the same ones that are *being recommended*.

Pizzato et al. (2010) consider the specific objective of *reciprocal communication*, which is partly motivated by a specific mechanism in the data they study (from a large Australian online dating website). That is, a recommendation of a user v to a user u should be considered successful only if u messages v, *and* v responds to their message.

Actual compatibility scores $f(u, v)$ in Pizzato et al. (2010) are estimated using a fairly simple feature-based strategy that looks for a match between u's preferences and v's attributes (some of which may be matched strictly, for example, if a user has historically expressed interest only in a certain gender). Following this the *reciprocal compatibility* is simply the harmonic mean of the two compatibility scores:

$$\text{reciprocal compatibility}(u, v) = \frac{2}{f(u, v)^{-1} + f(v, u)^{-1}}. \tag{6.5}$$

The harmonic mean here is preferable to (e.g.) the arithmetic mean as it does not allow either user's preference to 'dominate' the compatibility estimate, that is, two users are only compatible if *both* have high compatibility scores for each other.

Beyond the notion of reciprocity considered in Pizzato et al. (2010), online dating has certain 'balance' or 'diversity' constraints not yet seen in other problems, for example, we cannot identify a user with 'ideal' characteristics and recommend them to everyone (which might be perfectly reasonable for, say, movies); instead, the system only has utility if users both receive, and appear in, recommendations. We consider this type of constraint further when considering online advertising problems in Section 6.7.1.

6.3.2 Bartering Platforms

Rappaz et al. (2017) considered the problem of generating recommendation systems for *bartering* platforms, that is, settings in which users exchange goods.

They study several settings in which products are exchanged, including CDs and DVDs, though most of their analysis centers around three datasets, of books (from *bookmooch.com*), beers (from *ratebeer.com*), and video games (from *reddit.com/r/gameswap*).

On each of these websites, users have both a 'wishlist' W_u and a 'give-away' list G_u, that is, sets of items they wish to give or receive. Given this constraint on the problem, one might think that recommending compatible trades is as simple as identifying compatible pairs. However, surprisingly the data reveal that 'eligible' swapping partners are incredibly rare, and the vast majority of logged trades occur between items that were not expressly included in a user's wishlist; thus, there is a need to build a system that can model likely trading partners via latent preferences. They also note that users repeatedly trade with the same partners, indicating that there is a social component to trading.

Given the two factors above, the basic model combines a standard latent factor representation with a social term. Given a user u, an item i, and a potential trading partner v, their compatibility is modeled as

$$f(u, v, i) = \gamma_u \cdot \gamma_i + S_{u,v}. \qquad (6.6)$$

Here γ_u and γ_i are low-rank factors as in Equation (5.10), whereas $S_{u,v}$ is a (potentially full-rank) matrix $S \in \mathbb{R}^{|U| \times |U|}$; although S potentially encodes a large number of parameters, in practice it is very sparse (at least in their datasets) as the number of observed trading partners is limited.

Note that the this model captures only the interest of one user toward another's item; to model reciprocal interest, Rappaz et al. (2017) simply captures the average of interest in both directions (fig. 6.1):

$$f(u, i, v, j) = \frac{1}{2}(f(u, v, i) + f(v, u, j)). \qquad (6.7)$$

Other aggregation functions besides the arithmetic mean (such as the harmonic mean) can be used, though the arithmetic mean proved the most effective, indicating that a weak preference from one user can be made up for by a strong preference from another (in contrast to the online dating scenario from sec. 6.3.1). The model also includes a temporal term encoding timepoints when certain users are particularly active and certain items are particularly popular, though we leave the discussion of temporal models to Chapter 7.

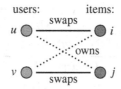

Figure 6.1 Basic idea behind reciprocal interest, as in Rappaz et al. (2017); in bartering settings, a strong preference from one user compensates for a potentially weaker one from the other. Compatibility is a function of the social cohesion between u and v, as well as their interest in the desired items (eqs. (6.6) and (6.7)).

Ultimately, the method is evaluated in terms of its ability to assign higher scores to observed interactions compared to non-observed ones (i.e., using a BPR-like training and evaluation scheme, as in sec. 5.2.2). The main conclusion of the experiments is that several components are important in bartering settings: reciprocal interest, a social history of trades, as well as temporal 'trends' across users and items.

6.4 Group- and Socially Aware Recommendation

Our opinions and decisions are influenced by our social connections. Within the context of recommendation. One possible dynamic is that of *social trust*: the fact that a friend has liked or purchased an item is a strong predictor of a user's future behavior (sec. 6.4.1). Alternately, in some contexts, recommendations must satisfy several users' interests simultaneously (e.g., selecting a movie for a group of users to watch) so that a user's preferences should be balanced against those of their friends (sec. 6.4.3).

More prosaically, social connections can simply be a way to harvest additional interaction data to improve the accuracy or cold-start performance of recommender systems. Given a paucity of data from a particular user, interactions from their social network can act as weak signals to augment the amount of data to be used for training. We explore a few representative approaches below, which we summarize in Table 6.2.

6.4.1 Socially Aware Recommendation

Several approaches have sought to incorporate signals from social networks to improve recommendation. The basic idea behind doing so is that social connections will help us to circumvent *sparsity* issues in interaction data. That is, even if a user has only a small number of observed interactions, we can (to

Table 6.2 *Comparison of socially aware recommendation techniques.*
References: Amer-Yahia et al. (2009); Ma et al. (2008); O'connor et al.
(2001); Pan and Chen (2013); Zhao et al. (2014).

Ref.	Social Data	Description
M08	*Epinions*	Trust links help to regularize γ_u, which must simultaneously explain rating and trust factors (sec. 6.4.1).
Z14	*Epinions, Delicious, Ciao, LibraryThing*	Friends' interactions act as additional *implicit signals* for recommendation (sec. 6.4.2).
O01	*MovieLens*	Studies the desirable characteristics of good interfaces for group recommendation (sec. 6.4.3).
A-Y09	*MovieLens*	Designs measures of *group consensus* and proposes recommendation algorithms to maximize them (sec. 6.4.3).
PC13	*MovieLens, Netflix*	Treats group preferences as weak signals to design pairwise sampling strategies for BPR (sec. 6.4.4).

some degree) leverage the interactions of their friends, whose opinions they are likely to trust.

Conceptually, the typical approach behind socially aware recommendation is to use social connections as a form of *regularizer*, which states that a user's preferences should be *similar to* those of their connections in a social network. For example, given a user with few interactions, we might assume that their preferences align with the (average of) their friends; this is a possibly better assumption than the regularizer of Equation (5.11), which in practice will essentially discard user latent factors (γ_u) for users with few interactions.

An early attempt to incorporate social networks into recommender systems extended the basic framework of a latent factor model (Ma et al., 2008). They looked at data from *Epinions*, which in addition to interaction data in the form of ratings (much like eq. (4.8)), includes a network of 'trust' and 'distrust' relationships. Unlike a typical social network, these are *signed* relationships, whereby a user explicitly indicates that they 'trust' (1) or distrust (-1) another user. That is, in addition to our interaction matrix, we have a (directed) adjacency matrix:

$$A = \left. \begin{bmatrix} 1 & \cdot & \cdot & -1 & 1 \\ \cdot & 1 & -1 & \cdot & \cdot \\ \cdot & 1 & 1 & -1 & \cdot \\ 1 & \cdot & 1 & \cdot & 1 \\ -1 & -1 & \cdot & 1 & 1 \end{bmatrix} \right\} \text{users.} \qquad (6.8)$$

$$\underbrace{\phantom{\begin{bmatrix} 1 & \cdot & \cdot & -1 & 1 \end{bmatrix}}}_{\text{users}}$$

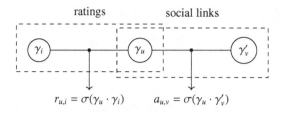

Figure 6.2 Social recommendation techniques often make use of a *shared parameter* (in this case γ_u) that simultaneously explains rating dimensions and social connections. In this way, social links can estimate preference dimensions even for users with few historical ratings.

Ultimately though, the distrust relationships are not used in Ma et al. (2008), as it is argued that the semantics of 'distrust' are somewhat more complex than (e.g.) users having different preference dimensions.

Thus, given a rating matrix R, and an adjacency matrix A, we want to predict ratings in R in such a way that A informs us about each user's likely latent preferences. The basic idea is to make use of a *shared parameter* γ_u for each user. For rating data, γ_u is no different from a user latent factor in a matrix factorization model, that is, it is combined with an item latent factor and used to predict the rating, in this case via a sigmoid function:[1]

$$r_{u,i} = \sigma(\gamma_u \cdot \gamma_i). \tag{6.9}$$

Next, the parameter γ_u is *re-used* to predict trust relationships in A:

$$a_{u,v} = \sigma(\gamma_u \cdot \gamma_v'). \tag{6.10}$$

The original paper allows A to be a weighted matrix, indicating varying degrees of social trust, but for simplicity we assume here that A contains only trust (1) and not-trust (0) values.

Note that while γ_u is a shared parameter, γ_v' is not; since the matrix A is directed, γ_u can be thought of as explaining why u trusts others, whereas γ_v' explains why v *is trusted by* others. In practice we are usually not interested in predicting entries $a_{u,v}$; rather, the trust relationships are additional data that should help us to calibrate γ_u more efficiently. This idea is depicted in Figure 6.2.

---

[1] The specific choice of the sigmoid function is an implementation detail, and ratings are scaled to be in the range [0, 1] to accommodate this choice.

The overall objective then takes the form

$$\underbrace{\sum_{(u,i)\in R} (r_{u,i} - \sigma(\gamma_u \cdot \gamma_i))^2}_{\text{rating prediction error}} + \lambda^{(\text{trust})} \underbrace{\sum_{(u,v)\in A} (a_{u,v} - \sigma(\gamma_u \cdot \gamma_v'))^2}_{\text{trust prediction error}} + \lambda\|\gamma\|_2^2, \qquad (6.11)$$

where $\lambda^{(\text{trust})}$ trades-off the importance of predicting the trust network (versus predicting ratings). Ultimately, experiments in Ma et al. (2008) show that the trust network helps to predict ratings more accurately than matrix factorization alone. Of course, it should be noted that trust relationships on *Epinions* are very closely tied to opinion dimensions, presumably more than in other social networks.

Note that the above is essentially a more complex form of cold-start (or 'cool-start') recommendation (as we saw in sec. 6.2), in the sense that we are leveraging a form of side-information (social connections) to make up for a paucity of interaction data. In the case of a user who has never rated an item (but has social connections), the system can still reasonably estimate γ_u from the preference dimensions of u's friends.

6.4.2 Social Bayesian Personalized Ranking

Above we showed how matrix factorization frameworks could be extended to incorporate signals from social networks. The intuition behind the idea simply stated that the same factors that explain preferences should also be able to explain 'trust' relationships.

Next, we will see how this idea can be adapted to predict interactions (rather than ratings), by incorporating social connections into the Bayesian Personalized Ranking framework from Section 5.2.2.

Conceptually, using social links to predict interactions relies on a possibly different assumption than we made above. Whereas our previous intuition above was based on some notion of trust, here we are simply assuming that a user is more likely to interact with items (e.g., to watch movies or read books) if their friends have previously interacted with them.

Zhao et al. (2014) attempted to adapt the assumptions made by Bayesian Personalized Ranking (BPR) to datasets involving social connections. Recall that BPR makes the assumption that a user's compatibility with items they've interacted with ($x_{u,i}$) should be higher than their compatibility with items they have not interacted with ($x_{u,j}$), which is captured via a sigmoid function:

$$x_{u,i} \geq x_{u,j} \quad \rightarrow \quad \sigma(x_{u,i} - x_{u,j}) \text{ should be maximized} \qquad (6.12)$$

(see eq. (5.30)). To adapt this to settings involving a social network, Zhao et al. (2014) assume a third type of feedback: for a user u, in addition to *positive* feedback i, and *negative* feedback j (as with BPR), we also have *social* feedback k, which consists of items consumed by u's connections in a social network.

Zhao et al. (2014) test two assumptions about how this social feedback should be incorporated. The first states that social interactions are weaker than positive interactions, but still stronger than negative interactions, essentially stating that users are somewhat more likely to interact with items their friends have interacted with:

$$\underbrace{x_{u,i} \geq x_{u,k}}_{\substack{\text{positive} \quad \text{social}}} ; \quad \underbrace{x_{u,k} \geq x_{u,j}}_{\substack{\text{social} \quad \text{negative}}} . \tag{6.13}$$

An alternate hypothesis states the opposite: if our friends have interacted with an item but we have not, this might instead be a signal that we know about the item, but deliberately chose not to interact with it; in this instance we drop the second assumption from Equation (6.13) and replace it with a weaker assumption:

$$\underbrace{x_{u,i} \geq x_{u,k}}_{\substack{\text{positive} \quad \text{social}}} ; \quad \underbrace{x_{u,i} \geq x_{u,j}}_{\substack{\text{positive} \quad \text{negative}}} . \tag{6.14}$$

Note that neither of these assumptions is 'better' than the other; rather they are simply hypotheses that must be tested by determining which best fits real datasets.

To train the model, a BPR-like objective (eq. (5.30)) is used, but which now involves two terms. For example, using the assumption from Equation (6.13):

$$\sum_{(u,i,k)\in\mathcal{T}} \log \sigma(x_{u,i} - x_{u,k}) + \sum_{(u,k,j)\in\mathcal{T}} \log \sigma(x_{u,k} - x_{u,j}) + \|\gamma\|_2^2, \tag{6.15}$$

where $\mathcal{T}$ is a training set consisting of positive, negative, and social feedback (i, j, and k) for each user u.

Ultimately, Zhao et al. (2014) show that both models outperform alternatives that do not leverage social connections. Several datasets besides *Epinions* are used, including data from *Ciao*, *Delicious*, and *LibraryThing* (product reviews, social bookmarks, and books). Overall, the assumption from Equation (6.14) slightly outperforms that of Equation (6.13) on all datasets.

6.4.3 Group-Aware Recommendation

Somewhat related to the topic of social recommendation is the idea of *group* recommendation, where recommendations should be made collectively to a group of users, rather than to an individual. Understanding group dynamics can help to improve recommendation accuracy, though another goal of the approaches below is to design evaluation criteria that correspond to group satisfaction.

Early work on this topic includes *PolyLens* (O'connor et al., 2001), though this work was mostly concerned with designing user interfaces for the purpose of group recommendation, rather than using group data to improve recommendation performance. Although focused on interface-building, the work shows the utility of group-based recommenders, which could help users to find items that are compatible with their group's mutual interests.

Later, Amer-Yahia et al. (2009) attempted to formalize the notion of group recommendation, by defining useful objectives that define how compatible a set of items is with a group. Given a pre-defined compatibility function $f(u, i)$ (e.g., the output of a latent factor model), a simple attempt to define group compatibility between a group of users G and an item i might consist of computing

$$\text{Average compatibility of } i: \quad rel(G, i) = \frac{1}{|G|} \sum_{u \in G} f(u, i). \tag{6.16}$$

Alternately, we could define the compatibility as that of the *least* compatible user in the group, known as *least misery*:

$$\text{Least misery:} \quad rel(G, i) = \min_{u \in G} f(u, i). \tag{6.17}$$

The latter is preferable in settings where users have constraints, for example, to avoid recommending a steakhouse to a group of users, some of whom are vegetarian.

Amer-Yahia et al. (2009) argue that in addition to maximizing relevance (or minimizing misery), it is also important that the group has some degree of *consensus* about the quality of an item. That is, users in a group should not drastically disagree about $f(u, i)$, separately from their actual scores. Two disagreement functions proposed are the average pairwise disagreement:

$$dis(G, i) = \frac{2}{|G|(|G| - 1)} \sum_{(u,v) \in G, u \neq v} |f(u, i) - f(v, i)|, \tag{6.18}$$

and disagreement variance:

$$dis(G, i) = \frac{1}{|G|} \sum_{u \in G} \left(f(u, i) - \underbrace{\frac{1}{|G|} \sum_{v \in G} f(v, i)}_{\text{average compatibility in } G} \right)^2. \tag{6.19}$$

Finally, Amer-Yahia et al. (2009) argue that a group *consensus function* should be a combination of both of these factors, that is, a relevance function (eq. (6.16) or (6.17)) and a disagreement function (eq. (6.18) or (6.19)):

$$\mathcal{F}(\mathcal{G}, i) = w_1 \times rel(\mathcal{G}, i) + w_2 \times (1 - dis(\mathcal{G}, i)), \qquad (6.20)$$

where w_1 and w_2 trade-off the relative importance of the two terms. *Group recommendation* then consists of finding suitable items (e.g., movies that no user in the group has seen) that maximize a (tuned) group consensus function.

Beyond defining notions of group consensus, Amer-Yahia et al. (2009) show how to efficiently select items that maximize the above criteria (note the large number of comparisons involved when performing optimization naively). They also demonstrate experimentally (via a *Mechanical Turk*-based user study of movie recommendations) that both *relevance* and *disagreement* are simultaneously important to achieve satisfaction within a group.

6.4.4 Group Bayesian Personalized Ranking

Much like Zhao et al. (2014) incorporated social links into Bayesian Personalized Ranking by treating friends' interactions as additional implicit signals, 'Group BPR' (Pan and Chen, 2013) seeks to treat group preferences as a form of implicit signal that can be used within a BPR framework.

While BPR assumes that a user u's compatibility with an observed interaction i is greater than their compatibility with an unobserved interaction j (i.e., $x_{u,i} > x_{u,j}$, as in eq. (5.25)), Pan and Chen (2013) assume that *group* preference acts as a similar form of implicit feedback. As with Social BPR (sec. 6.4.2), the goal of Group BPR is essentially to leverage weak signals from related users as a way of harvesting implicit pairwise preference feedback.

Specifically, if a group of users $\mathcal{G}$ has interacted with some item i, their *mutual preference* toward the item, defined as

$$x_{\mathcal{G},i} = \frac{1}{|\mathcal{G}|} \sum_{g \in \mathcal{G}} x_{g,i}, \qquad (6.21)$$

is assumed to be greater than a user u's preference toward an unseen item j (i.e., $x_{u,j}$). This notion of group preference is combined with the pairwise preference model from Equation (5.25), resulting in a preference model of the form:

$$\rho x_{\mathcal{G},i} + (1 - \rho)x_{u,i} > x_{u,j}, \qquad (6.22)$$

where ρ is a hyperparameter controlling the relative importance of individual versus group preference.

Interestingly, the training data used for evaluation by Pan and Chen (2013) consists of 'standard' interaction datasets that do not contain explicit groups; rather, groups are sampled randomly among users who have consumed a particular item. As such, Group BPR is perhaps best thought of as a different means of leveraging explicit and implicit signals in implicit feedback settings, rather than as a group method as such.

Experiments in Pan and Chen (2013) show that sampling pairwise preferences as in Equation (6.22) can improve performance over standard BPR on various benchmark datasets.

6.5 Price Dynamics in Recommender Systems

In spite of the obvious impact price has on user decisions, there is surprisingly little work that seeks to incorporate price features into personalized predictive models. Partly this owes to the lack of suitable datasets: the vast majority of the datasets we have studied so far (concerned with movies, books, restaurants, etc.) include few useful features from which to build a model of price.

Even in datasets that include a price variable, it is not obvious how this variable should be incorporated in to the types of algorithms we have seen so far (the difficulty of incorporating these variables is discussed in, e.g., Umberto (2015)). Naively one might think that price might be incorporated into (e.g.) a factorization machine (sec. 6.1) much like any other feature. While such a feature might help in cold-start settings, it is unlikely to improve predictive performance in general: to the extent that price explains significant variability in user preferences or item properties, it may already be captured by user or item latent factors. This form of ineffectiveness often comes as a surprise when implementing content-aware models: the features that explain the most variance (price, brand, genre, etc.) are precisely those that latent factor models already capture, and add little predictive capacity (see fig. 6.3). A notable exception to this is features that are not *static*: while a simple feature like the price of an item may already be 'baked in' to a latent factor representation, what our current models cannot tell us is how a user would react to a *change* in price. As such, much of the research we will explore below is concerned with questions of price variability, and modeling the impact that a *change* in price will have on user preference.

The models covered in this section are summarized in Table 6.3.

- Most of the settings we've considered in this chapter have essentially been forms of *cold-start*. In other words, features compensate for a lack of historical interaction data (from either the user or item side).
- Features are *unlikely* to be particularly useful in 'warmer' settings: even if a feature (price, brand, genre) explains variance, high-variance dimensions will already be captured by latent terms (i.e., γ_u and γ_i).
- An exception to the above is features which are not *static*. We study price variability in this chapter, and temporal dynamics more broadly in Chapter 7. Latent terms will struggle to capture this type of variability unless it is explicitly modeled.
- Another important use of features is for model *interpretability*: even features that yield a modest improvement in predictive performance may help us to understand the underlying dynamics of a particular problem better than we can from latent representations. We discuss such notions of interpretability (in the context of text-aware models) in Chapter 8.

Figure 6.3 When is side information useful for recommendation?

Table 6.3 *Comparison of price-aware recommendation techniques.*
References: Ge et al. (2011); Guo et al. (2017b); Hu et al. (2018); Wan et al.
(2017).

Ref.	Price Data	Description
G11	(Proprietary) data of travel tour purchases	Incorporates price and time constraints into travel tour recommendations (sec. 6.5.1).
G17	Various *Amazon* categories	Disentangles interactions in terms of preferences versus price compatibility (sec. 6.5.1).
H18	Purchase and browse data from *Etsy*	Forecasts a user's target purchase price from a sequence of browsed items (sec. 6.5.2).
W17	Purchases from Seattle grocery stores	Estimates how purchase decisions (item choice, quantity, etc.) are affected by price fluctuations (sec. 6.5.3).

6.5.1 Disentangling Prices and Preferences

Ge et al. (2011) consider price from the perspective of a user who wants recommendations that satisfy a *budget constraint*. They consider this problem in the context of recommending 'travel tours,' where a user has constraints in terms of time (the length of the vacation), and the amount they are able to spend. They note, however, that while the length and price of an actual travel package are observed, a user's constraints may not be, and as such must be modeled (or estimated) based on their historical activities.

To achieve this type of price-aware recommendation, Ge et al. (2011) consider a modification of a latent factor model that includes both a preference compatibility, and a price-compatibility term:

$$f(u, i) = \underbrace{S(C_u, C_i)}_{\text{price compatibility}} \cdot \overbrace{\gamma_u \cdot \gamma_i}^{\text{user preference}}. \tag{6.23}$$

γ_u and γ_i are user and item (travel tour)-related latent factors, as in Equation (5.10). C_u and C_i are cost-related factors; the cost for the tour (C_i) is assumed to be an observed, two-dimensional vector, encoding both time and price; C_u is assumed to be a corresponding latent compatibility encoding the user's price constraints; S is then a compatibility function, such as the (negative) Euclidean distance:

$$S(C_u, C_i) = 1 - \|C_u - C_i\|_2^2. \tag{6.24}$$

A few improvements to this basic model are proposed (including in a follow-up paper (Ge et al., 2014)); for example, different training strategies are proposed based on different types of explicit and implicit feedback; and the user factor C_u is carefully regularized (since, e.g., a trivial ℓ_2 regularizer would center user price constraints around zero).

Experiments (on a proprietary dataset of historical travel tour interactions) show that the model outperforms variants that fail to consider price information.

Guo et al. (2017b) also build a model to separately capture price and preference dynamics. Although the specific method is somewhat different from those we have discussed (a form of Poisson Factorization, see, e.g., Gopalan et al. (2013)), this approach has a common goal with Ge et al. (2011) of separating price and preference concerns. In essence, latent item properties γ_i are responsible for estimating ratings via $\gamma_u^{(\text{rating})} \cdot \gamma_i$ and also price compatibility via $\gamma^{(\text{price})} \cdot \gamma_i$; compatible items are then those that satisfy both of these concerns. This idea is similar to the use of shared parameters for social recommendation as in Figure 6.2.

6.5.2 Estimating Willing-to-Pay Prices within Sessions

Hu et al. (2018) also considered the effect that price has on users' purchasing decisions, but did so at the level of individual browsing sessions. That is, the sequence of products a user browses might provide some clue as to their purchase intent or their 'willing-to-pay' amount, for example, if they are comparison shopping among items within a certain price range.

Like Ge et al. (2011), the basic model of Hu et al. (2018) extends a latent factor model to incorporate a price-compatibility term:

$$f(u, i) = \gamma_u \cdot \gamma_i + \alpha_u C(u, p_i). \tag{6.25}$$

Here $C(u, p_i)$ encodes the compatibility between the user u and the price p_i of the item i, and α_u is a personalized measure of user u's sensitivity toward this term.

A trivial price-compatibility term might take the form

$$C(u, p_i) = \exp\left(-\omega(b_u - p_i)^2\right), \tag{6.26}$$

where p_i is the price of the item and b_u is a latent estimate of the user's budget; ω controls the bandwidth of the compatibility function. This function is essentially a variant of Equation (6.24).

To incorporate session dynamics, Hu et al. (2018) model price-compatibility in terms of a feature vector ρ_i, which is a one-hot encoding representing the *quantile* of the price p_i compared to the prices of previously viewed items in the session;[2] then the price-compatibility is merely $C(u, p_i) = \theta \cdot \rho_i$. This is further extended by using a *mixture model*, which essentially says that there could be different parameters θ_g for different (latent) users groups:

$$C(u, p_i) = \sum_g \underbrace{\frac{e^{\psi_{u,g}}}{\sum_{g'} e^{\psi_{u,g'}}}}_{\text{extent to which } u \text{ belongs to group } g} \overbrace{\theta_g \cdot \rho_i}^{\text{price-compatibility model for group } g}. \tag{6.27}$$

Hu et al. (2018) ultimately find that there are several different classes of user (based on latent group membership $\psi_{u,g}$): some tend to gradually browse toward more expensive items, some gradually browse toward cheaper items, and some consider a range of prices throughout a session.

6.5.3 Price Sensitivity and Price Elasticity

Notions such as *price sensitivity* and *price elasticity* (defined as the change in purchase quantity given a change in price) are well understood in economics and marketing (Case and Fair, 2007). Understanding such factors can help to guide custom marketing and promotion strategies (Zhang and Krishnamurthi, 2004; Zhang and Wedel, 2009).

However, they are less well understood in terms of their effectiveness in a *predictive* setting, that is, in terms of how price should be used to understand and forecast user actions (or to make recommendations).

Part of the reason that price has received relatively little attention (at least in academic literature) is presumably the lack of useful available data; even when price is observed, it is confounded by numerous other factors, such as brand or

---

[2] For example, $\rho_i = [0, 0, 0, 1]$ would indicate that the price p_i was among the top 25% of browsed prices.

manifest aspects of a product; moreover, even when price data is available, one rarely has *historical* data on price that allows for measurement of the impact of a *change* in price.

Wan et al. (2017) studied price in the context of grocery recommendation. Their research was mostly based on real transaction data from a physical grocery store (in Seattle), though it was also validated based on public data from *dunnhumby*. Both datasets contain price measurements, and critically measurements of price *variation* over time. As such the main questions center around the extent to which purchase decisions are affected by changes in price.

In the context of grocery shopping, potential questions include:

- Will a reduction in price cause a user to buy a *category* of product they otherwise would not have (e.g., would they buy milk at a discount if it was not on their shopping list)?
- Will a reduction in price cause users to buy a *specific item* that they otherwise would not have (e.g., would they buy a different brand of milk because of a discount)?
- Will a reduction in price cause users to buy a *larger quantity* of an item than they otherwise would have?

To study these questions, prediction is broken down into three subsequent choices:

$$p_u(\text{buy } q \text{ units of an item } i \text{ from category } c) =$$

$$p_u^{(\text{category})}(\text{buy a product from category } c)$$
$$\times p_u^{(\text{item})}(\text{buy product } i \mid \text{buying from category } c) \qquad (6.28)$$
$$\times p_u^{(\text{quantity})}(\text{buy } q \text{ units} \mid \text{buying item } i).$$

Each of these three prediction tasks (category, item, and quantity prediction) is based on a predictor $f(u, c, t)$, $f(u, i, t)$, and $f(u, q, t|i)$; the underlying method behind each is a latent factor model, as in Equation (5.10), including additional features associated with the time (e.g., what day of the week the trip occurs on). Each is passed through a different activation function, for example, quantity prediction is modeled via a *Poisson* function:

$$p(\text{quantity} = q | \text{buying item } i) = \frac{f(u, q, t|i)^{q-1} \exp(-f(u, q, t|i))}{(q-1)!}. \qquad (6.29)$$

Next, the change in purchase probability due to price is captured (for each of the three models) using a simple feature encoding the price at a particular point in time. Specifically (e.g., for quantity)

$$f'(u, q, t|i) = \underbrace{f(u, q, t|i)}_{u\text{'s compatibility with } q \text{ units of item } i \text{ at time } t} + \beta_{u,q} \log \underbrace{P_i(t)}_{\text{price of item } i \text{ at time } t}, \qquad (6.30)$$

where $P_i(t)$ is the price of the item at time t. $\beta_{u,q}$ is a coefficient encoding the price sensitivity, that is, the extent to which a particular user u, when purchasing q units of an item, will react to changes in price (e.g., a negative value of $\beta_{u,q}$ would indicate that a user is less likely to purchase a particular quantity given a price increase). All parameters are learned by training on purchase data, using a BPR-like training scheme.

Price-elasticity now reflects how much preferences change given a change in price, for example, for a particular item i; or *cross-elasticity* measures the extent to which a change in i's price will change a user's compatibility toward (e.g., probability of purchasing) a *different* product j. Price-elasticity and cross-elasticity are *measurements* after the model has been trained. The main finding of the model is that price-elasticity applies mostly to product choice, but not to category choice or quantity (i.e., a change in price may cause users to buy a *different* brand of eggs, but will not cause them to buy eggs when they otherwise would not have).

Ruiz et al. (2020) develop a somewhat similar model of consumer choice, also in a setting of grocery purchases. Like the above model, Ruiz et al. (2020) attempt to disentangle the various effects of item popularity, user preferences, and price dynamics, though also include additional terms involving seasonal effects. The main goal of the paper is to answer 'counterfactual' queries about price (i.e., what would the user have done if the price had been different?). By modeling how users will react to changes in price, they argue that the model is also able to detect interactions between products, namely in terms of which items are likely to be substitutable and complementary.

Finally, we mention attempts to use similar ideas within the context of dynamic pricing. Jiang et al. (2015) seek to combine ideas from pricing and recommendation in order to design optimal (i.e., profit-maximizing) promotion strategies. Conversely, Chen et al. (2016) analyze the characteristics of sellers on *Amazon*, in order to automatically detect the presence of algorithmic pricing.

6.6 Other Contextual Features in Recommendation

In this chapter, we have attempted a high-level treatment of the various ways features can be incorporated to develop richer models of interaction data. Naturally, we cannot give a complete presentation of all feature modalities, and as such we have only sought to cover some of the most common scenarios. Below we briefly survey a few of the other main directions for content-based recommendation.

6.6.1 Music and Audio

A number of scenarios we will explore later in the book involve interactions with music and audio data. First, interactions with music have significant sequential context, that is, the next interaction or recommendation should relate to the characteristics of the previous song (chap. 7, sec. 7.5.3). Second, music recommendations must carefully balance familiarity and novelty (chap. 10, sec. 10.5.1).

Given our focus in this chapter, we briefly explore the specific semantics of interaction data and the challenges involved in building content-aware models. We refer to, for example, Celma Herrada (2008) for a deeper survey of music recommendation.

Interaction signals in music can be quite different from those associated with the types of data we have seen so far (e.g., ratings and purchases). Feedback associated with music is often *implicit* and can be weak and noisy: for instance, we may know as little as whether a user finished a song or whether they skipped it (see, e.g., Pampalk et al. (2005)). Handling such signals is difficult as they do not obviously map to 'positive' and 'negative' signals.

Unlike most of the data we have studied so far, music interactions are also highly driven by *repeat consumption* (see, e.g., Anderson et al. (2014)). This requires specific techniques to understand under what conditions users might seek novelty versus more familiar options.

Extracting useful features from audio is also challenging. Wang and Wang (2014) note the difficulty of directly using high-dimensional audio features (e.g., based on spectrogram-based representations of audio) within a traditional feature-based recommender system. The solution they propose is to use a neural network-based representation (essentially a multilayer perceptron) to learn embeddings of songs that are useful for recommendation, that is:

$$\gamma_i = MLP(x_i). \tag{6.31}$$

Van Den Oord et al. (2013) adopt a similar approach based on a convolutional neural network (CNN) which operates on an audio *spectrogram*. Spectrograms are two-dimensional time/frequency representations of audio, so the approach is methodologically similar to using CNNs to develop content-aware models from images. We forego detailed discussion but note the similarity to image-based recommendation approaches such as those we develop in Chapter 9.

Like other recommendation domains, research in music recommendation has partly been driven by data. Popular music datasets include the *Million Song Dataset* and the *Taste Profile Dataset* (McFee et al., 2012), containing rich audio and interaction data, though various studies also make use of proprietary sources including data from *YouTube* (Anderson et al., 2014) and *Spotify* (Anderson et al., 2020).

6.6.2 Recommendation in Location-Based Networks

Several attempts have been made to incorporate geographical features into recommender systems. Actions are often guided by geographical constraints, whether due to a user operating within a certain geographical region, or due to sequential actions being highly localized.

Bao et al. (2015) survey attempts to model recommendations in *location-based social networks*, and highlights some of the main ideas and challenges in modeling this type of data:

- Locations are often used as a *contextual* feature, for example, users are likely to visit places (restaurants, hotels, landmarks, etc.) in the vicinity of those they have recently visited. We explore this type of assumption in the context of sequential recommendation in Chapter 7 (sec. 7.5.3).

- Appropriately extracting features from location data is difficult due to its hierarchical nature. For example, a restaurant belongs to a neighborhood, a city, a state, and a country. Strategies for extracting useful hierarchical representations from GPS data are covered in (e.g.) Zheng et al. (2009).

- Recommendation in such settings varies in terms of the data and goals involved. In addition to geo-tagged activities, data may include profile information, relations among users, and so on (Cho et al., 2011).

- Other familiar issues, such as cold-start, can be amplified in location-based data, where user activities can be sparse and data can grow rapidly.

As such, successful solutions to modeling in location-based social networks can incorporate several features, including those we have seen so far, for example, how to leverage social connections (as in sec. 6.4), and those we will see in later chapters, such as sequential dynamics. Bao et al. (2015) also highlight a number of data sources that are commonly used for the study of recommendation in location-based networks, including (e.g.) *Brightkite*, *Gowalla*, *Foursquare*, and so on.

6.6.3 Temporal, Textual, and Visual Features

So far we have covered content in recommender systems, including features ranging from price, geography, social signals, and audio. In the following chapters we will revisit content-aware recommendation techniques using features based on temporal and sequential dynamics (chap. 7), text (chap. 8), and images (chap. 9). These modalities require special attention, primarily to deal with the complex semantics of the data and high-dimensional signals involved. Exploring how to build personalized models based on these complex modalities of data is one of the main themes explored throughout the remainder of this book.

6.7 Online Advertising

Superficially, surfacing advertisements to users seems no different from any other form of personalized recommendation. That is, we can imagine learning user 'preferences' and advertisement 'properties' from (e.g.) clicked advertisements in much the same way that any other recommender system is trained.

While ad recommendation does indeed have many similarities to other forms of personalized recommendation, there are several properties that demand different solutions compared to what we have seen so far. In particular:

- Advertisers have budget constraints. In many recommendation settings we can tolerate considerable imbalance among the items that are recommended (e.g., a highly popular movie might be recommended to a substantial fraction of all users); this is impossible when recommending ads, given that each advertiser can afford to surface only a limited number of ads (and at the same time, we want to ensure that all advertisers have some ads recommended).
- Likewise, each user may only be shown a limited number of ads; while this seems a common enough feature in most recommendation scenarios, it is especially apparent when surfacing ads, as users are unlikely to explicitly request additional ads.
- Ad recommendations need to be made immediately. Again, this feature is common enough in many recommender systems, but is especially challenging given the considerations above: we cannot find a globally optimal solution that maximizes utility while satisfying advertisers' budget constraints. Instead, we must develop schemes that make local decisions in a way that approximates the globally optimal solution.
- Ad recommendation is highly contextual. Whereas most recommender systems rely heavily on user interaction histories, these are presumably less

reliable in ad recommendation scenarios (where users' interactions with ads are extremely sparse), if an interaction history is available at all. As such, one has to rely more heavily on user *context* (e.g., a user's query to a search engine).

- Even if a user is responsive to a certain type of ad, there is diminishing value in repeatedly showing similar ads. Instead, we must sometimes recommend ads with low expected utility in the hope of discovering new user interests (this is the basic principle behind a so-called *explore/exploit* tradeoff).

We will discuss a few of these issues as we briefly investigate systems for online advertising below. Note that in this section we will mostly ignore the question of how 'compatibility' between a user and an ad is estimated—this could itself be the output of a recommender system, or could simply be a bid that an advertiser places on a user or query. Our goal in this section is mostly to explore situations where we have constraints in terms of how many recommendations can be received by a user (or given of an item), and highlight some of the general differences and strategies used to build ad recommenders.

6.7.1 Matching Problems

A typical constraint in ad recommendation is what is known as a *matching* constraint, where each user can only be shown a fixed number of ads, and each ad can only be shown to a fixed number of users.

To begin with, we will consider the case where each ad is shown to exactly one user, and each user is shown exactly one ad. That is, we would like to select a function $ad(u)$ that maps users to ads, such that

$$ad(u) = ad(v) \to u = v. \tag{6.32}$$

Alternately, we could write this as an adjacency matrix A such that $A_{u,a} = 1$ if $ad(u) = a$. Then our constraint could be written as

$$\forall a \underbrace{\sum_u A_{u,a} = 1}_{\text{each advertiser shows one ad}} \quad ; \quad \forall u \underbrace{\sum_a A_{u,a} = 1}_{\text{each user sees one ad}}. \tag{6.33}$$

Then, we would like to choose the mapping that maximizes the utility between users and the ads they are shown:

$$\max_A \sum_{u,a} A_{u,a} f(u, a), \tag{6.34}$$

where $f(u, a)$ is a measure of the compatibility between a user and an ad (e.g., the output of a recommender system, a click probability, etc.).

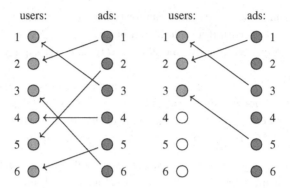

Figure 6.4 Ad recommendation can be viewed as a *bipartite matching problem* (left), where users are shown a fixed number of ads, and each ad is shown to a fixed number of users (in this figure each ad is shown to exactly one user, and *vice versa*). In an online setting (right), users arrive one at a time; we seek a solution that will be as close as possible to the solution we would have obtained in an offline setting at left.

This type of problem is known as a *matching problem*. Conceptually, it can be viewed as matching two sets of nodes to form a bipartite graph (fig. 6.4, left), where each possible edge has an associated weight (i.e., the compatibility between a user and an ad). Our constraint above now says that every node should be incident on one edge.

Outside of ad recommendation, this type of matching problem appears in many settings, for example, it is equivalent to the US's *National Residency Matching Program*, in which medical school students are matched to residency programs: each student can only be matched to a single residency, and each program has a limited number of slots; the matching should be chosen so as to optimize students' preferences for programs (and *vice versa*). Similar problems appear in various resource allocation settings (Gusfield and Irving, 1989); the original paper proposing the solution outlined below considered a setting related to college admissions (Gale and Shapley, 1962).

Although Equation (6.34) is a combinatorial optimization problem, it admits efficient approximation (the so-called stable marriage problem (Gusfield and Irving, 1989)) and a polynomial exact solution (see Kuhn (1955)).

6.7.2 AdWords

Above we discussed the issue of developing recommendation approaches that consider some notion of constraints or 'budgets' from the perspective of users and advertisers. While incorporating constraints is potentially useful in a variety of recommendation scenarios, our solution still does not fully address the setting of *ad* recommendation; in particular, when recommending ads, we are unlikely to see the entire set of users (or queries) in advance, before having to select advertisements.

As such, we desire algorithms that make decisions (i.e., assigns ads to users) one at a time, while still conforming to matching (or budget) constraints, as in Figure 6.4 (right).

Formally, the above describes the distinction between an *offline* and an *online* algorithm, that is, one which sees the entire problem in advance, versus one which must make predictions (or update model parameters) immediately in response to new interactions. We discussed this type of setting briefly in Section 5.7.

AdWords (Mehta et al., 2007) is a specific instance of this type of recommendation problem developed for *Google's* online advertising platform.

Mostly, the setting follows the one we described above, though includes a few additional components. Specifically,

- Each advertiser a has a *bid* $f(q, a)$ that they are willing to make for each query q.
- The bid generally refers to how much the advertiser will pay *if* the ad is clicked on; this is determined by an estimated *click-through-rate*, $ctr(q, a)$. As such the expected profit would be $f(q, a) \times ctr(q, a)$, which one can think of as being analogous to user-to-item compatibility (and could be estimated using a model such as one from Chapter 5).
- Each advertiser has a *budget* $b(a)$ (e.g., for a one-week period).
- As in Section 6.7.1, there is a limit on the number of ads that can be returned for each query.

Ultimately advertisers are selected via a function which considers both their bid amount $f(q, a)$ and the fraction of their budget remaining $r(a)$ compared to their initial budget $b(a)$. Specifically, advertisers are selected according to $f(q, a) \cdot (1 - e^{-\frac{r(a)}{b(a)}})$. Although the derivation of this specific formula is quite involved, it can be shown (see, e.g., Mehta et al. (2007)) that this tradeoff is in some sense optimal in terms of how closely the online algorithm approximates the offline solution.

Of course the actual implementation of *AdWords* contains many features not described here, for instance, *Adwords* uses a second-price auction (the winning advertiser pays the amount that the *second* highest bidder bid), and advertisers do not bid on exact queries, but rather are matched using 'broad matching' criteria that can include subsets, supersets, or synonyms of keywords being bid on. We refer to Rajaraman and Ullman (2011) for further description of these details, and Mehta et al. (2007) for a more detailed technical description.

Exercises

6.1   In Section 6.1 we introduced the factorization machine as a general-purpose technique for incorporating features into recommender systems. In this exercise we will incorporate a few features into a factorization machine to measure the extent to which they improve recommendation performance. *You could use any dataset for this exercise, so long as it includes a few features.* For example, using our beer dataset (as in sec. 2.3.1) we might include features such as:

- simple numerical features such as the ABV of the beer or the age of the user;
- the category of the item (one-hot encoded);
- the timestamp; this will require some care to encode, for example, you might use an encoding of the season or day of the week.

Using a few of these features (or similar features on another dataset), measure the extent to which they boost recommendation performance over a model which does not include them.[3]

6.2   In Section 6.2 we discussed the potential value of incorporating features (side information) into recommender systems, and argued that features may be most informative in *cold-start* scenarios. To assess this, conduct the following experiment (using your model from Exercise 6.1):

- for each user (or item) in the test set, count how many times that user appeared in the training set;
- plot the testing performance (y) of your model as a function of how many times that user appeared in the training set (x); this type of plot is shown in Figure 6.5;
- generate the same plot both with and without additional features in your factorization machine.

Naturally, our expectation is that performance will improve as users (or items) are less 'cold' (i.e., more training interactions). However, we expect the performance degradation to be more mild when features can compensate for a lack of historical interactions.

---

[3] Do not be surprised if the improvement is minimal; we will investigate this more in Exercise 6.2.

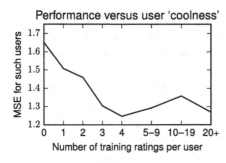

Figure 6.5 Performance (MSE) as a function of user coolness (defined as the number of times that user was seen during training). *Goodreads* 'graphic novels' data.

6.3 Before implementing a socially aware recommender, test the hypothesis that friends actually interact with more (or less) similar items compared to randomly chosen sets of users. Use any dataset that contains social interactions (such as those in Table 6.2). This hypothesis could be tested in various ways, for example, by computing the average Jaccard (or cosine, etc.) similarity between randomly chosen pairs of users, versus randomly chosen pairs of friends.

6.4 In Section 6.4 we explored a few ways to incorporate social signals into recommender systems. For the most part, these techniques amounted to ways of sampling negative feedback instances, for example, we might be more or less likely to interact with negative instances that our friends have already interacted with (eqs. (6.13) and (6.14)). Experiment with these sampling strategies (e.g., using the same dataset from Exercise 6.3) and determine which (if any) lead to improved performance over a traditional BPR implementation.

Project 5: Cold-Start Recommendation on *Amazon*

As we argued in Section 6.2, one of the main reasons to incorporate features into personalized recommendation approaches is to improve their performance in *cold-start* settings. Here, we will look at cold-start recommendation problems using data from *Amazon*, following data from (e.g.) Ni et al. (2019a). We select this dataset as it includes various types of item metadata (prices, brands, categories, etc.) that can potentially be useful in cold-start settings, though this project could be completed using any dataset that includes user or item metadata. For this project you'll likely want to select a specific sub-category (e.g., *Musical Instruments*, as we saw in sec. 4.3.2) which has informative features, and which is of an appropriate scale to build your model.

We will build our system for cold-start recommendation via the following steps:

(i) Start by implementing a 'vanilla' factorization machine to solve the prediction problem, that is, without incorporating any side-information. Note that this problem could be cast either as one of rating prediction (as in sec. 5.1) or as purchase prediction (as in sec. 5.2).

(ii) To build models for cold-start recommendation, it is useful to develop some evaluation metrics specifically for the purpose of evaluating cold-start (and 'cool-start') performance. To do so, try plotting the performance on the test set *as a function of the number of times the item appears in the training set* (as in Exercise 6.2)—this type of plot is shown in Figure 6.5 for a 'standard' latent factor model. Our hypothesis when incorporating side-information into recommendations is that performance improvements will be largest for the coldest items, and less useful for items with longer interaction histories. We will use this same type of plot to compare models in the following.

(iii) Several features could potentially be useful in cold-start scenarios. Consider how to encode the following: (a) the brand of the item; (b) the category (or categories) the item belongs to; and (c) the price of the item. Features describing relationships among items ('people who viewed X also viewed Y,' etc.) may also be useful (in much the same way as we considered user relationships in sec. 6.4).

For each cold-start feature you include, compare the performance of the model with and without that feature.

It may be worth revisiting this project as we explore more complex feature modalities in the later chapters, for example, you might consider more complex features based on the text of the product description, temporal information, or visual features. We will revisit these topics in Chapters 7 to 9.

7

Temporal and Sequential Models

Throughout Chapters 5 and 6 we gradually developed more refined arguments about the role that features (or 'side-information') play when modeling user interaction data. Our initial argument (started in sec. 5.1) was that latent user and item representations are sufficient to capture complex preference dynamics, and whatever features are most predictive (i.e., explain the most variability) of interactions will automatically emerge via our latent representations.

Later (e.g., in sec. 6.2), we refined our argument, noting that side-information *can* be useful, especially in settings where there is a paucity of interaction data from which to learn high-dimensional latent representations (i.e., *cold-start* settings).

However in both of the above cases we still assumed that our model of users and items was *stationary*. In practice, preferences and interactions can be non-stationary for a variety of reasons. For instance, no matter how many interactions we observe, and how many latent factors we fit, the models we have developed so far would struggle to tell us that a user might only buy swimsuits in summer, or that they are unlikely to watch the third film in a series until they have already seen the second.

In this chapter we explore techniques to build personalized models around user behavior that has *temporal and sequential dependencies*. Most straightforwardly, we might simply treat temporal and sequential information as additional features that can be modeled, for example, via the framework of a factorization machine as we developed in Chapter 6 (and indeed we will explore temporal models based on this type of approach). However as we will see in this chapter, a variety of complex and subtle temporal dynamics could be at play, for example:

- Dynamics could apply to users (e.g., users may 'grow out' of certain movies); items (e.g., a movie's special effects may become dated over time); or the *zeitgeist* of the entire community may shift over time.

177

- Temporal dynamics exist at multiple scales, for example, when modeling heart-rate data (sec. 7.8), dynamics can be short-term (e.g., a user running uphill), medium-term (e.g., a user getting tired) or long-term (e.g., a user becoming more fit).
- In addition to short- and long-term dynamics, dynamics can also be periodic (e.g. weekly or seasonal trends), or prone to bursts and outliers (e.g., purchases around a major holiday).

Our main focus in this chapter is to explore a wide variety of (personalized) models for temporally evolving data. As we will see, dynamics such as those above require carefully designed models (rather than simply including a temporal feature in a general-purpose model). As such, we focus on understanding the overall process and design considerations when building personalized models with temporal dynamics.

7.1 Introduction to Regression with Time Series

Before investigating more sophisticated models of temporal and sequential data, it is instructive to consider how much progress can be made with the techniques we have already developed.

To do so, we will consider developing predictors that estimate the next value in a sequence (or the next several values). In the simplest case, we are given a sequence of observations $y = \{y_1 \ldots y_n\}$, from which we would like to predict the next value (y_{n+1}). For example, one might want to estimate website traffic on the basis of historical traffic patterns.

To solve such a problem using a regression approach (or a classification approach for a binary outcome), we can imagine constructing features based on the previous observations ($\{y_1 \ldots y_n\}$) in order to predict the next one. Presumably, once we observe the true value of y_{n+1}, we would like to predict y_{n+2}, and so forth. Note that this blurs the line somewhat between 'features' and 'labels,' since the label for one prediction becomes a feature for the next.

Autoregression: This procedure is known as *autoregression* (referring to the fact that we are regressing on the same data that was used for prediction). As usual, we are typically interested in defining our regressor (or classifier) such that it minimizes some error between the predictions and the true values. That is, we want to define a predictor $f(y_1 \ldots y_n)$ that estimates the next value (y_{n+1}) in the sequence so as to minimize (e.g.) a MSE:

$$\frac{1}{n} \sum_{i=1}^{n} (f(y_1 \ldots y_i) - y_{i+1})^2. \tag{7.1}$$

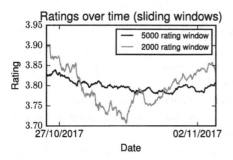

Figure 7.1 Moving-average plots of ~1 week of *Goodreads* fantasy novel ratings. Although not particularly effective as predictors, moving averages can be used to plot data and summarize overall trends.

Trivially, we might imagine several naive techniques for estimating the next value in a sequence, for example, we could predict the next value as a weighted sum of previous values:

$$\text{moving average:} \quad f(y_1 \ldots y_n) = \frac{1}{K} \sum_{k=0}^{K-1} y_{n-k} \tag{7.2}$$

$$\text{weighted moving average:} \quad f(y_1 \ldots y_n) = \frac{\sum_{k=0}^{K-1} (K-k) \cdot y_{n-k}}{\sum_{k=1}^{K} k}. \tag{7.3}$$

Although simple, one can imagine how these averages could potentially be better predictors than always predicting the next value to be equal to the previous one. These types of trivial predictors can also be used to plot trends in noisy data (fig. 7.1); averages over larger intervals (i.e., larger values of K) will produce smoother summaries of the data. Such averages can be efficiently computed for successive values via a dynamic programming solution; code to generate the plots in Figure 7.1 is presented below:

```
1   xSum = sum(x[:wSize]) # Given data x and y to plot, and a
        window size wSize
2   ySum = sum(y[:wSize]) # Sum of first wSize values
3   xSliding = []
4   ySliding = []
5
6   for i in range(wSize,len(x)-1):
7       xSum += x[i] - x[i-wSize] # Strip off oldest value and
            add newest one
8       ySum += y[i] - y[i-wSize]
9       xSliding.append(xSum / wSize)
10      ySliding.append(ySum / wSize)
```

The two trivial strategies above are heuristics for predicting the next value, capturing the intuition that it should be similar to recently observed values (eq. (7.2)), and possibly that more recent values should be more predictive than less recent ones (eq. (7.3)). However, a better strategy might be to *learn* which of the recent values are the most predictive, that is,

$$f(y_i \ldots y_n) = \sum_{k=0}^{K-1} \theta_k y_{n-k}. \qquad (7.4)$$

The values θ_k now determine which of the previous k values are most related to the next one. For example, in periodic data (e.g., network traffic, seasonal purchases), the most predictive values may include recent observations, observations from the same day last week, observations from the same day in the previous month, and so on.

For example, training a simple autoregressive model on a dataset of hourly measurements of bike rentals in the Bay Area[1] yields the following model:

$$y_n = \begin{aligned} & 0.471 y_{n-1} \\ & - 0.284 y_{n-2} \\ & + 0.106 y_{n-3} \\ & + 0.014 y_{n-4} \\ & - 0.021 y_{n-5} \\ & + 0.175 y_{n-24} \\ & + 0.540 y_{n-24 \times 7} \end{aligned} \qquad (7.5)$$

Here we see that the two most predictive observations are those from the previous hour (y_{n-1}) and from exactly one week ago ($y_{n-24 \times 7}$). Observe that we did not include *every* previous observation up to 24×7 hours ago as a feature, rather we only included those previous observations that we expected to be predictive.

Note that although the solution in Equation (7.4) uses *only* previous values in the sequence, one can of course include other features associated with the current timepoint or previous values, just like in a normal regression model.

Although a simple approach to regression and classification of time series data, the basic idea behind autoregression (i.e., to use previous observations to predict future values in a sequence) will reappear in many of the more complex models we develop, especially as we develop sequential models in Sections 7.5 and 7.6.

7.2 Temporal Dynamics in Recommender Systems

Several attempts have been made to improve recommendations by incorporating temporal dynamics. There are countless reasons why preferences, purchases, or interactions may change over time, or more simply why knowing the current timestamp may help us to more accurately predict the next

---

[1] Each observation y_h is a measurement of how many trips were taken during hour h.

interaction. Consider, for example, the following scenarios which could cause changes in movie ratings or interactions over time:

(i) Users who favor special effects may give lower ratings as a movie's special effects become dated.

(ii) Users may give higher ratings to older movies, for example, due to feelings of nostalgia.

(iii) Alternately, ratings of older movies may represent a biased sample of items that users had explicitly searched for (versus newer items which a user selected due to their being surfaced on a landing page).

(iv) A mundane change to a user interface, such as modifying the tool-tip text associated with a certain rating, may alter the rating distribution.

(v) A family member may borrow a user's account, and temporarily consume movies quite different from the account's typical activities.

(vi) Users may binge-watch a series, dominating their interaction patterns for a short period.

(vii) Action blockbusters may be more favored during summer (or Christmas movies during Christmas).

(viii) Users may want to consume (or avoid) content very similar to what they have previously interacted with.

(ix) Users may gradually develop an appreciation for certain characteristics of a movie as they consume more content from that genre.

(x) Users may be anchored by external forces, that is, the *zeitgeist* of what is currently popular in their community.

The above dynamics are quite varied in their sources and scale: Effects (i) and (ii) are gradual and long-term; (iii) and (iv) owe to vagaries of a changing user interface; (v) and (vi) are 'bursty' or short-term; (vii) is seasonal; (viii) is sequential; (ix) owes to user growth; and (x) is due to a changing community. One can imagine many other sources, especially in different settings subject to social dynamics, price variability, fashion, and so on. As we will see, understanding such dynamics is often key to making successful recommendations. Some may scarcely seem like 'temporal dynamics' at all: for example, a change to the user interface has little to do with user or item evolution. Nevertheless, we will argue that modeling even these trivial or mundane dynamics proves critical in order to disentangle them from the 'real' personalization dynamics in the data.

7.2.1 Methods for Temporal Recommendation

Methods for temporal recommendation fall broadly into two classes. The first make use of the actual *timestamps* of events. Each interaction (u, i) is augmented with a timestamp (u, i, t), and the goal is to understand how ratings $r_{u,i,t}$ vary over time. That is, our goal is to extend models such as the one in Section 5.1 (eq. (5.10)) so that parameters vary as a function of time, for example,

$$r_{u,i,t} = \alpha(t) + \beta_u(t) + \beta_i(t) + \gamma_u(t) \cdot \gamma_i(t). \qquad (7.6)$$

Modeling temporal dynamics in this way is effective at capturing long-term shifts of community preferences over time. Such a model can also capture short-term or 'bursty' dynamics, such as purchase patterns being affected by external events, or periodic events, such as purchases being higher at a particular time of day, day of week, or season.

A second class of methods discards the specific timestamps, but preserves only the *sequence* (or order) of events. Thus the goal is generally to predict the next action as a function of the previous one, that is,

p(user u interacts with item i | they previously interacted with item j). (7.7)

This type of model makes the assumption that the important temporal information is captured in the *context* provided by the most recent event. This is useful in highly contextual settings, such as predicting the next song a user will listen to, or other items they will place in their basket, and so on. In such settings knowing the most recent action (or most recent few actions) is more informative than knowing the specific timestamp.

These two classes of model are quite orthogonal, both in terms of the settings where they are effective, as well as the techniques involved. Below we will explore both settings via several case studies. First we will explore parametric temporal models (as in eq. (7.6)) through the example of the *Netflix Prize*, where temporal dynamics are carefully modeled to capture a wide variety of application-specific dynamics. We explore sequential models (as in eq. (7.7)) in Section 7.5 via several examples, starting with online shopping scenarios; these settings tend to be highly contextual, where the context of recent activities is often more informative than long-term historical activities.

Later, we will introduce *recurrent networks* as general-purpose models of sequence data (sec. 7.6), and as a potential approach to capture complex dynamics in evolving interaction sequences. Such models have the potential to overcome the limitations of traditional sequential models by learning complex semantics that persist over many steps. Such models (and variants based on different sequential architectures) arguably represent the current state-of-the-art for general purpose recommendation.

7.2.2 Case Study: Temporal Recommendation and the *Netflix Prize*

Careful modeling of temporal dynamics was one of the key features characterizing the strongest solutions to the *Netflix Prize* (which we described at the beginning of chap. 5). Several of the ideas that proved effective for modeling temporal dynamics on *Netflix* specifically are covered in Koren (2009) ('Collaborative Filtering with Temporal Dynamics'), which we summarize here.

As a motivating example, consider the two plots shown in Figure 7.2. At top, we see ratings over time averaged across weekly bins. We see several points where ratings appear to increase suddenly, followed by plateaus of relatively stable ratings; for example, at around week 210, average ratings appear to jump from around 3.5 stars to 3.6 stars.

Such long-term, population-level changes could owe to several explanations. Changes in rating patterns could be due to a changing user base, or from certain movies being added to *Netflix*; such changes could be due to world events exogenous to *Netflix*. Or, the change could owe to a factor as simple as a change in *Netflix*'s User Interface (UI), causing users to rate movies differently.

The bottom plot in Figure 7.2 shows another temporal trend, demonstrating that individual movies receive higher ratings the longer they have been available on *Netflix*. Again, such trends could be due to a variety of factors: users may be favorably biased toward older movies (e.g., by nostalgia); or again it could be a function of the UI: a user who specifically sought out an older movie may view it more favorably than a user who had discovered the same movie from the front page.

Whatever the underlying cause of these trends, they account for significant variability in the observed ratings. And as such, we should model these dynamics to predict ratings more accurately. Naively, one might simply discard (e.g.) older data that does not correspond to current rating trends. But, a more effective model would attempt to account for the differences between newer and older data, while learning from both.

To model the kinds of long term trends captured in Figure 7.2, Koren (2009) first focus only on temporally evolving bias terms, that is,

$$b_{u,i}(t) = \alpha + \beta_u(t) + \beta_i(t). \tag{7.8}$$

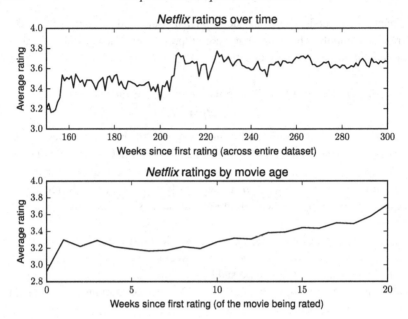

Figure 7.2 Temporal dynamics on *Netflix*. The top plot shows ratings averaged across each week over the lifetime of the dataset; the bottom plot shows how ratings change for newly introduced movies, showing that ratings gradually increase during the first few weeks the movie is on *Netflix*. These plots reveal a combination of sudden and gradual trends in movie ratings over time.

Starting with item biases, one can capture long-term, gradual variation simply by having different bias terms for different periods, that is,

$$\beta_i(t) = \beta_i + \beta_{i,\text{bin}(t)}. \tag{7.9}$$

Koren (2009) suggest ~ 30 bins corresponding to about 10 weeks each in the case of the *Netflix* data.

This basic idea of separating bias terms into bins could likewise be applied to capture periodic trends, much like we encoded periodic terms in Section 2.3.4. Here the bias term would again take the form of several bins:

$$\beta_i(t) = \beta_i + \beta_{i,\text{bin}(t)} + \beta_{i,\text{period}(t)}, \tag{7.10}$$

where period(t) could represent periodic effects at the level of different days of the week, or months of the year (etc.).

The above ideas are effective for modeling long-term and periodic dynamics, but are quite expensive: for example, the model in Equation (7.9) requires an additional 30 parameters *per item*; this is affordable for items on *Netflix* since the average item has over 5,000 ratings (100 million ratings of 17,770 titles).

However this would likely not be possible for users, as the average user has only around 200 ratings. Thus one needs a way of parameterizing user temporal dynamics that is considerably cheaper (i.e., involves fewer parameters).

A solution suggested in Koren (2009) is to use an 'expressive deviation' term for each user:

$$\mathrm{dev}_u(t) = \underbrace{\mathrm{sign}(t - t_u)}_{\text{before } (-1) \text{ or after } (1) \text{ the mean date}} \cdot |t - t_u|^x. \tag{7.11}$$

The term t_u represents the mean date amongst a particular user u's ratings, so that the term $(t - t_u)$ represents whether a particular point in time t is before or after the midpoint of the user's rating lifetime. The expressive deviation term is depicted in Figure 7.3; the exponent of 0.4 was found to work well on *Netflix* data. The deviation term augments the user bias term via a user-specific scaling term α_u, essentially controlling how strongly the deviation term applies to a specific user:

$$\beta_u(t) = \beta_u + \alpha_u \cdot \mathrm{dev}_u(t), \tag{7.12}$$

for example, a negative value of α_u would mean the user's ratings trend down over time, whereas a value $\alpha_u \simeq 0$ would mean that the user's overall bias is not subject to temporal variation. A similar strategy can also be used to capture variation at the level of individual latent dimensions, for example,

$$\gamma_{u,k}(t) = \gamma_{u,k} + \alpha_{u,k} \cdot \mathrm{dev}_u(t) + \gamma_{u,k,t}. \tag{7.13}$$

Note that the deviation terms in Equations (7.12) and (7.13) add only a single term per user (eq. (7.12)) or a single term per factor (eq. (7.13)). The final term $\gamma_{u,k,t}$ in Equation (7.13) (a temporally evolving term applied to a specific factor for a specific user) models highly local preference dynamics and can be used to model (e.g.) day-specific variability; this term is however highly expensive (in terms of the number of parameters introduced) so may only be feasible for some users.

When combined with the carefully chosen deviation term of Equation (7.11) this allows the model to capture quite complex dynamics while adding only a modest number of parameters; this basic design philosophy (a carefully-designed parametric model that costs only a small number of parameters) will prove a common theme when designing temporal models (sec. 7.2.3).

While the expressive deviation term is effective for users who have few interactions, for users who have more it can be useful to fit a more complex model. To do so, a spline function can be used to model gradual shifts in user biases. A spline function smoothly interpolates between a series of control points via the following function:

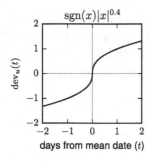

Figure 7.3 Expressive deviation term from Koren (2009)

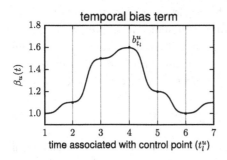

Figure 7.4 Spline interpolation of temporally evolving user bias

$$\beta_u(t) = \beta_u + \frac{\sum_{l=1}^{k_u} e^{\gamma|t-t_l^u|} b_{t_l}^u}{\sum_{l=1}^{k_u} e^{-\gamma|t-t_l^u|}}. \tag{7.14}$$

Here k_u is the number of control points for user u (which grows with the number of ratings that user has entered); t^u is a series of uniformly spaced time-points for each user; and $b_{t_l}^u$ is the bias associated with each control point. This type of interpolation is depicted in Figure 7.4.

The above term is a reasonably flexible way to capture gradual drift in user preferences, though still cannot handle sudden changes. Koren (2009) address this with a 'per day' user bias $\beta_{u,t}$, which can be useful for particular days in which users have a lot of activity. Note that such a bias is unlikely to be helpful when predicting future events; instead, by modeling outliers in this way, the model can essentially learn to 'ignore' events that are not useful for prediction. This too is a common design principle when building temporal models: the goal is not so much to forecast *future* trends but rather to adjust and account for *past* events appropriately.

The above ideas capture the essential components covered in Koren (2009); their work also includes an exploratory study of several alternative modeling approaches, including incorporating temporal dynamics into neighborhood-based models like those of Chapter 4.

7.2.3 What Can *Netflix* Teach Us about Temporal Models?

The model developed in the above case study involved several decisions that are quite specific to *Netflix*, and indeed the model was designed with the explicit goal of achieving strong performance on a single dataset. As such, many of the specific choices (such as the specific parametric form of the expressive deviation term) may not generalize to other settings. Nevertheless, there are several important lessons in the above study that apply generally when developing temporal models of user behavior:

- Successful solutions to the *Netflix Prize* highlighted the critical importance of temporal dynamics in recommendation settings. While the approaches we explored in Section 7.2.2 are quite *Netflix*-specific, they highlight a general philosophy followed when building temporal models: temporal models tend to be carefully designed around the dynamics of specific datasets and applications.
- One reason for the proliferation of many different hand-crafted temporal models is that temporal models are *expensive* in terms of the number of parameters required. As such a main focus when building temporal models is that of model *parsimony*: to prevent the parameter space from exploding, one must carefully choose models that capture the desired dynamics with as few parameters as possible.
- Temporal dynamics may range from 'lofty' concepts such as users becoming nostalgic toward older movies, to more mundane sources of variation, such as an overall shift in average ratings across the community. Both are important to model as both explain variance in the data: untangling even mundane dynamics is a critical step toward extracting meaningful personalization signals.
- Some specific lessons from *Netflix* generalize quite well, especially the importance placed on temporally evolving bias terms: the vast majority of temporal variation often owes to shifts in item popularity, user activity (etc.), and can be captured via evolving β_u or β_i; temporally evolving latent factors (γ_u or γ_i) play less of a role, or otherwise are simply too expensive to model.

Finally, we highlight that our goal in developing temporal models is typically not to *forecast* long-term trends. For example, our model of opinion dynamics on *Netflix* tells us nothing about what will be popular next year. Rather the goal is typically to account for discrepancies across different time periods so that interactions across time can be meaningfully compared. The resulting model thus gives a more accurate sense of *current* rating dynamics, if not future trends. See also Bell and Koren (2007) for further discussion.

Table 7.1 *Comparison of temporally aware recommendation techniques.*
References: Ding and Li (2005); Koren (2009); McAuley and Leskovec
(2013b); Xiang et al. (2010).

Ref.	Temporal Signal	Description
K09	Various	Uses a variety of parameteric functions and temporal bins, mostly to capture gradual drift in item biases and preferences (sec. 7.2.2).
DL05	Recency	Recent interactions are weighted more highly when determining relatedness against historical interactions (sec. 7.3.1).
X10	Sessions	Interactions within the same *session* are used as an additional signal of relatedness among items (sec. 7.3.2).
M13	Acquired tastes	Users acquire tastes toward certain items due to repeated exposure to related items (sec. 7.3.3).

7.3 Other Approaches to Temporal Dynamics

Our case study of temporal dynamics on *Netflix* demonstrated the general approach of building temporal models by carefully hand-crafting model components to account for the dynamics in a particular dataset or setting. Naturally, temporal dynamics can vary widely in other settings, demanding different modeling approaches. Below we outline a few of the main categories of temporal models and present a few specific examples which we summarize in Table 7.1.

7.3.1 Long-Term Dynamics of Opinions

Other than the methods we discussed above for temporal recommendation on *Netflix*, several papers studied the notion of gradually evolving concepts within the context of preferences and opinions.

Early works that deal with temporal dynamics explore the notion of *concept drift* (Tsymbal, 2004; Widmer and Kubat, 1996); early works on this topic are concerned with systems for classification in settings with temporally evolving data. Simple approaches consist of (e.g.) taking only a *window* of recent examples during training (much like we saw in fig. 7.1). More sophisticated approaches allow the context window size to adapt based on how 'stable' a particular concept is; or to reuse concepts that recur periodically; or to distinguish drifting concepts from noise. Models based on these ideas, along with theoretical results, are discussed in Widmer and Kubat (1996), among others.

Among temporal techniques for recommendation, early approaches incorporate temporal factors into heuristic techniques, such as the model from Equation (4.20). For example, in Ding and Li (2005), the basic idea is to weight related items in Equation (4.20) so that recent interactions are weighted more highly:

$$r(u, i) = \frac{\sum_{j \in I_u} R_{u,j} \cdot \text{Sim}(i, j) \cdot f(t_{u,j})}{\sum_{j \in I_u} \text{Sim}(i, j) \cdot f(t_{u,j})}. \qquad (7.15)$$

Here $t_{u,j}$ is the timestamp associated with the rating $R_{u,j}$, and $f(t_{u,j})$ is a monotone function of the timestamp. For example, relevance can decay exponentially for older items:

$$f(t) = e^{-\lambda \cdot t}. \qquad (7.16)$$

Godes and Silva (2012), while less focused on predictive modeling, attempt to characterize the long-term dynamics of opinions through online reviews. They studied book reviews on *Amazon*. Like our study of *Netflix* data (especially fig. 7.2), they study how ratings evolve over time, as well as how they evolve in terms of the age of a book (time since first review). The dynamics are quite different from those on *Netflix*, where both show a *decreasing* trend over time (in contrast to the 'nostalgia' effect we observed in fig. 7.2).

In addition to a difference in domain (books versus movies), *online reviews* potentially have quite different dynamics than ratings on *Netflix*, which Godes and Silva (2012) discuss in detail. For example, given that users see each other's reviews, they may be guided by social effects, for example, users may enter a review only if they perceive that it will affect the average rating (Wu and Huberman, 2008). They also discuss the importance of *self-selection*, where users who assign more value to a product tend to purchase it earlier (and thus are responsible for more positive early reviews) (Li and Hitt, 2008). Ultimately Godes and Silva (2012) argue that more complex dynamics may be at play once we appropriately control for these effects; ultimately their study again reveals that temporal dynamics can differ drastically as a function of a particular setting or dataset.

7.3.2 Short-Term Dynamics and Session-Based Recommendation

Most of the models of temporal dynamics we have discussed so far capture notions such as gradual drift, where models used a small number of parameters to describe gradually evolving parametric functions (fig. 7.3), sequential bins spanning several months (eq. (7.9)), or periodic effects (eq. (7.10)). While effective in the settings they were designed for, such models are limited to capturing broad, global trends. We touched briefly on models of short-term dynamics using per-day biases (Koren, 2009), though such terms are essentially forms of outlier detection.

Another pattern of short-term temporal variation arises due to users' specific context within an interaction *session*. Sessions may have a specific, narrow

users: items: sessions:

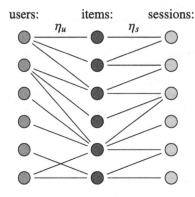

Figure 7.5 Session-based temporal graph (Xiang et al., 2010). Each session describes a sequence of interactions from a specific user.

focus that can be useful to predict future interactions in the short term, but which differ from users' overall patterns and can be discarded in the long term. 'Sessions' can be extracted in various ways, though are typically based on some simple heuristic such as setting session boundaries based on a threshold between successive interaction timestamps.

Xiang et al. (2010) attempt to combine models of long- and short-term dynamics by incorporating user sessions. Their model is based on random walk-based methods similar to those we studied in Section 4.4. Here, 'sessions' simply become additional nodes in the interaction graph, as in Figure 7.5. Edges now connect user-to-item interactions and session-to-item interactions. In terms of our random walk model, this means there are two mechanisms for information to propagate between related items. User-to-item and session-to-item terms are associated with different interaction weights η_u and η_s; roughly speaking, these control the relative importance of long-term user-level dynamics and short-term session-level dynamics. The model can also be tuned in terms of the granularity at which interactions are divided into sessions (with shorter sessions capturing more local dynamics). Xiang et al. (2010) show the value of this notion of short-term dynamics on user bookmark data (from *CiteULike* and *Delicious*).

We revisit session-based recommenders in more depth in Section 7.4 and Section 7.7 when we explore methods based on Markov chains and recurrent networks. Like Xiang et al. (2010), such models have a general goal of combining local dynamics from recent interactions with longer-term features extracted from users' interaction histories.

7.3.3 User-Level Temporal Evolution

Most of the sources of temporal dynamics we have explored so far owe to shifting properties of *items* (or how items are perceived over time, due to, e.g., nostalgia), or gradual shifts that apply to the community as a whole (including trivial dynamics such as a change in the user interface, which do not apply specifically to any user or item). Temporal drift could likewise occur at the level of individual users, for example, due to a user gradually gaining more experience with a certain type of item.

McAuley and Leskovec (2013b) sought to model this notion of 'acquired tastes' in recommendation datasets. They noted that in many settings, a user's preference toward a certain type of item may change due to the very act of consuming items of that type. This setting was motivated by data of beer and wine reviews (including the same datasets we have been using in examples throughout this book), though applies in various other settings: for example, a user will likely have a different opinion of *Seven Samurai* depending on whether it is the first or the fiftieth drama they've watched.

Note that this notion of temporal dynamics is not attached to an item, nor is it attached to the community as a whole (i.e., it is not a function of the precise timestamp); rather it is a function of a specific user's *expertise* at the time of their rating. McAuley and Leskovec (2013b) capture this type of dynamic by fitting two variables: γ_u^E captures user latent factors for users at different experience levels (where E belongs to a discrete set, for example, $E \in \{1 \ldots 5\}$). E is then fit for each user as a function of time (i.e., $E(u, t)$), with an additional constraint that $E(u, t) > E(u, t') \rightarrow t > t'$, that is, a user's 'experience level' must be non-decreasing over time.[2]

In addition to improving performance on certain datasets where acquired tastes play a key role, McAuley and Leskovec (2013b) argue that such a model can also be used to understand which specific types of items require expertise or experience for users to fully appreciate. Examples include IPAs (India Pale Ales), which users tend to gradually develop a preference toward, versus so-called adjunct lagers (e.g., *Bud Light*), which experienced users tend to dislike.

7.4 Personalized Markov Chains

The temporal models we saw in Section 7.2 directly modeled (or extracted features from) the *timestamps* associated with each interaction. We showed how features extracted from timestamps could include factors like seasonality, the day of the week, or nostalgia effects (etc.) on the *Netflix* dataset, and later we will revisit such models in the context of the temporal dynamics of fashion (sec. 9.2.1).

---

[2] This constraint forces the model to learn parameters resembling experience levels, in the sense that the model is forced to discover systematic 'stages' through which many users progress in common.

However in many settings, the best predictor of what a user will do next is simply what they did *last*. For example, if you click on a winter coat, then you might be interested in other winter clothing, regardless of whether those items are currently in-season.

Even trivial models such as the item-to-item recommenders which we saw in Section 4.3 implicitly made this assumption. For example, recommendations such as 'people who viewed X also viewed Y' can be made based purely on the context of what is currently being viewed; the user's historical interactions— or their preferences—are not considered. In contrast the approaches we explore below generally try to combine both personal and contextual factors.

Markov Chains: The assumption described above—that the next action is conditionally independent[3] of the interaction history given the previous action—describes exactly the setting of a *Markov Chain*. Formally, given a sequence of interactions (among a discrete set of items $i \in I$) $i^{(1)} \ldots i^{(t)}$, a Markov Chain assumes that the probability of the next interaction given the history can be written purely in terms of the previous interaction:

$$p(i^{(t+1)} = i \mid i^{(t)} \ldots i^{(1)}) = p(i^{(t+1)} = i \mid i^{(t)}). \tag{7.17}$$

Personalized Markov Chains generalize Equation (7.17) by allowing the probability of the next item to depend on both the previous item and the identity of the user u. That is, for a given user we have:

$$p(i_u^{(t+1)} = i \mid i_u^{(t)} \ldots i_u^{(1)}) = p(i_u^{(t+1)} = i \mid i_u^{(t)}). \tag{7.18}$$

What this means in practice is that when predicting a user's next action, our prediction should be a function of their previous action as well as their preference dimensions. Most of the time we can ignore the formalism of Markov Chains and more simply state that we are trying to fit a function of the form

$$f(\overbrace{u, i}^{\text{score associated with the next interaction}} \mid \underbrace{i_u^{(t-1)}}_{\text{given the user's previous interaction}}). \tag{7.19}$$

---

[3] Two variables a and b are said to be *conditionally independent* given a third variable c if $p(a, b|c) = p(a|c)p(b|c)$. Essentially c 'explains' any dependence a and b. In the case of Markov Chains, this assumption implies that the most recent event is sufficient to explain the next action's dependence on the history.

That is, where our previous models took a user and item as inputs (i.e., $f(u, i)$), or a user, item, and timestamp ($f(u, i, t)$), we now wish to model a user, an item, and the user's previous interaction. We might fit this function via a rating estimation framework (as in sec. 5.1), or a personalized ranking framework (as in sec. 5.2.2), and so on.

The key challenge in fitting models of the form in Equation (7.19) is that techniques like matrix factorization can no longer be straightforwardly applied. Whereas we previously modeled user/item interactions by factorizing a $U \times I$ matrix we must now factorize a $U \times I \times I$ *tensor* (i.e., interactions between the user, the item, and the previous item).

We will explore this idea by investigating specific implementations from case studies in the following section.

7.5 Case Studies: Markov-Chain Models for Recommendation

Below we describe various attempts to extend latent factor recommendation approaches to incorporate signals from the previous item. The main challenges involved include handling the large state space of interactions between users, items, and previous items; understanding the semantics that describe sequential relationships among items; and incorporating sequential dynamics with additional signals such as social information.

The models covered in this section are summarized in Table 7.2.

7.5.1 Factorized Personalized Markov Chains

An early paper that used Markov Chains for personalized recommendation was *Factorizing Personalized Markov Chains for Next-Basket Recommendation* (Rendle et al., 2010). Factorized Personalized Markov Chains (FPMC for short) predict what items a user will purchase next, based on the items in their previous basket; customer basket data from *Rossmann* (a German drugstore) was used to train and evaluate the model.

The basic premise of FPMC is that the contents of the previous basket should help to predict the contents of the next one, but also that the basket contents should be personalized to the user. This is achieved by fitting a function of the form

$$f(i|u, j), \tag{7.20}$$

Table 7.2 *Markov-chain models for personalized recommendation.*
References: Cai et al. (2017); Chen et al. (2012); Feng et al. (2015); He et al.
(2017a); Rendle et al. (2010).

Ref.	Method	Description
R10	Factorized Personalized Markov Chains (FPMC)	The next item should be compatible with the user, as well as the previous item (sec. 7.5.1).
C17	Socially Aware Personalized Markov Chains (SPMC)	Extends FPMC, incorporating a social term which states that the next item should be similar to our *friends'* previous items (sec. 7.5.2).
F15	Personalized Ranking Metric Embedding (PRME)	Similar to FPMC, but measures compatibility via similarity in a metric space (sec. 7.5.3).
C12	Factorized Markov Embeddings (FME)	Also uses a metric space, though items can have distinct 'start' and 'end' points (sec. 7.5.3).
H17	Translation-based Recommendation	Replaces the fixed user embedding γ_u with a translation operation in latent item space (sec. 7.5.4).

where u is a user, i is a potential item to be recommended, and j is an item from the user's previous basket.[4]

The paper discusses the difficulty of modeling sparse interactions of the form in Equation (7.20), and explains how this might be addressed with tensor decomposition. The decomposition used is essentially a generalization of the matrix factorization schemes we saw in Chapter 5, where $f(i|u, j)$ decomposes into a series of pairwise factors:

$$f(i|u, j) = \underbrace{\gamma_u^{(ui)} \cdot \gamma_i^{(iu)}}_{f(i|u)} + \underbrace{\gamma_i^{(ij)} \cdot \gamma_j^{(ji)}}_{f(i|j)} + \underbrace{\gamma_u^{(uj)} \cdot \gamma_j^{(ju)}}_{f(u,j)}. \qquad (7.21)$$

The three terms above denote the user's compatibility with the next item ($\gamma_u^{(ui)} \cdot \gamma_i^{(iu)}$), the next item's compatibility with the previous item ($\gamma_i^{(ij)} \cdot \gamma_j^{(ji)}$), and the user's compatibility with the previous item ($\gamma_u^{(uj)} \cdot \gamma_j^{(ju)}$). In practice, the latter expression cancels out when optimizing the model using a BPR-like framework (as we see in eq. (7.23), below), which is perhaps intuitive as the expression does not include the candidate item i; as such the factorization can be rewritten

---

[4] Although the original paper uses basket data, baskets are mostly a complication needed to handle their specific dataset. It is more straightforward to present the work by simply considering item sequences (which is how the method is often adopted by other papers). Where we write a term for a previous item, in Rendle et al. (2010) that expression would usually be replaced by a sum over items in the previous basket.

$$f(i|u, j) = \overbrace{\gamma_u^{(ui)} \cdot \gamma_i^{(iu)}}^{\text{user's compatibility with the next item}} + \underbrace{\gamma_i^{(ij)} \cdot \gamma_j^{(ji)}}_{\text{next item's compatibility with the previous item}}. \tag{7.22}$$

Intuitively, this factorization simply states that the next item should be compatible with both the user and the previous item consumed. Note that (as indicated by superscripts), item parameters are not shared between the terms $\gamma^{(ui)}$, $\gamma^{(iu)}$, $\gamma^{(ij)}$, $\gamma^{(ji)}$, that is, we use separate sets of factors when modeling how an item interacts with a user vs. another item.

Ultimately, the model is optimized using a BPR-like framework (sec. 5.2.2), that is, using a contrastive loss of the form

$$\sigma(f(i|u, j) - f(i'|u, j)), \tag{7.23}$$

where i' is a sampled negative item that the user did not consume.

Experiments compare two variants of FPMC, which exclude either the sequential or the personal term. That is, they model $f(i|u) = \gamma_u \cdot \gamma_i$ or $f(i|j) = \gamma_i \cdot \gamma_j$. Excluding the sequential term reduces the expression to regular matrix factorization (MF), as in Section 5.1. Excluding the personal term (which they term Factorized Markov Chains, or FMC), captures 'global' sequential dynamics that are common to all users. The experiments thus measure (albeit on a specific dataset) the extent to which future actions can be explained by the previous action, versus overall historical preferences.

Ultimately FPMC outperforms both variants, though interestingly FMC and MF outperform each other under different conditions. Importantly, FMC is particularly effective in *sparse* settings (i.e., few interactions per user/item) whereas MF works better on dense data.

We note briefly that methods like factorization machines (chap. 6, sec. 6.1) can relatively straightforwardly be used to implement FPMC-like models: in addition to embedding user and item encodings, one can simply augment the representation to include the previous item. We leave this as an exercise (Exercise 7.2), though also show how to implement FPMC in *Tensorflow* in Section 7.5.5.

7.5.2 Socially Aware Sequential Recommendation

Just as we saw how Bayesian Personalized Ranking can be augmented by sampling signals from social interactions in Section 6.4.2, sequential models like FPMC can also be improved by leveraging social information.

Socially Aware Personalized Markov Chains (SPMC) (Cai et al., 2017) extend FPMC (and Social BPR) by merging both temporal and social signals.

The basic idea is to extend Equation (7.22) from FPMC based on the reasoning that the user's next item should be similar to those that their friends have recently consumed:

$$f(i|u, j) = \gamma_u^{(ui)} \cdot \gamma_i^{(iu)} + \gamma_i^{(ij)} \cdot \gamma_j^{(ji)} + |S|^{-\alpha} \sum_{(v,k)\in S} \overbrace{\sigma(\gamma_u^{(uv)} \cdot \gamma_v^{(uv)})}^{\text{similarity between } u \text{ and } v} \overbrace{(\gamma_i^{(ik)} \cdot \gamma_k^{(ik)})}^{\text{next item's compatibility with friend's previous item}}. \quad (7.24)$$

Here the set S consists of only the most recent interactions k by each of u's friends v. The first term inside the summation $\sigma(\gamma_u^{(uv)} \cdot \gamma_v^{(uv)})$ measures the similarity between u and v, so that we only consider the effect of social influence if u and v are sufficiently similar. The term $|S|^{-\alpha}$ normalizes the expression so that social influence does not saturate the other terms for users with a large number of friends. Note that there is no term $\gamma^{(vu)}$ or $\gamma^{(ki)}$ in Equation (7.24) (i.e., only one set of representations is learned, rather than asymmetric representations as in eq. (7.22)); this is done simply to reduce the number of model parameters. Cai et al. (2017) show that including both temporal and social terms improves predictive performance over FPMC and Social BPR.

7.5.3 Locality-Based Sequential Recommendation

In Section 5.5.1, we briefly suggested that different aggregation functions (besides the inner product) could be useful in various contexts. This proves to be the case in various sequential recommendation settings, where sequential actions follow some notion of *locality*.

In Feng et al. (2015), sequential recommendation schemes were studied in the setting of Point-of-Interest recommendation. In such a setting, the context of the previous action is particularly informative, since the following action is likely to be (geographically) close. We briefly touched upon this assumption when introducing location-based social networks in Chapter 6 (sec. 6.6.2).

If the actual semantics of the problem demand some notion of locality, then arguably similarity in the latent space should also be based on locality (rather than, say, an inner product).

The framework of Feng et al. (2015), *Personalized Ranking Metric Embedding* (PRME), models sequential compatibility using an expression of the form:

$$f(i|j) = -d(\gamma_i - \gamma_j)^2 = -\|\gamma_i - \gamma_j\|_2^2. \quad (7.25)$$

Note two differences between this model (PRME) and FPMC (sec. 7.5.1):

- The main difference is the use of a distance (actually a squared distance) function, so that sequential activities exhibit locality in the latent space.

- Unlike FPMC, which used separate latent spaces $\gamma^{(ij)}$ and $\gamma^{(ji)}$ for the next and previous item, PRME uses only a single latent space (which saves parameters).

Like FPMC, PRME also includes an expression encoding the compatibility between the user and the item (again using a distance function), and also trains the model using a BPR-like framework (i.e., including a negative item i' as in eq. (7.23)). Other specific details include an explicit feature encoding geographical distance (based on latitude and longitude), and a temporal feature which down-weights the influence of the sequential term if sequential events are temporally far apart.

Though the authors of PRME argue that Euclidean distance is a more natural way of comparing sequential items (and show that PRME outperforms FPMC for POI recommendation), it should be noted that whether one similarity function is 'better' than the other largely depends on the semantics of the specific problem and dataset.

Another paper makes use of a similar model for personalized playlist generation (Chen et al., 2012). Like PRME, their model (Factorized Markov Embeddings, or FME) notes that sequential songs in playlists tend to be highly localized, such that a metric embedding is possibly well-motivated. The compatibility function given a user u, song i, and previous song j takes the form

$$f(i|u, j) = -d(\gamma_i^{(\text{start})} - \gamma_j^{(\text{end})})^2 + \gamma_u \cdot \gamma_i'. \tag{7.26}$$

Note a few differences between FME and PRME:

- FME uses a separate embedding for the next song ($\gamma^{(\text{start})}$) and the previous song ($\gamma^{(\text{end})}$). The basic idea being that songs in playlists should not just be highly local, but should gradually 'transition' from one song to the next, so that the 'start point' of the next song in latent space should be similar to the 'end point' of the previous song (fig. 7.6).
- FME uses a combination of both a distance function (for compatibility with the previous item) and an inner product (for compatibility with the user) in Equation (7.26). Again, this demonstrates that the correct choice of compatibility function is highly dependent on problem semantics.

7.5.4 Translation-Based Recommendation

Like FME (sec. 7.5.3), a third class of models for sequential recommendation are based on the principle of translation.

He et al. (2017a) built recommender systems using principles adapted from knowledge-base completion. Several techniques for knowledge base

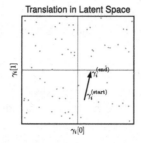

Figure 7.6 Some sequential models use the principle of translation to model sequential transitions between items

completion are based on the principle of learning low-dimensional embeddings that describe relationships among entities (Bordes et al., 2013; Lin et al., 2015; Wang et al., 2014). The basic idea is to represent both entities and relationships as vectors in a low-dimensional space, such that a relation vector encodes how to 'translate' between entities. For example, we might seek to learn vectors describing entities such as *'Alan Turing'* and *'England,'* such that given a vector describing the relation *'born in'* we should have

$$d(\overrightarrow{\text{Alan Turing}} + \overrightarrow{\text{born in}}, \overrightarrow{\text{England}}) \simeq 0, \qquad (7.27)$$

where d is a Euclidean distance.

Translation-based recommendation (He et al., 2017a) adapts this type of approach to personalized recommendation. Whereas for knowledge graph completion relations tell us how to traverse the space of entities, in a recommendation setting, *items* fulfil the role of entities, and *users* traverse the space of items. Then, given the previous item j and the next item i to be consumed in sequence,[5] we should have

$$d(\gamma_j + \gamma_u, \gamma_i) \simeq 0. \qquad (7.28)$$

Training such a model is quite similar to how we trained FME and PRME in Section 7.5.3: that is, we fit a compatibility function between a user, an item, and a previous item (much like eq. (7.26)):

$$f(i|u, j) = \beta_i - \|\gamma_j + \gamma_u - \gamma_i\|_2, \qquad (7.29)$$

where β_i is incorporated so that the method is capable of capturing overall item popularity as well as preferences. He et al. (2017a) further constrains

---

[5] In the original paper j is the *next* item and i is the previous, though we reverse the order to maintain notation across all methods.

item representations to live on a unit ball (i.e., $\|\gamma_i\|_2^2 = 1$), which was found to be effective in the knowledge graph completion settings above.

Conceptually, the above model corresponds to users following a 'trajectory' through their interactions over time (fig. 7.6). In principle, this ought to mean that related items (e.g., sequential songs in a playlist) should be aligned to form a chain of equally spaced items in the latent space. In practice, such complex dynamics are unlikely to emerge from the model; rather, like other temporal modeling approaches, the model benefits from its parsimony (i.e., it has much fewer parameters than other sequential models, due to the use of only a single latent space) but is still able to capture common sequential patterns even in sparse datasets.

7.5.5 FPMC in *Tensorflow*

Although several of the above models can be implemented via an appropriately designed factorization machine (Exercises 7.2 and 7.3), it is worth briefly describing how a sequential model might be implemented 'from scratch;' this will be useful when implementing variants that do not straightforwardly map to existing architectures (such as the factorization machine of sec. 6.1) or libraries.

Here we implement the Factorized Personalized Markov Chain (FPMC) method from Section 7.5.1, though the code can straightforwardly be adapted to implement other sequential methods discussed in Section 7.5.

We build our solution on top of our Bayesian Personalized Ranking implementation from Section 5.8.4. First, when parsing the data, we must be careful to process the timestamp:

```
1  for d in parse('goodreads_reviews_comics_graphic.json.gz'):
2      u = d['user_id']
3      i = d['book_id']
4      t = d['date_added'] # Raw timestamp string
5      r = d['rating']
6      dt = dateutil.parser.parse(t) # Structured timestamp
7      t = int(dt.timestamp()) # Integer timestamp
8      if not u in userIDs: userIDs[u] = len(userIDs)
9      if not i in itemIDs: itemIDs[i] = len(itemIDs)
10     interactions.append((t,u,i,r))
11     interactionsPerUser[u].append((t,i,r))
```

Note the use of the dateutil library to process the timestamp. The original timestamp in this dataset consists of raw strings (e.g., 'Wed Apr 03 10:10:41 - 0700 2013'); the operation dt = dateutil.parser.parse(t) converts this to a structured format; this can be used to extract features associated with the timestamp, for example, dt.weekday() reveals that this date is a Wednesday, which might be useful for extracting features for temporal models such as those in Section 2.3.4.[6] To build a sequential recommender, we are mainly interested in determining the *sequence order* of the interactions; to do so we call dt.timestamp(). For the date above this returns 1365009041, which represents the number of seconds since January 1, 1970 ('unix time'). Such a time representation, while seemingly fairly arbitrary, is useful when our goal is simply to sort observations chronologically, as we do when building sequential recommenders.

Next we sort each user's history by time, and augment our interaction data such that each interaction (u, i) includes the previous item j. We also add a 'dummy' item which acts as the previous item for the first observation:

```
12   itemIDs['dummy'] = len(itemIDs)
13   interactionsWithPrevious = []
14
15   for u in interactionsPerUser:
16       interactionsPerUser[u].sort()
17       lastItem = 'dummy'
18       for (t,i,r) in interactionsPerUser[u]:
19           interactionsWithPrevious.append((t,u,i,lastItem,r))
20           lastItem = i
```

Given these augmented interactions, we can modify the model from Section 5.8.4 to include the additional terms from Equation (7.22). Here we train in a BPR-like setting (i.e., including a sampled negative item k), though we could similarly adapt the model for rating prediction following code from Section 5.8.3. Omitting a few boilerplate elements, the model equation (eq. (7.23)) becomes:

```
21   gamma_ui = tf.nn.embedding_lookup(self.gammaUI, u)
22   gamma_iu = tf.nn.embedding_lookup(self.gammaIU, i)
23   gamma_ij = tf.nn.embedding_lookup(self.gammaIJ, i)
24   gamma_ji = tf.nn.embedding_lookup(self.gammaJI, j)
25   # (etc.)
26   x_uij = beta_i +\
27           tf.reduce_sum(tf.multiply(gamma_ui, gamma_iu), 1) +\
28           tf.reduce_sum(tf.multiply(gamma_ij, gamma_ji), 1)
29   x_ukj = beta_k +\
30           tf.reduce_sum(tf.multiply(gamma_uk, gamma_ku), 1) +\
31           tf.reduce_sum(tf.multiply(gamma_kj, gamma_jk), 1)
32   return -tf.reduce_mean(tf.math.log(tf.math.sigmoid(x_uij -
         x_ukj)))
```

The code above could be straightforwardly adapted to implement other sequential models, such as PRME (sec. 7.5.3) or translation-based recommendation (sec. 7.5.4).

---

[6] While fairly obvious in this instance, determining even such simple properties is difficult for certain date formats.

7.6 Recurrent Networks

A fundamental limitation of the Markov-Chain-based models we saw in Section 7.4 is that they have a very limited notion of 'memory,' due to the assumption that the next event is conditionally independent of all historical events, given the most recent observation. This assumption may be sufficient in certain scenarios, such as recommendation settings that are highly dependent on the context of the previously clicked item (e.g.). However, as we begin to model text data (chap. 8), or sequence data such as heart-rate logs (sec. 7.8), or more complex recommendation scenarios, we will need to handle longer-term semantics (such as grammatical structures in a sentence, or even an individual's level of 'fatigue' in a heart-rate trace).

Recurrent Neural Networks (RNNs) seek to achieve this notion of 'memory' by maintaining a 'hidden state' during each step.[7] The hidden state is a vector of latent variables that somehow capture the 'context' that the model needs to know to capture the long-term semantics of the problem. Formally, we can visualize the RNN as taking a sequence of inputs $(x_1 \dots x_N)$, and producing a sequence of outputs $(y_1 \dots y_N)$, and maintaining hidden states that update at each step $(h_1 \dots h_N)$. We might visualize this model as follows:

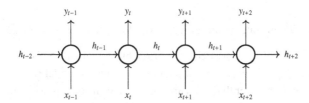

The RNN cell is now responsible for determining how the hidden state should change at each step, and what outputs should be generated.

More complex RNN models repeat this idea across multiple *layers*, so that RNN cells can be stacked, for example:

---

[7] Note that 'simpler' models attempt to accomplish the same goal within the framework of Markov–Chain-based models; see for example, Hidden Markov Models. However Recurrent Neural Networks are more typical of current practice and form the basis of models we develop later.

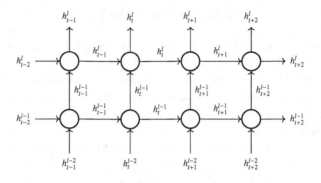

In this depiction (and in many treatments of the topic), the model is described only in terms of hidden states: the model receives an input, updates its hidden state, and passes this state to the next timestep and the next layer. The first layer may receive inputs (i.e., observed values x) while the last layer generates outputs (i.e., y).

When designing this cell, one might consider the types of dynamics required to model state transitions between successive steps:

- Based on the current hidden state, what output should be generated?
- How should the hidden state change as a function of the input that was just seen?
- What part of the hidden state should be preserved, and what part can be discarded?
- How can hidden state be preserved across long interaction sequences?

Below we describe one particular implementation of an RNN cell. Although there is nothing particularly sacred about the particular model we present, it is representative of the overall design approach, in terms of capturing the features described above.

7.6.1 The Long Short-Term Memory Model

The Long Short-Term Memory Model (Hochreiter and Schmidhuber, 1997) is a specific implementation of an RNN that has been popularized especially for use in text generation tasks, as we will discuss in Chapter 8.

A challenge in designing RNN cells as described above is how to encourage them to 'remember' state across long sequences. To achieve this, the LSTM cell (fig. 7.7) preserves the cell state (c in the equation below), mostly unmodified across steps. Other components are responsible for 'forgetting' part of the state (f), as a function of the current input and previous hidden state; updating

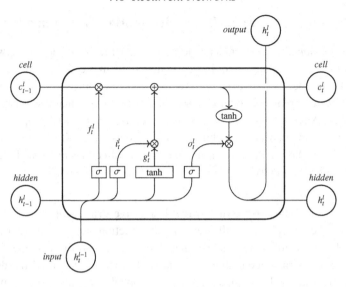

Figure 7.7 Visualization of an LSTM cell (eqs. (7.30) to (7.35))

the cell state (i and g); updating the hidden state (h); and determining what to output (o). Although not particularly relevant for the current discussion—the models discussed here could easily be replaced by different architectures—the specific form of these components in an LSTM cell is as follows:

$$f_t^l = \sigma(W_l^{(f)} \times [h_t^{l-1}; h_{t-1}^l]) \tag{7.30}$$

$$i_t^l = \sigma(W_l^{(i)} \times [h_t^{l-1}; h_{t-1}^l]) \tag{7.31}$$

$$o_t^l = \sigma(W_l^{(o)} \times [h_t^{l-1}; h_{t-1}^l]) \tag{7.32}$$

$$g_t^l = \tanh(W_l^{(g)} \times [h_t^{l-1}; h_{t-1}^l]) \tag{7.33}$$

$$c_t^l = g_t^l \times i_t^l + c_{t-1}^l \times f_t^l \tag{7.34}$$

$$h_t^l = \tanh(c_t^l) \times o_t^l. \tag{7.35}$$

Several variants of the above have been proposed to incorporate additional components, mostly consisting of specific differences to how the state is preserved and transformed among the equations above. It should be remarked though that the overall view of a 'cell,' in terms of inputs, outputs, and hidden states, is largely interchangeable across models in spite of differences in specific details.

7.7 Neural Network-Based Sequential Recommenders

Having developed a basic understanding of the structure of neural network-based models (including some 'basic' architectures in sec. 5.5.2 and recurrent networks in sec. 7.6), we now have the basic building blocks to understand how recurrent networks can be used to build personalized models of sequences. Although we will not present a full treatment of such approaches here (since some depend on techniques and models quite different from those covered in this book), here we outline the general directions explored by a few representative examples.

Relationship to Natural Language Processing

Many of the models we will study in this section are closely related to approaches used to model natural language. As we will discuss, the development of modern sequential recommenders has closely followed the development of state-of-the-art natural language models, ranging from recurrent networks (Hidasi et al., 2016), attention mechanisms (Li et al., 2017), self-attention (Kang and McAuley, 2018), and BERT-based models (Devlin et al., 2019).

The basic mechanism of applying natural language models to sequential data is fairly straightforward. In a natural language setting, documents are represented as sequences of discrete tokens (words); a model (such as that of sec. 7.6.1) might be trained to estimate the next word in a sequence. Likewise, in a recommendation setting, a user's sequence of actions can be represented as a sequence of discrete tokens (items). Via this analogy, state-of-the-art models from natural language can be fairly straightforwardly adapted to describe the dynamics of user interaction sequences. We will discuss this relationship more when designing models specifically for text in Chapter 8.

Conceptually, the appeal of neural network approaches to sequential modeling (and more broadly, the appeal of borrowing models from natural language) is that they allow models to capture complex *syntax* or *semantics* in sequential data. So far, when developing temporal and sequential recommenders we have mostly focused on either of (a) developing simple parametric functions to capture long-term dynamics, as we did in Section 7.2.2; or (b) modeling sequential dynamics using the context of previous interactions, following a Markov chain-like setup, as in Section 7.4. Both approaches have limitations: the former tends to require carefully hand-crafting models around specific dynamics, while the latter potentially captures only limited context (e.g., a single previous interaction). In principle, the techniques in this section aim to address these issues, by automatically uncovering both long- and short-term dynamics simultaneously, or potentially capturing complex interrelationships between items in a sequence.

'User-free' Sequential Recommendation

When introducing sequential models based on Markov Chains in Section 7.4, we argued that it was valuable to model *both* the compatibility between the user and the item, as well as the compatibility between adjacent items in a sequence. In short, both sources provide useful and complementary signals that each explain variation in users' activities.

However it is unclear whether this argument applies in the limit. Clearly, a single previous interaction does not provide the full context of a user's preferences; however, a model that includes *enough* historical interactions can possibly capture all of the necessary context without explicitly including any user term (we explored this idea a little when introducing FISM in sec. 5.3.2).

It is interesting to note that *none of the models we describe below learn explicit user representations*, relying instead on item representations plus a sufficient window of *context* to capture the dynamics of individual users. Doing so is conceptually appealing as an alternative to (e.g.) the cold-start models we discussed in Section 6.2: by eliminating the need for an explicit user term, we can quickly make effective recommendations by observing a few user actions, without needing to retrain the model (to fit user terms) or rely on side-information.

Such models fall somewhere in between the memory-based approaches we studied in Chapter 4 and model-based approaches we saw in Chapter 5: although item representations are learned from data, user representations must be captured implicitly by the model 'remembering' the context among their sequential actions.

The models covered in this section are summarized in Table 7.3.

7.7.1 Recurrent Network-Based Recommendation

An early paper to explore the use of recurrent networks for recommendation did so using the types of model we developed in Section 7.6.[8] Hidasi et al. (2016) explored the problem of *session-based* recommendation, where user interactions are divided into distinct 'sessions' (typically using some heuristic based on interaction timestamps). This setting is typical for recommenders

---

[8] Specifically they used a Gated Recurrent Unit, or GRU, though methodologically the approach is similar to the LSTM-based techniques we explored in Section 7.6.1.

Table 7.3 *Summary of deep-learning based sequential models. References:*
Hidasi et al. (2016); Kang and McAuley (2018); Li et al. (2017); Sun et al.
(2019).

Ref.	Method	Description
H15	Session-based Recommendation with RNNs	Item sequences are passed to a recurrent network; the network's hidden state is used to predict the next interaction (sec. 7.7.1).
L17	Neural Attentive Recommendation (NARM)	Combines an RNN (similar to that of Hidasi et al. (2016)) with an attention mechanism that operates on the sequence of network latent states in order to 'focus' on relevant interactions (sec. 7.7.2).
KM18	Self-Attentive Sequential Recommendation	Similar to NARM, but uses the principle of *self-attention* (i.e., a Transformer model) rather than a recurrent network (sec. 7.7.2).
S19	BERT4Rec	Also uses the principle of self-attention, though with a different architecture based on BERT (Devlin et al., 2019) (sec. 7.7.2).

based on recurrent networks (or more broadly, for recommenders that borrow techniques from natural language), since it allows sessions to be treated analogously to *sentences,* that is, short sequences of discrete tokens (items).

The method from Hidasi et al. (2016) seeks to pass sequences of items into a recurrent network (similar to that of sec. 7.6.1) such that the hidden state of the network is capable of predicting the next interaction.[9] As stated previously, this model (along with most of the related methods below) does not learn a user representation: rather the user 'context' is captured via the hidden state of the recurrent network. Hidasi et al. (2016) argue that a benefit of this type of approach is that it will work well in situations where long user histories are unavailable (e.g., on niche platforms or long-tailed datasets). In such cases, techniques like those we developed for the *Netflix Prize* (sec. 7.2.2) are unreliable as effective user representations (γ_u) cannot be learned from only a few interactions.

7.7.2 Attention Mechanisms

The main argument in favor of recurrent network-based approaches is that they can potentially capture longer-term sequential semantics compared to (e.g.) the

---

[9] The specific architecture used to achieve this passes the final hidden state into a feed-forward network (similar to those we studied in sec. 5.5.2), whose final layer estimates scores associated with all items; while computationally expensive, this is feasible for datasets with relatively small item vocabularies, for example, in the low tens-of-thousands for data in Hidasi et al. (2016).

Markov chain-based approaches we studied in Section 7.4. On the other and, the fact that simple Markov chain-based models are so effective in the first place suggests that even the context of a single recent item might be enough to capture a user's 'context' in many cases.

The basic intuition behind incorporating *attention mechanisms* into sequential recommender systems is to help the model to 'focus' on a small set of interactions among a relatively longer interaction sequence. Intuitively, this ought to allow the model to capture context from long interaction sequences, while still leveraging the fact that the *relevant* part of the context may only consist of a few interactions (Kang and McAuley, 2018). Attention mechanisms have been used in other settings such as image captioning (Xu et al., 2015) and machine translation (Bahdanau et al., 2014) (among others), where a small component of the input is 'attended on' when generating part of the output.

Neural Attentive Recommendation

Neural attentive recommendation (NARM) (Li et al., 2017) essentially seeks to extend and combine ideas from recurrent recommendation with the use of an attention mechanism. Their suggested model has two main components: a *global* encoder, which models sequential data from sessions in much the same way as a traditional RNN-based model (as described above); here the final hidden state of the RNN is responsible for (generating features capable of) predicting the user's next action. A second component, the *local* encoder, uses an attention mechanism over *all* of the hidden states in the sequence to build a feature. Roughly speaking, the local encoder's representation captures those specific actions in the user's recent history that best capture the user's intent.

Self-Attentive Sequential Recommendation

The approaches above essentially treat attention mechanisms as an *additional* component to extend existing recurrent models (i.e., NARM uses an attention mechanism to learn features from the latent representations from an RNN). A recent trend in natural language processing has been to rely more heavily on attention modules to capture complex structures in sentences, again with the attention mechanism retrieving relevant words in a source sentence to generate words in a target sentence (e.g., for machine translation). Recently, attention-based sequence-to-sequence methods, especially those based on the *Transformer* model (Vaswani et al., 2017), have emerged as the state-of-the-art for various general-purpose language modeling tasks. The overall goal of such models is much the same as we saw when developing recurrent networks in Section 7.6: to estimate an output sequence on the basis of an input sequence (or in the case of modeling interaction sequences, estimating the next item in the sequence based on the previous items). Whereas the recurrent networks we developed in Section 7.6 did so by successively passing and modifying a latent state across across network cells, the Transformer architecture instead relies purely on attention modules, so that the estimation of the next item in a sequence is a function of all previous items,[10] with attention determining which of the previous items is *relevant* to the next prediction.[11]

Kang and McAuley (2018) sought to apply the principle of self-attention to sequential recommendation problems; the method is a fairly straightforward adaptation of the Transformer architecture, whereby the next item in a sequence of user interactions is predicted on the basis of the previous items, with an attention module being responsible for determining which of the previous interactions are relevant to predicting the next one.

Other than the performance benefits of Transformer-based models (compared to recurrent networks and Markov chain models), Kang and McAuley (2018) attempt to visualize the attention weights of their model in order to understand which previous interactions the model 'attends on' when predicting the next item in a sequence. Not surprisingly they find that the most relevant item tends to be the previous item in the sequence, though interestingly, significant weight is given to more distant interactions. On some datasets these weights decay rapidly, while on others (such as *MovieLens*), relevance weights are more widely distributed across several historical interactions; collectively this suggests that while recommendations are subject to sequential context, this 'context' requires more than a single previous observation to capture.

BERT4Rec

While Kang and McAuley (2018) base their model on a 'standard' Transformer implementation, various extensions have been made to this architecture. For example, BERT4Rec (Sun et al., 2019) adapts BERT (Devlin et al., 2019), another Transformer-based model architecture. Without going into detail, this model is largely an architectural modification to the approach above; again superior performance in language modeling tasks appears to translate well to sequential recommendation problems. Overall this (and other related approaches) further highlight the general trend of applying state-of-the-art language models to build sequential recommenders.

---

[10] Up to some fixed maximum length.

[11] This description of the Transformer architecture is admittedly very rough, though a full description is quite involved; see the original paper (Vaswani et al., 2017) or one of many excellent tutorials that attempt to distill the core idea.

Attentional Factorization Machines

We also note that attention mechanisms have been applied in the context of traditional recommender systems. Attentional Factorization Machines (Xiao et al., 2017) apply attention mechanisms to factorization machines, as introduced in Chapter 6 (recall that such models are not necessarily sequential, though can encode sequential features). The application of attention mechanisms in this context is fairly straightforward. Recall from Chapter 6 that factorization machines aggregate pairwise interactions across (latent representations of) all features, as in Equation (6.2). Xiao et al. (2017) use attention to determine which pairwise interactions are most important in a particular context, which arguably helps the model not to focus on irrelevant interactions. Experiments show improvements over traditional factorization machines, and some of the deep learning-based recommendation approaches studied in Section 5.5.

7.7.3 Summary

Above we have only given a limited sample of recommendation methods based on recurrent networks and attention mechanisms. Although we have provided little detail about the specifics of each approach, we have highlighted the general trend of borrowing models from natural language and repurposing them for recommendation. The use of general-purpose language and sequence models for recommendation is increasingly representative of the current state-of-the-art; we will further visit this idea as we explore additional language modeling approaches in Chapter 8.

Note also that the above models in general have no explicit user representation: the input to the model is a sequence of items, based on which the next item is predicted. As such they can be thought of as contextual or memory-based models (though they do have *item* representations which are analogous to γ_i in traditional models). In principle, if long enough sequences are modeled, we can still capture the broad historical interests of the user, without a need for an explicit user term. In many cases the lack of a user term is a virtue of this type of model: when dealing with new users, we can make reasonable predictions based on a few sequential actions, without needing to resort to complex cold-start approaches, or retraining the model (though of course, attempts have been made to explicitly incorporate user terms into such sequential models, see, e.g., Wu et al. (2020)).

We will further revisit neural network based approaches at various points throughout the book. In Chapter 8 we consider neural network approaches to modeling text (including for text generation), following the same types of approaches we developed in Section 7.6. We also consider text representation approaches in Section 8.2, which can in turn be used to develop *item* representations for use in sequential recommendation (sec. 8.2.1). Finally in Chapter 9 we explore convolutional neural network approaches for image representation, recommendation, and generation.

7.8 Case Study: Personalized Heart-Rate Modeling

Other than building personalized sequence models for the purpose of recommendation as in Section 7.7, such models can also be used to capture dynamics in various other types of sequence data. In Chapter 8 we will explore using sequence models for personalized text generation; here we briefly examine how such models can be used to model heart-rate sequences.

Ni et al. (2019b) explored using personalized sequence models to estimate users' heart-rate profiles as they exercised using data from *EndoMondo*. That is, given the GPS route (latitude, longitude, and altitude) that a user intends to run (or walk, cycle, etc.), and a historical record of the user's previous activities, the goal of the model is to forecast the user's heart-rate profile as accurately as possible.

Modeling the dynamics of heart-rate sequences is particularly challenging for a few reasons, including:

- The dynamics are noisy, complex, and are highly dependent on external factors (e.g., the user's running speed, the altitude, etc.).
- These factors are a combination of both long- and short-term dynamics, for example, the user gradually becoming fatigued, versus the user encountering a hill.
- There is significant variation among individuals, to the point that a *non-*personalized model would be ineffective for the task.
- A large amount of training data is likely required to capture the complex factors involved in heart-rate dynamics. On the other hand, very few observations are likely to be available for each individual.

The model used by Ni et al. (2019b) is fairly similar to the recurrent network models we studied in Section 7.6, where a recurrent neural network (an LSTM in Ni et al. (2019b)) is augmented with low-dimensional embeddings capturing user characteristics, and contextual features describing the current activity: these embeddings are essentially analogous to user/item embeddings γ_u and γ_i. The argued benefit of low-dimensional user representations in this context is that one can learn a 'global' model to capture complex heart-rate dynamics from a large amount of data, along with a small number of user-specific parameters that allow the model to adapt to specific user characteristics from a limited number of observations. Again this is similar to personalized language models, where a high-dimensional language model is adapted via low-dimensional user and item terms.

In addition to user and contextual features, the recurrent network in Ni et al. (2019b) takes as input the GPS trace (latitude, longitude, altitude) of the route the user intends to complete. This sequence of variables is passed as an additional input to the model during each network step, so that the goal is to forecast heart-rate profiles as a function of the user, contextual variables (weather, time, etc.) and the intended route.

Ni et al. (2019b) show the benefit of such a model, over non-personalized alternatives and various alternative model architectures. Ultimately they argue that a system that can accurately make such forecasts can be used in various ways, for example,

- To recommend routes that will help a user to achieve a desired heart-rate profile.
- To recommend alternative routes that are semantically similar (in terms of heart-rate dynamics) to those they normally take, for example, if they want to maintain their routine while visiting a new city.
- To detect anomalies in the event that a user's heart-rate should significantly exceed the projected rate at any point.

Ultimately, we present the approach from Ni et al. (2019b) to highlight that personalized models of sequences have applications beyond 'traditional' recommendation settings that operate on (e.g.) click or purchase data. This case study highlights the potential application to settings such as personalized health.

7.9 History of Personalized Temporal Models

Although the *Netflix Prize* was one of the early drivers for the use of temporal models in recommendation scenarios, the basic idea of *concept drift*, in which the distribution of labels changes over time, dates back significantly further. For example, the *Dynamic Weighted Majority* algorithm (Kolter and Maloof, 2007) considers using an ensemble of classifiers ('experts'); the weighting of these classifiers' decisions changes over time as a function of the empirical performance of the classifiers. Kolter and Maloof (2007) also give a historical perspective on the problem of concept drift, dating back to early papers on the topic (e.g., Schlimmer and Granger (1986)).

While Koren (2009) showed the effectiveness of temporal factors on *Netflix* data, a few earlier efforts to use temporal dynamics in recommendation scenarios are notable. For example, Sugiyama et al. (2004) considered the problem of *personalized search*, though their solution to this problem is actually a form of recommender system. Theirs is an interesting case study in the use of simple similarity-based methods (like those of sec. 4.3.4 and eq. (4.22)) for a setting (personalized search) that does not immediately appear to be a recommender system. In terms of temporal dynamics, the main idea is to distinguish between 'persistent preferences' and 'ephemeral preferences' when building user profiles (from interaction histories), though this is mostly achieved by considering interactions within differently sized recency windows.

Following the success of modeling temporal dynamics on *Netflix*, there has been a proliferation of models that attempt to capture temporal dynamics in a variety of settings. As we described in Section 7.3, temporal dynamics may occur for a variety of reasons, ranging from long- and short-term dynamics (Xiang et al., 2010), community effects (Godes and Silva, 2012), or user evolution (McAuley and Leskovec, 2013b).

Exercises

7.1   Just as the autoregressive and sliding window techniques we introduced in Section 7.1 can be used for prediction, they can also be used for *anomaly detection*, that is, to determine which events in a sequence substantially deviate from our expectations. *Using any time-series dataset* (e.g., the bike rental data from sec. 7.1 or otherwise), train an autoregressive model and plot the model's residuals (i.e., the difference between the label and the prediction, as in eq. (2.34)) over time to find where the autoregressive prediction is least accurate. Creating such visualizations can be a good strategy to design additional model features: do the anomalies you find appear to occur at random, or can you design additional features to account for them?

7.2   In Chapter 6 we introduced factorization machines as a technique to incorporate various types of features into recommendation approaches (and discussed libraries to do so in sec. 6.1.2). When introducing Factorized Personalized Markov Chains in Section 7.5.1 we argued that this type of model can be represented via a factorization machine. Essentially, this can be done by concatenating representations for the item, the user (as in sec. 6.1), and the previous item. Following this approach, using any interaction dataset, compare models that use (a) only the sequential term $\gamma_i \cdot \gamma_j$; (b) only the preference term $\gamma_u \cdot \gamma_i$; and (c) both (i.e., FPMC). You could use either a regression (e.g., rating prediction) or implicit feedback setting, though if extending the code from Section 6.1.2 it is more straightforward to model the problem as one of rating prediction.

7.3 Likewise, FISM (sec. 5.3.2) can be implemented via a factorization machine. Here, the user term is replaced by a feature representing items the user has consumed (divided by the number of interactions), as in Equation (5.37). Incorporate such a feature into a factorization machine, that is,

$$f_i = \begin{cases} 1/|I_u| & \text{if } i \in I_u \\ 0 & \text{otherwise} \end{cases} . \tag{7.36}$$

When extracting a feature based on the interaction history, be sure to exclude the current interaction. Compare this model to the variants you trained in Exercise 7.2.

7.4 *Herding* effects occur when users' decisions (e.g., their ratings) are biased by those they've already seen: for example, a user may enter a high rating for an item simply because they see that ratings are already high. Investigate two types of models to determine the role of herding effects in recommendation data:

- An *autoregressive* model, in which previous item ratings are used to predict the next (with no personalization or item-specific terms).
- A recommendation-based approach, for example, by incorporating the most recent ratings as features in a factorization machine.[12]

Use these models to study under what conditions herding plays a role. For example, does it have a larger effect on high- or low-rated items, items with few ratings, and so on.

Project 6: Temporal and Sequential Dynamics in Business Reviews

In this project we will explore the various notions of temporal dynamics we covered in this chapter, and conduct a comparative study to determine which

---

[12] Consider how to deal with missing features (i.e., for observations with insufficient rating history), and whether any derived features (such as the historical average) may be useful.

notions work well in a particular setting. Specifically, we will consider consumption patterns of business reviews on *Google Local*, which has been used in various studies on temporal dynamics for recommendation (see, e.g., He et al. (2017a)). Business reviews are useful for the study of temporal dynamics, as activities have a combination of short-term, long-term, and sequential dynamics, though in principle this project could be conducted using any dataset that includes temporal information.

For most components in this project, you can base your implementation on the *factorization machine* framework we covered in Section 6.1 (e.g., using the *fastFM* library as in sec. 6.1.2). Others which do not follow this framework, such as models based on metric embeddings, are more challenging to implement.

We will explore this problem via the following steps:

(i) Start by training a (non-temporal) latent factor model for the task. Note that this problem could be cast either as one of rating prediction (as in sec. 5.1) or as visit prediction (as in sec. 5.2). Use this initial model to set up your learning pipeline and to find good initial values in terms of the number of latent factors, regularizers, and so on. Also consider how you might pre-process the dataset, for example, is it better to consider all businesses, or to consider only businesses within a specific category (such as restaurants)? If your setting requires negative samples (e.g., you are modeling visit prediction), consider how you will sample timestamps for the negative items.[13]

(ii) Next, we will incorporate temporal dynamics into our model via simple features. Consider how temporal dynamics might be at play in each of these settings, for example, ratings might vary on certain days of the week, or be more positive for new businesses, and so on. Process the timestamps associated with each activity to extract the day of the week, the month of the year, and the 'absolute' timestamp (which you may want to scale, for example, for the range [0, 1] to represent the lifetime of the dataset). Consider any other temporal features that might be useful in this dataset, for example, following ideas from Section 7.2.2.

(iii) Alternately, try including features based on sequential dynamics, for example, following the techniques from Exercises 7.2 and 7.3. Again you may use simple features (e.g., a one-hot encoding of the previous item, as in Exercise 7.2), or more complex ones (such as including several recent items, weighting in terms of recency or geographical distance, etc.).

---

[13] For instance, you could duplicate a timestamp from a positive instance from the same user.

(iv) Try to implement an alternate sequential model, such as one based on recurrent neural networks from Section 7.7. Although challenging to implement 'from scratch,' several of the cited papers have public code repositories on which you may base your implementation.

Although the main goal of the project is to build familiarity with and compare various temporal modeling techniques, consider also whether the temporal models you develop give you *insight* into the underlying dynamics of the data. For example, under what circumstances are users guided by temporal dynamics? Or what types of businesses are most subject to seasonal trends?

PART THREE

EMERGING DIRECTIONS IN PERSONALIZED MACHINE LEARNING

8

Personalized Models of Text

Throughout this book we have already worked with a wide variety of datasets involving text. Although we have made little use of this data so far, text can be useful both as a feature to improve the predictive performance of the types of method we have seen already, but can also be used to explore a variety of new applications.

As a feature to improve prediction, effectively making use of text is not straightforward. Text is noisy, varies in length, has complex syntax, and only a small fraction of words may be important to prediction. As such, we start this chapter with a primer on the types of feature engineering techniques that can be used to extract meaningful information from text (sec. 8.1).

Following this, we explore how text can be used to improve the types of personalized models we have developed in previous chapters. In the case of recommender systems, text ought to be helpful, as there is abundant text (e.g., product reviews) that can help us to 'explain' the underlying dimensions of users' preferences and items' properties; however effectively extracting these signals is not straightforward (sec. 8.3).

Having explored methods that use text as a feature to improve prediction, we also explore recent trends in natural language *generation*. The proliferation of language models based on recurrent networks, along with a slew of recent architectures for general-purpose language modeling and generation, have opened up a range of applications ranging from goal-oriented dialog (Bordes et al., 2017) to story (Roemmele, 2016) or poetry (Zhang and Lapata, 2014) generation. Naturally, such methods benefit from personalization, to better capture the context, preferences, or characteristics of individual users (Joshi et al., 2017; Majumder et al., 2020). We will explore such settings in the context of recommendation approaches that generate text to 'explain' recommendations to users (sec. 8.4.3), and systems that generate recommendation via natural language conversations with users (sec. 8.4.4).

Outside of recommendation, we also examine the use of text in other personalized or contextual settings, from simple forms of personalized retrieval (Project 7), to complex systems such as *Google*'s *Smart Reply* (sec. 8.5).

8.1 Basics of Text Modeling: The Bag-of-Words Model

In the following, we will explore the challenges involved in developing fixed-length feature vectors that describe text, as we develop the so-called *bag-of-words* representation. We will start by trying to develop text representations as naively as possible, and in doing so explore the various pitfalls and ambiguities involved.

8.1.1 Sentiment Analysis

To understand why modeling textual data is difficult, let us consider the seemingly simple task of predicting a rating based on the text of a review:

$$\text{rating} = x^{(\text{review})} \cdot \theta. \tag{8.1}$$

This is the same as the type of problem we set up in Chapter 2, except that our features X are derived from review text. Intuitively it makes sense that reviews should help us predict ratings, as they are specifically intended to explain a user's rating.

The task described in Equation (8.1) captures the basic setting of *sentiment analysis*, that is, learning what types of features are associated with 'positive' (i.e., high ratings) and 'negative' language. We discuss the importance of this task a little in Figure 8.1. The main challenge is how to appropriately extract meaningful features from text.

The first problem that we must deal with is that the features in Equation (8.1) are *fixed length* (i.e., X is a matrix), whereas text data is sequential. Later we will see how to establish more complex representations of text (sec. 8.2) but for now let us see how much progress we can make just by extracting a pre-defined set of features from each review.

Bag-of-words models attempt to solve this by composing X out of features that encode the presence or absence of certain words in a document. Thus it ignores key details such as the order in which words appear (see fig. 8.2).

A key component in the bag-of-words model is the *dictionary* that is used to build our feature vector. Our first attempt to build this dictionary might merely consist of compiling *every* word in a given corpus, for example:

Sentiment analysis, viewed superficially, may seem like an odd (or a 'toy') task: why would we ever want to predict ratings from reviews, given that in practice we never observe a review *without* a rating? Nevertheless, sentiment analysis is one of the core topics in natural language processing whose importance transcends the immediate task of predicting ratings. Sentiment analysis research is generally focused on:

- Understanding the socio-linguistic dimensions of sentiment, rather than the immediate task of predicting the rating.
- Building sentiment models that are *general purpose*, that is, models that can be trained on one corpus (e.g., of reviews), but can be used to predict sentiment in settings where ratings are not available.
- As a benchmarking task to test scalability, and the ability of NLP systems to understand detailed nuances in language.

Figure 8.1 What's the point of sentiment analysis?

```
1   wordCount = defaultdict(int)
2   for d in data:
3       for w in d['review/text'].split():
4           wordCount[w] += 1
5
6   nWords = len(wordCount)
```

Doing so on just the first 5,000 of our beer reviews reveals a total of *36,225* unique words. In other words, each review (on average) contains around seven previously unseen words. This number sounds large, but we might think that by the time we have seen 5,000 reviews that we would have 'saturated' the vocabulary of English words, and will not see too many more. However, if we repeat the same experiment for (e.g.) 10,000 reviews, we obtain 55,699 unique words—not quite double, but still a substantial increase, revealing that saturating the vocabulary happens slowly, if at all.

Looking at a few of the actual words in our dictionary, we see words like:

...the;   09:26-T04.;   Hopsicle;   beery;   #42; $10.65;   (maybe;   (etc.)

That is, we see words including proper nouns, unusual spelling, prices, punctuation, and so on. From this, we soon see that we will not quickly run out of unique 'words,' given any reasonable number of reviews.

To use a bag-of-words representation, we will need to reduce this dictionary to a manageable size. Some potential steps to do so include:

Removing Capitalization and Punctuation: Removing punctuation will reduce our dictionary size substantially, as word variants like '(maybe'

Loved every minute. So sad there isn't another! I thought JK really made Harry an even stronger archetypal hero - almost in a Paul Maud'Dib from Dune kind of way. He's fighting the ultimate evil, he's brave and takes risks, and believes in himself and doesn't give up despite many hardships.

risks, Paul and hardships. believes the almost sad ultimate kind up every - an there in brave hero I fighting Dune another! way. himself made really he's despite He's Loved from archetypal minute. and a Maud'Dib isn't even evil, of in many stronger So takes JK thought Harry give and doesn't

Figure 8.2 Bag-of-words models. The two reviews above have identical *bag-of-words* representations (the second randomly shuffles the words of the first). The review at right misses details that depend on syntax. Consider whether there is still enough information in the review at right to tell whether the overall sentiment is positive, or to predict other attributes (such as the genre).

(i.e., a word following a parenthesis) will be resolved to a common word. Likewise, we might ignore different capitalization patterns simply by converting all documents to lower-case.

Stemming: Stemming, that is, resolving similar words to their common word stems. Words like 'drink,' 'drinking,' and 'drinks' would all map to 'drink.'[1] Such techniques are mostly motivated by search and retrieval settings (i.e., to make sure results are retrieved even if a query uses a different word inflection than the result), though they could also be used to reduce our dictionary size. See, for example, Lovins (1968); Porter (1980) for examples of stemming algorithms.

Stopwords: Stopwords are common (English) words that likely carry (relatively) little predictive power compared to their frequency in a document. Standard stopword lists[2] include words such as 'am,' 'is,' 'the,' 'them,' and so on. Removing such words can reduce our dictionary size a little, or otherwise prevent our feature representations from being overwhelmed by common words (though we will see other ways to address this in sec. 8.1.3).

Decisions like whether to remove punctuation, whether to stem, or whether to remove stopwords, are largely dataset and application dependent. Characters like exclamation points could be predictive of sentiment;[3] or different word inflections (such as 'drinks' or 'drinker' in a corpus of beer reviews) may have

---

[1] Or words like 'argue,' 'arguing,' and 'argus' would map to 'argu'—the stem need not be an actual word.

[2] See, for example, `nltk.corpus.stopwords` in Python.

[3] Often, important punctuation characters are preserved by treating them like separate words, for example, the string 'great!' would be replaced by 'great!.'

different meanings; or stopwords like 'i' and 'her' could change the meaning of a sentence.

As such, the procedures above essentially amount to feature engineering choices: we should ultimately accept or reject the above procedures based on whether they improve performance for our given application (again, these are the kind of choices we would make with our validation set as in sec. 3.4.2).

For the moment, let us consider removing punctuation and capitalization, for example:

```
7   for d in data:
8       r = ''.join([c for c in d['review/text'].lower() if not
            c in string.punctuation])
9       for w in r.split():
10          wordCount[w] += 1
```

After removing them, we are left with 19,426 unique words. This is a reduction of nearly half compared to what we had before removing them, but is still a fairly large dictionary size.

A more straightforward way to reduce our dictionary to a manageable size is simply to include only the most commonly occurring words:

```
11  counts = [(wordCount[w], w) for w in wordCount]
12  counts.sort()
13  counts.reverse()
14
15  words = [x[1] for x in counts[:1000]]
```

Although perhaps not a completely satisfactory solution, this representation at least allows us to build a feature representation. A simple bag-of-words-based sentiment analysis model would now consist of predicting:

$$\text{rating} = \theta_0 + \sum_{w \in \mathcal{D}} \text{count}(w) \cdot \theta_w. \tag{8.2}$$

Here $\mathcal{D}$ is our *dictionary* (i.e., our set of words); θ is indexed by a word w, but in practice we would replace each word by an index (here from 1 to 1,000) for the sake of building a feature matrix.

Fitting such a model on our beer review dataset[4] yields a training MSE of 0.27 and a testing MSE of 0.51; this attests to both the expressive power of such models, as well as their ability to overfit.

Examining the coefficients θ, we find the five words associated with the most positive and most negative coefficients are:

---

[4] Here with an ℓ_2 regularizer with coefficient $\lambda = 1$, 4,000 data points for training and 1,000 for testing.

$$\theta_{\text{exceptional}} = 0.320; \qquad \theta_{\text{skunk}} = -0.364;$$
$$\theta_{\text{always}} = 0.256; \qquad \theta_{\text{oh}} = -0.312;$$
$$\theta_{\text{keeps}} = 0.234; \qquad \theta_{\text{skunky}} = -0.292;$$
$$\theta_{\text{impressed}} = 0.224; \qquad \theta_{\text{bland}} = -0.284;$$
$$\theta_{\text{raisins}} = 0.204; \qquad \theta_{\text{recommend}} = -0.267.$$

For example, every instance of the word 'skunk' (a negative association with beer) decreases our prediction of the rating by around one third of a star; likewise every instance of the word 'exceptional' increases our prediction by around the same amount. A few more observations:

- Words like 'skunk' and 'skunky' presumably convey the same information, indicating some redundancy in our representation; possibly this could be addressed by stemming.
- The word 'oh' is extremely negative, despite conveying little meaning by itself. Presumably, it occurs in phrases like 'oh no' (whereas 'no' itself appears in a wide variety of phrases so is not as negative); possibly we could account for such confounds by using N-grams (sec. 8.1.2).
- Likewise words like 'always' or 'keeps' are highly positive despite conveying little sentiment in isolation; the word 'raisins' possibly appears in the context of a specific popular item.
- The word 'recommend' is highly *negative*, in spite of seeming to convey positive sentiment. Presumably, this word frequently appears in negative phrases ('would not recommend,' etc.); we could account for such confounds by better handling of negation.

Finally, it is notable that the words 'skunk' and 'exceptional' are the 962nd and 991st most popular words in our corpus—that is, they are words we nearly discarded when we selected a 1,000 word dictionary. On the one hand, this might be an argument that our dictionary size was too small, since we nearly missed the most 'important' words. On the other hand, it is almost true by definition that the most predictive words will be rare ones: it is, after all, quite exceptional for an item to be described as 'exceptional.'

8.1.2 N-grams

Some of the oddities with the sentiment model we have developed so far possibly arose due to the simplifying assumptions made by the bag-of-words model. Critically, a bag-of-words model has no notion of *syntax* in a document, and as such cannot handle even simple concepts such as negation (e.g., 'not bad') or compound expressions that carry different meaning together than when alone (e.g., 'oh no').

N-gram models attempt to address some of these issues by considering words that frequently co-occur in sequence. That is, *bigrams* consist of pairs of words that are adjacent in a document; *trigrams* consist of groups of three words that appear consecutively in a document (etc.).

For example, the N-grams associated with the following sentence would be:

Sentence: 'Dark red color, light beige foam'
Unigrams: ['Dark,' 'red,' 'color,' 'light,' 'beige,' 'foam']
Bigrams: ['Dark red,' 'red color,' 'color, light,' 'light beige,' ...]
Trigrams: ['Dark red color,' 'red color, light,' 'color, light beige,' ...]
(etc.)

From the above example we can already see some potential benefits of using an N-gram representation, for example, several of the words in the above sentence are adjectives that modify the words 'color' and 'foam;' without an N-gram representation we might fail to correctly understand those nouns in context.[5] Similarly, negated terms (e.g., 'not bad' etc.) are readily handled by an N-gram representation.

N-grams are straightforward to extract in Python, for example:

```
16  sentence = 'Dark red color, light beige foam'
17  unigrams = sentence.split()
18  bigrams = list(zip(unigrams[:-1], unigrams[1:]))
19  trigrams = list(zip(unigrams[:-2], unigrams[1:-1], unigrams
        [2:]))
```

Having extracted N-grams, our approach to modeling the data is much the same as that of our bag-of-words model, that is, we extract counts associated with each N-gram, and use those counts as features to predict some outcome.

Note that generally we would not use (e.g.) bigrams exclusively, but rather would use a representation that included both unigrams and bigrams simultaneously. Much like our previous approach from Section 8.1.1, which simply found the most popular words (i.e., unigrams), we might count the popularity of unigrams and bigrams together.

On the same review corpus as in Section 8.1.1, the majority of popular terms are still unigrams—longer N-grams comprise 452 of the 1,000 most popular terms.

A few of the most popular N-grams include terms like 'with a,' 'in the,' 'of the,' and so on. At first glance, these do not look particularly useful, and are

---

[5] Though one could argue the opposite: if an adjective like 'beige' rarely occurs in any other context, then a regular bag-of-words representation may be sufficient to capture the relevant information.

To summarize our discussion in Section 8.1.2, N-grams are not always beneficial in language modeling tasks, partly because one has to trade off the predictive value of N-grams against the redundancy in encoding them. Some positive and negative points are summarized below:

- N-grams straightforwardly allow us to handle negation, and various forms of compound expressions, allowing us to handle relationships among words without having to resort to more complex models that explicitly handle syntax.
- Our dictionary size quickly multiplies when using N-grams. Assuming that we can handle a fixed dictionary size, in practice this sometimes means some informative unigrams will be replaced by uninformative N-grams.
- Stopwords, which made up a small fraction of our unigram dictionary, quickly multiply when building N-gram representations; thus there is additional redundancy in the N-gram representation.
- An N-gram representation may add substantial redundancy (or co-linearity) between features, for example, as informative unigrams are now duplicated among several N-gram features.

Figure 8.3 Arguments for and against N-grams

mostly combinations of stopwords. Likewise, few of the top N-grams appear to include negation—for example, among the top 1,000 terms, only eleven include the word 'not,' including, for example, 'but not,' 'not a,' 'is not,' 'not much,' 'not too,' and so on. Again these seem unlikely to be informative given that they do not modify meaningful terms.

The above example highlights that N-grams are not quite a simple panacea for the issues mentioned above about handling adjectives and negation (etc.). Indeed, one must carefully trade off the fact that N-grams introduce substantial redundancy into our feature vector with the possibility that they introduce some useful compound terms. Note that it is not straightforward to get the 'best of both worlds' in this scenario: assuming a dictionary of fixed size, we are potentially discarding informative unigrams (like 'exceptional' from sec. 8.1.1) in favor of less-informative N-grams. Again, these issues are model- and dataset-specific, and likely could be addressed by better accounting for stopwords (or possibly by using a larger dictionary). Mostly this example simply highlights that we must make extra considerations when incorporating N-grams into a model, and that they will not confer benefits unless carefully handled.

Some of these potential advantages and disadvantages of N-gram representations are summarized in Figure 8.3. Many of the disadvantages center around the redundancy of the representation, which can partly be mitigated by carefully selecting *important* features. We will revisit the topic of word importance in Section 8.1.3.

Finally, let us evaluate an N-gram representation on the same task from Section 8.1.1. Again we will build a 'bag-of-ngrams' model by taking the

1,000 most popular N-grams (for any value of N). Once extracted our model is again the same as that from Equation (8.2), the only difference being that our dictionary consists of a combination of N-grams of different lengths.

After fitting the model, performance in fact slightly degrades compared to the model from Section 8.1.1 (a test MSE of 0.54 compared to 0.51 in sec. 8.1.1). Examining some of the most predictive N-grams (i.e., largest and smallest values of θ_w) we find terms such as

$$\theta_{\text{pitch black}} = -0.397; \quad \theta_{\text{pitch}} = 0.354.$$

Upon further inspection, the word 'pitch' *always* appears in the expression 'pitch black,' to the point that the two terms will mostly 'cancel out'; again this highlights an issue of redundancy in our representation.

Possibly we can address this simply by further regularizing our model. Increasing the regularization coefficient to $\lambda = 10$ improves the performance somewhat (test MSE of 0.506), and results in more reasonable coefficients, such as:

$$\theta_{\text{wonderful}} = 0.177; \quad \theta_{\text{not bad}} = 0.174; \quad \theta_{\text{low carbonation}} = 0.137, \quad (8.3)$$

which appear to correctly handle negation ('not bad') and compound words ('low carbonation').

8.1.3 Word Relevance and Document Similarity

Suppose we wanted to build a system that recommends articles that are similar in content to ones a user had recently interacted with. As in Section 4.3, we might do so by defining an appropriate similarity metric between articles, and recommend those articles that are most similar:

$$f(i) = \arg\max_j \text{Sim}(i, j). \quad (8.4)$$

Given that our goal is to define similarity based on article *content* (rather than interaction histories as in Section 4.3), we might consider defining similarity based on the feature representations we developed so far in Section 8.1. For example, we could compare the cosine similarity of two bag-of-words representations x_i and x_j:

$$\text{Sim}(i, j) = \text{Cosine Similarity}(x_i, x_j). \quad (8.5)$$

However as we discussed in Section 8.1, the vectors x_i and x_j will be dominated by the most common words in the corpus (i.e., the largest magnitude words will likely be stopwords).

I read **this** after hearing from **a** few people that **it was** among their all-time favorites. **I was** almost put off when **I** saw **it was a** story **about** rabbits, originally written as a tale by a father **to** his children—but I'm glad **I** wasn't. **I** found **the** folk tales **about** El-ahrairah **to** be very impressive. **The** author clearly had **a** vivid imagination **to** create so much of **the** rabbits culture **and** history. But **I** think **this** book **was** worth reading as it's really **a** story **about** survival, leadership, **and** human nature. Oh **and** Fiver rocks. **And** BigWig is **the** man.

I was delighted by this book... the only fault is that it was too short! What a fantastic idea; a refuge for the children who have had adventures & now cannot fit back into the identity assigned to them. How many of us are not comfortable in the families we were born to? I loved the way the different doorways were sorted; one would think that adventures shared would be a bonding moment. Rivalries will be ever present; guess that is human nature. I don't want to describe too much & ruin the magic[...]

Figure 8.4 Term frequency and *tf-idf* comparison. On the left, the top 10 words by term frequency are bolded (i.e., the most common words in the review), and top 10 *tf-idf* words (based on a sample of 50,000 reviews) are underlined. A highly-similar review (based on cosine similarity of *tf-idf* vectors) is shown on the right.

In practice a user would probably not regard two documents as 'similar' just because they used words like 'the,' 'of,' or 'and' in similar proportions. As such, we presumably want a feature representation x_i that focuses on *relevant* terms.

In Figure 8.4 we see an example of a book review (of *Watership Down*) with the most frequently occurring words in boldface. Naturally, we would not say that the topic of this review was 'i' or 'a,' even though those words are the most frequently occurring.

Rather, we might argue that words like 'nature' or 'children' are more characteristic of the document, presumably because they do *not* occur in most documents. As such, we might consider words characteristic of a particular document to be those that occur frequently in that document but not in others.

To capture such a definition we should separately consider word frequency in a particular document, and frequency across a corpus at large. To do so we define two terms. First, the *term frequency* of a word w in a document d is simply the number of times that word appears in the document:

$$\text{Term Frequency}(w, d) = tf(w, d) = |\{t \in d \mid t = w\}|. \tag{8.6}$$

Note that this is essentially the same as the Bag-of-Words representation we developed in Section 8.1 (although the latter includes a fixed dictionary size).

Next, the *document frequency* measures how many documents in a corpus contain a particular word. In terms of a word w and a corpus $\mathcal{D}$:

$$\text{Document Frequency}(w, \mathcal{D}) = df(w, \mathcal{D}) = |\{d \in \mathcal{D} \mid w \in d\}|. \tag{8.7}$$

Now, for a word to be 'relevant' in a particular document, we want the term frequency $tf(w, d)$ to be high, and the frequency of the word across the entire corpus $df(w, \mathcal{D})$ to be relatively low. The *tf-idf* measure (term frequency-inverse document frequency) is a heuristic which achieves this goal via the following function:

$$\textit{tf-idf}(w, d, \mathcal{D}) = tf(w, d) \times \log_2\left(\frac{|\mathcal{D}|}{1 + df(w, \mathcal{D})}\right) \tag{8.8}$$

(the expression $1 + df(w, \mathcal{D})$ ensures that the denominator is never zero even for previously unseen terms). While the expression above captures our intuition that the term frequency should be high while the document frequency is relatively low, the specific expression may seem somewhat arbitrary (e.g., the inclusion of the $\log_2$ term). Indeed, this expression is merely a heuristic, as described in the original implementation (Jones, 1972). Later work has attempted to justify this choice, for example, by interpreting $\log_2 \frac{|\mathcal{D}|}{df(w,\mathcal{D})}$ as a log-probability of a word appearing in a document (Robertson, 2004), though these are post-hoc justifications for what was ultimately a heuristic choice.

Likewise, the term frequency is also a heuristic and is often modified for use in specific contexts. For instance, two alternate definitions of the term frequency include:

$$tf'(w, d) = \delta(w \in d) \tag{8.9}$$

$$tf''(w, d) = \frac{tf(w, d)}{\max_{w' \in d} tf(w', d)}. \tag{8.10}$$

Both of the above are essentially normalization schemes, intended to prevent *tf-idf* scores being higher for longer documents.

8.1.4 Using TF-IDF for Search and Retrieval

Although our interest in developing *tf-idf* is mostly to develop an effective, general-purpose feature representation of bag-of-words models of text, we briefly describe the general strategy when using this type of representation for document retrieval.

Tf-idf can be used relatively straightforwardly to retrieve *similar* documents, for example, by combining *tf-idf* representations with the cosine similarity (Figure 8.4, Exercise 8.4). However in a search or retrieval setting, the 'query' is not typically a document but rather a few user-specified keywords.

Okapi BM-25 (Robertson and Zaragoza, 2009) adapts *tf-idf*-based similarity measures to retrieval settings, essentially by treating terms in a query q and document d differently. While document words are represented using a *tf-idf* representation, all query words are regarded as being equally important. The specific scoring function between a query q and document d is defined as:

$$\text{score}(d, q) = \sum_{i=1}^{|q|} idf(q_i) \cdot \left(\frac{tf(q_i, d) \cdot (k_1 + 1)}{tf(q_i, d) + k_1 \cdot \left(1 - b + b \cdot \frac{|d|}{\text{avgdl}}\right)} \right). \tag{8.11}$$

Most terms are similar to those in Equation (8.8); k_1 and b are tunable parameters (e.g., $k_1 \in [1.2, 2.0]$ and $b = 0.75$, as in Schütze et al. (2008)). avgdl normalizes by the average document length (much like the normalization strategies in Equations (8.9) and (8.10)). The inverse document frequency score in Equation (8.11) also uses a custom normalization:

$$idf(q_i) = \log \left(\frac{|\mathcal{D}| - df(q_i, \mathcal{D}) + 0.5}{df(q_i, \mathcal{D}) + 0.5} + 1 \right). \tag{8.12}$$

Although we avoid an in-depth treatment of the topic, the above is merely to note the general difference in strategy between retrieval based on a query versus similar-document retrieval. We refer to Robertson and Zaragoza (2009) or Schütze et al. (2008) for further details.

8.2 Distributed Word and Item Representations

Word2Vec is a popular approach to developing *semantic representations* of words (Mikolov et al., 2013). Such representations are somewhat analogous to the user and item representations (γ_u and γ_i) we have been studying throughout this book. That is, just as our latent item representations give us a sense of which items are 'similar to' which others (likewise for users), we would like to find latent word representations γ_w that tell us which words are similar, or are likely to appear in the same context as each other.

These types of 'distributed' word representations are potentially useful for a variety of reasons:

- Unlike bag-of-words models (sec. 8.1), distributed representations offer a natural mechanism to handle synonyms. That is, words w and v that are synonyms of each other ought to have nearby representations γ_w and γ_v, since they will tend to appear in related contexts.
- Beyond synonyms, distributed representations might allow us better understand *relationships* among words.[6]

---

[6] See, for example, in Mikolov et al. (2013), where the word representation $\gamma_{king} - \gamma_{man} + \gamma_{woman}$ is close to that of γ_{queen}.

- In certain settings, distributed representations allow us to avoid dimensionality issues associated with bag-of-words models. For instance, when developing generative models of text (which we will touch on briefly in sec. 8.4), documents are typically represented as sequences of low-dimensional word vectors γ_w, rather than as vectors of (e.g.) word IDs via a bag-of-words model.

Below we briefly outline *word2vec* as described in Mikolov et al. (2013); in Section 8.2.1 we describe how this idea applies to learning item representations γ_i for recommendation. Although the latter and the former are essentially equivalent, the latter may feel more familiar, as it is similar to the way we learned item representations γ_i in user-free models models in Section 5.3.

Methodologically, *word2vec* seeks to model the probability that a word in a sequence w_t appears near words w_{t+j}, that is, $p(w_{t+j}|w_t)$. So, for a sequence of words $w_1 \ldots w_T$, we would like to learn word representations that maximize the (log) probability

$$\frac{1}{T} \sum_{t=1}^{T} \sum_{-c \le j \le c, j \ne 0} \log p(w_{t+j}|w_t). \tag{8.13}$$

Here c is the size of a *context window*, which determines how many neighboring words we consider; this is a hyperparameter that may be chosen to balance accuracy and training time, though potentially can vary depending on the word w_t. A simple way to define the probability $p(w_{t+j}|w_t)$ is to say that words w_{t+j} are likely to appear near words w_t with similar representations. In Mikolov et al. (2013) this is defined in terms of the inner product between representations:

$$p(w_o|w_i) = \frac{e^{\gamma_{w_o} \cdot \gamma_{w_i}}}{\sum_{w \in \mathcal{W}} e^{\gamma_w \cdot \gamma_{w_i}}} \tag{8.14}$$

where $\mathcal{W}$ is the set of words in the dictionary. The numerator in the above encodes the compatibility between the 'input' and 'output' words w_i and w_o; the denominator simply normalizes the value so that it corresponds to a probability over class labels.

Note also that we learn *two* representations, γ_w, and γ'_w for each word (referred to as the 'input' and 'output' representation, respectively). Although doing so doubles the number of parameters, this type of representation avoids symmetries, for example, a word is not likely to appear near itself. This is similar to the idea we saw when developing item-to-item recommender systems, and sequential recommender systems in Section 7.5, again the intuition being that an item is not likely to be co-purchased with itself (or appear nearby in a sequence).

Since the denominator in Equation (8.14) requires normalizing across all words in the dictionary $\mathcal{W}$, it is not efficient to compute. Mikolov et al. (2013) suggest a few schemes to overcome this issue, though the most straightforward is simply to sample a small number of 'negative' words, rather than normalizing over the whole dictionary. As such each computation of $p(w_o|w_i)$ is replaced by an approximation:

$$\log p(w_o|w_i) \simeq \log \sigma(\gamma'_{w_o} \cdot \gamma_{w_i}) + \sum_{w \in \mathcal{N}} \log \sigma(-\gamma'_w \cdot \gamma_{w_i}), \qquad (8.15)$$

where $\mathcal{N}$ is a sampled set of negative words. Mikolov et al. (2013) propose various schemes for choosing the sample $\mathcal{N}$, though most critically argue that the sampling probability should be proportional to the overall frequency of each word.

8.2.1 Item2Vec

Item2Vec (Barkan and Koenigstein, 2016) adapts the basic idea from *word2vec* as a means of learning item representations γ_i for recommendation settings. The main difference between item2vec and word2vec is simply that sequences of words in sentences/documents are replaced by ordered sequences of items that each user has consumed. In practice this simply means that the probability in Equation (8.15) is replaced by

$$\log p(i|j) \simeq \log \sigma(\gamma'_i \cdot \gamma_j) + \sum_{i' \in \mathcal{N}} \log \sigma(-\gamma'_{i'} \cdot \gamma_j), \qquad (8.16)$$

where $\mathcal{N}$ is a set of negative items, again sampled proportionally to overall item frequency.

Barkan and Koenigstein (2016) discuss the effectiveness of this type of item representation in the setting of item-to-item recommendation on a corpus of song listens from *Microsoft Xbox Music*. They show that the method naturally identifies latent dimensions that are associated with song genres; and they argue qualitatively that related items are semantically more meaningful than those produced by alternate item-to-item recommendation techniques.

8.2.2 Word2Vec and Item2Vec with Gensim

Finally, we show how *word2vec* and *item2vec* work in practice, using interaction and review data from beer reviews (as in sec. 8.1.1). To learn word representations, the input to the model is a list of documents (in this case reviews), each of which is a list of tokens (words). For this example we first remove capitalization and punctuation before tokenizing, as in Section 8.1.1.

Here we use the *Gensim* implementation of *word2vec*.[7] The model takes as input our tokenized reviews (in this case, we use a corpus of 50,000 reviews), a minimum word frequency, a dimensionality (i.e., $|\gamma_i|$), and a window size (i.e., c in eq. (8.13)). The final argument specifies which specific version of the model is used, which corresponds to the model presented above:

```
1  from gensim.models import Word2Vec
2
3  model = Word2Vec(reviewTokens,  # Tokenized documents
4                   min_count=5,   # Minimum frequency before
                    words are discarded
5                   size=10,       # Model dimensionality
6                   window=3,      # Window size
7                   sg=1)          # Skip-gram model
8
9  model.wv.similar_by_word('grassy')
```

In the final line, we retrieve the most similar words for a particular query; in *Gensim* this is based on the cosine similarity (eq. (4.17)) between the two word vectors:

$$\max_{w} \frac{\gamma_w \cdot \gamma_{grassy}}{\|\gamma_w\|\|\gamma_{grassy}\|} = \text{'citrus,'} \tag{8.17}$$

followed by 'citric,' 'floral,' 'flowery,' 'piney,' 'herbal,' and so on.

Similarly, we can use the same code to run *item2vec*, where our tokenized reviews are replaced by lists of items (i.e., product IDs) that each user has consumed (ordered by time).

After training a model on review histories, we find that the most similar beers to *Molson Canadian Light* are other light beers such as *Miller Light, Molson Golden, Piels, Coors Extra Gold, Labatt Canadian Ale,* (etc.). In Figure 8.5 we train a two-dimensional *item2vec* model for the sake of visualizing the data, which reveals that beers belonging to different categories tend to occupy different parts of the item space.[8]

8.3 Personalized Sentiment and Recommendation

The models for text we have explored so far, although they can be applied to user data like reviews, and can be used to recommend related documents, are ultimately not personalized.

---

[7] https://radimrehurek.com/gensim/.

[8] A more effective visualization might be produced by using higher-dimensional embeddings, followed by a distance-preserving visualization technique like *t-SNE* (Maaten and Hinton, 2008), though for here we plot the embedding dimensions directly for simplicity. We explore *t-SNE* a little further in Chapter 9.

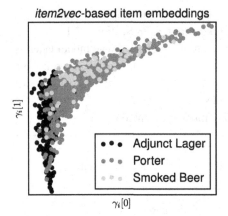

item2vec-based item embeddings

Figure 8.5 Item representations (γ_i) using a two-dimensional *item2vec* model. Representations for items from three distinct categories are shown.

Several attempts have been made to combine models of text with models of users and preferences, and in particular with recommendation approaches. For example, just as we saw techniques in Chapter 6 that improve recommender systems through the use of side-information, *text* can be useful to efficiently understand the dimensions of users' opinions.

Often there is a significant amount of textual data available in addition to interactions that might be leveraged to fit better models. Other than helping understand sentiment, text can help to understand the dimensions of items and preferences, for example, the different properties of products and the different aspects that users care about.

Text can also be helpful for model *interpretability*. So far, the recommender systems we have developed are essentially 'black boxes,' whose predictions (as in eq. (5.10)) are defined purely in term of latent factors. Models of text can be used to understand what aspects these latent dimensions correspond to (sec. 8.3.1), to synthesize reviews (sec. 8.4), or to explain recommendations (sec. 8.4.3).

However, extracting *meaningful* information from text is challenging. For example, most of the simple text representations we have seen so far (sec. 8.1) are high-dimensional and not particularly sparse; simply incorporating such features into general-purpose feature-aware models is possibly not effective, and one must instead design methods to work specifically with text. Below we cover a few representative approaches.

8.3.1 Case Studies: Review-Aware Recommendation

Product reviews are often used as a source of information to improve recommendation performance. Conceptually, reviews ought to tell us much more about preferences and opinions than (e.g.) a single rating can. This could be

Table 8.1 *Example of topics that explain variance in rating dimensions on Yelp (McAuley and Leskovec, 2013a)*

theaters	mexican	italian	medical	coffee	seafood
theater	mexican	pizza	dr	coffee	sushi
movie	salsa	crust	stadium	starbucks	dish
harkins	tacos	pizzas	dentist	books	restaurant
theaters	chicken	italian	doctor	latte	rolls
theatre	burrito	bianco	insurance	bowling	server
movies	beans	pizzeria	doctors	lux	shrimp
dance	taco	wings	dental	library	dishes
popcorn	burger	pasta	appointment	espresso	menu
tickets	carne	mozzarella	exam	stores	waiter
flight	food	pepperoni	prescription	gelato	crab

especially true for latent dimensions (γ_u and γ_i for users and items) since product reviews are intended to 'explain' the underlying dimensions behind users' decisions.

Roughly speaking, there are two schools of thought as to how reviews should be incorporated to improve recommendation performance. One option is to treat review text as a form of *regularization*, essentially to encourage the low-dimensional representations of users or items (via γ_u and γ_i) to be similar to low-dimensional representations extracted from text. Others seek to extract representations from text that can be used to improve feature-based matrix factorization methods. We give examples of both below.

Hidden Factors as Topics

An early attempt to incorporate text into recommender systems attempted to do so by making use of *topic models* applied to product reviews (McAuley and Leskovec, 2013a). Topic models (Blei et al., 2003) learn low-dimensional representations of text (essentially finding structure in the types of bag-of-words representations we covered in sec. 8.1). 'Topics' then correspond to sets or clusters of words that tend to co-occur together. For example, a topic model trained on movie reviews might discover that groups of words associated with 'action,' 'comedy,' or 'romance,' might tend to co-occur together, and therefore that these are distinct topics among movie reviews (we give examples of actual topics in Table 8.1).

The basic idea in McAuley and Leskovec (2013a) is that the low-dimensional structure among *reviews* should be related to the low-dimensional structure in *ratings*—after all, reviews are intended to explain why a user rated a product a certain way. Furthermore, even though a single rating can tell

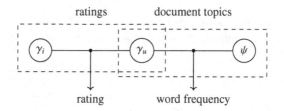

Figure 8.6 Similar to the social recommendation models from Section 6.4.1, personalized models of text often make use of a *shared* parameter that must simultaneously explain structure in interactions and documents

us very little about the underlying dimensions that explain a user's ratings, a single review potentially contains enough information to understand which dimensions are important to a user, or the characteristics of an item.

The method is somewhat reminiscent of the social recommendation approach we covered in Section 6.4.1 (Ma et al., 2008), in which a shared parameter γ_u was tasked with simultaneously explaining rating dimensions as well as social connections. The argument we made in Section 6.4.1 was that absent sufficient rating data, our estimate of γ_u can be informed from u's friends.

Likewise, McAuley and Leskovec (2013a) suggest that a shared parameter γ_u could simultaneously explain rating dimensions via a latent factor model, as well as the topics in reviews:

$$\underbrace{\sum_{(u,i)\in\mathcal{T}} (\alpha + \beta_u + \beta_i + \gamma_u \cdot \gamma_i - r_{u,i})^2}_{\text{rating error}} + \lambda \underbrace{\sum_{(u,i)\in\mathcal{T}} \sum_{w\in d_{u,i}} \log p(w|\gamma_u, \psi)}_{\text{topic likelihood}}, \quad (8.18)$$

where ψ is a set of additional (non-shared) parameters specific to the topic model (much like the approach in Section 6.4.1 had shared and non-shared social parameters). This idea is depicted in Figure 8.6.

Critically, the above model assumes an alignment between latent rating dimensions and review topics. In practice, there may be dimensions in reviews (i.e., topics) which are not related to rating dimensions (e.g., if a user discusses the plot in a book review, it may have little connection to their rating); likewise there may be 'intangible' latent dimensions that do not correspond to topics expressed in reviews. By assuming a one-to-one relationship between topics and latent dimensions, the model is useful in cold- (or cool-) start settings by forcing the topic model to discover *those topics that are capable of explaining the variation in ratings*. These topics in particular will be the ones that help us to quickly understand the dimensions that explain user ratings from a few interactions.

Examples of the types of topics discovered by this model are shown in Table 8.1; mostly, the discovered factors correspond to fine-grained product categories, which mostly reflect users' tendency to favor certain types of items over others.

Other Topic-Modeling Approaches

The above is a simple approach to combine low-dimensional representations of text (via a topic model) with low-dimensional representations of interactions (via a latent factor model). Several others have adopted a similar approach, typically by modifying how user factors γ_u and topic dimensions are related to each other.

Ling et al. (2014) and Diao et al. (2014) both consider the same setting as above, in which reviews are used to improve the performance of rating prediction models. Both note the limitations of assuming a simple one-to-one mapping between review topics and user preferences as in McAuley and Leskovec (2013a), and suggest more flexible ways to align topic and preference dimensions.

Wang and Blei (2011) proposed a similar approach to the problem of recommending scientific articles, where document representations are extracted from article text, and user preferences are modeled to predict which articles they will include in their libraries. This differs from the above formulation in that text is associated with items (documents) rather than users, and the setting is essentially an instance of 'one-class' recommendation (as in sec. 5.2), since one generally does not have explicit negative feedback about the articles a user did not read.

Neural-Network Approaches

Although our discussion above centered around 'traditional' models of text (such as topic models), more recent approaches learn representations of text using neural networks. Zheng et al. (2017) adopt a CNN based approach (based on *TextCNN* (Kim, 2014)), in which they treat user and item reviews as two separate 'documents,' based on which user and item representations (essentially γ_u and γ_i) are estimated. Later works extend this idea using attention mechanisms (which we discussed in Section 7.7.2), to infer which reviews are more relevant in a particular context (Chen et al., 2018; Tay et al., 2018).

8.4 Personalized Text Generation

In Section 7.6 we presented Recurrent Neural Networks as general-purpose models that can be used to estimate the next value in a sequence, or to generate sequences, based on some context and the sequence of tokens seen so far.

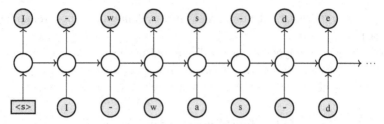

Figure 8.7 Recurrent neural network for text generation. At each step the network is responsible for generating the next token (in this case a character) on the basis of the tokens seen so far, and the network's current hidden state. '<s>' represents a 'start token' to begin generation (and generation would be terminated once the network generates an end token '<\s>').

Such models are routinely used to sample (or generate) realistic-looking text. Recurrent networks for text generation (see, e.g., Graves (2013)) follow essentially the same setup we saw in Section 7.6. At each step t, the network takes an input x_t (either a character, or a word representation), and updates its hidden states h_t based on the current input x_t and the previous step's hidden state h_{t-1} (as in sec. 7.6, multiple network layers can be stacked). The sequence of target outputs y is identical to x, but shifted by a single token, that is, the model is responsible for generating the *next* token in a sequence based on all the tokens seen so far. This type of setup is depicted in Figure 8.7.

While the above model will be capable of generating realistic-looking samples (i.e., documents that mimic those in the training set), the samples will not be context-dependent, and they will not be *personalized*.

Several papers have sought to adapt RNNs to generate *personalized* text, that is, text that mimics the context, preferences, or writing style of an individual user. We describe several such approaches below. Most are models of product reviews: partly because such data exhibits variation due to the user, item, and interaction between them, but also simply because such data is widely available. The models covered in this section are summarized in Table 8.2.

Why Generate Reviews?

Personalized text generation, especially when applied to datasets of product reviews, may seem an unusual task with no obvious application (beyond generating review spam): existing platforms are unlikely to surface generated reviews (such as the one in Figure 8.9) to users. However this task has more value when considering the broader context of personalized language generation. In practice, as we have seen elsewhere, reviews are often simply a convenient test-bed for training due to the wide availability of data. Other

Table 8.2 *Summary of personalized text generation approaches. References: Dong et al. (2017a); Li et al. (2017); Ni et al. (2017); Radford et al. (2017).*

Ref.	Goal	Description
R17	Sentiment analysis	Focuses on the task of generating user reviews, though is not personalized; the goal is mainly to learn disentangled representations and discover sentiment.
D17	Attribute-based generation	An encoder-decoder approach to generate reviews based on contextual attributes (such as the user, item, or rating).
L17	Abstractive tip generation	Generates short 'tips' (similar to review summaries), also based on an encoder-decoder approach; reviews are used during training to learn an intermediate representation.
N17	Personalized review generation	Generates reviews using a latent factor approach that takes user and item factors as inputs.

applications where personalized language generation could include dialog systems, assistive language tools, or natural language processing in other datasets with significant personal variability (e.g., clinical NLP).

Even within the context of reviews, a high-fidelity personalized language model can be used for other functions besides generation. For example, the model could be 'reversed' for personalized retrieval or search, that is, to retrieve items *that a user might describe in a particular way* (e.g., a query such as 'good dress for a summer wedding'). Personalized text generation can also be used within systems that explain or justify predictions, as we see in Section 8.4.3.

8.4.1 RNN-Based Review Generation

Radford et al. (2017) were among the first to explore the use of recurrent neural networks (and in particular, LSTM neural networks, as in Section 7.6.1) to generate reviews.

Although the model from Radford et al. (2017) is not personalized, the approach shows the effectiveness of recurrent networks to sample realistic-looking reviews. Below we explore several approaches that attempt to personalize reviews to individual users. 'Personalization' in this setting includes understanding an individual user's writing style, the context associated with a particular item, and the *interaction* between the two (which determines an individual user's reaction and their sentiment toward an item).

Conditional Review Generation

Given the promise of using recurrent networks to sample realistic-looking reviews from a background distribution, several papers have followed a similar

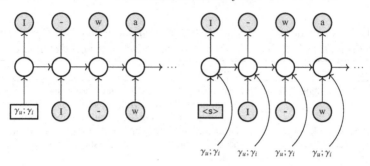

Figure 8.8 Personalized (or contextual) recurrent network architectures. Left: an encoder-decoder architecture; here the start token from Figure 8.7 is replaced by an input signal produced by (or jointly trained with) a previous model (in this case encoding user and item information). Right: the generative-concatenative network from Ni et al. (2017); here the contextual information is input during every step to help the model 'remember' the context over many steps.

approach to Radford et al. (2017) to generate reviews that are relevant to a specific context.

Conceptually, generating reviews to match a specific context follows ideas from *encoder-decoder* architectures which have proved useful in (e.g.) image captioning settings (Vinyals et al., 2015). Here, rather than passing a start token to the generator (as in fig. 8.7) one passes an encoding (i.e., a low-dimensional representation) of the context, such as an embedding representing an image; following this, decoding follows the same approach as in Figure 8.7, where the model's hidden states ought to retain the essential components of the context necessary to generate text conditionally. This type of encoder-decoder approach is depicted in Figure 8.8 (left).

Personalized Review Generation

Dong et al. (2017a) follow this type of encoder-decoder approach to accomplish 'attribute-based' conditional review generation. The approach follows the setting described above, whereby attributes are encoded and passed to an LSTM text generation model. The attributes used in their model include a user ID, an item ID, and the score associated with the review.[9]

Li et al. (2017) follow a similar approach to generate short 'tips,' that is, short summaries of reviews. The setting also follows an encoder–decoder approach, though is trained on data from *Yelp* and *Amazon* that includes

---

[9] Though this dependency on having the rating as an input could presumably be overcome by estimating it separately.

both reviews and summaries (or 'tips' on *Yelp*). While summaries are used as the model output, reviews are used during training to learn an effective intermediate representation that explains interactions between users and items.

The above methods generate reviews based on specific features or attributes, and as such can essentially be thought of as forms of 'contextual' personalization. Ni et al. (2017) designed text generation methods that directly model users (and items) in order to estimate reviews given only the context of a user and item ID.

The basic setup follows a latent factor approach, i.e., the 'input' to the model is a representation γ_u for the user and γ_i for the item. These latent user and item representations are trained jointly with the language model (in this case an LSTM, as in sec. 7.6.1); in practice these representations are concatenated onto the input tokens as in Figure 8.8 (right). Conceptually, rather than the latent factors γ_u and γ_i explaining user preferences and item properties that predict ratings (as in chap. 5), user factors must now account for patterns of variation in user writing styles (e.g., the structure used in their reviews), and item factors must account for the overall characteristics of items (e.g., their objective properties) that users are likely to write about. At the same time both the user and item factors must *jointly* explain the user's sentiment toward the item, for example, the positive or negative language that they will use.

An example of a review generated via this technique is shown in Figure 8.9. The review is surprisingly coherent and seems to capture (a) the user's writing style (e.g., they tend to write their reviews across separate paragraphs describing each aspect); (b) the item's overall characteristics (e.g., the category and flavor profile); and (c) the essential features of the user's preferences (leading to a lukewarm response for this item). Recall that as with a traditional recommender system although both the user and item have been seen during training, this specific user and item *combination* has not.

Extensions of this work combined latent user and item representations with observed attributes (Ni and McAuley, 2018). Doing so can help the model to use language that better captures specific item details (such as technical features of an electronics product). Further applications are proposed that use this type of technique for *assistive* review generation, for example, rather than generating reviews from scratch, the system could be used to help users write reviews based on a template or specific points or attributes, while still following their personalized writing style.

8.4.2 Case Study: Personalized Recipe Generation

So far, our study of personalized text generation has focused on product reviews. This is largely an opportunistic choice, as review corpora are a widely

12 oz. bottle, excited to see a new Victory product around, **A:** *Pours a dark brown, much darker than I thought it would be, rich creamy head, with light lace.* **S:** Dark cedar/pine nose with some dark bread/pumpernickel. **T:** This ale certainly has *a lot of malt,* bordering on Barleywine. *Molasses, sweet maple* with a clear *bitter* melon/white grapefruit hop flavour. Not a lot of complexity in the hops here for me. Booze is noticable. **M:** Full-bodied, creamy, resinous, nicely done. **D:** A good beer, it isn't exactly what I was expecting. *In the end above average,* though I found it monotonous at times, hence the 3. *A sipper for sure.*

A: *Pours a very dark brown* with *a nice finger of tan head that produces a small bubble and leaves decent lacing* on the glass. **S:** Smells like a nut brown ale. It has *a slight sweetness* and a bit of a woody note and a little cocoa. The nose is *rather malty* with some chocolate and coffee. The taste is strong but not overwhelmingly sweet. The sweetness is overpowering, but not overwhelming and is a pretty strong *bitter* finish. **M:** Medium bodied with a slightly thin feel. **D:** *A good tasting beer. Not bad.*

Figure 8.9 A real (left) and a synthetically generated review for the same user and item (right). Bold/italics added for emphasis.

available source of user-generated text. Here we focus on an alternative source of text data with user-level interactions, namely *recipes.*

Recipes have recently emerged as an interesting source of textual data, both for personalized retrieval, and more recently, generation (Majumder et al., 2019). Early systems to facilitate personalized interactions with recipes did so by helping users to search for recipes whose ingredients target specific health conditions (Ueta et al., 2011). Later systems approached the same task with explicit rules, and constraints of ingredients to avoid specific dietary restrictions (Inagawa et al., 2013). Other retrieval-oriented systems have sought to help users find recipes 'in the wild,' for example, by searching for recipes that correspond to a photo (Marin et al., 2019).

More recently, Majumder et al. (2019) considered whether personalized recipes can be synthesized using text generation frameworks. Here, the idea is to generate novel recipes that are consistent with a particular user's preferences (or specifically, their previous interactions). The setup is somewhat similar to that of Section 8.4, where we sought to generate personalized text conditioned on a (representation of a) user and an item. In Majumder et al. (2019), the training objective consists of a set of recipes a particular user has consumed, based on which the system should output (i.e., generate the text of) another recipe the user would consume.[10] In this way, the method can generate recipes that are consistent (in terms of, e.g., ingredients, cooking techniques, etc.) with those that the user would normally consume. An example of a recipe generated with this system is included in Figure 8.10.

---

[10] In practice, Majumder et al. (2019) input other metadata (such as a recipe title) to the method to overcome the difficulty of generating recipes 'from scratch.'

Name: Pomberrytini;

Ingredients: pomegranate-blueberry juice,
cranberry juice, vodka;

Figure 8.10 Example of a
personalized recipe, from
Majumder et al. (2019)

Combine all ingredients except for the ice in a
blender or food processor. Process to make a
smooth paste and then add the remaining vodka
and blend until smooth. Pour into a chilled glass
and garnish with a little lemon and fresh mint.

8.4.3 Text-Based Explanations and Justifications

So far, we have examined (a) textual data as a means of improving the *predictive accuracy* of personalized models (sec. 8.3); and (b) textual data as the *output* of a predictive model (sec. 8.4). Beyond these applications, text is also appealing as a means of *explaining* model predictions.

Text-based explanation connects to the more broad topics of *interpretability*, *explainability*, and *justification* of machine learning models. In the case of text-based explanations, the goal is to retrieve or generate a short text fragment that explains a model prediction. Such models bring us a little closer to the conceptual goal of producing 'human-like' explanations, that is, mimicking the way one person would justify a decision or recommendation to another.

As with the personalized text generation models above, much of the work in this space is focused on recommendations and review datasets, as review data serves as a convenient testbed to train models for personalized explanation. The more broad topic of (non-personalized) text-based explanation has been considered in other settings, such as text-based classification (Liu et al., 2019).

Extractive vs. Abstractive Approaches: Justification (and summarization) approaches can broadly be categorized as *extractive* or *abstractive*. 'Extractive' models use retrieval-like approaches to select text fragments (e.g., from a training corpus) that are relevant to a given context or query; 'abstractive' approaches generate novel text, either by paraphrasing the corpus or via a generative approach (as in sec. 8.4).

Crowd-Sourced Explanations

Prior to the use of generative models for text-based explanation, Chang et al. (2016) sought to use *crowd-sourcing* to generate personalized explanations for

Method	Type	Output
Personalized Retrieval	Extractive	*A great burger and fries*
Generated 'tip'	Abstractive	*This place is awesome*
Generated explanation	Abstractive	*breakfast sandwiches are overall very filling*

Figure 8.11 Examples of generated justifications for a recommendation of *Shake Shack* to a particular user. From *Yelp* data (Ni et al., 2019a).

movie recommendations. Since crowd workers are unlikely to be available to generate recommendations in real-time, Chang et al. (2016) adopt a template-based approach, where workers generate justifications based on users' interest in a particular aspect or tag (e.g., why should *Goodfellas* be recommended to a user who likes *drama*?). To help crowd-workers write explanations, workers are shown extracted review segments relevant to a particular tag, and are tasked with abstracting that text into a coherent explanation.[11]

Regardless of the practicality of crowd-sourcing such explanations, a main goal in Chang et al. (2016) is to confirm the overall value of text-based explanations to users (where human-generated explanations can be regarded as something of a gold-standard). They evaluate text-based explanations in terms of *efficiency* (acquainting users with the relevant properties of an item), *effectiveness* (helping users decide whether they want to watch a movie), *trust*, and *satisfaction*. They find that text-based explanations are preferred over more trivial tag-based explanations in terms of efficiency, trust, and satisfaction, though the change in terms of effectiveness is negligible.

Generating Explanations from Reviews

Ni et al. (2019a) explore abstractive approaches to justification generation. Overall, the model is similar to the methods we explored for review generation, in which a model is trained to generate a review given a particular user/item pair. Ni et al. (2019a) use a similar training setup, except that the target text used for training is text that has been identified as being suitable to surface as a recommendation justification. Ultimately this text is harvested from reviews, with a main challenge being how to identify suitable justification sentences among review text. Ni et al. (2019a) argue that training on this type of harvested text yields more effective justifications than models trained on reviews, tips, or retrieval-based techniques.

Examples of justifications generated using different techniques and training setups (from Ni et al. (2019a)) are shown in Figure 8.11.

---

[11] The complete pipeline from Chang et al. (2016) includes a few additional details, such as a step to vote on the best among several crowd-based explanations, among others.

Table 8.3 *Summary of approaches for conversational recommendation.*
References: Christakopoulou et al. (2016); Kang et al. (2019a); Li et al.
(2018); Mahmood and Ricci (2009); Thompson et al. (2004).

Ref.	Type	Description
T04	Query refinement	Elicits users' preferences and constraints with regard to item attributes.
MR09	Reinforcement learning	Queries users about recommendation attributes during each round; learns a policy to choose queries to efficiently yield a desirable recommendation.
C16	Iterative recommendation	Collects feedback about recommended items in order to iteratively learn user preferences; explores various query strategies to elicit preferences quickly.
L18	Free-form conversation	Collects conversational data in which a 'recommender' suggests movies and a 'seeker' provides feedback. Trains a dialog model to mimic the role of the recommender.
K19	Free-form conversation and reinforcement learning	Similar to the above, though trained using reinforcement learning so that the 'recommender' and 'seeker' exchange information to arrive at a target recommendation.

8.4.4 Conversational Recommendation

Arguably, our implicit goal when developing systems for text-based explanation or justification above is to mimic the ways humans explain or justify their decisions. Following this, perhaps an ideal system for interactive recommendations might mimic the paradigm of *conversation*.

Conversational recommender systems combine ideas from dialog generation, explainability, and interactive recommendation. The precise paradigm of 'conversation' varies widely: early methods facilitate simple iterative feedback from users (Thompson et al., 2004), while more recent methods more closely represent free-form conversation (Kang et al., 2019a).

Below we survey a few representative approaches; we refer to Jannach et al. (2020) for a more thorough survey. The models covered in this section are summarized in Table 8.3.

Query Refinement

Early approaches for conversational recommendations essentially treat 'conversation' as a form of iterative query refinement. In Thompson et al. (2004) users are asked questions that attempt to determine their preferences or constraints toward a fixed set of attributes (e.g., cuisine type, price range, etc.);

as such a user model is simply a weighting over potential attribute values. Retrieval then consists of selecting items whose attributes most closely match user preferences.

Other early approaches to 'conversational' recommendation are essentially forms of interactive recommendation, in which a system can query users or gather feedback from users during each round (Mahmood and Ricci, 2007, 2009). Mahmood and Ricci (2009) adopt a reinforcement learning approach to interactive recommendation. During each step, the system may perform a number of actions, including asking users more detail about specific attributes, or asking them for feedback on a panel of recommendations. Reinforcement learning techniques are used to select an optimal policy in terms of what actions the system should perform under a given state.

Interactive Recommendation

Christakopoulou et al. (2016) follow a similar strategy to those above, but combines an interactive recommendation framework with a latent factor model, similar to those we studied in Chapter 5. Here, the goal is to use a conversational strategy to quickly infer users' preferences γ_u toward item properties γ_i. Interactions consist of a one-sided form of 'conversation' in which the system asks simple questions to the user about their preferences; a main goal of Christakopoulou et al. (2016) is to understand the ideal characteristics of questions that should be asked to users in order to elicit their preferences efficiently. Questions can be *absolute* (ask a user whether they like or dislike an item), or *pairwise* (ask a user which of two items they prefer). Question selection strategies consist of determining which items should be evaluated during each step. Strategies include selecting random items, items with the highest estimated compatibility, or items whose compatibility has the most uncertainty. After each question, compatibility scores are recomputed based on question responses, resulting in a model that gradually becomes more accurate during successive rounds.

Free-form Conversation

More recent approaches try to follow the conversational paradigm more literally. Ideally, conversations should be *free-form*, in which both the system's question and the user's response take the form of free text. Li et al. (2018) attempted to formulate conversational recommendation in this form, for the specific task of movie recommendation. A major challenge which they overcome is to build appropriate ground-truth data for this task. Their approach builds on previous attempts to build dialog datasets, including dialogs specifically focused around movies (Dodge et al., 2016). Dialogs are constructed by crowd workers, who assume roles of a *recommender* or *seeker*; conversations between the recommender and the seeker are tagged in terms of the movies mentioned, as well as explicit feedback (has the seeker seen the movies mentioned and did they like them). Around 10,000 such conversations are collected.

Having collected such data, Li et al. (2018) then seek to train a dialog generation model that can fulfil the role of the recommender. Their solution combines ideas from dialog generation with a recommender system, so that users' preferences can be estimated and the output controlled to reference specific movies.

A potential limitation of Li et al. (2018) is that it relies on explicit movie mentions and feedback to learn user preferences; as such their method could not straightforwardly recommend a movie based on a simple goal, such as a user requesting 'a good sci-fi movie.' Kang et al. (2019a) seek to build conversational recommenders following this 'goal oriented' view of recommendation. To collect data, a conversation game is conducted, where both the seeker and recommender ('expert') are given prompt movie sets: the seeker's set represents their ostensible interests, while the expert's set is a collection of movies, one of which matches the seeker's preferences (determined offline based on a similarity metric). The expert's goal is to determine *which* movie in their set matches the user's preferences via repeated conversation turns. Kang et al. (2019a) note that while in principle the expert could simply enumerate movies in their set until they reach the 'correct' one, in practice this rarely happens, and players tend to engage in free-form conversation, asking about general attributes and qualities.

Like Li et al. (2018), Kang et al. (2019a) then train dialog agents to play the game. During play, the expert can either engage in a dialog turn or select one of the movies from their set; the goal is for the expert to identify the target movie in as few moves as possible.

8.5 Case Study: *Google's Smart Reply*

Google's Smart Reply is a system developed for *GMail* to automatically recommend short responses for e-mail. Given an e-mail thread as input, the system is tasked with surfacing (three) likely responses; although the goal is ultimately to maximize engagement with the feature, the system is trained by taking a large corpus of thread/response pairs, and learning to predict (or maximize the likelihood of) users' historical responses to a given e-mail thread.

As a case study in personalized text generation, this system is interesting for several reasons:

- As a form of personalized machine learning, *Google*'s solution does not have explicit user parameters; rather, 'personalization' is done implicitly by learning from the context already present in the e-mail thread.
- They describe two successive—and quite different—solutions to this problem in a sequence of papers. The first is based on a sequence-to-sequence language model (i.e., a text generation framework); the second is a seemingly more trivial retrieval-based solution.
- Other interesting facets of the studies include how they deal with scalability, diversification, the appropriateness of suggesting a reply for a given context, and so on.

The models we discuss are described in Kannan et al. (2016) and Henderson et al. (2017). The first solution (Kannan et al., 2016) uses an LSTM-based sequence-to-sequence model, similar to those we described in Section 7.6.1. The model reads a sequence of tokens from the original message, which are used to generate a hidden state, which is then used to begin generation of the target response (the model can be used to rank predetermined response candidates as well as for generation). Several issues must be dealt with (in both of the solutions from Kannan et al. (2016) and Henderson et al. (2017)):

- The system must be trained in such a way that private/sensitive data is not used during training (and likewise decoding must not leak sensitive data).
- When selecting among response candidates, the generated responses must be semantically diverse. Even responses with quite different syntax may be redundant in terms of intent; this is achieved using a *semantic clustering* approach.
- Even for messages that tend to receive positive responses, candidates should include a combination of positive and negative responses.
- Finally, the system should only be used in situations where an automatic response is likely to be appropriate.

In a follow-up paper, Henderson et al. (2017) suggested alternative methods based on multilayer perceptrons. The overall problem setting is similar: to select a small set of responses given an input e-mail. However given that a multilayer perceptron cannot *generate* responses, a large set of response candidates is collected, such that the system is merely responsible for scoring or ranking candidates.

The main thesis in Henderson et al. (2017) is simply to argue that given a large enough set of candidate responses, a *retrieval*-based approach has performance on-par with a *generation*-based approach—while being significantly more straightforward, and facilitating faster inference (retrieval).

Several details are incorporated in order to achieve the desired result, that mimic several of the strategies we have explored in this book, for instance:

- How to effectively represent text (e-mails) using fixed length features. Henderson et al. (2017) use a bag-of-words representation based on N-grams (sec. 8.1.2).
- How to select negative instances (i.e., non-replies); as in Section 5.2.2 one cannot compare *all* negatives to a given positive instance, and must instead rely on sampling.
- How to perform efficient inference (retrieval). After query and response pairs are embedded via a multilayer perceptron, they are scored via an inner product operation. Thus finding the most compatible reply resembles *maximum inner product search*, as in Section 5.6.

Ultimately, this case study reveals (or reinforces) the notion that simple solutions can often be as effective as more complex ones, and that complex, real-world systems can be developed from exactly the kind of 'standard' techniques we have studied.

Exercises

8.1 *The exercises below may be conducted using any dataset that includes reviews associated with numerical ratings.* Implement a sentiment analysis pipeline based on a bag-of-words model, as in Section 8.1, Equation (8.2). You may follow the code provided as a starting point to build a model based on the 1,000 most common unigrams.

8.2 Several choices must be made when building feature representations from text. Extending your model from Exercise 8.1, and using a validation set, experiment with various modeling choices (in addition to the regularization hyperparameter λ). Possible modeling choices include:

- the dictionary size;
- whether to use unigrams, bigrams, or a combination of both.[12]
- whether to remove capitalization, punctuation, or to treat punctuation characters as separate words;
- whether to use *tf-idf* (eq. (8.8));
- how to handle stopwords, stemming, and so on.

---

[12] That is, all unigrams *and* bigrams can be sorted by popularity; certain common bigrams (such as common negations) will then have higher frequency than some unigrams and will be included in the model.

8.3   In Section 8.2.1 we presented Item2vec as an alternate means of item-to-item recommendation. Much as we did in Chapter 4 (Exercise 4.3), consider how this item-to-item model can be used to make recommendations based on a user's history, and compared against alternate recommendation approaches. Several methods in *Gensim* could be helpful to retrieve related items based on an interaction sequence.

8.4   As discussed in Section 8.1.4, *tf-idf* representations of documents can be used to retrieve documents that are semantically similar to each other. For this exercise, we will use all reviews of a single item as a single 'document.' First, compute the *tf-idf* representations of all items, and compute the most similar item (in terms of cosine similarity between *tf-idf* vectors) given a particular query (e.g., the first item in the dataset). Compare this to similarity computed on bag-of-words representations.

8.5   In Chapter 4 (Exercise 4.4), we considered using similarity functions to predict ratings for user/item pairs. Adapt one of those predictors (e.g., the predictor from Equation (4.22)) to estimate ratings using a text-based item-to-item similarity function, such as the one you developed in Exercise 8.4 or the Item2vec model from Exercise 8.3.[13]

Project 7: Personalized Document Retrieval

The models we developed in the above exercises use features derived from text, but most are not *personalized*. Here, we will explore how to personalize these models following the approaches we developed in this chapter. This project could be conducted using any dataset involving ratings and user reviews, as in the above exercises.

As a starting point, we will build a personalized model of sentiment analysis; your model can extend the one you developed in Exercises 8.1 and 8.2. Perhaps the simplest form of personalization consists of fitting bias terms for each user, much like the bias terms we included when developing recommender systems in Chapter 5. Such a term can account for the fact that one user may regard (e.g.) a three-star rating as positive (and therefore use positive language) whereas anther user may regard it as negative. This term can be incorporated by extending a model like that in Equation (8.2):

$$\alpha + \beta_u + \sum_{w \in \mathcal{D}} \text{count}(w; \mathcal{D}) \cdot \theta_w. \tag{8.19}$$

[13] Given that repeatedly computing item-to-item similarities for high-dimensional text features is likely quite computationally intensive, it is most likely feasible to evaluate your method only on a small sample of user/item pairs.

This model could be fit either by (a) treating the user identity as a one-hot vector, and treating the problem as an ordinary linear regression problem, or (b) by gradient descent, much as we fit bias terms when developing recommender systems in Chapter 5.

Having fit this model, investigate the extent to which the addition of the bias term improves performance (e.g., in terms of the MSE), and the extent to which it alters the weights associated with the most positive and negative words.

Following this, we would like to develop a more complex model that estimates personalized compatibility with (the words in) a particular document. Fitting a model θ_w per-user would be impractical (we likely would not have enough interactions per user). Instead, develop a model that estimates a user's compatibility with a document in terms of latent factors. Rather than associating latent factors with individual documents, we will associate them with *words* in documents, augmenting our bag-of-words model from Equation (8.19):

$$\alpha + \beta_u + \sum_{k=1}^{K} \sum_{w \in \mathcal{D}} \text{count}(w; \mathcal{D}) \cdot \gamma_{u,k} \theta_{k,w}. \tag{8.20}$$

Here K is essentially a set of *topics*: $\gamma_{u,k}$ measures the extent to which user u is interested in topic k; $\theta_{k,w}$ measures the extent to which the word w is relevant to topic k; and $\text{count}(w; \mathcal{D})$ measures how many times a word appears in a particular document.

Again, the above model could be implemented via gradient descent, though alternately consider how you might fit a similar model using a factorization machine (sec. 6.1). Equation (8.20) essentially captures latent interactions between word embeddings (via a bag-of-words model), and users.[14]

Compare the performance of your model from Equation (8.20) to a bias-only (eq. (8.19)) and non-personalized (eq. (8.2)) model. The model could easily be extended to incorporate N-grams, or additional features from text.

---

[14] Roughly speaking, we're replacing the item in the design matrix from Equation (6.1) with a bag-of-words representation of a document.

9

Personalized Models of Visual Data

Traditional models of visual data deal with problems like classification, detection, or (more recently) image generation, though the bulk of approaches are not personalized: discriminative models (classifiers, detectors) are usually concerned with identifying some objective label in an image, or generative models are concerned with learning a background distribution governing the overall dynamics of a large corpus of data. On the other hand, many of our decisions and interactions can be guided by visual factors, and preferences toward visual attributes can be highly subjective.

The situation above is much as we saw when introducing models for text in Chapter 8. Just as we saw in Section 8.3 that text can be used to improve both the fidelity and interpretability of recommendations, visual data can likewise be included to improve the accuracy of models in settings where personal preferences are significantly guided by visual signals.

Visual data are critical in domains like fashion, where preferences are largely guided by visual factors. Problems like recommendation in such settings are highly personalized, and problems like compatibility among items depend on complex factors that are hard to precisely define. Furthermore, recommendation in such scenarios frequently suffers from *cold-start* (or 'cool start') problems, given the long-tail of new and rarely consumed items.

We will begin this chapter by exploring personalization in 'traditional' settings like image search and retrieval (sec. 9.1). Following this we will explore how to incorporate visual data into recommendation approaches (sec. 9.2). Much of our discussion will be centered around domains like fashion recommendation, where visual features naturally play a key role, though we will also look at other visually guided scenarios ranging from art to home decor.

Following this we will explore new recommendation modalities involving visual data. Item-to-item, or set-based recommendation are particularly important in settings involving visual data, again including settings like outfit generation in fashion (sec. 9.3).

Finally we will explore personalized *generative* models of images (sec. 9.4). Just as we saw models that generate personalized text in Chapter 8, there are a few settings where one might wish to generate images that are personalized to a user's preferences or context, such as systems for personalized design.

9.1 Personalized Image Search and Retrieval

Before studying the use of visual data in the context of recommendation, it is worth briefly considering how visual data is handled in 'traditional' settings like image search and retrieval, and how those settings can be personalized. We will explore two representative approaches that have common elements with methods we have seen in previous chapters, namely the use of latent factor representations to describe users and queries, and the use of joint embeddings. These same themes will reappear as we develop more complex personalized models in later sections.

Latent Factors: Wu et al. (2014) personalize image retrieval by identifying trending searches that are relevant to a particular user. After finding trending queries (based on an approach from Al Bawab et al. (2012)), they estimate compatibility between a user and a query using a latent factor approach. The setting is one of implicit feedback (we only observe positive instances, that is, historical queries), and Wu et al. (2014) adopt an instance reweighting scheme similar to those we saw in Section 5.2.1. Here they fit latent factors associated with a user (γ_u) and a query (γ_q) as follows:

$$\sum_{u,q} c_{u,q}(R_{u,q} - \gamma_u \cdot \gamma_q)^2 + \Omega(\gamma). \tag{9.1}$$

Here $R_{u,q}$ is a binary interaction matrix measuring whether the user has ever issued query q during training. The weight matrix c controls our instance reweighting strategy (see eq. (5.19)); the basic idea is that higher importances should be associated with trending instances.

Joint Embeddings: In Chapter 8 we saw the use of joint embeddings to capture hidden factors that are shared between interaction and review data (see, e.g., fig. 8.6). Similar ideas are used in image retrieval settings, in this case to learn a shared embedding between a query q and an image i:

$$d(q, i) = \|g(q) - g(i)\|_2^2. \tag{9.2}$$

For example, in Pan et al. (2014), $g(q)$ and $g(i)$ were based on simple linear embeddings of (textual) query features f_q and (visual) image features f_i:

$$g(q) = f_q W^{(\text{query})}; \quad g(i) = f_i W^{(\text{image})}. \tag{9.3}$$

$W^{(\text{query})}$ and $W^{(\text{image})}$ are trained so that distances in Equation (9.2) are minimized based on click-through data. That is, distances should be small between query/image pairs associated with a large number of clicks.[1]

We will see a similar setting in Section 9.3.1, in which a query image is projected into a low-dimensional 'style space' (eq. (9.8)) so that neighboring images can be retrieved. The query-based retrieval approach of Equation (9.3) operates on a similar principle, except that query features are extracted from text (as we studied in sec. 8.3.1).

9.2 Visually Aware Recommendation and Personalized Ranking

Much as we saw with text in Chapter 8 (sec. 8.3), visual data is difficult to incorporate directly into recommender systems, given that feature representations are high dimensional, and dense.

Personalized recommendation problems involving visual content (e.g., clothing) have been studied for several years, with initial attempts ignoring visual data altogether. For example, an early system for clothing recommendation (Hu et al., 2014) learns a user's 'style' in order to recommend clothing, but does so using 'likes' rather than any analysis of visual features. Likewise, *YouTube's* early recommendation approaches (Davidson et al., 2010) are based on heuristic 'relatedness scores' based on co-visitation (essentially a form of neighborhood-based approach, as in sec. 4.3), though some features based on video metadata are included in the model; newer solutions (based on deep learning) adopt more complicated candidate generation and ranking strategies, though again make little if any use of explicit visual signals (Covington et al., 2016).

Below we focus on a few of the main approaches that explicitly incorporate visual data into recommendation and personalized ranking models.

9.2.1 Visual Bayesian Personalized Ranking

Initial attempts to incorporate visual signals into ranking models follow the Bayesian Personalized Ranking framework from Section 5.2.2 to incorporate

---

[1] Note that this approach assumes that query and click data is available at training time, presumably from a method *not* based on visual embeddings.

observed image features f_i associated with each item, such as a product image. That is, we want to define a compatibility function $x_{u,i,j} = x_{u,i} - x_{u,j}$ (as in eq. (5.24)) that estimates which of two items i and j are more compatible with the user.

Starting with a simple latent factor-based compatibility model, we might first consider simply replacing our (latent) item representations γ_i with our observed image features, that is,

$$x_{u,i} = \alpha + \beta_u + \beta_i + \gamma_u \cdot f_i. \tag{9.4}$$

In this way, γ_u would now determine which features are most compatible with each user (in fact, this is a linear model as in chap. 2). Although conceptually reasonable, the issue in doing so becomes quickly apparent once we consider that image features are typically very high dimensional. For instance, the visual features used in the study below (extracted from ImageNet) are 4,096-dimensional. Incorporating them directly into $x_{u,i}$ as in Equation (9.4) would thus require fitting thousands of parameters *per user*, which is not feasible in datasets that typically consist of only (e.g.) tens of interactions per user.

Visual Bayesian Personalized Ranking (He and McAuley, 2015) attempts to address this by projecting images into a low-dimensional embedding space via a matrix E. Here E is $|f_i| \times K$ matrix (e.g., $4096 \times K$), which projects the image into a K-dimensional space. Following this, the projected image dimensions can be matched to user preference dimensions:

$$x_{u,i} = \alpha + \beta_u + \beta_i + \gamma_u \cdot (E f_i). \tag{9.5}$$

Note that the projected features $E f_i$ fulfil much the same role as γ_i in a typical latent factor model, except that they are learned based on features rather than historical interactions (and as such can be used in cool- or cold-start settings).

Note that $E f_i$ is a *learned* embedding, and is fit so as to maximize the probability of observed interactions, as with all other terms in Equation (9.5). Note also that while E is high dimensional (e.g., around 40,000 parameters if $|f_i| = 4096$ and $K = 10$), it is a *global* term that is shared among all items; thus for a large enough dataset it accounts for only a small fraction of the model's parameters.

Because the embedding is low-rank, we are assuming that users' preferences toward these visual dimensions can be explained via a small number of factors. While this is similar to the assumption made by a 'standard' latent factor model (e.g., as in eq. (5.10)), we are further assuming that these factors can be explained by visual dimensions. However in practice there could be several latent factors *not* explainable by visual features (e.g., factors due to price, material, brand, etc.). To address this the original paper includes *both* latent item factors γ_i as well as visual item factors Ef_i:

$$x_{u,i} = \alpha + \beta_u + \beta_i + \overbrace{\gamma_u(Ef_i)}^{\text{visual preference dimensions}} + \underbrace{\gamma'_u \cdot \gamma_i}_{\text{latent preference dimensions}} + \overbrace{\beta^{(f)} \cdot f_i}^{\text{visual bias}}. \tag{9.6}$$

Correspondingly, there are two sets of user terms: γ_u, which explains preferences toward visual factors, and γ'_u, which explains preferences toward non-visual factors. Intuitively, the two terms will play different roles depending on how 'cold' an item is: for a cold (or 'cool') item, visual features will be much more reliable than latent factors; whereas for 'hot' items (i.e., those with many associated interactions) γ_i will be able to capture additional non-visual dimensions. Equation (9.6) also includes a 'visual bias' term $\beta^{(f)} \cdot f_i$ ($\beta^{(f)}$ is an $|f_i|$-dimensional vector) that is able to estimate item biases in cold scenarios.

Several other considerations must be made to implement such an algorithm efficiently. For instance, accessing (high-dimensional) image features at random (e.g., within a stochastic gradient descent algorithm), leads to poor caching performance; likewise computing the projection Ef_i is expensive. In practice these issues are dealt with by pre-computing all projections Ef_i (which can be performed as a single matrix-matrix product), and updating E only periodically during gradient descent.

Visual Bayesian Personalized Ranking is effective in settings where items have few associated interactions (which He and McAuley (2015) note is common in fashion recommendation scenarios). In the original paper the model is demonstrated on a clothing dataset from *Amazon*, as well as a clothing trading dataset (*Tradesy*). The latter is particularly challenging because traded items are not associated with long transaction histories, meaning that model predictions must largely rely on visual signals.

Modeling the Visual Evolution of Fashion Trends

He and McAuley (2016) extended the above ideas from Visual Bayesian Personalized Ranking to incorporate temporal dynamics. Modeling temporal dynamics in this setting is interesting partly because the patterns of temporal variation in (e.g.) clothing purchases are different from those that were successful in other settings, such as on *Netflix* (sec. 7.2.2). Such models are interesting as a means of analyzing historical trends in fashion over time.

The main idea in He and McAuley (2016) is simply to break the training dataset into a sequence of *epochs*, each of which have their own parameters. These epochs are somewhat akin to the 'bins' used to model long-term temporal dynamics on *Netflix*, though a key difference is that the bin sizes are variable and placed at learned intervals (using a dynamic programming procedure); given that the model has a large number of parameters, this helps to ensure that fewer bins are used during time periods with little temporal variation, whereas more (and smaller) bins are used during periods which are more dynamic.

9.3 Case Studies: Visual and Fashion Compatibility

In Section 9.2 we saw how visually aware recommender systems can be used to match items (or images of items) to users' preferences. Earlier, in Chapter 4 (sec. 4.3) we discussed several types of recommendation approaches that considered similarity between items; such measures guide 'item-to-item' recommendation approaches (e.g., 'people who bought X also bought Y'). Here, we would like to develop similar approaches that establish visual similarity (or compatibility) between items. Rather than basing similarity on interaction histories as we did in Section 4.3, here we can base similarity directly on the visual appearance of items.

Many studies on visual compatibility are specifically concerned with *fashion images*. Estimating compatibility in such a domain has obvious applications to specific tasks like outfit generation and recommendation, or even to generate 'wardrobes' of mutually compatible items. More simply, in settings like fashion, visual compatibility with past interactions or purchases is a strong predictor of future interactions.

Some of the specific characteristics that make this problem difficult (and different from other forms of item-to-item recommendation), are as follows:

- It is challenging to construct datasets that act as 'groundtruth' for visual compatibility, that is, pairs of items that are known to 'go well' together.
- Further to the above, any groundtruth of compatible items is bound to be highly noisy, and highly subjective; successful methods need to account for these challenges, and possibly learn compatibility in a personalized way.
- The features that make items visually compatible in settings like fashion could be subtle, and could be quite different from the information available in co-purchase data, or even in most visual feature descriptors.
- Finally, the notion of 'compatibility' is semantically quite different from 'similarity.' For example, clothing items that go together should be similar in some ways but complementary in others.

Approaches to these problems mainly differ in their specific solutions to the problems above. We describe a few key approaches below.

9.3.1 Estimating Compatibility from Co-purchases

Early approaches to estimating visual compatibility built datasets from co-purchases, for example, using publicly available datasets of reviews from *Amazon*.

McAuley et al. (2015) crawled data from *Amazon*'s surfaced recommendations ('people who bought X also bought Y', etc.) and, in the case of clothing, treated these as 'groundtruth' examples of items that are visually compatible.

Having defined such a compatibility function, the goal is to learn an appropriate distance function, such that frequently co-purchased items tend to be closer together than others. The distance function is then used in a simple binary classification framework (similar to logistic regression) to predict:

$$p(i \text{ co-purchased with } j) = \sigma(c - d(i, j)). \tag{9.7}$$

In Chapter 7, we considered how to learn distance functions for problems such as next Point-of-Interest recommendation (sec. 7.5.3). When doing so, items (and users) were projected into a latent space via parameters γ. To recommend compatible clothing, we might instead use features extracted directly from (the product images of) i and j: first, general-purpose visual features are readily available, and are likely to be informative in fashion compatibility scenarios; second, reliance on features is desirable in cold-start settings, which might be common in settings (like fashion) where item vocabularies are large and changing; third, a model based only on visual features can be more straightforwardly *transferred* to settings where user data is not available.

Given image features associated with the items f_i and f_j, McAuley et al. (2015) discuss several strategies for establishing visual similarity. Trivially, one could directly consider the (squared) distance between f_i and f_j (i.e., $\|f_i - f_j\|_2^2$), however general-purpose image features may not focus on attributes that are relevant to fashion.

A second solution is to learn a weighted distance function that discovers which features are relevant and discards those that are not, that is, $\sum_k w_k(f_{i,k} - f_{j,k})^2$. However it is argued that in fashion scenarios 'compatibility' cannot be captured by modeling similarity between features—for example, a user generally would not select a shirt because it looks 'similar' to a pair of pants. To address this, a similarity function is proposed which projects the images into a low-dimensional 'style space':

$$d(i, j) = \|s_i - s_j\|_2^2; \quad \text{where} \quad s_i = E \times f_i. \tag{9.8}$$

In the case of McAuley et al. (2015) f_i is a 4096-dimensional image descriptor, extracted from a model trained on ImageNet (Jia et al., 2014); E is then a

$4096 \times K$ vector, where K is some small embedding dimension (on the order of $K = 10$). Ultimately the embedded vector $s_i = E \times f_i$ is analogous to the latent vectors γ_i from previous models (and very closely matches the embedding approach of sec. 9.2.1), in the sense that it captures the underlying dimensions that explain variation in co-purchases.

The method is then trained using a dataset C of complementary pairs, along with a set of *non-complementary* pairs C^- (which in practice are sampled randomly). The model is then trained using a logistic regression-like setup to distinguish complementary and non-complementary pairs:

$$\underbrace{\sum_{(i,j) \in C} \log \sigma(c - d(i, j))}_{\text{complementary pairs}} + \overbrace{\sum_{(i,j) \in C^-} \log(1 - \sigma(c - d(i, j)))}^{\text{non-complementary pairs}}. \tag{9.9}$$

Finally, although the approach is mainly designed for item-to-item recommendation (and as such is not *personalized*), a personalized version can be developed by adding a user latent vector γ_u that encodes which dimensions of this 'style space' are important to each user:

$$d_u(i, j) = \sum_k (\gamma_{u,k} s_{ik} - \gamma_{u,k} s_{jk})^2 \tag{9.10}$$

(in this case, the model is trained on triples (u, i, j) of co-purchases of items by each user u).

McAuley et al. (2015) show that this type of model can be used in several ways. First, it can predict co-purchases accurately, especially when predictions are personalized. Second, the use of image data is effective at *visualizing* the parameters of the model, that is, determining what are the primary dimensions that explain variance in users' 'styles.' Finally, since the model (as in eq. (9.8)) takes only images as input, it can be transferred to assess compatibility (and arguably, 'fashionability') of outfits outside of the original training data.

Veit et al. (2015) made use of the same co-purchase data to solve the same task, but did so directly from the 'pixel level,' that is, by training a Convolutional Neural Network, rather than using a pre-trained image representation. This type of architecture is depicted in Figure 9.1: two input images (items), labeled as 'compatible' or 'incompatible,' are passed through two CNNs, both of which share the same parameters. The CNNs learn low-dimensional representations $\phi(x)$ and $\phi(y)$ for the two items; these are essentially equivalent to the 'style space' embeddings of Equation (9.8), except that they are learned from the pixel level, and therefore could potentially capture subtle characteristics not available in pre-trained representations. Like Equation (9.8), the model

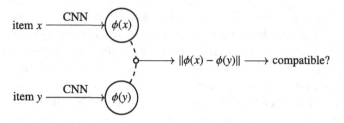

Figure 9.1 Basic siamese setup for item-to-item compatibility

is trained to learn a metric, so that compatible items have nearby embeddings and incompatible items do not.

He et al. (2016a) showed that prediction performance can be improved in fashion settings by using separate embeddings for the 'query' and 'target' items i and j, that is,

$$d(i, j) = \|\gamma_i - \gamma'_j\|_2^2. \tag{9.11}$$

Critically, by using two different latent spaces, 'compatibility' need not follow the assumptions of a metric space, for example, an item need not be compatible with itself. In this way the model can learn which aspects should be systematically different when matching items—such as blue pants going with brown shoes.

9.3.2 Learning Compatibility from Images in the Wild

The above papers showed that visual data can be effective when predicting co-purchases in domains like fashion. However, it is arguable whether such models actually learn a useful notion of 'fashionability.' For one, a co-purchase is a very noisy indicator of whether two items are compatible: in practice, two purchases on one account may not even be for the same person. Secondly, the images in such datasets (e.g., product images from *Amazon*) are not 'wild' images (they are usually scaled, centered objects on a white background), so might struggle to capture the fashionability of an outfit in a photo (e.g.).

Kang et al. (2019b) try to address this issue by developing models of fashionability that operate directly on images in the wild. At training time, the approach consists of an image (or 'scene') that is known to contain a particular item; each item also has a 'clean' product image much like those in Section 9.3.1. The basic idea is then that the item must be compatible with other objects in the scene.

To build a training set, the known items are cropped from each training image, each resulting in a scene image that does *not* contain the known item, but ought to contain compatible objects. Ultimately, this means that we have a set of training pairs consisting of an item plus a (cropped) scene that is known to be compatible with the object (but does not contain it). From here, fashion compatibility can be estimated by learning a relationship between the scene (s) and product (p) images:

$$d(s, p) = \|f(s) - f(p)\|_2^2. \tag{9.12}$$

Much like Equation (9.8), this distance function is based on learned embeddings of the scene and product images. Several differences exist between these embeddings and those used in Section 9.3.1, mostly to account for the fact that the scene image likely contains a large number of *irrelevant* objects. Critically, the method uses an *attention mechanism* (as in sec. 7.7.2, see also, e.g., Xu et al. (2015)), which is used to identify regions of the scene image that are relevant for compatibility detection. For example, in an outdoor image, the attention mechanism may learn to focus on the person in the image and their outfit, while ignoring 'background' objects in the surrounding scene.

Note that the above is ultimately not a *personalized* model, that is, there are no parameters associated with the individual users. However the system is arguably more useful than that of Section 9.3.1 from a personalization perspective, in the sense that it would allow a user to upload an image of themselves and receive recommendations that complement their personal style. As such, it is an example of *contextual* or non-parametric personalization.

In addition to experiments on personalized fashion, Kang et al. (2019b) show that the same technique can be used for complementary item recommendation in other settings, such as recommending compatible furniture based on items in a living room.

9.3.3 Generating Fashionable Wardrobes

The papers above consider *pairwise* compatibility among items as a proxy for selecting sets of items that will form compatible outfits.

Hsiao and Grauman (2018) consider the more challenging problem of finding *collections* of items that can be used to generate compatible outfits (called 'capsule wardrobes'). Their specific notion of a 'wardrobe' is a set of items belonging to fixed sets of categories (or 'layers'), for example, tops, bottoms, outerwear. The suggested quality of a good wardrobe is that it should be capable of generating many outfits, that is, a large number of sets of items should be mutually compatible. At the same time, a wardrobe should have a wide *variety* of items (e.g., many nearly identical pairs of jeans and t-shirts would generate many outfits but would not be a good wardrobe).

First Hsiao and Grauman (2018) define a measure to determine the compatibility of items in a single outfit. Their specific approach is based on *topic modeling* which we studied a little in Section 8.3.1. Essentially, an outfit is represented by a low-dimensional vector; each dimension of this vector in turn corresponds to a mixture over certain visual attributes (e.g., an outfit dimension might correspond to 'floral patterns,' and this dimension might be associated with visual attributes describing appearance, shape, cut, etc.).[2] A set of items is said to constitute a good outfit if their collective attributes resemble those of training outfits.

Hsiao and Grauman (2018) explore the relationship between these interacting components (outfits, wardrobes, versatility, as well as personalization of these components), and develop optimization schemes to circumvent the combinatorial nature of the problem.

Perhaps the most important contributions in Hsiao and Grauman (2018) are simply the creative use of training data, and the formalization of what it means for a set of items to be 'good' in terms of compatibility. Hsiao and Grauman (2018) make the argument that this type of model and training procedure is preferable to other techniques that rely on (e.g.) pairwise compatibility relationships; a topic model-based approach results in a holistic notion about the overall qualities of an outfit, and allows for training on complete outfit images rather than collecting training data from co-purchases (as in sec. 9.3.1), which may be subject to noise or otherwise not representative of real fashion compatibility.

9.3.4 Domains Other than Fashion

The visual dynamics of fashion items are often the focus of studies on personalized visual models, though fashion is not the only domain in which visual features play a key role.

A few others have sought to study personalized visual dynamics in related domains. Bell and Bala (2015) learned models of visual compatibility of home decor items collected from *Houzz*; the model is similar to the fashion compatibility models we studied in Section 9.3.1, with the main goal being to learn a similarity function between images via a Siamese network. At training time, the problem is essentially cast as a form of visual search: that is,

---

[2] 'Outfits' and 'attributes' are roughly analogous to 'documents' and 'words' in the original topic model formulation (Blei et al., 2003).

given a scene containing an item, identify the item. This is achieved by training on a dataset of image pairs, where one image consists of an item in a scene while the other consists of a clean (or 'iconic') product image. As such, the learned distance metric simply attempts to map both *in-situ* images and clean images to the same point. Although the main application for this task is visual search (i.e., find the item in this image, or find images containing this item), other potential applications are discussed that make use of the learned metric, such as identifying stylistically compatible items across categories.

Kang et al. (2019b) also adapted their model (which we studied in sec. 9.3.2) to the problem of furniture / home decor recommendation. The technique is essentially the same as that described in Section 9.3.2, but is trained on a dataset of interior design and home decor items from *Pinterest*. Here, rather than estimating a clothing item which completes an outfit (by withholding that item from the scene during training), the method is used to identify home decor items which are visually compatible (or complementary to) others in the scene.

He et al. (2016b) considered visual dynamics in the context of *art* recommendation. Their setting is an online art community (*Behance*), where personalized preferences can potentially be guided by a variety of visual, temporal, and social factors. Spiritually, the modeling approach is similar to that used to model the temporal dynamics of fashion (as in sec. 9.2.1), that is, by combining pre-trained image embeddings with a variety of application-specific temporal dynamics. The main component of their temporal model is a Markov chain-based approach (as in sec. 7.5), whereby interactions are largely guided by recent context. He et al. (2016b) also observe that art recommendation has a significant social component, whereby preferences can be estimated based on the identity of the artist as much as from the art itself (as in, e.g., sec. 6.3.2).

9.3.5 Other Techniques for Substitutable and Complementary Product Recommendation

While much of the work on substitutable and complementary item recommendation is motivated by applications in fashion (where such recommendations can naturally be used to generate outfits, etc.), a few others have considered the problem more broadly, either to consider different modalities of data (besides visual features), or to consider complementarity in settings other than fashion.

Learning Non-Metric Item Relationships

Wang et al. (2018) also studied the problem of recommending substitutable and complementary products, proposing several modifications to the approaches we studied above.

First, as we saw in Section 9.3, a good model for complementary product recommendation ought to recognize that 'complementarity' should ideally not be captured by a similarity function. That is, complementary items have systematically *different* characteristics, and in particular an item is not complementary with itself.

Following this logic, we might train a complementarity model consisting of two sets of factors γ_i and γ'_j (much like that of eq. (9.11)) for complementary pairs i and j:[3]

$$\underbrace{\sum_{(i,j)\in C} \log \sigma(\gamma_i \cdot \gamma'_j)}_{\text{complementary pairs}} + \overbrace{\sum_{(i,j)\in C^-} \log \sigma(\gamma_i \cdot \gamma'_j)}^{\text{non-complementary pairs}}. \qquad (9.13)$$

Several other extensions are proposed, mostly to handle data sparsity issues and cold-start scenarios. Wang et al. (2018) leveraged knowledge about the specific semantics of substitutable items; for example, if complementary pairs tend to belong to specific sub-categories (e.g., shirts are often compatible with jeans), this acts as a weak signal that other products within these categories are also complementary. Likewise, substitutable relationships might be *transitive* (e.g.), that is, if i is substitutable for j, and j is substitutable for k, then i is likely substitutable for k; various 'soft' constraints of these types ultimately help to improve performance.

Diversifying Complementary Item Recommendation

Although complementary recommendations are intended to be distinct from the query item, this does not necessarily mean that recommended complements will be distinct from *each other*. For example, it would presumably not be useful to recommend only t-shirts as a complement for a pair of jeans; instead, one might wish to recommend a combination of shirts, belts, shoes, and so on.

Although we will revisit the notion of diversity in depth in Chapter 10, here we discuss some approaches that consider the problem within the specific context of complementary item recommendation.

---

[3] Note that in practice, complementary pairs $i \to j$ are *directed*, for example, a large fraction of camera purchases are paired with a memory card, whereas only a small fraction of memory card purchases are paired with a camera.

He et al. (2016a) considered that a good set of complementary items might be represented as a *mixture* over different notions or 'modes' of compatibility c. They start with a simple pairwise compatibility model between items i and j of the form

$$d_c(i, j) = \|\gamma_i - \gamma_j^{(c)}\|_2^2, \tag{9.14}$$

where γ_i and $\gamma_j^{(c)}$ are based on image embeddings. This is similar to the model of Equation (9.8), though includes *separate* embeddings γ and $\gamma^{(c)}$ for the 'query' item i and complementary item j; using separate embeddings breaks the symmetry between i and j, which is desirable for complementary items (e.g., an item should not be complementary with itself).[4]

Next, He et al. (2016a) note that Equation (9.14) captures only a single notion of compatibility; if a model is trained using such a function, this will presumably correspond to the predominant mode of compatibility in the data, but will not be diverse. To address this, He et al. (2016a) proposed treating the compatibility relationships in the data as a probabilistic mixture over several competing notions. This idea borrows from a mathematical framework known as a *mixture of experts* (Jacobs et al., 1991). Specifically:

$$d(i, j) = \sum_{c=1}^{C} \underbrace{p(c|i)}_{\text{relevance of compatibility function } c \text{ to query } i} \cdot d_c(i, j). \tag{9.15}$$

Here, $p(c|i)$ measures which types of compatibility relationships $d_c(i, j)$ are most likely to be relevant for a query item i; while written as a probability, this can more simply be thought of as a function that is used to combine compatibility relationships with different weights. Here

$$p(c|i) = \frac{\exp(\theta_c f_i)}{\sum_{c'} \exp(\theta_{c'} f_i)}, \tag{9.16}$$

where f_i is a feature vector describing the image i, and θ_c is a parameter vector associated with the cth compatibility function.

Ultimately this model learns C separate embeddings $\gamma_i^{(c)}$ for each item (along with the query embedding γ_i), each corresponding to a different notion of compatibility or 'complementarity.' In principle, this means the model is able to capture several different modes of compatibility that interact simultaneously. At test time, diverse lists of compatible items can be generated by sampling from different compatibility functions $d_c(i, j)$ according to their relevance $p(c|i)$.

---

[4] As such, Equation (9.14) is no longer a distance function.

Incorporating Item Types

Hao et al. (2020) noted that both accuracy and diversity of complementary product recommendation can be achieved my making explicit use of available category data. Instead of directly predicting which items j are compatible with a query item i, the approach first attempts to estimate which of several *categories* are relevant to a given query; following this, the method generates complements via several category-specific compatibility functions, similar to $d_c(i, j)$ form Equation (9.14).

9.3.6 Implementing a Compatibility Model in *Tensorflow*

Most of the compatibility models we saw in the previous section are relatively straightforward to implement on top of pre-trained image features.

Below we assume a feature matrix X such that x_i is an image feature describing item i (e.g., a feature from ImageNet as in He and McAuley (2015)), and that each pair (i, j) is associated with a label y determining whether the pair is compatible ($y = 1$) or not ($y = 0$). The model then projects the images into 'style space' via $s_i = E_i x_i$ and $s_j = E_j x_j$ (similar to eq. (9.5)); here we use two separate embeddings so that the model can learn asymmetric relationships. Finally compatibility is evaluated via $\sigma(c - d(s_i - s_j))$ (similar to Equation (9.9)):

```
1  class CompatibilityModel(tf.keras.Model):
2      def __init__(self, featDim, styleDim):
3          super(CompatibilityModel, self).__init__()
4          # Embeddings for the query item (Ei) and target item
                (Ej)
5          self.E1 = tf.Variable(tf.random.normal([featDim,
                styleDim],stddev=0.001))
6          self.E2 = tf.Variable(tf.random.normal([featDim,
                styleDim],stddev=0.001))
7          # Offset term as in Equation 9.9
8          self.c = tf.Variable(0.0)
9
10     def predict(self, x1, x2):
11         # Style-space embeddings γi and γj
12         s1 = tf.matmul(x1, self.E1)
13         s2 = tf.matmul(x2, self.E2)
14         return tf.math.sigmoid(self.c - tf.reduce_sum(tf.
                math.squared_difference(s1,s2)))
15
16     # Given image features x1 and x2, and label y (0/1)
17     def call(self, x1, x2, y):
18         # Shorthand for Equation 9.9
19         return -tf.math.log(self.predict(x1,x2)*(2*y - 1) -
                y + 1)
20
21 model = CompatibilityModel(4096, 5)
```

Similarly, we could modify the code to use the compatibility based on the inner product:

```
22  def predict(self, x1, x2):
23      s1 = tf.matmul(x1, self.E1)
24      s2 = tf.matmul(x2, self.E2)
25      return tf.math.sigmoid(self.c - tf.matmul(s1,tf.
            transpose(s2)))
```

Finally, we train the model by sampling compatible and incompatible pairs from our training set and computing gradients:[5]

```
26  def trainingStep(compat):
27      with tf.GradientTape() as tape:
28          (i1,i2,y) = random.choice(compatiblePairs)
29          x1,x2 = X[i1],X[i2]
30          objective = model(x1,x2,y)
31      gradients = tape.gradient(objective, model.
            trainable_variables)
32      optimizer.apply_gradients(zip(gradients, model.
            trainable_variables))
```

9.4 Personalized Generative Models of Images

In Chapter 8, we examined personalized models of text from two directions: first, we used text within *predictive* tasks, for example, we saw how text can be used for regression problems (sec. 8.1), and to improve the performance of recommender systems (sec. 8.3). Second, we saw how to personalize *generative* models of text (sec. 8.4), that is, to generate text that matches a user's writing style or preferences.

Likewise, our discussion of visual data has so far considered using images to improve predictive performance; it is worth spending a little time exploring how to personalize *generative* models of images.

Briefly, the basic framework we will consider extending is that of the *Generative Adversarial Network*, or GAN.

Generative Adversarial Networks are an unsupervised learning framework in which two components 'compete' to generate realistic looking outputs (in particular, images) (Goodfellow et al., 2014). One component (a generator) is trained to generate data, while another (a discriminator) is trained to distinguish real versus generated data. Thus the generated data are trained to look

---

[5] Although this example is simple enough to allow reasonably fast training, there are several ways that this code could be made more efficient, for example, the embeddings of all images in X could be computed simultaneously.

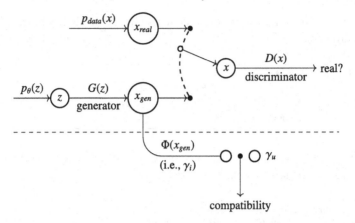

Figure 9.2 Basic setup of a generative adversarial network (GAN), and a personalized GAN. The components above the dotted line depict the 'standard' GAN setup, in which a generator competes with a discriminator to generate images that are indistinguishable from real data. Components below the dotted line are used to develop a personalized GAN that encourages the generated image to be compatible with a particular user.

'realistic' in the sense that they are indistinguishable from those in the dataset. Such systems can also be conditioned on additional inputs, in order to sample outputs with certain characteristics (Mirza and Osindero, 2014).

The basic setup of a Generative Adversarial Network is depicted in Figure 9.2. Here x_{real} is an image sampled from a dataset, whereas x_{gen} is a synthetically generated image. The discriminator $D(x)$ is then given an image x, and is responsible for predicting whether it is a sample from the dataset or is a synthetic image. For image generation, the discriminator is typically a form of convolutional neural network (CNN), whereas the generator is a series of *deconvolution* operators, essentially operating via a similar principle as the CNN, but in reverse. The generator takes as input a latent code z, a random input which allows the generator to produce distinct images (z is essentially a *manifold* which describes patterns of variation in image data so as to capture the variability in the training dataset). The discriminator D and generator G are trained simultaneously, such that the generator gradually becomes better at generating images that are capable of 'fooling' a better and better discriminator.

The above type of architecture has been used to generate various types of realistic images, including artwork, clothing, and human faces. Kang et al. (2017) sought to develop *personalized* GANs, that would generate images that capture the preferences of individual users.

The approach from Kang et al. (2017) essentially combines the GAN framework with a personalized image preference model, similar to that of Visual Bayesian Personalized Ranking (sec. 9.2.1). The basic idea is depicted in Figure 9.2 (bottom). Once a GAN is trained (as above), the image $G(z)$ generated by a given latent code is passed to both the discriminator (D) as well as a personalized preference model. For the preference model, the image is represented via $\Phi(G(z))$; this is analogous to γ_i, or Ef_i as in Equation (9.5), though unlike VBPR (sec. 9.2.1) the synthetic image is not associated with any particular item i. A user's preference toward this synthetic item is then estimated via $\gamma_u \cdot \Phi(G(z))$. Ultimately, the objective is that a generated image should be simultaneously plausible (according to $D(G(z))$), but also desirable to the user (according to $\gamma_u \cdot \Phi(G(z))$):

$$\arg\max_z \underbrace{\gamma_u \cdot \Phi(G(z))}_{\text{user preference toward generated image}} - \overbrace{\eta(D(G(z)) - 1)^2}^{\text{'plausibility' of generated image}}. \qquad (9.17)$$

Kang et al. (2017) argue that a model such as that above can be used in several ways. Most straightforwardly, it can be used to generate designs (or images) that match the preferences of individual users; Equation (9.17) can be straightforwardly modified to find optimal designs for a *population* of users (e.g., by taking an average over users $\sum_u \gamma_u \cdot \Phi(G(z))$). Alternately, given an existing image (rather than a generated image $G(z)$), Equation (9.17) (or rather, its gradient) can be used to suggest *local modifications* to the image that will make it preferable to a user or population.

Exercises

9.1 Starting from the code from Section 9.3.6, and using a small dataset of compatible (and non-compatible) pairs (e.g., from *Amazon* clothing products, as in McAuley et al. (2015)), set up a pipeline for estimating compatibility relationships (e.g., 'also bought' or 'also viewed' products). Tune the model (e.g., in terms of the number of embedding dimensions, regularization, etc.) and measure its accuracy (in terms of its ability to successfully distinguish compatible from non-compatible items).

9.2 The model from Exercise 9.1 is based on a distance (or similarity) function of the form $\|s_i - s'_j\|_2^2$. Note that there is nothing particularly special about this specific choice of similarity function (much as we discussed in sec. 5.5.1). Consider whether variants of this model might lead to better performance, for example:

- Is a squared distance preferable to an inner product, or other choices of distance function?
- The model from Section 9.3.6 embeds image features f_i into a latent space via $s_i = E f_i$. Is this superior to a purely latent embedding (γ_i)? How do they compare for cold versus warm items?
- Different categories could have different compatibility semantics. Is it useful to learn different embeddings E_c per category?

9.3 A challenging aspect of learning a compatibility model between images is that of generating negative samples (i.e., pairs of items believed to be incompatible). If we naively generate samples by randomly choosing incompatible items, we may learn a trivial solution which merely predicts that (e.g.) men's shoes do not tend to be compatible with women's dresses. In other words, the model may have learned to do little more than to indirectly categorize items. Such a model may be accurate, but would hardly have learned the semantics of what combinations are *fashionable*. Alternately, try training a compatibility model that for each positive (compatible) pair (i, j) selects a more challenging negative pair (i, k) where k has *the same category* as j; this will force the model to rely on aspects like color, texture, patterns (etc.) rather than simply learning to categorize items. Evaluate your solution by training both models (randomly sampled, and within-category), and comparing their performance on a within-category test set.

9.4 When studying notions like fashion compatibility (or indeed, any latent item representation in a recommender system), it is worth exploring whether the learned representations semantically correspond to our intuitive notion of similarity. To assess this, it helps to visualize latent item representations γ_i in two dimensions (for the sake of plotting them). In Figure 8.5 we did this simply by learning two-dimensional item representations, though by doing so we are likely visualizing a suboptimal model. Various techniques exist that learn distance-preserving embeddings for the sake of visualizing data.[6] Below we show code for embedding a matrix of representations via *t-SNE* (McInnes et al., 2018):

```
1  import numpy as np
2  from sklearn.manifold import TSNE
3
4  X_embedded = TSNE(n_components=2).fit_transform(X) # X
         is a matrix of all item representations γᵢ
```

[6] That is, so that we can embed K-dimensional data into two dimensions such that 'similar' items in the original space are still nearby once they are embedded.

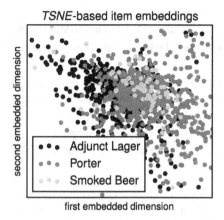

TSNE-based item embeddings

Figure 9.3 Ten-dimensional item representations (γ_i) embedded into two dimensions via *t-SNE*; this is a ten-dimensional version of the model from Figure 8.5

Using this (or an alternative embedding) strategy, visualize the embeddings you fit in the above exercises. To understand the semantics of the embeddings, it can be useful to visualize them by category (as in fig. 9.3) or some other feature (price, brand, etc.).

Project 8: Generating Compatible Outfits

In this project we will explore various ways to build outfit recommenders, following similar strategies to those we developed in Section 9.3.

First, consider how you would generate a training dataset of compatible items. It is probably most realistic to start by considering *pairwise* compatibility, that is, to generate a training dataset of pairs of items (i, j) that are mutually compatible (as in sec. 9.3 or sec. 9.3.6). Even then, several options are available for mining pairwise compatibility data. For example:

- Co-purchase relationships (e.g., 'people who bought i also bought j'), as in McAuley et al. (2015).
- Directly mining co-purchased items from user interaction histories (e.g., if a user u purchased both items i and j, this is an indication that they might be compatible). This strategy was also explored in McAuley et al. (2015).
- Both of the above approaches are highly noisy, as items are not necessarily co-purchased with the intention of being worn together. A third approach consists of mining explicit relationships from actual outfit data. For example, as in Section 9.3.2.

Consider the advantages and disadvantages of each of the above approaches. For example, which will allow you to collect the most data, and which will be the least noisy? Further consider how you should select samples, for example, you probably want to avoid pairs (i, j) where both items belong to the same category, or might further restrict your dataset to certain categories of interest.

Similarly, you should choose an appropriate strategy to generate *negative* samples for training, that is, pairs (i, j) that do *not* go together. Trivially, such samples could be generated from pairs of random items, though more 'difficult' negatives could be generated by selecting pairs from specific categories.

Having built your dataset, there are several potentially interesting directions for study. For example:

(i) What is an appropriate model to use to estimate compatibility relationships? A good starting point may be a model such as that from Equation (9.13), since compatibility relationships are likely to be asymmetrical in this context.

(ii) Consider whether it is worthwhile to incorporate visual features to estimate compatibility via an embedding strategy (e.g., following the code from sec. 9.3.6) or whether it is sufficient to model compatibility in a latent space (e.g., as in eq. (9.11)).

(iii) Consider whether it is useful to incorporate other features, such as brands, prices, features from text, and so on.

(iv) Is there value to training a *personalized* model for this task, that is, rather than predicting whether a pair of items (i, j) are compatible, can you predict whether i and j are compatible *for a particular user u*. Think carefully whether the identity of the user explains a significant amount of variation in compatibility relations, and whether enough data can be mined to fit a personalized model (similar to the approach in Equation (9.10)).

Finally, consider ways to visualize the model (or its predictions), either by representing items in a low-dimensional space (as in Exercise 9.4), or by building a simple interface to explore compatible items.

Note that other than the use of visual features, the above steps could be used to build item-to-item compatibility models for *any* types of data (e.g., dishes in a menu, songs in a playlist), and are not limited to outfit generation.

10

The Consequences of Personalized Machine Learning

So far, we have largely viewed personalized machine learning as a 'black-box' task. That is, given a user, their context, and some potential stimulus, can we estimate how the user will react to that stimulus?

This black-box view of machine learning, while effective for building accurate models, ignores the potential real-world consequences of how such models are applied.

Broadly, the dangers of blindly applying machine learning models are well-studied: ML algorithms can perpetuate, mask, or amplify biases in training data, or have low accuracy for underrepresented groups. Detecting and mitigating these types of biases largely describes the study of 'fairness' in machine learning (see, e.g., Dwork et al. (2012)).

Within the context of *personalized* machine learning, black-box models, if applied carelessly, can also hide or amplify biases or other issues. Below we highlight a few examples, to be studied throughout this chapter:

- A recommender system, although ostensibly designed to aid *discovery*, may actually have a 'concentration' effect, where users are gradually locked into a 'filter bubble' containing only a narrow set of items (sec. 10.2).

- Alternately, by recommending content that maximally aligns with a user's interests, a system may gradually push them toward more and more 'extreme' content (sec. 10.2).

- Recommender systems may have reduced utility for users (or groups of users) who are underrepresented in the training data; for instance, 'popular' items that are widely recommended may merely reflect what is popular among the majority group (sec. 10.7).

- Recommendations may focus only on a user's predominant interest, while failing to capture the diversity and breadth of their interactions (sec. 10.6.3).

273

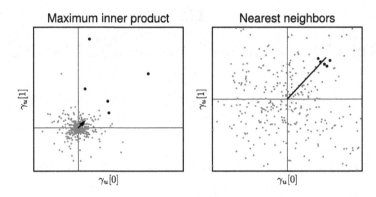

Figure 10.1 Recommendations selected for a user by maximizing an inner product (left) or taking nearest neighbors (right)

- Likewise, systems could disadvantage vendors (or content creators, etc.) by failing to recommend products in the long-tail (sec. 10.7.1).

To conceptually demonstrate some of the above issues, Figure 10.1 highlights the ways in which a recommender system, if applied naively, may lead to a 'concentration' or 'extremification' effect. At left we show personalized recommendations generated by maximizing an inner product ($\gamma_u \cdot \gamma_i$), as in Section 5.1; at right we show item-to-item recommendations generated by finding similar items (i.e., nearest neighbors of γ_i). When maximizing an inner product (fig. 10.1, left), the recommended items are on the 'fringe' of the item space; roughly speaking, if I know that a user likes action movies (e.g.), then I might recommend movies with *the most* action. While this might make sense in the context of movie recommendation, when recommending (e.g.) political videos on *YouTube*, such a strategy may drive users toward fringe or 'extreme' content. Alternately, when choosing nearest neighbors (fig. 10.1, right), users' recommendations are concentrated around very similar content, which may lead to a 'filter-bubble' effect.

While the above is merely a conceptual demonstration, in the following sections we will examine empirical studies (e.g., from *YouTube* and *Facebook*) that analyze filter bubbles and extremification in the context of deployed recommendation settings. We will also look further into issues of diversity, bias and fairness, exploring a wide variety of potential consequences of personalized model training.

These ideas connect to the broader topic of fairness and bias in machine learning, though as we will see the issues in personalized settings can be quite different. Much of our focus when introducing these issues is to present strategies to address them, in order to build personalized models that are more diverse, unbiased, and fair.

10.1 Measuring Diversity

Before exploring case studies measuring the effect of recommendations on diversity (and filter bubbles, extremification, etc.), it is useful to briefly consider how we might assess such effects on top of of recommenders like those we have developed in previous chapters. We will look at two main concepts: first, across *all* users, do recommended items follow the same *distribution* as the set of items that were consumed? Second, among individual users, are the recommended items more or less diverse than their historical consumption trends?

We first train a recommender (here using comic books from *Goodreads*), following the code presented in Section 5.8.2 (i.e., using a model based on Bayesian Personalized Ranking).

Next we generate a set of example recommendations from the model and compare those with the original interaction data. For each user, we generate as many recommendations as they have interactions in the original data, so that each user is represented the same number of times in both our interaction data and our empirical recommendation data:

```
countsPerItem = defaultdict(int)

for u in range(nUsers):
    # Given a matrix of interactions X, as in Section 5.2
    recs = model.recommend(u, Xui, N = len(itemsPerUser[u]))
    for i, score in recs:
        countsPerItem[i] += 1
```

Next we compare the measurements above to the same measurements derived from the interaction data. In particular, do popular items (based on the number of historical interactions) frequently appear among recommendations; and conversely, are frequently recommended items popular? We plot these comparisons in Figure 10.2.

The two seem to match reasonably closely, that is, popular items tend to get recommended frequently, and items that are frequently recommended tend to be popular; though there are some differences, for example, the interaction distribution appears to be less 'peaked.' There are various ways we could formally measure the discrepancy between these two distributions, or compute summary statistics that help us to compare them. In the context of item

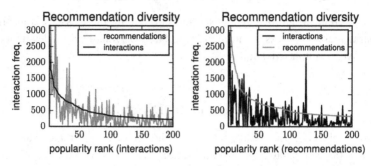

Figure 10.2 Distribution of interactions compared to recommendations (based on an implicit-feedback model trained on comic books from *Goodreads*). The left plot measures the *recommendation* frequency of the 200 most popular items (as measured by the number of interactions in the training set); the right plot measures the *interaction* frequency of the 200 most recommended items.

recommendations, we might be interested in whether one of the two distributions is more *concentrated* than the other, that is, whether recommendation frequencies are highly peaked around a few popular items (versus a flatter, or longer-tailed distribution). One measure (that we will see used in some of the studies below) is the *Gini coefficient*, a measure of statistical dispersion. Given a set of measurements y (in this case, frequencies associated with each item), the Gini coefficient measures the *average (absolute) difference between frequencies*, that is:

$$G(y) = \frac{\sum_{i=1}^{N} \sum_{j=1}^{N} |y_i - y_j|}{2N^2 \bar{y}}. \tag{10.1}$$

Highly concentrated data will have a large coefficient, while flatter distributions will have $G(y)$ close to zero (the presence of $2\bar{y}$ in the denominator scales the expression to be in the range $[0, 1]$).

In practice the coefficient can be computed approximately, that is, by sampling rather than enumerating all possible pairs of items:

```
8   def gini(y, samples=1000000):
9       m = sum(y) / len(y) # average
10      denom = 2 * samples * m
11      numer = 0
12      for _ in range(samples):
13          i = random.choice(y)
14          j = random.choice(y)
15          numer += math.fabs(i - j)
16      return numer / denom
```

In the case of this particular experiment, the interaction data yields a Gini coefficient of $G \simeq 0.72$ while the recommendations yield $G \simeq 0.77$. In other words, this particular recommendation algorithm has resulted in recommendations that are somewhat more 'concentrated' compared to historical interaction data.

10.2 Filter Bubbles, Diversity, and Extremification

The idea that recommender systems trap users in 'filter bubbles' (Pariser, 2011) amplify existing biases toward popular items, or guide users toward extreme content, are often reported in popular media and discussed anecdotally, though such concepts are often not precisely defined. It is also difficult to measure these types of dynamics empirically, as one rarely has the ability to analyze the counterfactual scenario in which the recommender was not in place.

Below we explore several attempts to measure diversity (and related notions such as filter bubbles and extremification) more precisely, either through simulation, or by empirically measuring the interaction patterns of real users.

10.2.1 Exploring Diversity Through Simulation

An early paper that attempted to define and analyze the impact that recommender systems have on interaction diversity did so via simulation (Fleder and Hosanagar, 2009). They noted the existence of two competing hypotheses as to why recommender systems might encourage or discourage diversity: on the one hand, recommender systems can guide content *discovery*, which can increase the diversity of item interactions (Brynjolfsson et al., 2006); on the other hand, recommender systems might reinforce the popularity of already-popular products, thus reducing diversity (Mooney and Roy, 2000). Their attempt to resolve this question built a simple simulation which generates recommendations, in which the probability of an item being recommended, or the probability of a user accepting it, can be controlled. By varying the controllable parameters, they show that under almost all conditions (i.e., except in edge cases), the recommender system leads to a concentration effect (i.e., results in a reduction in interaction diversity), as measured by the Gini coefficient.

Of course, the above is not necessarily true of *every* recommender system; indeed as we will see in Section 10.3, one can design a recommender system so as to explicitly target the diversity of recommended items. Rather, the above result is simply a demonstration that under fairly minimal conditions, recommender systems *can* lead to a concentration effect.

10.2.2 Empirically Measuring Recommendation Diversity

Following Fleder and Hosanagar (2009), which studied the possibility of filter bubbles via simulation, Nguyen et al. (2014) present an initial attempt to empirically measure the effect of recommender systems on content diversity in a real setting.

The research questions in Nguyen et al. (2014) are similar to the ones studied via the simulations above, namely: do recommender systems gradually expose users to narrower content over time; and, how does this effect vary as a function of how receptive users are to recommendations.

Diversity in Nguyen et al. (2014) is defined in terms of a 'tag genome,' which is a collection of tags assigned to movies. Standard similarity measures (e.g., cosine similarity) are then used to measure the similarity (or spread) between recommended and consumed movies.

Empirically, Nguyen et al. (2014) found reduced diversity over time, both for recommendations and users' actual interactions. Interestingly though, the effect is mitigated for users who tend to interact with (i.e., rate) the system's recommendations. As such, while there appears to be an overall concentration effect in users' interaction patterns, it is not entirely clear what role the recommender system plays. We will investigate this question a little further via a more recent empirical study on *Facebook* in Section 10.5.2.

Zhou et al. (2010) conducted a similar empirical study of recommendations on *YouTube*, and argued that *YouTube*'s recommendations (specifically the 'related videos' feature) have a positive impact on content diversity. They showed that recommendations drive a large fraction of views on *YouTube*, and that views driven by recommendations have higher diversity than views from a popularity-driven system.[1]

10.2.3 Auditing Pathways to Extreme Content

Ribeiro et al. (2020) attempted to empirically analyze the pathways via which users arrive at extreme content on *YouTube*. The authors used curated lists of channels (for their study, of 'alt-right' political channels) in order to establish a ground-truth of what is meant by 'extreme' content; they also collected less extreme content ('alt-lite,' general media, etc.), in order to determine whether there are systematic pathways from less- to more-extreme content (by tracking users' commenting histories) over time.

Their main finding is that there appears to be a trajectory where users migrate from less (e.g., 'alt-lite') to more extreme content, and that users who interact with extreme content can often be traced to an earlier point in time where they primarily interacted with more moderate channels. They also

---

[1]   Note however that it is hard to argue that recommendation-driven views are therefore 'diverse,' given that popularity-driven views would presumably lead to high concentration, and as such are arguably not a particularly diverse baseline.

consider the role that recommendations play in this radicalization process, noting that there tend to be pathways from more moderate communities to more extreme content (though this pathway tends to be through channel rather than video recommendations). Although they cannot assess the role of *personalization* in this process (as they do not have access to the actual recommendations surfaced to users), this suggests that even simpler item-to-item recommenders can still guide users to extreme content.

10.3 Diversification Techniques

Having argued in theory how recommenders might guide users to niche, highly similar, or extreme content (fig. 10.1), and having assessed the same problems empirically through the case studies above, we now turn to strategies that can be used to mitigate these consequences. Here we study techniques that attempt to balance relevance with *diversity*. Diversification strategies generally seek to optimize the aggregate quality of a set of results by ensuring that none are excessively self-similar. Diversity is just one of several 'beyond accuracy' metrics we will consider (we will explore several others in sec. 10.6). Such metrics are in some sense largely qualitative: to the extent that we optimize and evaluate models based on relevance (ratings, likelihood of purchasing, etc.), here we are generally seeking to improve some subjective notion of aggregate usefulness (in this case, that a set of results should not be too self-similar). One theme we will see when designing diversification techniques is that we can significantly increase diversity (and other metrics) with only a minimal reduction in relevance. We will see more detailed strategies for evaluating these types of methods via case studies in Section 10.5.

The methods discussed in this section (and another we will discuss later) are summarized in Table 10.1.

10.3.1 Maximal Marginal Relevance

A simple notion of diversity that is commonly used in document retrieval scenarios is that among a (ranked) list of retrieved documents, each retrieved item should simultaneously be relevant, but at the same time not too similar to the already-returned items.

This notion is captured by the *Maximal Marginal Relevance* (Carbonell and Goldstein, 1998) procedure (MMR). The approach was originally designed for retrieving sets of text passages that best summarize a document (with respect to some query): each document should be similar to the query, but also dissimilar from the documents already retrieved.

Table 10.1 *Summary of diversification techniques. References: Adomavicius and Kwon (2011); Carbonell and Goldstein (1998); Steck (2018); Wilhelm et al. (2018); Zhang et al. (2012).*

Ref.	Technique	Description
CG98	Maximal Marginal Relevance	Recommended items should balance utility against diversity compared to already-recommended items (sec. 10.3.1).
AK11	Aggregate Diversity	Recommended items should be those that have high compatibility for a particular user, but low aggregate compatibility (e.g., popularity); this will lead to *aggregate* diversity of recommendations across the entire population (sec. 10.3.2).
W18	Determinantal Point Processes	Balances utility and diversity (as with MMR above), but using a set-based objective (sec. 10.3.3).
Z12	Serendipity	Recommendations should be relevant, but unexpected compared to those in the user's history (sec. 10.6.1).
S18	Calibration	Recommendations should exhibit the same distribution of attributes (e.g., in terms of recommended categories) as users' historical interactions (sec. 10.6.3).

The same concept can straightforwardly be applied in recommendation scenarios, given that we have notions of both *relevance* and *similarity* available, for example, relevance might be the output of a latent factor model, while similarity could be defined in terms of cosine similarity, or as an inner product between item representations γ_i and γ_j.

To apply the concept to recommendation, we would define the Maximal Marginal Relevance as follows:

$$MMR = \underset{i \in R \backslash S}{\arg\max} \Big[\lambda \underbrace{Sim^{\text{user}}(i, u)}_{\text{relevance to the user}} - (1 - \lambda) \overbrace{\underset{j \in S}{\max} Sim^{\text{item}}(i, j)}^{\text{similarity to already-recommended items}} \Big], \qquad (10.2)$$

where R is an initial candidate set of recommendations (most trivially, e.g., a list of items the user has not already interacted with), and S is a set of items retrieved so far. Sim^{user} and Sim^{item} are item-to-user and item-to-item similarity functions (respectively); the former is presumably the compatibility function returned by a recommender system; the latter is any item-to-item similarity measure.

Note that the above is computed iteratively, that is we add one result at a time by maximizing the MMR until the list S has the desired size. Finally, λ trades off the extent to which we care about compatibility versus diversity.

10.3.2 Other Re-ranking Approaches to Diverse Recommendation

Similar to Maximal Marginal Relevance, several approaches have been specifically designed for re-ranking in recommendation scenarios. *Re-ranking* approaches, including MMR, assume that we are given an initial ranking function which we trust to find items of high relevance, but which lack diversity; thus we wish to re-rank these initial results to balance the two concerns.

One such re-ranking approach for recommendation was proposed in Adomavicius and Kwon (2011). The approach assumes the presence of three components: first, a compatibility score, for example, a rating prediction $r(u, i)$. Second, a *relevance-oriented* ranking technique, $\text{rank}_u(i)$; this could be any ranking function (though most trivially one might simply order predictions by $r(u, i)$). And third, another 'diversity oriented' ranking function; conceptually, this should focus on recommending items to users that they would *not* normally consider.

An example of a diversity-oriented loss from Adomavicius and Kwon (2011) is to sort items by popularity, with the *least* popular items being ranked first:

$$\text{rank}^{(\text{pop})}(i) = |U_i|. \tag{10.3}$$

Recommending *unpopular* items does not at first appear to be a particularly effective recommendation strategy; however this ranking is used in conjunction with the prediction score $r(u, i)$. Specifically, to encourage diversity we want to find *unpopular* items that *this* user is likely to enjoy. Spiritually, this is somewhat reminiscent of our *tf-idf* approach to finding important words in documents (sec. 8.1.3).

The specific (re-)ranking objective from Adomavicius and Kwon (2011) then looks like

$$\text{rank}'_u(i, t) = \begin{cases} \text{rank}^{(\text{pop})}(i) & \text{if } r(u, i) \geq t \\ \alpha_u + \text{rank}_u(i) & \text{otherwise} \end{cases}. \tag{10.4}$$

Here t is a threshold term, essentially determining whether one of the low-popularity recommendations has a high enough score to recommend; α_u is an offset term ensuring that the popularity-based recommendations appear first in the ranking before those of $\text{rank}_u(i)$.

Adomavicius and Kwon (2011) show that as the threshold t is changed, the system gradually trades-off between recommendation precision and diversity. Several different ranking functions are considered, for example, to replace popularity-based ranking by alternatives based on the average rating, rating variance, and so on.

They also note that the type of diversity achieved by this ranking mechanism is quite different from that in Section 10.3.1, as it does nothing to encourage diversity (or dissimilarity) among an individual user's item list. Instead, they discuss the related notion of *aggregate diversity*, which defines diversity across the item vocabulary itself, that is, recommendations across *all* users should have reasonable coverage of the complete item vocabulary. This is related to the notion of *P*-fairness that we will discuss in Section 10.7.1.

10.3.3 Determinantal Point Processes

So far, we have we discussed various approaches that attempt to balance accuracy and diversity via what are essentially 'heuristic' strategies that greedily select items that maximize utility while being sufficiently novel compared to the rest.

Determinantal Point Processes (or DPPs) (Kulesza and Taskar, 2012) are a *set-based* optimization technique that can be used to identify subsets of items that simultaneously maximize item quality and diversity among items. Specifically, given a set of items I, a DPP assigns a probability $p(S)$ to every subset $S \subseteq I$. The goal is then to model (i.e., parameterize) this probability, either globally or for individual users, such that finding the subset of items which maximizes $p(S)$ has an optimal tradeoff between utility and diversity.

Wilhelm et al. (2018) studied the application of DPPs to diversify recommendations on *YouTube*.

The method assumes a few inputs. First, as with previous diversification techniques, we assume a utility or 'quality' estimate $f(u, i)$ is given (e.g., from a pre-trained recommender system), which encodes the probability that user u will interact with item i given i's features; we also assume a predefined distance function $d(i, j)$ between two items.

Next, we have historical sets of items that have been surfaced to the user (i.e., the outputs of an existing system), along with subsets of items that the user selected (indicated by binary labels $y_{u,i}$). The goal is to select subsets of items that will maximize the total number of interactions, which in practice is trained by maximizing the Cumulative Cain:

$$\sum_u \sum_i \frac{y_{u,i}}{\text{rank}_u(i)}, \tag{10.5}$$

where $\text{rank}_u(i)$ is the new rank assigned by the proposed algorithm. That is, items the user interacted with ($y_{u,i} = 1$) should have high rank (see sec. 5.4.3).

Note that the above seems reminiscent of 'traditional' approaches to recommendation, that is, we are ranking items such that positive interactions should have high rank (which seems similar to what we saw in sec. 5.4.3). The main difference here is simply the observation that the total number of interactions will be maximized when utility and diversity are balanced (e.g., a user will quickly become bored if recommendations cover only one of their interests).

Next, given a candidate set of N items, we define a matrix $L^{(u)}$ such that diagonal entries $L_{i,i}^{(u)}$ encode the utility of an item i and off-diagonal entries $L_{i,j}^{(u)}$ encode the similarity of two items i and j. The specific parameterization used in Wilhelm et al. (2018) is:

$$L_{i,i}^{(u)} = f(u, i)^2, \tag{10.6}$$

$$L_{i,j}^{(u)} = \alpha f(u, i) f(u, j) \exp\left(-\frac{d(i, j)}{2\sigma^2}\right) \quad \text{for } i \neq j. \tag{10.7}$$

Now, the quality of a subset S is proportional to the determinant of the submatrix of L induced by S, $\det(L_S)$. Specifically:

$$p(S) = \frac{\det(L_S)}{\sum_{S' \subseteq I} \det(L_{S'})}. \tag{10.8}$$

Critically, the denominator of the above equation can be computed efficiently as

$$\sum_{S' \subseteq I} \det(L_{S'}) = \det(L + I), \tag{10.9}$$

where I is the identity matrix.

To understand (roughly) why the determinant is diversifying, it helps to consider the trivial example where S consists of only two items i and j; then the determinant is given by

$$\det\left(\begin{bmatrix} L_{i,i} & L_{i,j} \\ L_{j,i} & L_{j,j} \end{bmatrix}\right) = L_{i,i} L_{j,j} - L_{i,j} L_{j,i}; \tag{10.10}$$

this value will be maximized when the utility is high ($L_{i,i} L_{j,j}$) and the similarity is low ($L_{i,j} L_{j,i}$).

In spite of the relatively simple form of Equation (10.8), it is still not practical to solve the (NP-hard) problem of finding the optimal subset. In Wilhelm et al. (2018) this is addressed by a simple greedy algorithm (similar to that of sec. 10.3.1, among others), in which one starts with the empty set of videos $S = \emptyset$, and iteratively adds the item i which maximizes the determinant $\det(L_{S \cup \{i\}})$.

Note that the parameterization in Equation (10.7) includes two tunable parameters, α and σ. Intuitively these parameters control the relative weight of utility versus diversity (α), and the 'tightness' of the similarity function (σ). These parameters are selected globally, but in principle could be learned per-user.

Ultimately, the experiments find that implementing the above DPP on a user's video feed increases user satisfaction (as measured by session duration), compared to various other diversification strategies.

10.4 Implementing a Diverse Recommender

Here we will briefly describe an implementation of a diversified recommender. Our implementation is based on the *maximal marginal relevance* method of Section 10.3.1, though could be straightforwardly adapted to implement other re-ranking strategies from Section 10.3.2.

We start by building a few utility data structures. First we collect the list of candidate recommendations, excluding any items the user has already consumed. Next we compute compatibility scores between a user u and all items. Here our compatibility scores (i.e., $Sim^{user}(i, u)$ in eq. (10.2)) are simply the output of a latent factor recommender (here we use a batch-based prediction function as in sec. 5.8.5). We sort these in order from the highest- to the lowest-rated items. In practice we might want to re-rank only the top few hundred items rather than computing diversity scores for extremely low-compatibility items.

```
1  candidates = list(itemSet.difference(itemsPerUser[u]))
2  compatScores = list(zip([float(f) for f in model.
       predictSample([userIDs[u]]*len(candidates), [itemIDs[i]
       for i in candidates])], candidates))
3
4  compatScores.sort(reverse=True)
```

Next we implement a function to determine the similarity between a candidate recommendation and others already in the list (i.e., $\max_{j \in S} Sim^{item}(i, j)$ from eq. 10.2). itemEmbeddings is a lookup table containing embeddings γ_i for each item. The similarity function (sim) is the cosine similarity (not shown), though other similarity functions could be substituted (including simple alternatives such as checking whether items belong to the same category):

```
1  itemEmbeddings = dict(zip(candidates, tf.nn.embedding_lookup
       (model.gammaI, [itemIDs[i] for i in candidates])))
2
3  def maxSim(itemEmbeddings, i, seq):
4      if len(seq) == 0: return 0
5      return max([sim(itemEmbeddings,i,j) for j in seq])
```

To implement the iterative re-ranker we define a method that takes the list of recommendations generated so far (seq), and generates the next item to be added to the list, based on the weighted combination from Equation (10.2).

Table 10.2 *Diversified recommendations (maximal marginal relevance)*

rank	Low diversity	Medium diversity	High diversity
1	Founders KBS (Kentucky Breakfast Stout)	Founders KBS (Kentucky Breakfast Stout)	Founders KBS (Kentucky Breakfast Stout)
2	Two Hearted Ale	Samuel Smith's Nut Brown Ale	Samuel Smith's Nut Brown Ale
3	Bell's Hopslam Ale	Two Hearted Ale	Salvator Doppel Bock
4	Pliny The Elder	Bell's Hopslam Ale	Oil Of Aphrodite - Rum Barrel Aged
5	Samuel Smith's Oatmeal Stout	Kolsch	Great Lakes Grassroots Ale
6	Blind Pig IPA	Drax Beer	Blue Dot Double India Pale Ale
7	Stone Ruination IPA	A Little Sumpin' Extra! Ale	Calistoga Wheat
8	Schneider Aventinus	Odell Cutthroat Porter	Dogwood Decadent Ale
9	The Abyss	Miner's Daughter Oatmeal Stout	Traquair Jacobite
10	Northern Hemisphere Harvest Wet Hop Ale	Rare Bourbon County Stout	Cantillon Gueuze 100% Lambic

λ is passed as an argument to the function to trade-off the importance of compatibility and diversity:

```
1  def getNextRec(model, compatScores, itemEmbeddings, seq,
       lamb):
2      scores = [(lamb * s - (1 - lamb) * maxSim(itemEmbeddings
           ,i,seq), i) for (s,i) in compatScores if not i in
           seq]
3      (maxScore,maxItem) = max(scores)
4      return maxItem
```

Note that the above implementation is inefficient and even on a modestly sized dataset (in terms of the size of the item vocabulary) requires several seconds to generate recommendations. Several strategies might be used to improve its performance, including efficient retrieval techniques (as in sec. 5.6), or by exploiting certain structure in our compatibility or diversity functions that would obviate the need to exhaustively compute all scores.

Examples of Diversified Recommendations: Table 10.2 shows examples of diversified recommendations on beer review data. Different values of λ are chosen to control the compatibility/diversity trade-off (for a randomly chosen user). The first set of recommendations ($\lambda = 1$) optimizes only for compatibility: the user is recommended a selection of rich stouts and IPAs. Decreasing λ by a little (middle column) introduces a few 'lighter' yet similar beers;

decreasing λ further results in beers from a wide variety of categories (wheat beers, lambics, scotch ales, etc.).

Note that the ideal value of λ depends on a variety of factors, including our specific choices of compatibility and diversity functions.[2] The solution can also be sensitive to hyperparameters (e.g., the number of factors and how strongly we regularize). In practice the optimal amount of diversity may simply be guided by what 'looks right.'

10.5 Case Studies on Recommendation and Consumption Diversity

In Section 10.2.2, we saw an empirical study of diversity on *YouTube*, which argued that recommender systems led to diverse views, though this analysis was limited in that the point of comparison was a popularity-based alternative (which is likely not diversity-inducing). Below we explore a few additional case-studies that study diversity within the context of music (sec. 10.5.1) and news (sec. 10.5.2) recommendation, attempting to characterize users in terms of their consumption patterns, and potentially how to guide users to more diverse content.

10.5.1 Diversity on *Spotify*

Anderson et al. (2020) sought to empirically study the effect that recommendation algorithms have on diversity, and more critically to understand how different types of users respond to diverse recommendations.

The paper considers the listening patterns of around 100 million users on *Spotify*. Unlike (e.g.) Fleder and Hosanagar (2009), which defined 'diversity' in terms of the Gini coefficient (i.e., the statistical dispersion of *which* items get consumed), Anderson et al. (2020) define diversity in terms of song representations, that is, essentially the γ_i values in a recommender system.[3]

The specific embeddings γ_i on *Spotify* are estimated using an *item2vec*-like method (as we saw in sec. 8.2.1). The *musical diversity* of a user u's listening activity is defined in terms of a score which they term *generalist-specialist* (or *GS*), following previous work (Waller and Anderson, 2019). Specifically, we start by defining the centroid of a user's *listening history* (which we will term γ_u) as

---

[2] Which may not even be on the same scale: in our case one is a rating (in the range $[1, 5]$) and the other is a cosine similarity (in the range $[-1, 1]$).

[3] Of course, this version of 'diversity' has its own limitations, as it assumes that the learned latent space accurately captures semantic diversity among items.

$$\gamma_u = \frac{1}{|H|} \sum_{j=1}^{|H|} \gamma_{H_j}, \tag{10.11}$$

where H is a list of songs in the user's listening history, with repetition, such that repeated listens will count more to the average. Then the *GS*-score is defined as the average cosine similarity between the user representation γ_u and the items they listen to:

$$GS(u) = \frac{1}{|H|} \sum_{j=1}^{|H|} \frac{\gamma_{H_j} \cdot \gamma_u}{\|\gamma_{H_j}\|\|\gamma_u\|}. \tag{10.12}$$

Intuitively, *specialists* (high $GS(u)$) tend to have songs γ_i in their listening history oriented primarily in a certain direction; *generalists* (low $GS(u)$) do not, ostensibly corresponding to a broader range of preferences.

Part of the analysis in Anderson et al. (2020) is a study of the relationship between diversity (as measured by $GS(u)$) and various other attributes. For example, less active users tend to be specialists (high $GS(u)$), generalist users are less likely to abandon the system ('churn'), and more likely to subscribe to the 'premium' version of the product.

However the main feature in the analysis is to study the relationship between recommendations and diversity, and in particular how generalists and specialists respond differently to algorithmic recommendations. This is measured experimentally by exposing real users on *Spotify* to different recommendation conditions. Three types of recommender system are used: one which merely ranks songs (within a specific predefined subgenre) by popularity; one which is a simple relevance ranker based on user-to-item similarity (essentially a form of heuristic recommendation); and one which is a learned recommender specifically trained to maximize the probability that a user will listen to a song to completion.

First, compared to popularity, recommendation approaches lead to a substantial increase in the number of songs streamed for both groups (they also lead to an increase in the number of songs *skipped*, but this is more than made up for in additional streams). That is, users could be said to be more *engaged* when interacting with recommendations compared to a popularity baseline. Second, the benefit of recommendations appears across both groups (generalists and specialists), though is significantly more pronounced for specialists: this aligns with the paper's hypothesis in the sense that specialists are more sensitive to songs matching their personal relevance criteria. Finally, the learned ranker confers a slight additional benefit over the relevance ranker, though the benefit is surprisingly modest, indicating that simple relevance ranking is sufficient in this context.

Guiding Users to More Diverse Content

In a follow-up paper, Hansen et al. (2021) also consider consumption patterns on *Spotify*, and broadly explore the trade-offs involved in terms of algorithmic choices, diversity methods, and user satisfaction. They note (as we have seen throughout this chapter) that several ranking approaches bias recommendations toward highly popular content that closely resemble interactions from users' histories; like Anderson et al. (2020) they also find evidence that users can in many cases be satisfied by recommendations that are more diverse and less popular.

Several diversification techniques are explored, each of which essentially attempts to trade-off a relevance versus a diversity term. Hansen et al. (2021) explore the merits of each; they broadly favor reinforcement learning-based approaches as a means of swaying users toward diverse content, but note the difficulties involved in productionizing such systems.

10.5.2　Filter Bubbles and Online News Consumption

Much of the discussion of 'filter bubbles' has been in the context of online news, where concerns generally center around whether recommender systems (or more simply, algorithmic ranking techniques) will limit the ideological diversity of content users consume.

Bakshy et al. (2015) study the extent to which users on *Facebook* tend to consume news that conforms to their political ideology. The analysis begins by training a supervised learning system to label news articles as 'liberal,' 'conservative,' or 'neutral,' based on shares by users who volunteer their political affiliation as part of their profile.

The main questions of interest center around the extent to which users are exposed to (or choose to interact with) content that is aligned with their own ideology versus content which is 'cross-cutting.' 'Exposure' refers to algorithmic feed ranking surfacing the content, whereas 'interaction' refers to a user's choice to click on exposed content.

There are many confounding factors in such an analysis, which the study attempts to control for. For example, users' social networks are primarily composed of friends who share a common ideology, so naturally the content users could potentially be exposed to via their social network is predominantly not cross-cutting. Likewise, users' tendency to interact with (i.e., click on) content is confounded by the fact that the feed ranker already factors in click probability when determining which (and how prominently) content is surfaced to the user in the first place.

After attempting to control for these effects, the study's main findings are that algorithmic ranking indeed exposes users to less ideologically diverse news than would be expected by the ideological makeup of their social group, however users interact with ideologically diverse content at an even lower rate than their rate of exposure. Based on this, the authors argue that individual choice plays the largest role in users' exposure to content that is ideologically homogeneous.

However, the argument above does not refute the possibility of a 'filter bubble' of online news consumption, it merely argues that its primary cause (in the case of *Facebook*) is not necessarily algorithmic.

Diversity Across Consumption Channels

Flaxman et al. (2016) sought to measure the impact that new forms of consumption (news aggregators, social recommendation, etc.) have on the diversity and extremity of news consumption. Their analysis is based on 50,000 users who have the *Bing Toolbar* plugin installed, which allows for their interaction patterns to be tracked.

The main goal of the paper is to measure how diversity differs across users who interact with news via different consumption channels. *Direct* consumption (directly visiting a URL or accessing a bookmark); *aggregator*-based consumption (specifically, visiting links from *Google News* in the case of their study); *social* consumption (consumption from *Facebook*, *Twitter*, or e-mail); and *search* (consumption via queries on *Google*, *Bing*, and *Yahoo* search). Various mundane aspects must also be dealt with to determine which links correspond to news articles, versus opinion pieces, and so on. Much of the data collection effort centers around determining the ideological stance of articles and publishers (for which there is no ground truth); the ideological stance of individuals is then measured in terms of the articles they consume.

Consumption from these four sources is measured in various ways. First, *segregation* measures the average distance in polarity scores between two randomly chosen users who consume news via the same channel. These scores reveal that consumers of opinion pieces are more segregated than consumers of news across all four channels, with social media and search traffic being the most segregated. This arguably aligns with the concept of a filter bubble, to the extent that these media lead to ideologically more segregated groups.

Counter to this result, they also find that users who consume media from search engines and social media *also* experience higher exposure to ideologically diverse news (as opposed to users who consume news from aggregators or via direct consumption). Flaxman et al. (2016) argue that most online news consumption mimics patterns of traditional media consumption, with users predominately visiting homepages of their preferred mainstream outlets; ultimately, to the extent that 'filter bubbles' exist in online news, their dynamics are not as straightforward as they might first appear.

Filter Bubbles on *Google News*

Haim et al. (2018) conducted an exploratory study of recommendation on *Google News*, in order to determine the effects of personalization on content diversity. Like Bakshy et al. (2015), they broadly argue that the effects of filter bubbles are somewhat overstated, or otherwise that the patterns of bias in recommendations are not the same as what is anecdotally understood to be a 'filter bubble.'

They conduct two studies, to look at 'explicit' and 'implicit' personalization. Both are based on empirical observation of the actual news recommendations provided by *Google News*, sampled from several synthetic user accounts. Recommendations are then compared against 'traditional' (i.e., non-personalized, curated) news sources in terms of topic and content diversity.

In the 'explicit' setting, they make use of a *Google News* feature that allows users to specify the types of news they are interested in, among a set of broad categories (e.g., sports, entertainment, politics). Annotators then labeled recommended articles according to these categories in order to quantify the alignment between the explicit preferences and the recommended articles.

The first finding is simply that *Google News* does indeed respect users' explicit preferences, in the sense that the proportion of recommended articles matching the desired topic far exceeds their proportion in a non-personalized setting.

Haim et al. (2018) also evaluate recommendations in terms of source diversity (i.e., in terms of the original news sources that *Google News* aggregates). Here, they find surprisingly that a few somewhat niche news sources dominate recommendations, whereas more mainstream sources are underrepresented; this result is relatively consistent across each of the personalized accounts.

In the 'implicit' setting, Haim et al. (2018) made use of several social media accounts, corresponding to users with specified (but synthetic) demographics and preferences (such as a marketing manager, an elderly conservative, etc.). Each of these simulated agents then interacts with social media (liking articles on *Facebook*, *Google+*, etc.), after which their *Google News* recommendations are compared.

The main conclusion of this second study is simply that implicit personalization has little effect on the recommended results (though there is evidence that some results are indeed personalized).

Ultimately while both Bakshy et al. (2015) and Haim et al. (2018) argue against a 'filter bubble' as such, both point to potential issues of bias in recommendations; Bakshy et al. (2015) suggest that recommendations do indeed present an overall more biased perspective compared to users' broader social groups, while Haim et al. (2018) show that certain niche sources tend to be over-represented in news recommendations.

10.6 Other Metrics Beyond Accuracy

So far, we have considered diversity in terms of the trade-off between recommending the highest relevance items (e.g., highest click probability) while ensuring that recommended items are not too similar to each other. Other than relevance, diversity among items is only one desirable characteristic to trade-off.

Besides relevance and diversity, other desirable features of a recommendation list might include:

- Items should be *novel* to the user, that is, the recommender system should balance *discovery* of new items against recommending items with high interaction probability, but which are already known to the user.
- Rather than being internally diverse, we might have goals such as mutual compatibility among items (e.g., Hao et al. (2020)).
- Recommended items should have good *coverage*, that is, they should represent a broad range of categories or features; or they should be *balanced*, in terms of matching the category distribution from the user's history.
- Other goals could be more nebulous, such as perceived unexpectedness, serendipity, or overall user satisfaction.

Kaminskas and Bridge (2016) broadly survey these alternate optimization criteria for recommender systems, focusing in particular on diversity, serendipity, novelty, and coverage. We briefly survey some of their main findings (as well as more recent work) below.

Many of the approaches to diverse recommendation discussed in Kaminskas and Bridge (2016) are *re-ranking* strategies, similar to maximal marginal relevance (sec. 10.3.1) and other techniques we have discussed so far. They also discuss other settings where diversity might be desirable, such as conversational recommendation (sec. 8.4.4) and the relationship to more traditional work in 'portfolio optimization' from information retrieval (Markowitz, 1968).

10.6.1 Serendipity

Various attempts have been made to define 'serendipity' in the context of recommendations. Kaminskas and Bridge (2016) start with the core property of 'surprise' (i.e., recommendations should be different from one's expectations); Kotkov et al. (2018) state that serendipity should be a combination of relevance, novelty and unexpectedness.

Each of these competing elements is difficult to define precisely, and some (like a recommendation being 'surprising') are likely subjective. Below we discuss a few specific attempts to incorporate serendipity into recommendations, and to understand what it means to users in practice.

Serendipity in Music Recommendation

Zhang et al. (2012) consider how music recommendations can be improved by balancing goals of accuracy, diversity, novelty, and serendipity. Their specific approach combines many of the ideas we have seen already: *diversity* is measured in terms of the cosine similarity between items in a recommendation list (as in sec. 4.3.3); *novelty* or 'unexpectedness' is defined in terms of overall item popularity (as in sec. 10.3.2); serendipity (or 'unserendipity,' since low values mean high serendipity) is defined using a novel function, which essentially measures how similar recommended items are to those in the user's interaction history:

$$\text{Unserendipity} = \frac{1}{|U|} \sum_{u \in U} \frac{1}{|I_u|} \sum_{i \in I_u} \sum_{j \in R_u} \frac{\text{Cos}(i, j)}{|R_u|}, \qquad (10.13)$$

where R_u is a set of items recommended to the user and I_u is the item history for user u. This measure takes a low value if recommended items are on average different from those that appeared in users' histories.

Given these three metrics (diversity, novelty, and serendipity), Zhang et al. (2012) seek recommendation techniques that can optimize them without overly compromising accuracy. While metrics such as that of Equation (10.13) cannot straightforwardly be incorporated into the optimization scheme directly, various models are designed to ensure that recommendations are topically diverse or belong to distinct clusters. Quantitatively, Zhang et al. (2012) study the trade-off between accuracy, diversity, novelty, and serendipity under different configurations of this model. They also conduct a user study to evaluate the qualitative aspects of the model, revealing that subjective notions of 'serendipity' and 'usefulness' can be improved without overly harming user enjoyment.

Investigating Serendipity via User Studies

Given the ambiguous nature of the precise definition of serendipity, Kotkov et al. (2018) attempted to assess what it means to users via a survey. They survey commonly proposed notions for diversity, ranging from items the user simply has not heard of, did not expect to be recommended, or are highly dissimilar to what they usually consume. They found that serendipitous recommendations are effective in broadening user preferences, though do not have a significant impact in terms of satisfaction. They investigate the key feature of *unexpectedness* and its different definitions in the literature (a few of which we study in sec. 10.6.2). In particular they find that items a user did not expect to be relevant (or did not expect to like) tend to have a negative effect in terms of user satisfaction, and are not as effective at broadening preferences compared to other notions of unexpectedness.

Wang et al. (2020) also studied serendipity via a large-scale user study, asking users directly what type of item features contributed to the perceived serendipity of a recommendation. They found that while perceived serendipity is positively influenced by lower popularity (similar to the principle from our simple diversification technique in eq. (10.4)), characteristics such as being from a distant category, or separated temporally from similar recommendations, do not contribute to perceived serendipity. That 'serendipitous' results can be close in time and category compared to previous interactions is somewhat surprising, given our efforts to define serendipity above. Wang et al. (2020) hypothesize that this is due to the rapidly evolving nature of user preferences, where distant interactions rapidly lose meaning. They also find that (perceived) serendipity is not static across user demographics (older and/or male users tend to perceive recommendations as more serendipitous, younger users are more sensitive to item popularity, etc.); one hypothesis is that this relates to overall familiarity with the particular shopping platform.

10.6.2 Unexpectedness

Adamopoulos and Tuzhilin (2014) attempt to define the notion of 'unexpectedness' as it relates to (movie) recommendations. They note that one cannot target unexpectedness in isolation, or one could trivially generate poor-quality but unexpected recommendations. As such they seek a notion of *utility* that balances unexpectedness against traditional metrics of recommendation quality. They define unexpectedness (for a user u and item i) as a distance between i and the set of items the user u 'expects' to receive. They further assume that there is some optimal value for this distance (which could be different for each user): recommendations that are too expected are uninteresting, while recommendations that are too unexpected will be regarded as irrelevant; 'quality' is defined more straightforwardly in terms of ratings.

Several quantities must then be determined: each user's personal tolerance for unexpectedness, the ideal trade-off between unexpectedness and utility, and finally the definition of what is 'expected.' For the latter Adamopoulos and Tuzhilin (2014) use a definition based on content similarity in terms of movie attributes (movies with similar attributes are 'expected'). The goal of Adamopoulos and Tuzhilin (2014) is not to fit these values (which are largely subjective quantities) but to evaluate the performance of recommendation approaches under various hypothetical scenarios. The most promising finding is that optimizing this type of joint utility need not harm performance compared to methods that target quality exclusively.

Li et al. (2020) define unexpectedness in terms of clustering: users' consumption histories (γ_i) are clustered in latent space. An 'unexpected' item j is one that is not close to any cluster. To prevent the model from simply recommending outlying or 'fringe' items (which might trivially maximize unexpectedness), a unimodal distribution over desired utility values is introduced. Unexpectedness is then balanced against utility, weighted according to a personalized factor measuring the extent to which each user tends to favor unexpectedness over relevance.

10.6.3 Calibration

A related notion to diversity is that of *calibration* of predictions or recommendations. Whereas a diversity metric might suggest (e.g.) that we should expose users to a wide distribution of recommendations, which potentially span beyond their explicit preferences, *calibration* refers to the idea that recommendations should be made *in proportion* to expressed preferences. For instance, if a user watches 40% sci-fi movies and 60% romantic comedies, they should not exclusively be recommended romantic comedies, as might happen when naively recommending by maximizing compatibility.

Steck (2018) introduce such a notion of *calibrated recommendations*, in the context of movie recommendations on *Netflix*. Their work discusses metrics to assess calibration, as well as methods to calibrate the outputs of an existing recommender system.

Their notion of calibration operates over a pre-defined set of item *genres*, described using a stochastic genre vector $p(g|i)$ (e.g., a movie might be categorized as 80% 'action' and 20% 'sci-fi'); this could potentially be adapted to other attributes toward which one desired calibration. The basic idea behind a calibration metric is then that the distribution of genres g among a user's history $i \in I_u$ should match the distribution of *recommended* items $i \in R_u$. The two terms are defined (respectively) as:

$$\text{historical:} \quad p(g|u) = \frac{\sum_{i \in I_u} w_{u,i} \cdot p(g|i)}{\sum_{i \in I_u} w_{u,i}}, \quad (10.14)$$

$$\text{recommended:} \quad q(g|u) = \frac{\sum_{i \in R_u} w_{r(i)} \cdot p(g|i)}{\sum_{i \in R_u} w_{r(i)}}. \quad (10.15)$$

Both expressions include a 'weighting' term w. In the case of the historical distribution $w_{u,i}$ might weight items according to recency (e.g.), or for the case of recommendations $w_{r(i)}$ might weight recommendations according to their position in a list (i.e., their ranking); either term could also be ignored.

Now, the goal is to generate a set of recommended items R_u such that the two distributions should match closely. The difference between the two distributions can be measured by (e.g.) the Kullback–Leibler divergence:

$$KL(p, q) = \sum_g p(g|u) \log \frac{p(g|u)}{q(g|u)}. \qquad (10.16)$$

Of course, in addition to being well-calibrated, recommendations should also be highly compatible according to the recommender system itself. This is achieved in Steck (2018) with a simple expression that trades off recommendation utility and calibration (via a trade-off hyperparameter λ):

$$R_u = \underset{R}{\arg\max}\, \underbrace{(1 - \lambda) \cdot \sum_{i \in R} f(u, i)}_{\text{compatibility}} - \underbrace{\lambda \cdot KL(p, q(R))}_{\text{calibration}}. \qquad (10.17)$$

Steck (2018) note that the above is a hard combinatorial optimization problem, but can be approximated greedily (with a certain optimality guarantee), by iteratively adding one item at a time to R so as to optimize the above criterion until the desired number of items is reached.

An appealing property of this approach is that it can be applied in a purely post-hoc fashion to the outputs of any recommender system that associates scores between users and items. The experiments in Steck (2018) show (by varying λ in eq. (10.17)) that a reasonable degree of calibration can be achieved with minimal loss in recommendation utility.

10.7 Fairness

Fairness in machine learning is often defined in terms of predictions and protected characteristics. For example, when building a classifier to aid in hiring decisions, we might be interested in ensuring that men and women are ranked as 'qualified' at approximately the same rate. Or, a system for predicting recidivism should not be biased against individuals of a certain race (Chouldechova, 2017).

Typically, we might desire that the outputs of our classifier $f(x_i)$ do not depend on some protected feature $x_{i,f}$ (indicating race, gender, etc.). Some common definitions include, for example, *demographic parity*, which states that the probability of a positive prediction (e.g., being ranked as 'qualified') should be the same whether one has the protected feature or not:

$$p(f(x_i) = 1 | x_{i,f} = 1) = p(f(x_i) = 1 | x_{i,f} = 0). \qquad (10.18)$$

The related notion of *equal opportunity* allows for the possibility that the target variable depends on the protected feature, and states that *among the qualified* ($y_i = 1$) *or unqualified* ($y_i = 0$) *individuals*, the probability of a positive prediction should be the same whether or not one has the protected features:

$$p(f(x_i) = 1 | x_{i,f} = 1, y_i = y) = p(f(x_i) = 1 | x_{i,f} = 0, y_i = y). \qquad (10.19)$$

These are just two examples out of dozens of possible notions of fairness that may be of interest, see, for example, Mehrabi et al. (2019) for a comprehensive survey.

A classifier may violate the above rules for a variety of reasons. For example, the training data may exhibit historical bias against a certain group; or, a classifier trained on highly imbalanced data may simply make inaccurate (or imbalanced) predictions for groups that are poorly represented in the data (we already saw a simple example of this for an imbalanced dataset in sec. 3.3.1). Several machine learning techniques have been proposed to mitigate unfairness in such scenarios, for example, by pre-processing the biased data (Kamiran and Calders, 2009), or by altering the classifier itself (Zafar et al., 2017).

In the contexts of recommendations and personalized predictions, one may have slightly different definitions and goals in terms of building a 'fair' model. Yao and Huang (2017) attempt to adapt notions of fairness to personalized recommendation contexts. They consider a running example of course recommendation, where course evaluations in Computer Science (e.g.) may primarily represent the preferences of the predominantly male population; models trained on such data (or even simple statistics or heuristics based on popularity, etc.) may merely reflect the preferences or activities of the majority group.

Yao and Huang (2017) introduce several metrics of fairness with respect to the outputs of a recommender system, and show that these metrics can be straightforwardly incorporated into the training objective (meaning that the model can be discouraged from making unfair predictions). Their metrics are defined by dividing users into groups g_u, which are assumed to be binary, though in the studied case of gender g_u can simply be divided into the over-represented group (male) and the under-represented group (non-male).

Value Unfairness measures the extent to which one group tends to have their ratings over- or under-predicted compared to the other:

$$U_{\text{val}} = \frac{1}{|I|} \sum_{i=1}^{|I|} \left| \left(\underbrace{\mathbb{E}_g[y]_i}_{} - \overbrace{\mathbb{E}_g[r]_i}^{\text{average } rating \text{ for group } g \text{ on item } i} \right) - \left(\mathbb{E}_{\neg g}[y]_i - \mathbb{E}_{\neg g}[r]_i \right) \right|. \qquad (10.20)$$

expected *prediction* for group g on item i

Note that since both sides take expectations (or averages), the measure is invariant to size differences between the two groups.

Value unfairness could occur in a latent factor model (like that of eq. (5.10)) if, for example, predictions are dominated via the bias terms β_i; in a model in which one group is over-represented, the bias terms may essentially reflect the preferences only of the over-represented group.

Absolute Unfairness replaces differences in expectation (from eq. (10.20)) with absolute values:

$$U_{\text{abs}} = \frac{1}{|I|} \sum_{i=1}^{|I|} \left| \left| \mathbb{E}_g[y]_i - \mathbb{E}_g[r]_i \right| - \left| \mathbb{E}_{\neg g}[y]_i - \mathbb{E}_{\neg g}[r]_i \right| \right|. \tag{10.21}$$

Following this change, absolute unfairness now captures the extent to which one group has their ratings *mispredicted* (in an absolute sense) more than the other. This essentially measures a difference in the system's *utility* between the two groups, in the sense that if one group routinely receives recommendations with high error then the system is unlikely to be useful to them.

Next, Yao and Huang (2017) define *under-* and *over-estimation* unfairness to assess the model's tendency to either under- or over-predict the true ratings:

$$U_{\text{under}} = \frac{1}{|I|} \sum_{i=1}^{|I|} \left| \max\{0, \mathbb{E}_g[r]_i - \mathbb{E}_g[y]_i\} - \max\{0, \mathbb{E}_{\neg g}[r]_i - \mathbb{E}_{\neg g}[y]_i\} \right|, \tag{10.22}$$

$$U_{\text{over}} = \frac{1}{|I|} \sum_{i=1}^{|I|} \left| \max\{0, \mathbb{E}_g[y]_i - \mathbb{E}_g[r]_i\} - \max\{0, \mathbb{E}_{\neg g}[y]_i - \mathbb{E}_{\neg g}[r]_i\} \right|. \tag{10.23}$$

These definitions are somewhat analogous to related concepts we saw when evaluating ranking models in Section 3.3; consistently underpredicting is analogous to having low recall (failing to retrieve relevant items), whereas overpredicting is analogous to having low precision (retrieving items that are not relevant). Both can potentially reduce the utility of the recommender system for one of the groups.

Ultimately, Yao and Huang (2017) show that each of the above metrics can be incorporated into recommender systems of the form given in Equation (5.14). That is, they can be combined via a trade-off term so that the model is accurate while minimizing unfairness, for example:

$$\frac{1}{|\mathcal{T}|} \sum_{(u,i)\in\mathcal{T}} \underbrace{(\alpha + \beta_i + \beta_u + \gamma_i + \gamma_u - R_{u,i})^2}_{\text{accuracy}} + \lambda \underbrace{U_{\text{abs}}}_{\text{(absolute) fairness}}. \tag{10.24}$$

Optimization remains straightforward, as each fairness metric is differentiable with respect to the model parameters. The main finding of the paper is then that fairness metrics can be optimized while paying only a minimal price in terms of overall model accuracy.

In addition to presenting the above objectives, Yao and Huang (2017) also show that real data do in fact exhibit biases with respect to the above metrics. They do so using data from *MovieLens* across different genres where women or men are over-represented; finally they show that such biases can be mitigated using the above techniques.

10.7.1 Multisided Fairness

A separate attempt to introduce fairness metrics into recommendation problems is described in Burke (2017). In comparison to the fairness metrics defined above, the main difference is to consider fairness from both the perspective of users of the system ('consumers') as well as content providers ('producers'). As a motivating example, they consider a hypothetical recommendation scenario on the microfinancing website *Kiva.org*, where it may be desirable that proposals from different businesses receive somewhat balanced representation among recommendations. More broadly, this is an instance of recommendation in a 'matchmaking' setting where both sides (in this case, users and businesses) are being matched to each other; in such cases, fairness should not be defined in terms of one 'side' only, but should consider the needs of both types of stakeholders. Other examples are cited including online advertising, the sharing economy, or online dating (as in sec. 6.3.1).

To achieve this notion of fairness, they consider fairness separately from the perspective of consumers and producers, which they term *C*- and *P*-fairness. Following these definitions, the fairness metrics we studied above would be examples of *C*-fairness. Burke (2017) note that *C*- and *P*-fairness are not merely symmetric definitions, and that *P*-fairness may have requirements not encountered when studying *C*-fairness, such as in the examples above. For example, in a product recommendation setting, if we wanted to encourage sales diversity, the producers are *passive* in the sense that they are not actively seeking out recommendations in the system.

Finally, Burke (2017) consider settings of *CP*-fairness, where fairness must be considered from the perspectives of both sides simultaneously. We will revisit examples of *P*-fairness and *CP*-fairness as we examine case studies of gender bias in Section 10.8.

A selection of the fairness objectives from this section (as well as our case studies in Section 10.8) is summarized in Table 10.3.

Table 10.3 *Comparison of personalized fairness objectives. References: Ekstrand et al. (2018b); Wan et al. (2020); Yao and Huang (2017).*

Ref.	Objective	Description
YH17	Value Unfairness	Neither of two groups should have their compatibility over- or under-predicted more than the other (sec. 10.7).
YH17	Absolute Unfairness	Neither of two groups should have their compatibility mispredicted more than the other (sec. 10.7).
E18	Demographic parity among recommendations	Demographics (e.g., author gender) should be reasonably balanced (or should match the training distribution) among the items being recommended (sec. 10.8.2).
W20	Marketing fairness	Individuals underrepresented in marketing media (e.g., images) should not have reduced recommendation utility (sec. 10.8.3).

10.7.2 Implementing Fairness Objectives in *Tensorflow*

Part of the appeal of the fairness objectives we have developed in this section is that they can straightforwardly be incorporated into the learning objectives of standard recommenders.[4] Below we will implement 'absolute unfairness' as in Section 10.7. We will use data from beer reviews (this is the same data we used in Section 2.3.2) which includes user gender information and in which male users are substantially over-represented. First, we read the data, recording user gender along with each interaction:

```
5   for d in parse('beer.json.gz'):
6       if not 'user/gender' in d: continue # Skip users who
            didn't specify gender
7       g = d['user/gender'] == 'Male'
8       u = d['user/profileName']
9       i = d['beer/beerId']
10      r = d['review/overall']
11      if not u in userIDs: userIDs[u] = len(userIDs)
12      if not i in itemIDs: itemIDs[i] = len(itemIDs)
13      interactions.append((g,u,i,r))
```

Next, we build some utility data structures to store interactions for each item according to group membership (g and $\neg g$ for males and females):

---

[4] This is in contrast to fairness objectives in some classical settings. For example, when balancing hiring decisions with respect to gender it may not be permissible for the algorithm to base the decision on the protected attribute (see, e.g., Lipton et al. (2018)).

```
14   interactionsPerItemG = defaultdict(list)
15   interactionsPerItemGneg = defaultdict(list)
16
17   for g,u,i,r in interactions:
18       if g: interactionsPerItemG[i].append((u,r))
19       else: interactionsPerItemGneg[i].append((u,r))
```

We also store item sets for each group for sampling:

```
20   itemsG = set(interactionsPerItemG.keys())
21   itemsGneg = set(interactionsPerItemGneg.keys())
22   itemsBoth = itemsG.intersection(itemsGneg)
```

Finally, we implement the absolute (un)fairness objective. This implementation computes the fairness objective for a single item (i.e., one term in the summation in eq. 10.21). During training, this objective can be called for a small sample of items, and added to the accuracy term:

```
23   def absoluteUnfairness(self, i):
24       G = interactionsPerItemG[i]
25       Gneg = interactionsPerItemGneg[i]
26       # Compute the terms from Equation 10.21
27       rG = tf.reduce_mean(tf.convert_to_tensor([r for _,r in G
             ])) # 𝔼_g[r]_i
28       rGneg = tf.reduce_mean(tf.convert_to_tensor([r for _,r
             in Gneg])) # 𝔼_¬g[r]_i
29       pG = tf.reduce_mean(self.predictSample([userIDs[u] for u
             ,_ in G], [itemIDs[i]]*len(G))) # 𝔼_g[y]_i
30       pGneg = tf.reduce_mean(self.predictSample([userIDs[u]
             for u,_ in Gneg], [itemIDs[i]]*len(Gneg))) # 𝔼_¬g[y]_i
31       Uabs = tf.abs(tf.abs(pG - rG) - tf.abs(pGneg - rGneg))
32       return self.lambFair * Uabs
```

10.8 Case Studies on Gender Bias in Recommendation

Just as Yao and Huang (2017) used gender imbalance as a motivating example to study fairness and bias with regard to under-represented groups in recommender systems, several studies have investigated specific scenarios where recommenders exhibit significant bias, or have reduced utility for a specific gender.

10.8.1 Data Resampling and Popularity Bias

Ekstrand et al. (2018a) study a similar problem to Yao and Huang (2017) (sec. 10.7), also noting that there is a substantial *utility gap* between the majority versus under-represented groups (i.e., closest to *absolute unfairness* as in eq. (10.21)). Bias is reported with respect to both gender and age attributes, both of which are self-reported by users in datasets of movies and songs (from *MovieLens* (Harper and Konstan, 2015) and *Last.FM* (Celma Herrada, 2008)).

Unlike Yao and Huang (2017), where this type of bias is corrected using a joint objective that balances overall utility with unfairness (eq. (10.24)), Ekstrand et al. (2018a) use a *data resampling* approach to correct for bias. This type of approach is borrowed from Kamiran and Calders (2009) where it was used in the context of fair classification. The basic idea is to resample the data so as to achieve equal representation among groups; practically speaking, this is fairly similar to the reweighting schemes we explored in Section 3.3.2.

Ekstrand et al. (2018a) also raise the potential issue of *popularity bias* in recommender systems (also discussed in Bellogin et al. (2011)), in which algorithms that work well for popular items will generally be favored over algorithms which *personalize* better (but whose performance is worse for popular items). To address this, they introduce evaluation metrics that control for the effect of popularity, so that algorithms can be compared according to their degree of personalization rather than their tendency to select popular items.

10.8.2 Bias and Author Gender in Book Recommendations

Ekstrand et al. (2018b) explore bias from the perspective of book *authors*. This is somewhat analogous to the idea of *P*-fairness from Section 10.7.1, given that we are interested in how recommendations could be biased against 'producers' (in this case, authors of a certain gender).

Book reviews and metadata are collected from *BookCrossing* (Ziegler et al., 2005), *Amazon* (McAuley et al., 2015), and *Goodreads* (Wan and McAuley, 2018). An interesting component of the study is how these datasets can be augmented to incorporate the gender of each author, which is not a feature immediately available in any of the above datasets; author gender information is compiled from external sources, which is matched to records in each of the datasets.

Ekstrand et al. (2018b) begin by analyzing the overall gender distribution of authors in the datasets, as compared to the gender distribution among reading histories of individual users. Beyond this, they seek to study how gender bias is 'propagated' by recommendation algorithms, that is, the extent to which users who exhibit a moderate tendency toward authors of a certain gender will tend to have recommendations in which that gender is more extremely over-represented. Finally, they analyze the extent to which these issues can be mitigated algorithmically.

Ultimately, the study concludes that authors in all three datasets (at least those whose identities could be resolved) are predominantly male. In terms of rating histories by users, the distribution is less skewed. In terms of recommendation algorithms, results are quite mixed, with certain algorithms and datasets leading to more or less skewed recommendations, or otherwise recommendations that mimic users' own gender preferences.

Finally, the authors find that gender imbalance in recommendations can be mitigated easily via simple re-ranking strategies, with minimal impact on performance. This analysis bears some similarity to our study of filter bubbles (sec. 10.5.2), or the techniques used to calibrate recommendations (in this case to match a desired gender distribution rather than a genre distribution) from Section 10.6.3.

10.8.3 Gender Bias in Marketing

Wan et al. (2020) investigate bias in terms of how products are *marketed*. For example, a user may be more (or less) inclined to purchase a clothing item if it is modeled by somebody sharing their gender, weight, age, skin-tone, and so on. In some instances, these features may be directly relevant to the suitability of the item, but in others they may not be. If users are disinclined to interact with items simply because their own identity is not represented, this reduces the utility of the system to the users, represents a missed opportunity in terms of sales, and raises broader issues of representation in marketing. 'Fairness' from this perspective is an instance of *CP*-fairness from Section 10.7.1, as both producers and consumers face consequences from unfair treatment.

Like Ekstrand et al. (2018b), Wan et al. (2020) start by assessing the extent to which these types of biases can be found in historical interactions (in their case, purchases). They consider two settings: clothing, using a dataset from *ModCloth*, and electronics, using data from *Amazon*. On *ModCloth*, they are interested in whether users are less inclined to buy items if the model has a different body type than the user (e.g., the user is plus-size, but the model is not, even though the item is available in plus-sizes). On *Amazon*, they are interested in whether ostensibly 'genderless' products have different sales patterns among male and female users, based on their marketing images.

Again, the study faces difficult issues of augmenting the data since gender and size attributes of users are not readily available. *ModCloth* specifies the size of the models in marketing images, and user sizes are inferred from their historical tendency to purchase only items of a certain size. Data augmentation is more difficult on *Amazon*: gender attributes in marketing images must be inferred using computer vision techniques; gender attributes of users are inferred from their purchases in the *clothing* category.[5]

---

[5] Of course, clothing purchases are a rough proxy for gender identity, and users whose purchases span both gender categories are not considered.

Indeed, the study determines that there is significant correlation between users' attributes and their purchase patterns (e.g., male users tend to purchase electronics items marketed by male models). Of course, as with gender in book recommendations (sec. 10.8.2), it is hard to disentangle 'bias' or 'unfairness' from users' intrinsic preferences or legitimate marketing choices (e.g., the reason that women tend to buy women's watches may be largely practical). However the goal is to determine whether bias is *amplified* by recommender systems, and whether this effect can be mitigated.

The specific question that is asked is whether recommendation *errors* are correlated with market segments and marketing images. This bears passing similarity to the notion of *absolute unfairness* as in Equation (10.21), though that measure considers unfairness only from the perspective of the *user's* identity, whereas the question asked here concerns both user and item 'identity' simultaneously. Specifically, four possible types of error are investigated:

$$\text{Product Image} \begin{cases} \text{Female} \\ \text{Male} \end{cases} \underbrace{\begin{bmatrix} \bar{e}_{F,F} & \bar{e}_{M,F} \\ \bar{e}_{F,M} & \bar{e}_{M,M} \end{bmatrix}}_{\substack{\text{Female} \quad \text{Male} \\ \text{User Identity}}} \cdot \tag{10.25}$$

Under a null model, the errors should not be correlated with market segments (this can be measured via a specific statistical test).

Finding that these errors are indeed significantly correlated with market segments, Wan et al. (2020) seek to address this via a loss which balances model error and error correlation:

$$\overbrace{\sum_{u,i}(f(u,i) - r_{u,i})^2}^{\text{prediction error}} + \alpha \underbrace{\mathcal{L}_{corr}}_{\text{error parity on market segments}} \cdot \tag{10.26}$$

Again, this joint loss can be optimized much like the one in Equation (10.24), satisfying the fairness objective with minimal loss in prediction accuracy.

Ultimately, the above case-studies demonstrate that even with regard to a single characteristic (gender), the potential fairness consequences are surprisingly varied and require careful attention to resolve.

Exercises

10.1 In this exercise we will explore recommender systems that balance relevance with diversity. You may base your implementation on the code and data from Section 10.4. Start by experimenting with a variety of diversity objectives. For example:

- Replacing the cosine similarity (sim) with other similarity functions based on item representations.
- Use similarity functions based on item *features*. For example, a simple diversity function might simply measure whether two items belong to a different category, or have a different ABV (etc.).
- Replace the Maximal Marginal Relevance criterion with an alternative from Section 10.3, for example, as in Equation (10.4) or Equation (10.8).

Evaluating diversification techniques is difficult, since they make a qualitative improvement at the cost of a quantitative metric. Evaluate your diversification techniques by plotting a relevance metric (such as those in Section 5.4) as the diversity parameter (e.g., λ in eq. (10.2)) changes. Does your plot contain an 'elbow,' that is, a region in which diversity is significantly increased without sacrificing relevance?

10.2 In addition to issues of diversity as we saw in Exercise 10.1, we also studied *concentration* effects in Sections 10.2.1 and 10.2.2, whereby a recommender system can skew the distribution of recommended items toward a smaller set of items than those represented in the training data. In Section 10.1 we measured concentration in terms of the Gini coefficient (eq. (10.1)) of historical data versus recommendations. Consider some strategies to reduce the concentration among recommendations. For example:

- Explicitly penalize highly popular (or highly recommended) items from being recommended too often (e.g., by adding a small negative bias to popular items).
- Incorporate a diversification strategy such as one from Exercise 10.1.
- Add some small amount of randomization into recommendations.

Note that one can trivially produce recommendations that are less concentrated simply by recommending uniformly at random. As in Exercise 10.1, see if you can produce a strategy that improves concentration (in terms of the Gini coefficient) without significantly harming relevance metrics.

10.3 In Section 10.7 we developed various fairness objectives for personalized recommender systems; although we will explore these objectives more in Project 9, for the moment let us consider the notion of *demographic parity* as in Equation (10.18). In Ekstrand et al. (2018b) demographic parity is measured with respect to gender (of book authors), though for the purpose of this exercise you could consider any attribute associated with the items (e.g., whether a beer is low or high ABV). For a few such attributes, compare the training distribution (i.e., proportion of historical interactions having that attribute) to the recommendation distribution. Consider whether you can design simple strategies to correct any disparity, for example, by systematically assigning higher relevance scores to items from an under-represented class.

Project 9: Diverse and Fair Recommendations

In this project we will consider how we can improve the outputs of the types of recommendation approach we originally developed in Chapter 5. Select a dataset that includes a gender attribute, such as the beer data we used in Section 2.3.2, or others from Section 10.8. A suitable dataset would be one that:

- Contains a gender attribute and is imbalanced with respect to this attribute (e.g., the majority of users are male); in such a dataset we might be concerned that recommendations will have reduced utility for the underrepresented group.
- Contains item metadata, such as categories, prices, or other item attributes, which can be used to measure recommendation diversity, calibration, and so on.

In principle this project could be completed with any similar dataset that includes (a) an attribute of interest with respect to which we can measure bias, such gender, age, and so on; and (b) item metadata with respect to which we can measure diversity.

Use this dataset to analyze diversity and fairness from the following perspectives:

(i) Implement a recommender system to predict ratings in the dataset, for example, a latent factor model as in Section 5.1.

(ii) Using the above model, compute the four fairness metrics from Section 10.7 (i.e., value unfairness, absolute unfairness, under- and overestimation unfairness), comparing male (g) to non-male ($\neg g$) users.[6]

(iii) Next, assess recommended items in terms of diversity. Diversity could be measured in several ways, for example, you could measure diversity with respect to the distribution of recommend items, or with respect to some attribute (e.g., the style or brand). This could be a formal measure of dispersion such as the Gini coefficient (as in eq. (10.1)), or a plot of recommendation versus interaction frequency as in Figure 10.2.

---

[6] Or whichever group g is over-represented.

References

Abdollahpouri, Himan, Burke, Robin, and Mobasher, Bamshad. 2017. Recommender systems as multistakeholder environments. In: *UMAP '17: Proceedings of the 25th Conference on User Modeling, Adaptation and Personalization.* ACM.

Adamopoulos, Panagiotis and Tuzhilin, Alexander. 2014. On unexpectedness in recommender systems: Or how to better expect the unexpected. *ACM Transactions on Intelligent Systems and Technology,* **5**(4), 1–32.

Adomavicius, Gediminas and Kwon, YoungOk. 2011. Improving aggregate recommendation diversity using ranking-based techniques. *IEEE Transactions on Knowledge and Data Engineering,* **24**(5), 896–911.

Al Bawab, Ziad, Mills, George H, and Crespo, Jean-Francois. 2012. Finding trending local topics in search queries for personalization of a recommendation system. In: *KDD '12: Proceedings of the 18th ACM SIGKDD International Conference on Knowledge Discovery and Data Mining.* ACM.

Amer-Yahia, Sihem, Roy, Senjuti Basu, Chawlat, Ashish, Das, Gautam, and Yu, Cong. 2009. Group recommendation: Semantics and efficiency. *Proceedings of the VLDB Endowment,* **2**(1), 754–65.

Anderson, Ashton, Kumar, Ravi, Tomkins, Andrew, and Vassilvitskii, Sergei. 2014. The dynamics of repeat consumption. In: *WWW '14: Proceedings of the 23rd International World Wide Web Conference.* ACM.

Anderson, Ashton, Maystre, Lucas, Anderson, Ian, Mehrotra, Rishabh, and Lalmas, Mounia. 2020. Algorithmic effects on the diversity of consumption on Spotify. In: *WWW '20: Proceedings of The Web Conference 2020.* ACM.

Bachrach, Yoram, Finkelstein, Yehuda, Gilad-Bachrach, Ran, Katzir, Liran, Koenigstein, Noam, Nice, Nir, and Paquet, Ulrich. 2014. Speeding up the Xbox recommender system using a Euclidean transformation for inner-product spaces. In: *RecSys '14: Proceedings of the 8th ACM Conference on Recommender Systems.* ACM.

Bahdanau, Dzmitry, Cho, Kyunghyun, and Bengio, Yoshua. 2014. Neural machine translation by jointly learning to align and translate. *arXiv preprint arXiv:1409.0473.*

Bakshy, Eytan, Messing, Solomon, and Adamic, Lada A. 2015. Exposure to ideologically diverse news and opinion on Facebook. *Science,* **348**(6239), 1130–2.

Bao, Jie, Zheng, Yu, Wilkie, David, and Mokbel, Mohamed. 2015. Recommendations in location-based social networks: A survey. *GeoInformatica*, **19**, 525–65.

Barkan, Oren and Koenigstein, Noam. 2016. Item2vec: Neural item embedding for collaborative filtering. In: *2016 IEEE 26th International Workshop on Machine Learning for Signal Processing*. IEEE.

Bayer, Immanuel. 2016. fastfm: A library for factorization machines. *The Journal of Machine Learning Research*, **17**(184), 1–5.

Bell, Robert M and Koren, Yehuda. 2007. Lessons from the Netflix prize challenge. *ACM SIGKDD Explorations Newsletter*, **9**(2), 75–9.

Bell, Sean and Bala, Kavita. 2015. Learning visual similarity for product design with convolutional neural networks. *ACM Transactions on Graphics*, **34**(4), 1–10.

Bellogin, Alejandro, Castells, Pablo, and Cantador, Ivan. 2011. Precision-oriented evaluation of recommender systems: An algorithmic comparison. In: *RecSys '11: Proceedings of the Fifth ACM Conference on Recommender Systems*. ACM.

Bennett, James, Lanning, Stan, et al. 2007. The Netflix prize. In: *Proceedings of the KDD Cup and Workshop*, p. 35.

Bentley, Jon Louis. 1975. Multidimensional binary search trees used for associative searching. *Communications of the ACM*, **18**(9), 509–17.

Blei, David M, Ng, Andrew Y, and Jordan, Michael I. 2003. Latent Dirichlet allocation. *Journal of Machine Learning Research*, **3**, 993–1022.

Bobadilla, Jesús, Ortega, Fernando, Hernando, Antonio, and Gutiérrez, Abraham. 2013. Recommender systems survey. *Knowledge-Based Systems*, **46**, 109–32.

Bordes, Antoine, Usunier, Nicolas, Garcia-Duran, Alberto, Weston, Jason, and Yakhnenko, Oksana. 2013. Translating embeddings for modeling multi-relational data. In: *Advances in Neural Information Processing Systems 26 (NIPS 2013)*, Neural Information Processing Systems Foundation.

Bordes, Antoine, Boureau, Y-Lan, and Weston, Jason. 2017. Learning end-to-end goal-oriented dialog. *arXiv preprint arXiv:1605.07683*.

Bottou, Léon. 2010. Large-scale machine learning with stochastic gradient descent. In: *Proceedings of COMPSTAT 2010. Springer*.

Brin, Sergey and Page, Lawrence. 1998. The anatomy of a large-scale hypertextual web search engine. *Computer Networks and ISDN Systems*, **30**(1–7), 107–17.

Broder, Andrei Z. 1997. On the resemblance and containment of documents. In: *Proceedings. Compression and Complexity of Sequences 1997*. IEEE.

Brynjolfsson, Erik, Hu, Yu Jeffrey, and Smith, Michael D. 2006. From niches to riches: Anatomy of the long tail. *Sloan Management Review*, **47**(4), 67–71.

Burke, Robin. 2002. Hybrid recommender systems: Survey and experiments. *User Modeling and User-Adapted Interaction*, **12**, 331–70.

Burke, Robin. 2017. Multisided fairness for recommendation. *arXiv preprint arXiv:1707.00093*.

Cai, Chenwei, He, Ruining, and McAuley, Julian. 2017. SPMC: Socially-aware personalized Markov chains for sparse sequential recommendation. In: *IJCAI '17: Proceedings of the 26th International Joint Conference on Artificial Intelligence*. International Joint Conferences on Artificial Intelligence.

Carbonell, Jaime and Goldstein, Jade. 1998. The use of MMR, diversity-based rerank-ing for reordering documents and producing summaries. In: *SIGIR '98: Proceed-ings of the 21st Annual International ACM SIGIR Conference on Research and Development in Information Retrieval*. ACM.

Case, Karl E and Fair, Ray C. 2007. *Principles of Microeconomics*. Pearson Education.

Celma Herrada, Òscar. 2008. *Music recommendation and discovery in the long tail*. Ph.D. thesis, Universitat Pompeu Fabra.

Chang, Shuo, Harper, F Maxwell, and Terveen, Loren Gilbert. 2016. Crowd-based per-sonalized natural language explanations for recommendations. In: *RecSys '16: Proceedings of the 10th ACM Conference on Recommender Systems*. ACM.

Charikar, Moses S. 2002. Similarity estimation techniques from rounding algorithms. In: *STOC '02: Proceedings of the 34th Annual ACM Symposium on Theory of Computing*. ACM.

Chen, Chong, Zhang, Min, Liu, Yiqun, and Ma, Shaoping. 2018. Neural attentional rating regression with review-level explanations. In: *WWW '18: Proceedings of the 2019 World Wide Web Conference*. ACM.

Chen, Le, Mislove, Alan, and Wilson, Christo. 2016. An empirical analysis of algo-rithmic pricing on Amazon Marketplace. In: *WWW '16: Proceedings of the 25th International Conference on World Wide Web*. ACM.

Chen, Shuo, Moore, Josh L, Turnbull, Douglas, and Joachims, Thorsten. 2012. Playlist prediction via metric embedding. In: *KDD '12: Proceedings of the 18th ACM SIGKDD International Conference on Knowledge Discovery and Data Mining*. ACM.

Cheng, Heng-Tze, Koc, Levent, Harmsen, Jeremiah, Shaked, Tal, Chandra, Tushar, Aradhye, Hrishi, Anderson, Glen, Corrado, Greg, Chai, Wei, Ispir, Mustafa, et al. 2016. Wide & deep learning for recommender systems. In: *DLRS 2016: Pro-ceedings of the 1st Workshop on Deep Learning for Recommender Systems*, 7–10.

Cho, Eunjoon, Myers, Seth A, and Leskovec, Jure. 2011. Friendship and mobility: User movement in location-based social networks. In: *KDD '11: Proceedings of the 17th ACM SIGKDD International Conference on Knowledge Discovery and Data Mining*. ACM.

Chouldechova, Alexandra. 2017. Fair prediction with disparate impact: A study of bias in recidivism prediction instruments. *Big Data*, 5(2), 153–63.

Christakopoulou, Konstantina, Radlinski, Filip, and Hofmann, Katja. 2016. Towards conversational recommender systems. In: *KDD '16: Proceedings of the 22nd ACM SIGKDD International Conference on Knowledge Discovery and Data Mining*. ACM.

Cortes, Corinna and Vapnik, Vladimir. 1995. Support-vector networks. *Machine Learning*, 20, 273–97.

Covington, Paul, Adams, Jay, and Sargin, Emre. 2016. Deep neural networks for You-Tube recommendations. In: *RecSys '16: Proceedings of the 10th ACM Conference on Recommender Systems*. ACM.

Dacrema, Maurizio Ferrari, Cremonesi, Paolo, and Jannach, Dietmar. 2019. Are we really making much progress? A worrying analysis of recent neural recommen-dation approaches. In: *RecSys '19: Proceedings of the 13th ACM Conference on Recommender Systems*. ACM.

Davidson, James, Liebald, Benjamin, Liu, Junning, Nandy, Palash, Van Vleet, Taylor, Gargi, Ullas, Gupta, Sujoy, He, Yu, Lambert, Mike, Livingston, Blake, et al. 2010. The YouTube video recommendation system. In: *RecSys '10: Proceedings of the Fourth ACM Conference on Recommender Systems*. ACM.

Devlin, Jacob, Chang, Ming-Wei, Lee, Kenton, and Toutanova, Kristina. 2019. BERT: Pre-training of deep bidirectional transformers for language understanding. In: *Proceedings of NAACL-HLT 2019*. Association for Computational Linguistics.

Diao, Qiming, Qiu, Minghui, Wu, Chao-Yuan, Smola, Alexander J, Jiang, Jing, and Wang, Chong. 2014. Jointly modeling aspects, ratings and sentiments for movie recommendation (JMARS). In: *KDD '14: Proceedings of the 20th ACM SIGKDD International Conference on Knowledge Discovery and Data Mining*. ACM.

Ding, Yi and Li, Xue. 2005. Time weight collaborative filtering. In: *CIKM '05: Proceedings of the 14th ACM International Conference on Information and Knowledge Management*. ACM.

Dodge, Jesse, Gane, Andreea, Zhang, Xiang, Bordes, Antoine, Chopra, Sumit, Miller, Alexander, Szlam, Arthur, and Weston, Jason. 2016. Evaluating prerequisite qualities for learning end-to-end dialog systems. *arXiv preprint arXiv:1511.06931*.

Dong, Li, Huang, Shaohan, Wei, Furu, Lapata, Mirella, Zhou, Ming, and Xu, Ke. 2017a. Learning to generate product reviews from attributes. In: *Proceedings of the 15th Conferences of the European Chapter of the Association for Computational Linguistics*. Association for Computational Linguistics.

Dong, Yuxiao, Chawla, Nitesh V, and Swami, Ananthram. 2017b. metapath2vec: Scalable representation learning for heterogeneous networks. In: *KDD '17: Proceedings of the 23rd ACM SIGKDD International Conference on Knowledge Discovery and Data Mining*. ACM.

Dwork, Cynthia, Hardt, Moritz, Pitassi, Toniann, Reingold, Omer, and Zemel, Richard. 2012. Fairness through awareness. In: *ITCS '12: Proceedings of the 3rd Innovations in Theoretical Computer Science Conference*. ACM.

Ekstrand, Michael D, Tian, Mucun, Azpiazu, Ion Madrazo, Ekstrand, Jennifer D, Anuyah, Oghenemaro, McNeill, David, and Pera, Maria Soledad. 2018a. All the cool kids, how do they fit in? Popularity and demographic biases in recommender evaluation and effectiveness. In: *Proceedings of the 1st Conference on Fairness, Accountability and Transparency*. ML Research Press.

Ekstrand, Michael D, Tian, Mucun, Kazi, Mohammed R Imran, Mehrpouyan, Hoda, and Kluver, Daniel. 2018b. Exploring author gender in book rating and recommendation. In: *RecSys '18: Proceedings of the 12th ACM Conference on Recommender Systems*. ACM.

Feng, Shanshan, Li, Xutao, Zeng, Yifeng, Cong, Gao, and Chee, Yeow Meng. 2015. Personalized ranking metric embedding for next new POI recommendation. In: *IJCAI'15: Proceedings of the 24th International Conference on Artificial Intelligence*. AAAI Press/International Joint Conferences on Artificial Intelligence.

Flaxman, Seth, Goel, Sharad, and Rao, Justin M. 2016. Filter bubbles, echo chambers, and online news consumption. *Public Opinion Quarterly*, **80**, 298–320.

Fleder, Daniel and Hosanagar, Kartik. 2009. Blockbuster culture's next rise or fall: The impact of recommender systems on sales diversity. *Management Science*, **55**(5), 697–712.

Friedman, Jerome, Hastie, Trevor, Tibshirani, Robert, et al. 2001. *The Elements of Statistical Learning*. Springer.

Gale, David and Shapley, Lloyd S. 1962. College admissions and the stability of marriage. *The American Mathematical Monthly*, **69**(1), 9–15.

Ge, Rong, Lee, Jason D, and Ma, Tengyu. 2016. Matrix completion has no spurious local minimum. In: *NIPS '16: Proceedings of the 30th International Conference on Neural Information Processing Systems*. Neural Information Processing Systems Foundation.

Ge, Yong, Liu, Qi, Xiong, Hui, Tuzhilin, Alexander, and Chen, Jian. 2011. Cost-aware travel tour recommendation. In: *KDD'11: Proceedings of the 17th ACM SIGKDD International Conference on Knowledge Discovery and Data Mining*. ACM.

Ge, Yong, Xiong, Hui, Tuzhilin, Alexander, and Liu, Qi. 2014. Cost-aware collaborative filtering for travel tour recommendations. *ACM Transactions on Information Systems*, **32**(1), 1–31.

Godes, David and Silva, José C. 2012. Sequential and temporal dynamics of online opinion. *Marketing Science*, **31**(3), 448–73.

Goodfellow, Ian, Pouget-Abadie, Jean, Mirza, Mehdi, Xu, Bing, Warde-Farley, David, Ozair, Sherjil, Courville, Aaron, and Bengio, Yoshua. 2014. Generative adversarial nets. In: *NIPS '14: Proceedings of the 27th International Conference on Neural Information Processing Systems*. Neural Information Processing Systems Foundation.

Gopalan, Prem, Hofman, Jake M, and Blei, David M. 2013. Scalable recommendation with Poisson factorization. *arXiv preprint arXiv:1311.1704*.

Graves, Alex. 2013. Generating sequences with recurrent neural networks. *arXiv preprint arXiv:1308.0850*.

Guo, Huifeng, Tang, Ruiming, Ye, Yunming, Li, Zhenguo, and He, Xiuqiang. 2017a. DeepFM: A factorization-machine based neural network for CTR prediction. In: *IJCAI '17: Proceedings of the 26th International Joint Conference on Artificial Intelligence*. International Joint Conferences on Artificial Intelligence.

Guo, Yunhui, Xu, Congfu, Song, Hanzhang, and Wang, Xin. 2017b. Understanding users' budgets for recommendation with hierarchical Poisson factorization. In: *IJCAI '17: Proceedings of the 26th International Joint Conference on Artificial Intelligence*. International Joint Conferences on Artificial Intelligence.

Gusfield, Dan and Irving, Robert W. 1989. *The Stable Marriage Problem: Structure and Algorithms*. MIT Press.

Haim, Mario, Graefe, Andreas, and Brosius, Hans-Bernd. 2018. Burst of the filter bubble? Effects of personalization on the diversity of Google News. *Digital Journalism*, **6**(3), 330–43.

Hansen, Christian, Mehrotra, Rishabh, Hansen, Casper, Brost, Brian, Maystre, Lucas, and Lalmas, Mounia. 2021. Shifting consumption towards diverse content on music streaming platforms. In: *WSDM '21: Proceedings of the 14th ACM International Conference on Web Search and Data Mining*. ACM.

Hao, Junheng, Zhao, Tong, Li, Jin, Dong, Xin Luna, Faloutsos, Christos, Sun, Yizhou, and Wang, Wei. 2020. P-Companion: A principled framework for diversified complementary product recommendation. In: *CIKM '20: Proceedings of the 29th ACM International Conference on Information and Knowledge Management*. ACM.

Harper, F Maxwell and Konstan, Joseph A. 2015. The MovieLens datasets: History and context. *ACM Transactions on Interactive Intelligent Systems*, **5**(4), 1–19.

He, Ruining and McAuley, Julian. 2015. VBPR: Visual Bayesian personalized ranking from implicit feedback. In: *AAAI '16: Proceedings of the 30th AAAI Conference on Artificial Intelligence*. AAAI Press.

He, Ruining and McAuley, Julian. 2016. Ups and downs: Modeling the visual evolution of fashion trends with one-class collaborative filtering. In: *WWW '16: Proceedings of the 25th International Conference on the World Wide Web*. ACM.

He, Ruining, Packer, Charles, and McAuley, Julian. 2016a. Learning compatibility across categories for heterogeneous item recommendation. In: *2016 IEEE 16th International Conference on Data Mining*. IEEE.

He, Ruining, Fang, Chen, Wang, Zhaowen, and McAuley, Julian. 2016b. Vista: A visually, socially, and temporally-aware model for artistic recommendation. In: *RecSys '16: Proceedings of the 10th ACM Conference on Recommender Systems*. ACM.

He, Ruining, Kang, Wang-Cheng, and McAuley, Julian. 2017a. Translation-based recommendation. In: *RecSys '17: Proceedings of the 11th ACM Conference on Recommender Systems*. ACM.

He, Xiangnan and Chua, Tat-Seng. 2017. Neural factorization machines for sparse predictive analytics. In: *SIGIR '17: Proceedings of the 40th International ACM SIGIR Conference on Research and Development in Information Retrieval*. ACM.

He, Xiangnan, Liao, Lizi, Zhang, Hanwang, Nie, Liqiang, Hu, Xia, and Chua, Tat-Seng. 2017b. Neural collaborative filtering. In: *WWW '17: Proceedings of the 26th International Conference on the World Wide Web*. ACM.

Henderson, Matthew, Al-Rfou, Rami, Strope, Brian, Sung, Yun-Hsuan, Lukács, László, Guo, Ruiqi, Kumar, Sanjiv, Miklos, Balint, and Kurzweil, Ray. 2017. Efficient natural language response suggestion for smart reply. *arXiv preprint arXiv:1705.00652*.

Hidasi, Balázs, Karatzoglou, Alexandros, Baltrunas, Linas, and Tikk, Domonkos. 2016. Session-based recommendations with recurrent neural networks. *arXiv preprint arXiv:1511.06939v4*.

Ho, Tin Kam. 1995. Random decision forests. In: *Proceedings of 3rd International Conference on Document Analysis and Recognition*. IEEE.

Hochreiter, Sepp and Schmidhuber, Jürgen. 1997. Long short-term memory. *Neural Computation*, **9**(8), 1735–80.

Hsiao, Wei-Lin and Grauman, Kristen. 2018. Creating capsule wardrobes from fashion images. In: *Proceedings of the IEEE Conference on Computer Vision and Pattern Recognition*. IEEE.

Hu, Diane, Louca, Raphael, Hong, Liangjie, and McAuley, Julian. 2018. Learning within-session budgets from browsing trajectories. In: *RecSys '18: Proceedings of the 12th ACM Conference on Recommender Systems*. ACM.

Hu, Diane J, Hall, Rob, and Attenberg, Josh. 2014. Style in the long tail: Discovering unique interests with latent variable models in large scale social e-commerce. In: *KDD '14: Proceedings of the 20th ACM SIGKDD International Conference on Knowledge Discovery and Data Mining*. ACM.

Hu, Yifan, Koren, Yehuda, and Volinsky, Chris. 2008. Collaborative filtering for implicit feedback datasets. In: *2008 Eighth IEEE International Conference on Data Mining*. IEEE.

Hug, Nicolas. 2020. Surprise: A Python library for recommender systems. *Journal of Open Source Software*, **5**(52), 2174.

Inagawa, Yuma, Hakamta, Junki, and Tokumaru, Masataka. 2013. A support system for healthy eating habits: Optimization of recipe retrieval. In: *HCI International 2013 – Posters' Extended Abstracts*. Springer.

Indyk, Piotr and Motwani, Rajeev. 1998. Approximate nearest neighbors: Towards removing the curse of dimensionality. In: *STOC '98: Proceedings of the 30th Annual ACM Symposium on Theory of Computing*. ACM.

Ingrande, Jerry, Gabriel, Rodney A, McAuley, Julian, Krasinska, Karolina, Chien, Allis, and Lemmens, Hendrikus JM. 2020. The performance of an artificial neural network model in predicting the early distribution kinetics of propofol in morbidly obese and lean subjects. *Anesthesia & Analgesia*, **131**(5), 1500–9.

Jacobs, Robert A, Jordan, Michael I, Nowlan, Steven J, and Hinton, Geoffrey E. 1991. Adaptive mixtures of local experts. *Neural Computation*, **3**(1), 79–87.

Jannach, Dietmar, Manzoor, Ahtsham, Cai, Wanling, and Chen, Li. 2020. A survey on conversational recommender systems. *arXiv preprint arXiv:2004.00646*.

Jennings, Andrew and Higuchi, Hideyuki. 1993. A user model neural network for a personal news service. *User Modeling and User-Adapted Interaction*, **3**, 1–25.

Jia, Yangqing, Shelhamer, Evan, Donahue, Jeff, Karayev, Sergey, Long, Jonathan, Girshick, Ross, Guadarrama, Sergio, and Darrell, Trevor. 2014. Caffe: Convolutional architecture for fast feature embedding. In: *MM '14: Proceedings of the 22nd ACM International Conference on Multimedia*. ACM.

Jiang, Yuanchun, Shang, Jennifer, Liu, Yezheng, and May, Jerrold. 2015. Redesigning promotion strategy for e-commerce competitiveness through pricing and recommendation. *International Journal of Production Economics*, **167**, 257–70.

Jones, Karen Sparck. 1972. A statistical interpretation of term specificity and its application in retrieval. *Journal of Documentation*, **60**(5), 493–502.

Joshi, Chaitanya K, Mi, Fei, and Faltings, Boi. 2017. Personalization in goal-oriented dialog. *arXiv preprint arXiv:1706.07503*.

Kabbur, Santosh, Ning, Xia, and Karypis, George. 2013. FISM: Factored item similarity models for top-n recommender systems. In: *KDD '13: Proceedings of the 19th ACM SIGKDD International Conference on Knowledge Discovery and Data Mining*. ACM.

Kaminskas, Marius and Bridge, Derek. 2016. Diversity, serendipity, novelty, and coverage: A survey and empirical analysis of beyond-accuracy objectives in recommender systems. *ACM Transactions on Interactive Intelligent Systems*, **7**(1), 1–42.

Kamiran, Faisal and Calders, Toon. 2009. Classifying without discriminating. In: *2009 2nd International Conference on Computer, Control and Communication*. IEEE.

Kang, Dongyeop, Balakrishnan, Anusha, Shah, Pararth, Crook, Paul, Boureau, Y-Lan, and Weston, Jason. 2019a. Recommendation as a communication game: Self-supervised bot-play for goal-oriented dialogue. In: *Proceedings of the 2019 Conference on Empirical Methods in Natural Language Processing*. Association for Computational Linguistics.

Kang, Wang-Cheng and McAuley, Julian. 2018. Self-attentive sequential recommendation. In: *2018 IEEE International Conference on Data Mining*. IEEE.

Kang, Wang-Cheng, Fang, Chen, Wang, Zhaowen, and McAuley, Julian. 2017. Visually-aware fashion recommendation and design with generative image models. In: *2017 IEEE International Conference on Data Mining*. IEEE.

Kang, Wang-Cheng, Kim, Eric, Leskovec, Jure, Rosenberg, Charles, and McAuley, Julian. 2019b. Complete the look: Scene-based complementary product recommendation. In: *2019 IEEE Conference on Computer Vision and Pattern Recognition*. IEEE.

Kannan, Anjuli, Kurach, Karol, Ravi, Sujith, Kaufmann, Tobias, Tomkins, Andrew, Miklos, Balint, Corrado, Greg, Lukacs, Laszlo, Ganea, Marina, Young, Peter, et al. 2016. Smart reply: Automated response suggestion for email. In: *KDD '16: Proceedings of the 22nd ACM SIGKDD International Conference on Knowledge Discovery and Data Mining*. ACM.

Kim, Yoon. 2014. Convolutional neural networks for sentence classification. In: *Proceedings of the 2014 Conference on Empirical Methods in Natural Language Processing*. Association for Computational Linguistics.

Kingma, Diederik P and Ba, Jimmy. 2014. ADAM: A method for stochastic optimization. *arXiv preprint arXiv:1412.6980.*

Kleinberg, Jon M. 1999. Hubs, authorities, and communities. *ACM Computing Surveys*, **31**(4es), 5–es.

Koenigstein, Noam, Ram, Parikshit, and Shavitt, Yuval. 2012. Efficient retrieval of recommendations in a matrix factorization framework. In: *CIKM '12: Proceedings of the 21st ACM International Conference on Information and Knowledge Management*. ACM.

Kolter, J Zico and Maloof, Marcus A. 2007. Dynamic weighted majority: An ensemble method for drifting concepts. *Journal of Machine Learning Research*, **8**, 2755–90.

Konstan, Joseph A, Riedl, John, Borchers, A, and Herlocker, Jonathan L. 1998. *Recommender Systems: A GroupLens Perspective. AAAI Technical Report WS-98-08.* AAAI Press.

Koren, Yehuda. 2009. Collaborative filtering with temporal dynamics. In: *KDD '09: Proceedings of the 15th ACM SIGKDD International Conference on Knowledge Discovery and Data Mining*. ACM.

Koren, Yehuda, Bell, Robert, and Volinsky, Chris. 2009. Matrix factorization techniques for recommender systems. *Computer*, **42**(8), 30–7.

Kotkov, Denis, Konstan, Joseph A, Zhao, Qian, and Veijalainen, Jari. 2018. Investigating serendipity in recommender systems based on real user feedback. In: *SAC '18: Proceedings of the 33rd Annual ACM Symposium on Applied Computing*. ACM.

Kuhn, Harold W. 1955. The Hungarian method for the assignment problem. *Naval Research Logistics Quarterly*, **2**(1–2), 83–97.

Kulesza, Alex and Taskar, Ben. 2012. Determinantal point processes for machine learning. *Foundations and Trends in Machine Learning*, **5**(2–3), 123–286.

Lakkaraju, Himabindu, McAuley, Julian J, and Leskovec, Jure. 2013. What's in a name? Understanding the interplay between titles, content, and communities in social media. In: *7th International AAAI Conference on Weblogs and Social Media*. AAAI Press.

Li, Jing, Ren, Pengjie, Chen, Zhumin, Ren, Zhaochun, Lian, Tao, and Ma, Jun. 2017. Neural attentive session-based recommendation. In: *CIKM '17: Proceedings of the 2017 ACM Conference on Information and Knowledge Management*. ACM.

Li, Ming, Dias, Benjamin M, Jarman, Ian, El-Deredy, Wael, and Lisboa, Paulo JG. 2009. Grocery shopping recommendations based on basket-sensitive random walk. In: *KDD '09: Proceedings of the 15th ACM SIGKDD International Conference on Knowledge Discovery and Data Mining*. ACM.

Li, Pan, Que, Maofei, Jiang, Zhichao, Hu, Yao, and Tuzhilin, Alexander. 2020. PURS: Personalized unexpected recommender system for improving user satisfaction. In: *RecSys '20: 14th ACM Conference on Recommender Systems*. ACM.

Li, Raymond, Kahou, Samira, Schulz, Hannes, Michalski, Vincent, Charlin, Laurent, and Pal, Chris. 2018. Towards deep conversational recommendations. In: *NIPS '18: Proceedings of the 32nd International Conference on Neural Information Processing Systems*. Neural Information Processing Systems Foundation.

Li, Xinxin and Hitt, Lorin M. 2008. Self-selection and information role of online product reviews. *Information Systems Research*, **19**(4), 456–74.

Lin, Yankai, Liu, Zhiyuan, Sun, Maosong, Liu, Yang, and Zhu, Xuan. 2015. Learning entity and relation embeddings for knowledge graph completion. In: *Proceedings of the 29th AAAI Conference on Artificial Intelligence*. AAAI Press.

Linden, Greg, Smith, Brent, and York, Jeremy. 2003. Amazon.com recommendations: Item-to-item collaborative filtering. *IEEE Internet Computing*, **7**(1), 76–80.

Ling, Guang, Lyu, Michael R, and King, Irwin. 2014. Ratings meet reviews, a combined approach to recommend. In: *RecSys '14: Proceedings of the 8th ACM Conference on Recommender Systems*. ACM.

Lipton, Zachary C, Chouldechova, Alexandra, and McAuley, Julian. 2018. Does mitigating ML's impact disparity require treatment disparity? In: *NIPS '18: Proceedings of the 32nd International Conference on Advances in Neural Information Processing Systems*. Neural Information Processing Systems Foundation.

Liu, Dong C and Nocedal, Jorge. 1989. On the limited memory BFGS method for large scale optimization. *Mathematical Programming*, **45**, 503–28.

Liu, Hui, Yin, Qingyu, and Wang, William Yang. 2019. Towards explainable NLP: A generative explanation framework for text classification. In: *Proceedings of the 57th Annual Meeting of the Association for Computational Linguistics*. Association for Computational Linguistics.

Liu, Nathan N and Yang, Qiang. 2008. EigenRank: A ranking-oriented approach to collaborative filtering. In: *SIGIR '08: Proceedings of the 31st Annual International ACM SIGIR Conference on Research and Development in Information Retrieval*. ACM.

Lovins, Julie Beth. 1968. Development of a stemming algorithm. *Mechanical Translation and Computational Linguistics*, **11**(1–2), 22–31.

Ma, Hao, Yang, Haixuan, Lyu, Michael R, and King, Irwin. 2008. SoRec: Social recommendation using probabilistic matrix factorization. In: *CIKM '08: Proceedings of the 17th ACM Conference on Information and Knowledge Management*. ACM.

Maaten, Laurens van der and Hinton, Geoffrey. 2008. Visualizing data using t-SNE. *Journal of Machine Learning Research*, **9**, 2579–605.

Mahmood, Tariq and Ricci, Francesco. 2007. Learning and adaptivity in interactive recommender systems. In: *ICEC '07: Proceedings of the 9th International Conference on Electronic Commerce*. ACM.

Mahmood, Tariq and Ricci, Francesco. 2009. Improving recommender systems with adaptive conversational strategies. In: *HT '09: Proceedings of the 20th ACM Conference on Hypertext and Hypermedia.* ACM.

Majumder, Bodhisattwa Prasad, Li, Shuyang, Ni, Jianmo, and McAuley, Julian. 2019. Generating personalized recipes from historical user preferences. In: *Proceedings of the 2019 Conference on Empirical Methods in Natural Language Processing.* Association for Computational Linguistics.

Majumder, Bodhisattwa Prasad, Jhamtani, Harsh, Berg-Kirkpatrick, Taylor, and McAuley, Julian. 2020. Like hiking? You probably enjoy nature: Persona-grounded dialog with commonsense expansions. In: *Proceedings of the 2020 Conference on Empirical Methods in Natural Language Processing.* Association for Computational Linguistics.

Marin, Javier, Biswas, Aritro, Ofli, Ferda, Hynes, Nicholas, Salvador, Amaia, Aytar, Yusuf, Weber, Ingmar, and Torralba, Antonio. 2019. Recipe1m+: A dataset for learning cross-modal embeddings for cooking recipes and food images. *IEEE Transactions on Pattern Analysis and Machine Intelligence*, **43**(1), 187–203.

Markowitz, Harry M. 1968. *Portfolio Selection.* Yale University Press.

McAuley, Julian and Leskovec, Jure. 2013a. Hidden factors and hidden topics: Understanding rating dimensions with review text. In: *RecSys '13: Proceedings of the 7th ACM Conference on Recommender Systems.* ACM.

McAuley, Julian, Leskovec, Jure, and Jurafsky, Dan. 2012. Learning attitudes and attributes from multi-aspect reviews. In: *2012 IEEE 12th International Conference on Data Mining.* IEEE.

McAuley, Julian, Targett, Christopher, Shi, Qinfeng, and Van Den Hengel, Anton. 2015. Image-based recommendations on styles and substitutes. In: *SIGIR '15: Proceedings of the 38th International ACM SIGIR Conference on Research and Development in Information Retrieval.* ACM.

McAuley, Julian John and Leskovec, Jure. 2013b. From amateurs to connoisseurs: Modeling the evolution of user expertise through online reviews. In: *WWW '13: Proceedings of the 22nd International Conference on World Wide Web.* ACM.

McFee, Brian, Bertin-Mahieux, Thierry, Ellis, Daniel PW, and Lanckriet, Gert RG. 2012. The million song dataset challenge. In: *WWW '12 Companion: Proceedings of the 21st International Conference on World Wide Web.* ACM.

McInnes, Leland, Healy, John, Saul, Nathaniel, and Großberger, Lukas. 2018. UMAP: Uniform manifold approximation and projection. *Journal of Open Source Software*, **3**(29), 861.

Mehrabi, Ninareh, Morstatter, Fred, Saxena, Nripsuta, Lerman, Kristina, and Galstyan, Aram. 2019. A survey on bias and fairness in machine learning. *arXiv preprint arXiv:1908.09635.*

Mehta, Aranyak, Saberi, Amin, Vazirani, Umesh, and Vazirani, Vijay. 2007. Adwords and generalized online matching. *Journal of the ACM*, **54**(5), 22-es.

Mikolov, Tomas, Sutskever, Ilya, Chen, Kai, Corrado, Greg S, and Dean, Jeff. 2013. Distributed representations of words and phrases and their compositionality. In: *NIPS '13: Proceedings of the 26th International Conference on Neural Information Processing Systems.* Neural Information Processing Systems Foundation.

Mirza, Mehdi and Osindero, Simon. 2014. Conditional generative adversarial nets. *arXiv preprint arXiv:1411.1784.*

Mooney, Raymond J. and Roy, Loriene. 2000. Content-based book recommending using learning for text categorization. In: *DL '00: Proceedings of the 5th ACM Conference on Digital Libraries*. ACM.

Narayanan, Arvind and Shmatikov, Vitaly. 2006. How to break anonymity of the Netflix prize dataset. *arXiv preprint cs/0610105*.

Ng, Nathan H, Gabriel, Rodney A, McAuley, Julian, Elkan, Charles, and Lipton, Zachary C. 2017. Predicting surgery duration with neural heteroscedastic regression. In: *Proceedings of the 2nd Machine Learning for Healthcare Conference*. ML Research Press.

Nguyen, Tan and Sanner, Scott. 2013. Algorithms for direct 0–1 loss optimization in binary classification. In: *Proceedings of the 30th International Conference on Machine Learning*. ML Research Press.

Nguyen, Tien T, Hui, Pik-Mai, Harper, F Maxwell, Terveen, Loren, and Konstan, Joseph A. 2014. Exploring the filter bubble: The effect of using recommender systems on content diversity. In: *WWW '14: Proceedings of the 23rd International Conference on World Wide Web*. ACM.

Ni, Jianmo and McAuley, Julian. 2018. Personalized review generation by expanding phrases and attending on aspect-aware representations. In: *Proceedings of the 56th Annual Meeting of the Association for Computational Linguistics*. Association for Computational Linguistics.

Ni, Jianmo, Lipton, Zachary C, Vikram, Sharad, and McAuley, Julian. 2017. Estimating reactions and recommending products with generative models of reviews. In: *Proceedings of the 8th International Joint Conference on Natural Language Processing*. AFNLP.

Ni, Jianmo, Li, Jiacheng, and McAuley, Julian. 2019a. Justifying recommendations using distantly-labeled reviews and fine-grained aspects. In: *Proceedings of the 9th International Joint Conference on Natural Language Processing*. Association for Computational Linguistics.

Ni, Jianmo, Muhlstein, Larry, and McAuley, Julian. 2019b. Modeling heart rate and activity data for personalized fitness recommendation. In: *WWW '19: The World Wide Web Conference*. ACM.

Ni, Jianmo, Hsu, Chun-Nan, Gentili, Amilcare, and McAuley, Julian. 2020. Learning visual-semantic embeddings for reporting abnormal findings on chest x-rays. In: *Empirical Methods in Natural Language Processing*. Association for Computational Linguistics.

Ning, Xia and Karypis, George. 2011. Slim: Sparse linear methods for top-n recommender systems. In: *2011 IEEE 11th International Conference on Data Mining*. IEEE.

O'connor, Mark, Cosley, Dan, Konstan, Joseph A, and Riedl, John. 2001. PolyLens: A recommender system for groups of users. In: *ECSCW 2001: Proceedings of the 7th European Conference on Computer-Supported Cooperative Work*. Springer.

Pampalk, Elias, Pohle, Tim, and Widmer, Gerhard. 2005. Dynamic playlist generation based on skipping behavior. In: *ISMIR 2005: 6th International Conference on Music Information Retrieval*.

Pan, Rong, Zhou, Yunhong, Cao, Bin, Liu, Nathan N, Lukose, Rajan, Scholz, Martin, and Yang, Qiang. 2008. One-class collaborative filtering. In: *2008 Eighth IEEE International Conference on Data Mining*. IEEE.

Pan, Weike and Chen, Li. 2013. GBPR: Group preference based bayesian personalized ranking for one-class collaborative filtering. In: *IJCAI 13: Proceedings of the 23rd International Joint Conference on Artificial Intelligence*. AAAI Press/International Joint Conferences on Artificial Intelligence.

Pan, Yingwei, Yao, Ting, Mei, Tao, Li, Houqiang, Ngo, Chong-Wah, and Rui, Yong. 2014. Click-through-based cross-view learning for image search. In: *SIGIR '14: Proceedings of the 37th International ACM SIGIR Conference on Research and Development in Information Retrieval*. ACM.

Pariser, Eli. 2011. *The Filter Bubble: What the Internet is Hiding from You*. Penguin.

Park, Seung-Taek and Chu, Wei. 2009. Pairwise preference regression for cold-start recommendation. In: *RecSys '09: Proceedings of the Third ACM Conference on Recommender Systems*. ACM.

Pizzato, Luiz, Rej, Tomek, Chung, Thomas, Koprinska, Irena, and Kay, Judy. 2010. RECON: A reciprocal recommender for online dating. In: *RecSys '10: Proceedings of the Fourth ACM Conference on Recommender Systems*. ACM.

Porter, Martin F. 1980. An algorithm for suffix stripping. *Program*, **14**(3), 130–7.

Radford, Alec, Jozefowicz, Rafal, and Sutskever, Ilya. 2017. Learning to generate reviews and discovering sentiment. *arXiv preprint arXiv:1704.01444*.

Rajaraman, Anand and Ullman, Jeffrey David. 2011. *Mining of Massive Datasets*. Cambridge University Press.

Rappaz, Jérémie, Vladarean, Maria-Luiza, McAuley, Julian, and Catasta, Michele. 2017. Bartering books to beers: A recommender system for exchange platforms. In: *WSDM '17: Proceedings of the 10th ACM International Conference on Web Search and Data Mining*. ACM.

Rashid, Al Mamunur, Albert, Istvan, Cosley, Dan, Lam, Shyong K, McNee, Sean M, Konstan, Joseph A, and Riedl, John. 2002. Getting to know you: Learning new user preferences in recommender systems. In: *IUI '02: Proceedings of the 7th International Conference on Intelligent User Interfaces*. ACM.

Rendle, Steffen. 2010. Factorization machines. In: *2010 IEEE International Conference on Data Mining*. IEEE.

Rendle, Steffen and Schmidt-Thieme, Lars. 2008. Online-updating regularized kernel matrix factorization models for large-scale recommender systems. In: *RecSys '08: Proceedings of the 2008 ACM Conference on Recommender Systems*. ACM.

Rendle, Steffen, Freudenthaler, Christoph, and Schmidt-Thieme, Lars. 2010. Factorizing personalized Markov chains for next-basket recommendation. In: *WWW '10: The 19th International World Wide Web Conference*. ACM.

Rendle, Steffen, Freudenthaler, Christoph, Gantner, Zeno, and Schmidt-Thieme, Lars. 2012. BPR: Bayesian personalized ranking from implicit feedback. In: *UAI '09: Proceedings of the 25th Conference on Uncertainty in Artificial Intelligence*. ACM.

Rendle, Steffen, Krichene, Walid, Zhang, Li, and Anderson, John. 2020. Neural collaborative filtering vs. matrix factorization revisited. In: *RecSys '20: 14th ACM Conference on Recommender Systems*. ACM.

Ribeiro, Manoel Horta, Ottoni, Raphael, West, Robert, Almeida, Virgílio AF, and Meira Jr, Wagner. 2020. Auditing radicalization pathways on YouTube. In: *FAT* '20: Proceedings of the 2020 Conference on Fairness, Accountability, and Transparency*. ACM.

Robertson, Stephen. 2004. Understanding inverse document frequency: On theoretical arguments for IDF. *Journal of Documentation*, **60**(5), 503–20.

Robertson, Stephen and Zaragoza, Hugo. 2009. The probabilistic relevance framework: BM25 and beyond. *Foundations and Trends in Information Retrieval*, **3**(4), 333–89.

Roemmele, Melissa. 2016. Writing stories with help from recurrent neural networks. In: *AAAI '16: Proceedings of the 30th AAAI Conference on Artificial Intelligence*. ACM.

Ruiz, Francisco JR, Athey, Susan, Blei, David M, et al. 2020. SHOPPER: A probabilistic model of consumer choice with substitutes and complements. *Annals of Applied Statistics*, **14**. 10.1214/19-AOAS1265.

Sachdeva, Noveen, Manco, Giuseppe, Ritacco, Ettore, and Pudi, Vikram. 2019. Sequential variational autoencoders for collaborative filtering. In: *12th ACM International Conference on Web Search and Data Mining*. ACM.

Sarwar, Badrul, Karypis, George, Konstan, Joseph, and Riedl, John. 2001. Item-based collaborative filtering recommendation algorithms. In: *WWW '01: Proceedings of the 10th International Conference on World Wide Web*. ACM.

Schlimmer, Jeffrey C and Granger, Richard H. 1986. Incremental learning from noisy data. *Machine Learning*, **1**, 317–54.

Schütze, Hinrich, Manning, Christopher D, and Raghavan, Prabhakar. 2008. *Introduction to Information Retrieval*. Cambridge University Press.

Sedhain, Suvash, Menon, Aditya Krishna, Sanner, Scott, and Xie, Lexing. 2015. Autorec: Autoencoders meet collaborative filtering. In: *WWW '15 Companion: Proceedings of the 24th International Conference on World Wide Web*. ACM.

Smith, Brent and Linden, Greg. 2017. Two decades of recommender systems at Amazon.com. *IEEE Internet Computing*, **21**(3), 12–8.

Steck, Harald. 2018. Calibrated recommendations. In: *RecSys '18: Proceedings of the 12th ACM Conference on Recommender Systems*. ACM.

Sugiyama, Kazunari, Hatano, Kenji, and Yoshikawa, Masatoshi. 2004. Adaptive web search based on user profile constructed without any effort from users. In: *WWW '04: Proceedings of the 13th International Conference on World Wide Web*. ACM.

Sun, Fei, Liu, Jun, Wu, Jian, Pei, Changhua, Lin, Xiao, Ou, Wenwu, and Jiang, Peng. 2019. BERT4Rec: Sequential recommendation with bidirectional encoder representations from transformer. In: *CIKM '19: Proceedings of the 28th ACM International Conference on Information and Knowledge Management*. ACM.

Tay, Yi, Luu, Anh Tuan, and Hui, Siu Cheung. 2018. Multi-pointer co-attention networks for recommendation. In: *KDD '18: Proceedings of the 24th ACM SIGKDD International Conference on Knowledge Discovery and Data Mining*. ACM.

Thompson, Cynthia A, Goker, Mehmet H, and Langley, Pat. 2004. A personalized system for conversational recommendations. *Journal of Artificial Intelligence Research*, **21**(1), 393–428.

Tsymbal, Alexey. 2004. The problem of concept drift: Definitions and related work. Computer Science Department, Trinity College Dublin. TCD-CS-2004-15.

Ueta, Tsuguya, Iwakami, Masashi, and Ito, Takayuki. 2011. A recipe recommendation system based on automatic nutrition information extraction. In: *KSEM: International Conference on Knowledge Science, Engineering and Management*. Springer.

Umberto, Panniello. 2015. Developing a price-sensitive recommender system to improve accuracy and business performance of e-commerce applications. *International Journal of Electronic Commerce Studies*, **6**(1), 1–18.

Van Den Oord, Aäron, Dieleman, Sander, and Schrauwen, Benjamin. 2013. Deep content-based music recommendation. In: *NIPS '13: Proceedings of the 26th International Conference on Neural Information Processing Systems*. Neural Information Processing Systems Foundation.

Van Rijsbergen, Cornelius Joost. 1979. *Information Retrieval*. Butterworth-Heinemann.

Vaswani, Ashish, Shazeer, Noam, Parmar, Niki, Uszkoreit, Jakob, Jones, Llion, Gomez, Aidan N, Kaiser, Lukasz, and Polosukhin, Illia. 2017. Attention is all you need. In: *NIPS '17: Proceedings of the 31st International Conference on Neural Information Processing Systems*. Neural Information Processing Systems Foundation.

Veit, Andreas, Kovacs, Balazs, Bell, Sean, McAuley, Julian, Bala, Kavita, and Belongie, Serge. 2015. Learning visual clothing style with heterogeneous dyadic co-occurrences. In: *2015 IEEE International Conference on Computer Vision*. IEEE.

Vinyals, Oriol, Toshev, Alexander, Bengio, Samy, and Erhan, Dumitru. 2015. Show and tell: A neural image caption generator. In: *2015 IEEE Conference on Computer Vision and Pattern Recognition*. IEEE.

Waller, Isaac and Anderson, Ashton. 2019. Generalists and specialists: Using community embeddings to quantify activity diversity in online platforms. In: *WWW '19: The World Wide Web Conference*. ACM.

Wan, Mengting and McAuley, Julian. 2018. Item recommendation on monotonic behavior chains. In: *RecSys '18: Proceedings of the 12th ACM Conference on Recommender Systems*. ACM.

Wan, Mengting, Wang, Di, Goldman, Matt, Taddy, Matt, Rao, Justin, Liu, Jie, Lymberopoulos, Dimitrios, and McAuley, Julian. 2017. Modeling consumer preferences and price sensitivities from large-scale grocery shopping transaction logs. In: *WWW '17: Proceedings of the 26th International Conference on World Wide Web*. ACM.

Wan, Mengting, Wang, Di, Liu, Jie, Bennett, Paul, and McAuley, Julian. 2018. Representing and recommending shopping baskets with complementarity, compatibility and loyalty. In: *CIKM '18: Proceedings of the 27th ACM International Conference on Information and Knowledge Management*. ACM.

Wan, Mengting, Ni, Jianmo, Misra, Rishabh, and McAuley, Julian. 2020. Addressing marketing bias in product recommendations. In: *WSDM '20: Proceedings of the 13th International Conference on Web Search and Data Mining*. ACM.

Wang, Chong and Blei, David M. 2011. Collaborative topic modeling for recommending scientific articles. In: *KDD '11: Proceedings of the 17th ACM SIGKDD International Conference on Knowledge Discovery and Data Mining*. ACM.

Wang, Ningxia, Chen, Li and Yang, Yonghua. 2020. The impacts of item features and user characteristics on users' perceived serendipity of recommendations. In: *UMAP '20: Proceedings of the 28th ACM Conference on User Modeling, Adaptation and Personalization*. ACM.

Wang, Xinxi and Wang, Ye. 2014. Improving content-based and hybrid music recommendation using deep learning. In: *MM '14: Proceedings of the 22nd ACM International Conference on Multimedia*. ACM.

Wang, Yining, Wang, Liwei, Li, Yuanzhi, He, Di, and Liu, Tie-Yan. 2013. A theoretical analysis of NDCG type ranking measures. In: *Proceedings of the 26th Annual Conference on Learning Theory*. MLR Press.

Wang, Zhen, Zhang, Jianwen, Feng, Jianlin, and Chen, Zheng. 2014. Knowledge graph embedding by translating on hyperplanes. In: *AAAI '14: Proceedings of the 28th AAAI Conference on Artificial Intelligence*. AAAI Press.

Wang, Zihan, Jiang, Ziheng, Ren, Zhaochun, Tang, Jiliang, and Yin, Dawei. 2018. A path-constrained framework for discriminating substitutable and complementary products in e-commerce. In: *WSDM '18: Proceedings of the 11th ACM International Conference on Web Search and Data Mining*. ACM.

Wasserman, Larry. 2013. *All of Statistics: A Concise Course in Statistical Inference*. Springer Science & Business Media.

Widmer, Gerhard and Kubat, Miroslav. 1996. Learning in the presence of concept drift and hidden contexts. *Machine Learning*, **23**, 69–101.

Wilhelm, Mark, Ramanathan, Ajith, Bonomo, Alexander, Jain, Sagar, Chi, Ed H, and Gillenwater, Jennifer. 2018. Practical diversified recommendations on YouTube with determinantal point processes. In: *CIKM '18: Proceedings of the 27th ACM International Conference on Information and Knowledge Management*. ACM.

Wu, Chun-Che, Mei, Tao, Hsu, Winston H, and Rui, Yong. 2014. Learning to personalize trending image search suggestion. In: *SIGIR '14: Proceedings of the 37th International ACM SIGIR Conference on Research and Development in Information Retrieval*. ACM.

Wu, Fang and Huberman, Bernardo A. 2008. How public opinion forms. In: *Internet and Network Economics*. Springer.

Wu, Liwei, Li, Shuqing, Hsieh, Cho-Jui, and Sharpnack, James. 2020. SSE-PT: Sequential recommendation via personalized transformer. In: *RecSys '20: 14th ACM Conference on Recommender Systems*. ACM.

Xiang, Liang, Yuan, Quan, Zhao, Shiwan, Chen, Li, Zhang, Xiatian, Yang, Qing, and Sun, Jimeng. 2010. Temporal recommendation on graphs via long-and short-term preference fusion. In: *KDD '10: Proceedings of the 16th ACM SIGKDD International Conference on Knowledge Discovery and Data Mining*. ACM.

Xiao, Jun, Ye, Hao, He, Xiangnan, Zhang, Hanwang, Wu, Fei, and Chua, Tat-Seng. 2017. Attentional factorization machines: Learning the weight of feature interactions via attention networks. In: *IJCAI '17: Proceedings of the 26th International Joint Conference on Artificial Intelligence*. AAAI Press/International Joint Conferences on Artificial Intelligence.

Xu, Kelvin, Ba, Jimmy, Kiros, Ryan, Cho, Kyunghyun, Courville, Aaron, Salakhudinov, Ruslan, Zemel, Rich, and Bengio, Yoshua. 2015. Show, attend and tell: Neural image caption generation with visual attention. In: *Proceedings of the 32nd International Conference on Machine Learning*. MLR Press.

Yang, Jaewon, McAuley, Julian, Leskovec, Jure, LePendu, Paea, and Shah, Nigam. 2014. Finding progression stages in time-evolving event sequences. In: *WWW '14: Proceedings of the 23rd International Conference on World Wide Web*. ACM.

Yao, Sirui and Huang, Bert. 2017. Beyond parity: Fairness objectives for collaborative filtering. In: *NIPS '17: Proceedings of the 31st International Conference on Neural Information Processing Systems*. Neural Information Processing Systems Foundation.

Yildirim, Hilmi and Krishnamoorthy, Mukkai S. 2008. A random walk method for alleviating the sparsity problem in collaborative filtering. In: *RecSys '08: Proceedings of the 2008 ACM Conference on Recommender Systems*. ACM.

Yu, Hsiang-Fu, Hsieh, Cho-Jui, Si, Si, and Dhillon, Inderjit. 2012. Scalable coordinate descent approaches to parallel matrix factorization for recommender systems. In: *2012 IEEE International Conference on Data Mining*. IEEE.

Zafar, Muhammad Bilal, Valera, Isabel, Rogriguez, Manuel Gomez, and Gummadi, Krishna P. 2017. Fairness constraints: Mechanisms for fair classification. In: *Proceedings of the 20th Artificial Intelligence and Statistics*. MLR Press.

Zhang, Guijuan, Liu, Yang, and Jin, Xiaoning. 2020. A survey of autoencoder-based recommender systems. *Frontiers of Computer Science*, **14**, 430–50.

Zhang, Jie and Krishnamurthi, Lakshman. 2004. Customizing promotions in online stores. *Marketing Science*, **23**(4), 561–78.

Zhang, Jie and Wedel, Michel. 2009. The effectiveness of customized promotions in online and offline stores. *Journal of Marketing Research*, **46**(2), 190–206.

Zhang, Shuai, Yao, Lina, Sun, Aixin, and Tay, Yi. 2019. Deep learning based recommender system: A survey and new perspectives. *ACM Computing Surveys*, **52**(1), 1–38.

Zhang, Xingxing and Lapata, Mirella. 2014. Chinese poetry generation with recurrent neural networks. In: *Proceedings of the 2014 Conference on Empirical Methods in Natural Language Processing*. Association for Computational Linguistics.

Zhang, Yuan Cao, Séaghdha, Diarmuid Ó, Quercia, Daniele, and Jambor, Tamas. 2012. Auralist: Introducing serendipity into music recommendation. In: *WSDM '12: Proceedings of the Fifth ACM International Conference on Web Search and Data Mining*. ACM.

Zhao, Tong, McAuley, Julian, and King, Irwin. 2014. Leveraging social connections to improve personalized ranking for collaborative filtering. In: *CIKM '14: Proceedings of the 23rd ACM International Conference on Information and Knowledge Management*. ACM.

Zheng, Lei, Noroozi, Vahid, and Yu, Philip S. 2017. Joint deep modeling of users and items using reviews for recommendation. In: *WSDM '17: Proceedings of the 10th ACM International Conference on Web Search and Data Mining*. ACM.

Zheng, Yu, Zhang, Lizhu, Xie, Xing, and Ma, Wei-Ying. 2009. Mining interesting locations and travel sequences from GPS trajectories. In: *WWW '09: Proceedings of the 18th International Conference on World Wide Web*. ACM.

Zhou, Ke, Yang, Shuang-Hong, and Zha, Hongyuan. 2011. Functional matrix factorizations for cold-start recommendation. In: *SIGIR '11: Proceedings of the 34th International ACM SIGIR Conference on Research and Development in Information Retrieval*. ACM.

Zhou, Renjie, Khemmarat, Samamon, and Gao, Lixin. 2010. The impact of YouTube recommendation system on video views. In: *IMC '10: Proceedings of the 10th ACM SIGCOMM Conference on Internet Measurement*. ACM.

Ziegler, Cai-Nicolas, McNee, Sean M, Konstan, Joseph A, and Lausen, Georg. 2005. Improving recommendation lists through topic diversification. In: *WWW '05: Proceedings of the 14th International Conference on World Wide Web*. ACM.

Index

abstractive, 243
accuracy, 50, 54
ad recommendation, 170
Adam optimizer, 71
Adobe, 8
AdWords, 172
aggregate diversity, 282
Amazon, 5, 8, 20, 82, 88, 95, 100, 167, 175,
    189, 240, 256, 258, 260, 269, 301, 302
anomaly detection, 212
area under the ROC curve (AUC), 115, 116,
    120, 122, 142, 143
attention mechanism, 204, 206, 207, 209, 237,
    261
    self-attention, 140, 204, 206, 208
autoencoder, 128
    denoising autoencoder, 129
AutoRec, 120, 129
autoregression, 178, 212

bag-of-words representation, 220, 221,
    223–225, 227, 229, 235, 249, 251
balanced error rate (BER), 56, 76
Bayesian Personalized Ranking (BPR), 114,
    134, 135, 137, 142, 199, 275
    Group BPR, 161
    Social BPR, 158
    Visual BPR (VBPR), 254, 269
Behance, 263
BERT, 140, 204
    BERT4Rec, 208
bigram, 225, 249
bilinear, 133, 150
Bing, 289
bipartite graph, 97, 99, 172

BookCrossing, 301
bookmooch.com, 154
BrightKite, 169

calibration, 294
case studies, 100, 183, 193, 210, 234, 241,
    247, 257, 286, 300
Ciao, 156
Cinematch, 122
CiteULike, 190
cold-start, 6, 130, 133, 144, 145, 149–151,
    155, 158, 162, 169, 174, 175, 177, 205,
    209, 252, 255, 258, 264
collaborative filtering, 86, 127, 183
computational social science, 11
concentration, 14, 273, 274, 277, 278, 304
concept drift, 188, 211
conditional independence, 192, 201
conversational recommendation, 12, 219, 245,
    246, 291
convolutional neural network (CNN), 130,
    168, 259, 268
cosine similarity, 90, 92, 100, 118, 132, 136,
    227–229, 233, 250, 278, 280, 287, 292,
    304
Criteo, 140
crowd-sourcing, 243
csv, 135
cumulative gain, 124

dateutil, 199
decision tree, 53, 152
deep learning, 3, 32, 44, 54, 70, 125, 130, 140,
    147, 209, 254
Delicious, 156, 159, 190

322

Printed in the United States
by Baker & Taylor Publisher Services